THE TOP 500 HEAVY METAL SONGS OF ALL TIME

Published by ECW PRESS
2120 Queen Street East, Suite 200, Toronto, Ontario, Canada M4E 1E2

NATIONAL LIBRARY OF CANADA CATALOGUING IN PUBLICATION DATA

Popoff, Martin
The top 500 heavy metal songs of all time: Martin Popoff.

ISBN 1-55022-530-8

1. Heavy Metal (Music) — History and criticism. I. Title.
II. Title: Top five hundred heavy metal songs of all time.

ML3534.P829 2002 781.66 C2002-902176-6

Editor: Michael Holmes
Cover and Text Design: Darren Holmes
Typesetting: Gail Nina
Production: Mary Bowness
Printing: Transcontinental

This book is set in Utopia and Ice Age

The publication of *The Top 500 Heavy Metal Songs Of All Time* has been generously supported by the Canada Council, the Ontario Arts Council, and the Government of Canada through the Book Publishing Industry Development Program. Canada

DISTRIBUTION
CANADA: Jaguar Book Group, 100 Armstrong Avenue, Georgetown, ON, L7G 5S4

UNITED STATES: Independent Publishers Group, 814 North Franklin Street, Chicago, Illinois 60610

EUROPE: Turnaround Publisher Services, Unit 3, Olympia Trading Estate, Coburg Road, Wood Green, London N2Z 6T2

AUSTRALIA AND NEW ZEALAND: Wakefield Press, 1 The Parade Way West (Box 2066), Kent Town, South Australia 5071

PRINTED AND BOUND IN CANADA

ECW PRESS
ecwpress.com

THE TOP 500 HEAVY METAL SONGS OF ALL TIME

MARTIN POPOFF

ECW PRESS

Acknowledgments

In terms of the work put in, this book was virtually co-authored by my dad, Harry Popoff. He was the assembler, keeper and updater of the database, coming up with a system I still don't understand. I think he learned about four times as much about metal as he would have wanted to throughout this process. My deep thanks go to him for the many hours put in. The book's got 500 songs listed, and sortable — again to his credit and ingenuity — by a number of variables. But there were approximately 4500 songs which received votes, so you can imagine the work involved beyond past what you see here. Again, dad, thanks for everything.

Special Thanks

Most of the artist quotes throughout this book are from interviews I have personally conducted with the rock dude concerned. I wanted these quotes as fresh as possible and I wanted them to come from my archives. It's a point of pride.

However, my deepest appreciation goes out to two buds, for kind permission to snag a few from their chats with rock stars.

Drew Masters, through his legendary M.E.A.T. magazine was an essential Torontonian and Canadian source of international metal info from the late '80s into the mid-'90s. One of the things that was fascinating to me in flipping through the legacy, was how deeply he felt about trumpeting the plight of homegrown independent acts, dozens upon dozens of hopefuls getting their most treasured encouragement in the pages of M.E.A.T. Drew was in fact, one of my biggest influences in terms of getting me into this rock journalism business in the first place. Heavy hails are in order. Drew can be reached at: drewmasters@sympatico.ca.

When Drew moved on, one of his staffers, Tim Henderson started up Brave Words & Bloody Knuckles, today, eight years later, recognized as one of the top metal mags in the world, with a website (www.bravewords.com), that is also award-winning. Through his many efforts, Tim is probably the single most influential promoter of metal today.

It's all about family: Beth and Trevor; mom, dad, Brad; my large, extended family to the east!

Thanks

Mikael Akerfeldt, Eric Alper, Angie Aue, Anna, John and Karen at The Aylmer Express, Ed Balog, Marco Barbieri, Tracy Barnes and www.hardradio.com, Carl Begai, Mike Bell, Greg Below, Paul Bergeron, Keith Bergman, James Bickers, Mike Blackburn, Al Block, Matt Bower, Adrian Bromley, www.bwbk.com, Chris Bruni, Peter Burnside, Brave Scotty Cairns, the ever capable gang at Century Media, the good folk at Chart, Chip, Jen, Mark and Brett at Chipster PR, Classic Rock, Jeb Wright from Classic Rock Revisited (www.classicrockrevisited.com), Brian Coles, Rob, Ric, Pat and Steve at Collector's Guide Publishing, Eric Coubard, Neil Cournoyer, Crook'd Records, Neil Deas, Phil Dellio, Evelina Dimitrova, Mike Drew, Earache, Jack, Mary, Joy, and Michael at ECW PRESS, Chuck Eddy, Anastasia Saradoc and the the staff at EMI, Andreas at The End, Scott Floman, Charles Florio, Tommy Floyd, Simon Fateux at Fusion, Alan Gilkeson, Jim and Derek at www.gemm.com, Kerry Goulding, Gritz, Jeremy Hainsworth, Tom at Hypnotic, Scott Hefflon and Lollipop, Greg Loescher at Goldmine, Mark Gromen, Alan Grusie, Guitar World, Michael Hannon and the best power trio in the world American Dog, Devin and Tracy at HevyDevy, Paula Hogan, Maurizio Iacono, Jim Pitulski at InsideOut, Billy James, Montreal dynamo Mitch Joel, Kevin Julie, Carol Kaye, Paul Kennedy and Krause Communications, Jeff Kitts, Alan Klit: best guitarist I ever played with, Chuck Klosterman, Borivoj Krgin, Blaise Laflamme, Hugues Laflamme, Mitch Lafon, John and Steve Larocque, Anne Leighton, Dave Ling, Lion Music, Matthias Mader at Iron Pages, Dan and Pete at Magna Carta Records, Jasun Mark, Rhodes Mason, Michael and Deb at Mazur PR, Joel McIver, Brian, Mike, Tracy and the staff of Metal Blade, Metal Sludge (www.metalsludge.com), Metal Update, John Moran, Dave Murphy, Bob Nalbandian, Jess and Victoria at Neat, Lance King at Nightmare Records, Noel E. Noel, Nuclear Blast, Meredith Ochs, Brian O'Neill, Outsider, David Perri, Steve at PHD, Greg Pratt, Naiden Kolchev at Pro-Rock, Chris Purdy, Record Collector, Bryan Reesman, the Relapse crew, Alex Ristic, Claudio and the staff of Roadie Crew, Henry Rollins, Mark Roper, Matt at Sanctuary, Jon Satterley, Geoff Savage, J.J. at Scrape, Adam Sewell, Garry Sharpe-Young, Dale Sherman, Jackie Short, Rose Slanic, Aaron and Wendy Small, Sony, Dan 'n' Matt Kieswetter at Space In Your Face, Dennis, Rosie, Jon and Paul at Spitfire, SPV, Forrest Toop, my bandmates in Torque: Sammy, Mark, Rader, Kurt Torster, Underdogma, Universal, Unretrained!, Jamie and Sharon Vernon, Matt Walker, Mick Wall, Steven Ward, Joanna Dine at Warner, Adam Wasylyk, Marc Weisblott, Eddie Williamson, Josh Wood, Scott Woods.

Introduction

Always loved lists. As terrible teens, we used to sit and compile them seven ways to Sunday, sometimes starting on Saturday. I'm not going to say too much here about what you are about to see, 'cos it's pretty self-explanatory. Plus, git on over to the end, and you'll see a few appendices of analysis, ranging from the trite to the loamy substantial.

But yeah, the reason I did this is as follows. I've always wanted to write about specific songs, and I figured, why not let YOU pick the songs? Massage in what is hopefully an admirable element of objectivity, although you will see that not all my song reviews are gleefully supportive of your collective bad taste! And I always wanted to know the answer to this particular question. And what I think I'm gathering from the responses, is that what we have is quite statistically valid, the extended thought being that, since this is OF ALL TIME, I only see subtle shifts occurring when or if we revisit this in a few years. But those shifts are bound to occur, most notably, with more select bits of more recent material becoming "classic" and certain old classics being forgotten with the sands of time (sigh).

Of course, another reason I wanted to do this was to make use of the 600 or so interviews I've done with these bands. I had to rely on some help from a few friends (see Acknowledgements) but for the most part, I've tapped my own well. These quotes, when possible, are specific to the song at hand, but many are general as well. Hopefully these general ones capture at least the essence of the band sweating out the song, or perhaps they capture one of the contexts of the song, for example, the album from whence it sprung phoenix-like and perched in the collective consciousness of the metal nation. I didn't want to include any quotes from anybody that I didn't know personally. And so I said hey, no problem, a few of these listings will have no artist quote. When I hunt down someone from Humble Pie or Hendrix's band or Steppenwolf or get Page or Plant to talk to me, well, you'll get a quote. Next time.

As a few notes of explanation, within the body text only, albums are bolded, songs are italicized. Label and year of release: I've tried, hopefully with very few errors or inconsistencies, stuck with the label name at country of origin (some may be U.S. parent org.) as well as the date of release for that heavy home territory. Points is points, and like I say, it's a little complicated based on the above mentioned four ways the lists came in, not to mention the slightly subjective mathematical adjustments that needed to be made the odd time someone sent a list of 14, or said the top two were a tie, or the top five are ranked and the rest aren't. You have no idea what people will come up with. As well, you will see some lists from the artists as well. Consider them all unranked unless otherwise noted. Most of these were collected on the fly in interviews I had with the rock dude his bad-ass self, but some were email answers. Although I've assigned no ranking number, these artist lists are indeed subtly ranked, as they are for the most part presented in the order in which the artist dredged them from their tour-addled memories. And finally, you will see a few single/EP/12 shots. These are merely for eye-candy. There are no album shots because it's a book about songs. Pretty pictures of albums will be in the next book.

So, without further ramblin' on, here are the final tallies for the Top 500 Heavy Metal Songs Of All Time. Here also are my silly comments, along with those from one of the guys who officially was in the pop combo who performed said life-altering statement.

1 PARANOID BLACK SABBATH

3588 points

from Paranoid (Warner '70)

Well, well, here we have it, the greatest heavy metal song of all time as picked by you, the mop-headed minions, Black Sabbath's *Paranoid* distilling, leaching, compressing, focusing, magnifying the abstract idea of heavy metal into a brief, frighteningly tossed-off, psychologically uneasy smudge of temporal space. The song is all business, chugging pan-evidence to the power of the distortion box, the powerful effect of a mind under synaptic stress, the power of bass rattling the eardrums, the power of a resolutely rock 'n' roll 4/4 beat satanically forged in the '50s. Defiant as the music it somewhat unwillingly represents (a defiance in its own right), *Paranoid* offers very little to go on, scant, absentminded information flitted, fitted and departed. It is short, simple, the razor's edge of metal's razor. It asks the metal naysayer to filter out all of the Rolling Stone-splodge they've ever heard about metal and listen to the wind, a wind that is only a little more than the core movement of Elvis, the Beatles and the rock 'n' roll experience in general. That little more is found in the vacuum between this song's fuzz and its chug, Iommi also very modestly dresses the dossier with another key metal-quality riff — which causes the neck-craning of those who may embrace and of those who may scorn — perked and pricked attention in the first dozen seconds — only to have this scythe-like guitar pattern disappear mischievously, enigmatically, illogically, chemically and through malnutrition, poverty and malcontent, for the remainder of the song's 2:46 cat-pounce. Oz plays the character with all too much knowledge of the song's mental profiling, Geezer plays bass — really plays bass — like a '60s guy, Bill adds to the definition of the new music by articulating stomp, and Tony, well, he simply adds an extra paragraph to the pages and pages he, his guitar and his shop-damaged fingers would write on the subject. You picked *Paranoid* because it is a meeting place so specific and small nobody would waste time getting lost trying to hook up with their buddies — they are in the same uneasy box with you and their chemicals are shared. But, as I've concentrically come around to in the spoo above, there's a residual and fortunate side effect of picking such a brief, stupid, underdogged piece of music as fleeting frame of the big powerful picture (I'm smugly glad it edged out *Master of Puppets*), and the effect is this: it allows one to mentally block out the noise pollution of metal's whirring, buzzing, braying three decades thus far, and focus the mind on the power of metal's ultimate weapon — the pure and pounded power chord as the dependable chassis for a whole, beloved genre of music.

Geezer Butler on *Paranoid* . . .

> "We'd finished the album and had packed up all our gear and the management said they needed an extra three or four minutes to put on the album and we said we didn't have anything and they said, 'Can you write something?' And Ozzy would literally be singing the lyrics as I wrote them. I was looking through the basement the other day and I found all the original lyrics from the **Paranoid** album, and verses from the song *Paranoid* that weren't used. It might be interesting for people to see the original versions some day. But it's just getting the time to do it. Lyrically, *War Pigs, Iron Man, Paranoid* . . . I used to try and give a message of hope or something at the end of each song and now I don't bother. Now I realize I can't change anything!"

2 MASTER OF PUPPETS METALLICA

3578 points *from Master of Puppets (Elektra '86)*

Title track of an album considered a classic but slightly imperfect in this writer's opinion for arguably rehashing **Ride the Lightning**, *Master of Puppets* is the hardest working clang banger therein enclosed, a tight, taut, mid-paced thrasher with a unique stop-and-go signature, primed for air guitar and air drums, many of which were smuggled into the seminal gigs that marked Metallica's first arena (well, hockey barn) tour, Metal Church in distressed tow. It is also 8:38 in scope, predicting the sprawl of . . . **And Justice for All**. But all the parts fit, indeed Hetfield's memorable "Master, master" showing up in two totally different riffs. Themes recur, and other than the silly mellow chunk, new themes dovetail nicely. In effect, it doesn't feel 8:38 long, given the many verses, the involved pre-chorus and equally elaborate chorus. The song simply takes a long time to work through its necessary elements. And it's all wrapped in an aura of youthful energy, the band leaping around the flame of their first fame, gleefully bringing mosh-heavy punked-out metal to the masses, getting famous and getting to clear-conscious proselytize for the cause at the same time.

Lars Ulrich on becoming more rock than metal . . .

> "We called ourselves Rocktallica before anyone else ever did. I guarantee you we were joking about that in the studio before anyone else caught on. It's really hard to talk about. It's such a part of my everyday life. It's like getting up in the morning and putting on a pair of socks; it's something you don't even think about. It's like when you say, do you ever think about Metallica been limiting? Of course, I'm proud of the name. At the end of the day, it's just a fucking name. Is it so sacred that we can't change the way it's written? Of course it's not. Can we write it upside down and stand it on its head? Of course we can, because it's our fucking name. We can do whatever we want, but at the same time, it means a lot to me because it's basically been every day of my life for 15, 16 years. At the end, it's completely indispensable because it's just nine letters that form a sound."

3 ACE OF SPADES MOTÖRHEAD

3165 points *from Ace of Spades (Bronze '80)*

Frantic, sleepless, agitated, punk rocker than you . . . *Ace of Spades* found Motörhead at their warmongering best, this track bringing to fruition the guitar crunch, saw and slash that was so often lost on past Motörhead anthems and sub-anthems. The track works because there is a polluted profusion of distinctive Fast Eddie work, riffs and riff pieces that grab you by the throat, while Lemmy just does his thing, playing lead bass, all on top of a percussion attack from Phil that sounds like a football riot. Lyrically, Lemmy gets to play his card, hollering and hollowing out his autobiography in hoary haiku-like pieces, direct, down the gullet, track one, side one. Late in the game (and it's a short home team route: 2:47 of it), Eddie rips off one of his more aggressive solos, before the band drops heads-down into another round of verse violence, advancing towards an end that is only the start of a record full of slip-shoddy shoot 'em ups.

Fast Eddie Clarke on *Ace of Spades* . . .

"Well, there is another version that came out on a bootleg album. It's called The Original Version. When we first did it, we were doing some eight-track recordings in our rehearsal room where we were, to see how the songs were sounding. One of those songs was *Ace of Spades*, but it was a completely different riff at that time (sings the recorded and the original version). It went like that. So once we got into the studio, Lemmy actually said, 'Listen, what can we do with that riff?' So we riffed around with it a little bit and then we came up with the alternative. So when it first got written, it was just something we were jamming on. Lemmy had a rough vocal for it but once we got into the studio with the producer, Vic Maile, who did **Ace of Spades** and **No Sleep**, he kind of hustled us a bit to kind of alter things to get things working. Which hadn't happened before. So a lot of *Ace of Spades* came out of the actual recording sessions and a couple of other ones on there did as well. We had gotten to a point where we really couldn't sort of finish things properly, you know what I mean? So we had to do it in the studio where we could look at it and see what it was sounding like and do the adjustments."

4 CRAZY TRAIN
OZZY OSBOURNE

2940 points *from Blizzard of Ozz (Jet/CBS '80)*

A track beloved by mulleted millions around the world, *Crazy Train* digs into Ozzy's scrambled egg psyche like none of the man's many other incredulous confessionals. And indeed, the musical soundtrack is a bit left field, the verse pumping along to a disco crime nursery rhyme, set to a sort of fiddle as Rome burns melody. But we find its emotional strings set us up for a shambolic fall, a breakthrough, as Ozzy's eerie, impassioned, somewhat compressed vocal launches into a mournful, impatient pre-chorus and chorus, zinger being the oncoming hell-bound truth from which Sgt. Sharon, in the nick of time, saves the man. Props to the band for risking such a strange set of melodies, and props to Ozzy for selling us on his insanity through the abstraction of the only tool he has, his injured set of peerless pipes.

Bob Daisley on *Crazy Train* . . .

> "I remember one review that said that we were the thinking man's heavy metal. I was really proud of that. Whether people knew it or not, I knew it. I knew that I had written the lyrics. What I am most proud of is *Crazy Train*. Randy came up with the riff and Ozzy came up with the vocal melody and I wrote the lyrics and the musical section that Randy soloed over in the middle. It's become a rock 'n' roll anthem and I am really proud of that. That used to be one of my rock 'n' roll ambitions when I was with Rainbow. I wanted to write a hit single or be involved in writing one with somebody else. In Rainbow, Ritchie and Ronnie wrote everything and they didn't need anyone else. When **Blizzard of Ozz** happened it was great because I got to realize one of my ambitions. *Crazy Train* is really a peace song about how crazy it is that people are brainwashed and mind-controlled by the powers that be over fucking stupid religion

and stuff like that. We've inherited all the bullshit from all of the cold wars and all of the crap. The young people inherited it and back then I was still young (laughing). The bass note thing at the beginning was planned. Ozzy used to like different songs starting different ways. He used to say, 'Let's start this one off with the drums.' I think it was probably Ozzy's idea to start the song like that. The 'all aboard' came later in the studio when we were overdubbing vocals."

5 ANGEL OF DEATH SLAYER

2936 points *from Reign in Blood (Def Jam '86)*

Beloved for so many reasons, *Angel of Death* is the longest track and first track on death metal's crowning classic, or more accurately, a classic that is many a fan's favourite thrash, death and/or black metal album. Everything about the new, forever seminal Slayer is enclosed in this Nazi tale, which, like many a death treatise, doesn't so much glorify as display for all to see how truly abysmal man can be if he really puts his Icke-reptillian shape-shifting mind to it. Nearly five minutes long on Slayer's most famous half hour knifing, *Angel of Death* is a ripping speed machine, rot through with grooves that are all drum tornado Lombardo. Araya is enunciating very clearly this cautionary tale of Auschwitz, and solos positively exploded in an atonal wandering key style that is now the norm in death metal. You couldn't occupy a more sacred spot in the Slayer catalogue than track one, side one on **Reign in Blood**, and *Angel of Death* doesn't disappoint, slapping the listener around before tossing him into the interrogation chair, the victim's head spinning as he's force-fed this off-the-rails realization of death metal's previously caged, uptight, latent power. As with the genre-defining closer *Raining Blood*, metaphors for all of the album's characteristics are contained within this coal-impenetrable trend-killer. I mean, forget the carping about the 28-minute Slayer album; *Angel of Death* is a sharp shocking five-minute Slayer album in itself.

Dave Lombardo on *Angel of Death . . .*

"Absolutely brutal. The drum break that everybody, you know, kind of pinpoints when they talk to me, that came from a drum solo I used to do. I used to break in the middle of the drum solo and just do double bass, and Kerry liked that. He said, 'Hey, let's put that in the song' and I said OK."

Kerry King from Slayer
Pantera — *Becoming*
Slipknot — *Get This*
Slayer — *Disciple*
Black Sabbath — *Megalomania*
AC/DC — *Highway to Hell*
AC/DC — *If You Want Blood (You've Got it)*
Judas Priest — *Stained Class*
Metallica — *Damage Inc.*
Sepultura — *Propaganda*
Slayer — *Raining Blood*

6 THE NUMBER OF THE BEAST
IRON MAIDEN

2896 points *from The Number of the Beast (EMI '82)*

The sonic equivalent of the band's natty leg-warmer and tights ensembles, the opening riff to *The Number of the Beast* is a mite gay, very British and of utmost importance to the career aspirations of many of today's big metal lugans. Truth be told, it's one of the most dramatic track intros of all time (OK, within a subset called primary-coloured metal), playing, toying with the drama that is to come, a drama that once it does come, further obfuscates with a hiccuped 7/4 rhythm. It is a happy Satan song, its riff the red-headed stepsister of the dollhouse melody that drives *Crazy Train*. But still, *The Number of the Beast* is a fine introduction to the thespian adrenaline skills of Bruce Dickinson, whose admonishing chorus-leading "666"s stick in the craw over what is the song's second happy-go-tweedle-dum riff. And with a twist of a slumlord moustache, it is a very mischievous song that wades right into the middle of the witch hunt hysteria of the mid-'80s, bellowing a big, "Hey, we're evil, too!" Reverent snickering hails to this rushed, flawed, melodically sweet and sour anthem for driving, one flat tire and all, so high up into the heart of darkness of our chart.

Bruce Dickinson on recording *The Number of the Beast* . . .

> "Steve writes a lot of the riffs just into a little tape recorder by humming, and then he just transfers it to the bass, which is probably why the riff sounds a bit singsongy, because that's probably what he was doing at the time. Other than that, I had one of the most frustrating three hours of my life singing the first two lines of that song. Could not get it right. I mean, it's only whispering, really. We were going round and round and round and I was getting more and more frustrated. I had been singing the song in rehearsals over and over again and I just wanted to get on with the rest of the song. And the producer, Martin Birch, wouldn't let me get beyond the first two whispered lines. And it was like, if we can't get these first two lines right, we can't work on the rest of the song. Got to get these first two lines right, got to get the right vibe. So I didn't know what he meant, and he sat down and told me a story about Ronnie Dio, the song *Heaven and Hell*. And the opening line to the song is, 'Sing me a song, you're a singer.' So Ronnie came into the studio and sang the opening lines, and Martin said 'Stop!' And Ronnie goes, 'What's wrong?' Martin says, 'No, do that again.' And Ronnie goes, 'What's wrong with it?' 'It's not quite right.' 'But I sang it in rehearsal tons of times.' And Martin said, 'No, think about what you're saying. Here you are, Heaven and Hell, and you're walking out between Heaven and Hell, and you're saying, "Sing me a song, you're a singer," right? So you've got to sum up your entire life in those few words. Think you've done it?' And then he went to me, 'And now you have to do those two lines the same way.' That's kind of what it was like working with Martin Birch."

7 HALLOWED BE THY NAME
IRON MAIDEN

2591 points *from The Number of the Beast* (EMI '82)

Ah yes, you get what's going on here? **The Number of the Beast** as an album is such an emotional fan favourite, and *Hallowed Be Thy Name* is that record's serious epic, its stirring kitchen sink workhorse, its non-obvious dark vortex of thrusting skill, its grave home of intricate, Priest-improving twin leads. So a convergence of the fond album and Maiden's reason to be — the long dong song — takes place like a total eclipse. Bruce gets to do some large and laser-slicing vocal work as well, clarion-calling to the metal minions one of those slippery lyrics that implies messing about with dark forces and the subsequent woes that imprint themselves on those (these?) who meddle. Musically, this ominous personal tragedy is enforced by curly Q riffs that are baroque-en for you, ornate, innate patterns that drill through Dante's layers in search of forbidden meaning, just like the title track.

Bruce Dickinson on *Hallowed Be Thy Name* . . .

> "What I remember most is that it was blindingly obvious from the moment we started playing it in rehearsal, that it was going to be classic. It was one of those songs that was just instant. The biggest Maiden epic before that was *Phantom of the Opera*, and I remember Steve came in and said, that's it, I've got the new *Phantom of the Opera* and that was *Hallowed*."

8 WAR PIGS
BLACK SABBATH

2355 points *from Paranoid (Warner '70)*

Pregnant pauses like **Rosemary's Baby**, flailing air drums like a Rush convention . . . *War Pigs* is metal audacity personified, Sabbath inventing plain deer-in-the-headlights prog, segueing horrifically, zigzagging badly and grandly. The lyrics to this one are famously off the cuff, which in itself is a lark, Ozzy pushing out alone into the battle plain, encouraged only by Bill Ward hi-hat tap-tapping a warning of chords to come. Ostensibly against war, *War Pigs* is more like punk rock bellyaching, us and theming, something to yak about on the dole, set to a blister blunderbuss of occurrences, the band blindly building to a series of wind-ups, culminating in the ultimate tape acceleration effect, the direct opposite of the song's agonizingly point-void opening head-spread.

Geezer Butler on his lyrical hot buttons . . .

> "It's just a reflection of society, real life. Everyone has their point of view. I used to write like that. *War Pigs, Lord of This World*, even *Paranoid*. It's just an observation of society. I'm not preaching or trying to come up with any answers. But *War Pigs* is such a strong song. That's why we start concerts with that song. It has absolutely everything in it. It's a great song and it gets you up to play the whole concert. From there it's like, full steam ahead."

9 BACK IN BLACK
AC/DC

1995 points *from Black in Black (Atlantic '80)*

The new ground zero for copious bubbly fluid intake, *Back in Black* basically snatched that brown bottle (coincidentally) from another AC/DC song, *Highway to Hell*, folks gleeful that the death of Bon didn't mean drinking was to be outlawed or even discouraged. It's odd to think this could have been, and was going to be, sung by Bon. What was he mourning? And if it ain't about mourning, AC/DC isn't exactly a goth band. And besides, where was Brian "Beano" Johnson "back" from? Was he following some sort of beery decline from all that fame and critical acclaim with Geordie? I know, it's a "we"; it's a team. In any event, Malc and Angus shock us once again with simplicity, large empty spaces, plain nothingness, on a track producer Mutt Lange didn't want on the album because he didn't get it, snickers Angus.

Angus Young on a new era . . .

> "Well with Mutt Lange, it was the first time he had ever worked with us, and I don't even think at that point that he had even had a big album, a big success. I think he'd had a few single successes in this part of the world but he hadn't had a major album, and for us it was our first time really working with someone else as a producer. But we felt it was a good combination because we had wanted to try a few different things. Up until that point we had made a lot more in your face rock 'n' roll and we wanted to try a couple of medium-style rock tracks. We had a lot of ideas even from touring on **Highway to Hell** that we felt we should finish off what we had been working on. You never know, after Bon died, we could have said this is it. We may have stopped, but we still felt that we should have finished off, hence even the cover of **Back in Black**. You can see it; we made it in black for the colour, called it **Back in Black**, and even put the bell on the front. Obviously it was different after Bon's death. I suppose to some people they would have probably viewed you as a whole new act, and in one way, it was like starting again because you don't know what's coming, you don't know how it's going to be received. You think, is this ethical? That was our tribute to Bon."

10 IRON MAN BLACK SABBATH

1915 points *from Paranoid (Warner '70)*

The protruding forehead riff to end all Neanderthal clubbings, *Iron Man* is the lorry-driving, industrial wastelandlubbing ne'er-welcome uncle of *Smoke on the Water*, which two years later would become the new power chord poop on the rug. But 1970 and 1971 belonged to the reticent, hirsute, sideways-glancing noise terrorists in Sabbath, who lead with this flashy monster tale, creepy cartoon voice announcing the sturm and drang to come, the band thenceforth delivering the triumphant doom of heavy metal, which in the larger world of music, would quickly be pronounced a pariah of a genre, puerile and grating persona non grata. People who put *Iron Man* down forget all the parts, the song's modestly dramatic and erratic mood swings, most folks keying on that end-stop of a riff. But they shouldn't. Sabbath were indeed a creative power trio, on *Iron Man*'s back half, the band operating in the tradition of Cream or The Who or Van Halen, configuring this and that, laying it down live . . . er, are you buying any of this?

Geezer Butler on *Iron Man* . . .

> "I thought it was a really stupid concept (laughs), but it was from a comic book, *Iron Man*, and it was all about this being. It was an ecological theme. We were all very environmental at the time, and it was about this entity that turns into metal and is incapacitated at the end, just lying there. He can't talk at the end of it but he has all this knowledge that can save the earth from catastrophe. But yeah, I think science fiction played a big part in things like *Iron Man*, science fiction and fantasy and the supernatural and a lot of politics as well in our lyrics. The one thing we didn't want to do was normal love songs, because everybody in the world was doing them. And our whole band was against all that anyway, everybody talking about splitting up with their girlfriend and stuff. The reason we got together and made our music in the first place was because nobody else was doing it. So I just wrote about things that were interesting to me at the time. If I'd read a particularly good book, I'd condense that down to a song."

11 HEAVEN AND HELL BLACK SABBATH

1835 points *from Heaven and Hell (Warner '80)*

Heaven and Hell is the perfect Black Rainbow song, a divine synthesis between Ronnie's lyrics and melodies, with the massive heave of Tony's fossilized, Valhalla-cracking riffery. Its ambiguity is the cauldron of life itself, Ronnie summing up the complexity of things, the foreboding shadows in all of living's corners, the good, the bad, the strings-attached rewards that come from the bad, and the bad that comes from blind acceptance of the good (think *Don't Talk to Strangers*). So lyrically, as well as musically, it's a small and very loud nation-state, a landscape, a terrain, characterized by peaks and valleys. Later on, there is a pitched battle within one of those valleys, a fast break that is the only part on the album that matches *Die Young* for emotional connectivity, the band rising above the smoke as one, spurred on by Bill Ward's militaristic snare intro. It is an epic crafted precisely to be one, the precision evidenced by the fact that at under seven minutes (one could argue that it's over by six), it isn't all that long, even if you feel like you've been through a war.

Ronnie James Dio on *Heaven and Hell* . . .

> "I had the idea for *Heaven and Hell,* the feel for the song. I knew where I wanted to take it lyrically and melodically. Tony came up with the riff and the other parts in between. That one really flowed. We were knocked out by that one ourselves. When we started rehearsing that one we couldn't stop playing it. We played it every day for hours and went, 'Yeah, this is great!' Finally, after enjoying it so much we realized that we had to finish it. It is just a great song. That happens a lot when you work with people that you have not worked with before. The first projects are usually the most stunning because you have a collection of ideas that are drastically different from each other. So you write and it seems to flow more than it actually did. It was an easy album to write because everybody was given their chance to do what they needed to do and what they wanted to do. As we carried on, we got a little more finite about it because we had so much success with **Heaven and Hell**. We started looking more at the next album and began saying things like, 'I don't really like what you did there. Maybe you could do it more like this.' Your freedom really stops flowing at that point. You're concerned about what somebody else wants."

12 PAINKILLER JUDAS PRIEST

1784 points *from Painkiller* (CBS '90)

Count me floored that this manic panic button of a scream dream has perched its wind tunnel self high upon high as the top Priest track of all time. It points to the fact that fans will reward a white hot metal return, no matter the demographic or dreary song cycle of the times. This is supposed to be a Priest more in need of painkillers than writing them, but there you go, Priest inexplicably delivering a vicious thrash metal maelstrom, over which Halford unleashes a heady metal mania that finds him shredding his upper register. No question drummer Scott Travis has forcefully pumped new blood into the band, who seem downright giddy at having a 'merican double bass drum machine kicking their doddering pasty English butts, against their tea-time wills, into the not yet non-metal '90s.

Ian Hill on *Painkiller* . . .

> "Well, there you go (laughs). That's a progression from *Screaming for Vengeance*, *Freewheel Burning*. Right up until we stopped there (laughs), that was the end of the line for the big fast aggressive songs, a great track. Up until that point, it was the hardest thing we had ever done. Rob's performance was great, as it was on the whole album. He did a great job. His voice came across very powerfully on *Painkiller*, much bigger, not that it wasn't before, but there was much more presence in his voice."

13 ONE
METALLICA

1758 points *from . . . And Justice for All (Elektra '88)*

I think *One* kicks way up the list because of a mass compulsive disorder where people are hysterically afraid out of their heads that if they don't vote for this, *One* will happen to them. It is indeed horrific, the story of a guy blown up by a land mine, left with no arms, legs, sight, speech, hearing or most importantly, the ability to commit suicide. The anti-war tale is set to an abrasive progressive rock soundtrack, notoriously oddly recorded, featuring stadium-stumbly drums, electric guitar with all the tricks turned off (easier than locating an acoustic) and occasionally, big rusty power chords. The back end is a big thrash blazeout, I guess the true soundtrack to the celebrated visual of the much-vaunted video of the song. But perhaps the biggest insult to the protagonist of the story is the fact that those with arms and legs could waltz to the verses and emphatically pound fists into the cool hockey barn air to the fast bits. Also, look away from the horrid mellow guitar solos or licks or whatever you want to call 'em (Kirk imagining what soft music sounds like). But then again chop 'n' change Lars ain't exactly easing anybody into the blues zone either.

Jason Newsted on the *One* video . . .

> "Ever since I've been in the band we've been interested in doing a video, because we're all into movies and stuff but we knew that it had to be just right. *One* really started off as an experimental thing; we found a movie, **Johnny Got His Gun**, that thematically fit the song, so we came up with the cool plot for the video. So we went out one afternoon with one camera to a warehouse and had ourselves shot live and then we turned it over to the director and he edited it together with the movie pieces. We saw it develop bit by bit, minute by minute, and when it was finished, we all said 'wow.' It turned out really intense and we're all proud

of it; it's not a typical rock video with girls and rain, it's an emotional statement about war. A bit grim for some, but totally unique for a rock vid. There's three or four different versions out because MTV originally rejected the first edit, giving us a hard time and making a stink about it. Finally it came down to them being overwhelmed with requests. Their lines were flooded! So they gave in and finally played the whole version. There's now a new one that is just us playing with the movie."

14 HIGHWAY STAR DEEP PURPLE

1729 points *from Machine Head (Warner '72)*

Pulsating hard rock purity, *Highway Star* is the supreme example of Deep Purple's keyboard/guitar alchemy. Ritchie and Jon grind out a disciplined straight-line antidote to white line fever — a frothy wave of adrenaline laced with aerial ballets from both aforementioned engine room employees. Lord's solo is elegiac, ornate, well-reasoned, intellectual, and Ritchie matches wits with the lord of organ chords, carving out turf that would, through mounting evidence, become his signature castle rock sound. And let's not forget that neither would be able to hold the fort without the rock-solid groove laid down by Ian Paice, who continues to prove his subtle touch, even when addressing a song so boldly drawn.

Ian Gillan on *Highway Star* . . .

"There were some journalists on the bus asking some very penetrating questions like, 'How do you write a song?' and Ritchie went duh, duh, duh, duh . . . on an acoustic guitar and said, 'Like this.' And as we were driving down to Portsmouth, I started singing, 'Nobody's gonna take my car.' We did it in the show that night at Portsmouth Guild Hall in England. So that evolved; songs just evolve. You don't sit down and write them as such."

15 BLACK SABBATH BLACK SABBATH

1700 points

from Black Sabbath (Warner '70)

Bulldozing into the sinister ministry of the times, *Black Sabbath*, that long dong of a green-faced hexing song, is for many a metal watershed, the sand-swept holy land for heavy-osity. Besides the triple witching hour of its name, *Black Sabbath* straps you down and forces you to contemplate the long drone of metal mindfulness, Iommi selling the nothing and the everything of nothing more than an electric guitar tortured specifically this new way. And of course, the Sabs are accidentally or instinctually too smart to leave us clinging to that premise alone, later turning on the jets for some mod metal riffery and psych prog tomfoolery. But it really is a loud capital letter, neatly perched at the start of 1970, a song so convincingly about the durability and utility of open wound power chords, that the music world couldn't help but be changed forever.

Geezer Butler on *Black Sabbath* . . .

> "Our very first song, *Black Sabbath*, was another bass riff. We knew it was different then because it was a different approach. I don't think bass players wrote stuff before like that. At the time Paul McCartney was the most famous, but the Beatles didn't write riffs on bass. So I think we sort of set a precedent for the way we were writing from then on. Everything was sort of bass riffs. Even when Tony wrote them on guitar, it was like how the bass would be. The lyric writing came about because no one else in the band could do it. Ozzy did some lyrics. I think he did like two sets of lyrics on the first album. For *Black Sabbath*, he just like ad libbed those lyrics, but then when it came down to coming up with something else, he was stuck (laughs). Tony couldn't do lyrics, Bill couldn't do them, so it was left to me. So I sort of got the knack for them. I think when we did the song *Black Sabbath*, I think we knew we were definitely onto something different — just by the audience reaction at the pubs we were playing at at the time. We loved the heavier stuff. We were all into Hendrix and Cream and Zeppelin. I don't know. The one thing that appealed to us was taking that sound and maybe making it heavier than everybody else. I don't know, it just fitted our feeling at the time. We started out as a blues band and many of the songs on the first album were quite blues-based. But there were never

any songs where we were thinking about another band or their style. Our biggest influence was Led Zeppelin though."

16 HOLY WARS . . . THE PUNISHMENT DUE MEGADETH

1692 points *from Rust in Peace (Capitol '90)*

Serving as microcosm for the album as a whole, *Holy Wars* was involved, committed, immersed in the idea of serious literature-inspiring metal. Its elongated intro speaks of minds occupied and cluttered, blessed with a previously unknown bounty of creativity, as does the fact that after four short verses, the song collapses into a rude and rudimentary break before the sublime and elegant *The Punishment Due,* which is followed by a return to the triumphant opening themes. All in all, it's a masterful way to begin what is widely hailed as Megadeth's best album, *Holy Wars* being an unconventional mini-epic, surprisingly stingy on instant gratification, pay-off riffs, hooks or money shots. And it's a discomforting lyric, as is the sharp steel frame on which Dave's rant sits. Yet this bubbling cauldron nourishes with purpose, priming the mind pliable for the challenging corporate and corporate-slaying (snake eats itself) shred to follow.

Dave Mustaine on *Holy Wars . . . The Punishment Due . . .*

"*Holy Wars* was a song that I wrote. I woke up in Dublin, Ireland and the night before I was in Antrim. I had been drinking Guinness. And some guy in the audience was selling bootleg Megadeth T-shirts, and I said go get the stuff. I'm not against people, if they want to be part of our team, earning money with us, if they want to work with us. But taking from us is taking from our families and it's hurting our band and hurting our ability to take our music to the masses. So I don't support bootleg merchandise at all; I don't appreciate it at all. It doesn't have anything to do with me not having enough money. It has to do with, first off, the merchandise is usually shit, and second off, the people who are usually doing it are sneaky bastards. So in this case, it was totally unrelated to what I just described. So in this case, it was someone selling T-shirts for the cause. And I thought, well what the hell is the cause? And I'm already like two Guinness pints into this thing. And they say if you draw a happy face in the foam in the top of the Guinness, you'll have a drinking partner for the night. So I'm drawing smiley faces in there and I'm getting absolutely tanked. And I asked this Irish guy . . . and I'm part Irish. I'm a little different than most American Irish people when I go to Ireland. When American Irish people go there they go, 'Oh, I'm Irish, I'm part Irish!' and the real Irish people don't give a fuck. They don't want to hear about you being a sliver Irish. But because we have a lot of fans there, and I'm of Irish ancestry, they're glad for the fact I have some heritage from there. So I get away with it a little bit that I think I kind of was being a little bit too nosy when I was there. And I asked the guy what the cause was about. And he made it sound so, so beautiful. It was so eloquently described. All he said was, 'It's the Protestants and the Catholics. They have a problem with each other and they both think their religion is better than the other. And it's basically just prejudiced religion.' And I went, 'Oh, that's simple.' He didn't say that they're bombing each other, killing one another, that they're throwing Molotov cocktails at cars and children are dying and innocent people are getting killed all the time and all the things that are involved with it. And I didn't even know what side of the cause he's fighting for. So I get up onstage, and I said 'This one's for the cause. Give Ireland back to the Irish. Anarchy in Ireland.' Now Paul fucking McCartney can say, 'Give Ireland back to the Irish.' Dave Mustaine can't. So I say that and that's the last thing I remember. And the next morning I go out for breakfast and David Ellefson won't talk to me and I said, 'What's your problem?' And he says, 'There were three fucking bomb threats last night and they had to clear the venue three times with dogs, come in their sniffing for bombs, because of you and your fucking IRA statement.' And I said, 'What IRA statement?' He said, 'Give Ireland back to the Irish. This one's for the cause.' And I went 'What?!' And I couldn't believe I'd done that. So we get to Nottingham Rock City and it was in England and I just put pen to paper and everything just came out. And the most important part for me was that killing for religion is something I don't understand. And then the other relevant part of it was fools like me who cross the seas, come from a foreign land, and then ask the sheep, the followers, for their beliefs. And I asked the guy, and instead of just being the entertainer, playing my songs and shutting up, I said something I shouldn't have talked about. And that's one of our most popular songs. The second half of the song, *Punishment Due* is about a comic, **The Punisher**. The first part is about Antrim."

17 VICTIM OF CHANGES JUDAS PRIEST

1665 points *from Sad Wings of Destiny (Gull '76)*

This massive metal stone helped change the rules of metal, and its charms and innovations were subtle, offering no great shakes over top-level Sabbath or Deep Purple, just this fresh, progressive sophisticated stacking of dependable metal chords. It moves through menace and sorrow back into menace, until Halford's piercing screams announce the new threshold for vocalists up cloudward where the new guitar plateau now existed, courtesy of bandmates K. K. and Glenn, a couple of blokes better at doing than articulating what they've done. Through black hill and dark dale, *Victim of Changes* resolutely established the Priest as the new metal worldbeaters, not yet the kings of fast science, but already more sinister and leaden and intelligent than their main youthful competitors Rainbow and Scorpions.

Ian Hill on *Victim of Changes* . . .

"*Victim of Changes* started life as *Whiskey Woman*. It was written by Ken and Alan Atkins originally, the original vocalist for the band who left. It was sort of put on the back burner for the first album and it ended up being put on **Sad Wings** in a very, very revamped way. Robert put some new lyrics to it, and Glenn got involved and worked closely with Ken and changed the rhythm and the format of the song. And that one is evergreen; that is a song we could not drop (laughs). It's one of those songs that we would get lynched if we dropped it. It's one of the all-time classic songs. It's got everything, the rock, the melody; it's got two great lead breaks. It's what Priest were and are known for really, the light and shade, the heaviness, the aggression and it's all summed up in that one song, really."

Ripper Owens from Judas Priest
Judas Priest — *Victim of Changes*
Black Sabbath — *Heaven and Hell*
Iron Maiden — *Children of the Damned*
Pantera — *Cowboys from Hell*
Alice In Chains — *It Ain't Like That*
Queensryche — *Operation Mindcrime*
Judas Priest — *Hell is Home*
Soundgarden — *Outshined*
Savatage — *Hall of the Mountain King*
Black Sabbath — *Children of the Grave*

18 ELECTRIC EYE JUDAS PRIEST

1643 points *from Screaming for Vengeance* (CBS '82)

Sending hesher tingles and jingles all up and down metalhead spines within a very pivotal year for metal, *Electric Eye* announced with laser precision that Priest were at least thinking about their extreme roots, closing (maybe) the toothless tollbooth at the **Point of Entry**. After what is a grand, dramatic, tension-building Maiden-me-too intro called *The Hellion, Electric Eye* bounds into the room and starts flipping over furniture. It is a song that reads and roams like a screenplay, underscored with purpose and pacing but zagged o'ertop with emotional jags. Ultimately it is perhaps the first fast heavy track from Priest as they existed deep into their commercial, cynical, jaded all-too-aware years. As a result, it reflects, somewhere between arguably and abstractly, maturity, as well as maturity's subplots: hook, pacing, sequencing and melody.

Rob Halford on *Electric Eye* . . .

> "Well, *Electric Eye* is relevant because it talks about an invasion of privacy by spy satellites, but the cool thing is that I revisited that approach and wrote *Cyberworld* on the **Resurrection** CD,

and it just talks about the way that no matter where we go and what we do in the world, we're always under a microscope, and that there is no such thing as 100 percent privacy in your life."

19 WELCOME TO THE JUNGLE
GUNS N' ROSES

1611 points *from Appetite for Destruction (Geffen '87)*

More like welcome to the backstabbing hell that is the hypertense L.A. metal scene in the late '80s. That's the tight definition of the song, the expanded including ruthless L.A. ambition in all fields, the further expanded including the soul-destroying stresses of city life in general. The lasting impression is one of rhythmic punch, slashed by Slash, multiple stab wounds courtesy of Axl's plastic-burning whine. The song serves as the philosophical anchor to the album, the self-proclaimed welcome mat to a record vastly overrated in my mind. Still, what do I know? Half the album made the Top 500.

Duff McKagan on *Welcome to the Jungle* . . .

"That was a song written about a time when Axl had hitchhiked, either in a part of Queens or Brooklyn or maybe even the Bronx, where these little kids were swinging sticks at him (laughs). He found himself in this place where he just shouldn't have been. And then there were some old guys, you know, like, 'You're in the jungle; you're gonna die.' He's like, 'Fuck, let's get out of here.'"

20 RAINING BLOOD
SLAYER

1564 points *from Reign in Blood (Def Jam '86)*

Man, they could have stopped with the title, folded up their arms and mumbled, "Righteous, wicked. . . ." But they wrote a song, and it is a flaming epic of frenzied death, a better song than the record's only beef-eating brethren *Angel of Death* because *Raining Blood* is ultimately less topical, more surreal, crammed to overflowing with better riffs. It is a track more extreme in every way, faster, slower, thrashier, high tension-fraught and diamond-destroyed by solos that howl like small deadly bugs. It's over four minutes long but it positively and constantly swipes with a big hunting knife at conclusion, one that is forgone, a return to storm clouds of blood, if you can imagine that (Slayer apparently can). If you want to know what happens when **God Hates Us All**, Slayer take a lusty draw on green smoke and offer an exhaled suggestion.

Kerry King on **Reign in Blood** . . .

> "Definitely a high point in thrash history. I think in most people's eyes, in terms of albums, that's the record of records. And you know, we didn't think anything of it when we put it out. We thought, yeah, this record is cool, I'm digging it. And that's as far as we expected it to go at that point. We were just at the top of our game as far as speed goes. Probably the intense speed of **Reign in Blood** made **South of Heaven** so slow, because we just wanted to do something different."

Devin Townsend from Strapping Young Lad
Judas Priest — *Sinner*
Iron Maiden — *Back in the Village*
Warrior — *Fighting for the Earth*
Slade — *Run Runaway*
Metallica — *Ride the Lightning*
Metallica — *Leper Messiah*
Carcass — *Heartwork*
Fear Factory — *Scapegoat*
Anthrax — *Among the Living*
Keel — *The Right to Rock*

21 CREEPING DEATH METALLICA

1539 points *from Ride the Lightning (Music For Nations '84)*

Coulda called this one *Master of Master of Puppets*, *Creeping Death* presaging Metallica's ability to write long, involved songs that can still soothe any drooling headbanger. *Creeping Death*'s secret strength is its unique speed: faster than your average clunking Anthrax mosh, but not as fast as thrash or speed. It is indeed merely quick, hurrying at a clip that engages the heart. The song's other draw is its riff, Hetfield and Hammett rock 'n' rolling conventionally then all of a sudden stuffing in a bunch of notes, turning an obvious and plain headbang into something remarkable. Finally, *Creeping Death* sticks in the craw due to its cheerleading call-and-response vocal, the imaginative fan easily visualizing even the non-vocalists in the band rushing up to the mike on cue for a quick simple beery bark before getting back to what they do better.

Lars Ulrich on the modern, less extreme Metallica . . .

> "I'm very comfortable with it. There are so many taboos for a lot of people about hard rock and it's such a conservative and one-sided approach that a lot of these people have. The kids always love to incite shit all the time and then run away from it. And I love doing that with a lot of these things. Like the whole thing last year, when we came out wearing makeup. It was really to kind of fuck with people, because I really wanted to make sure that people didn't pigeonhole us and I did not think they knew exactly where we were at."

22 FADE TO BLACK METALLICA

1489 points *from Ride the Lightning (Music For Nations '84)*

Metallica's first shot at a dirge turns out, years and imported beers later, to have been one of their better attempts, *Fade to Black* finding a melody that isn't forced, the band's acoustic riffs sounding inspired like Randy Rhoads doing *Dee* or *Goodbye to Romance*. As well, teenage despair and suicide are subjects well-suited to this new blue thing called a Metallica ballad. And of course, it's a pretty kick-ass ballad, offering big Manowar pronouncements and later a state-of-the-art staccato riff at two speeds: slog and cruise (please compare with Saxon's *The Eagle Has Landed*), closing with Sabbath-sobbing twin leads and a heavy ears-a'-ringin' fade to black.

Lars Ulrich on changing times . . .

> "Obviously, my head is in a different place than it was in 1985. If we went out and didn't give you an exact picture of where our heads were at right now, then that really wouldn't be Metallica and that really wouldn't be fair. Every time, we've given you a picture of our heads. Every time we've given you a record, it's always been what that particular timeframe has been about for us. I think that's one of the things we're best at. We are best at not shielding our motions and instincts and just letting them come out. Whether you like what we do or don't like what we do, you can never take that away from us. That's probably the thing that I'm proudest of."

23 HIGHWAY TO HELL AC/DC

1469 points *from Highway to Hell (Atlantic '79)*

With what is likely the simplest guitar riff nestled inside the simplest drum pattern you'll ever hear, *Highway to Hell* was the Humble Pie-eyed heavy metal incarnation of the idea of Everyman. Folks on the right were scared of this song and for good reason. If it wasn't literally about Hell (it was actually written in dedication to the rigours of touring), it captured the wilful happy dead brain cell downward spiral of the messed-up partying metalhead through use of Satan's primal, primary poetic musical charms, the track ultimately being structured on near nothingness, oblivion. Again it is a dare from this atom-level, atom-sized band to please, look everywhere, under the cushions, behind the potted palm . . . we dare you to find a trace of ego in these songs.

Angus Young on independence . . .

> "Well you stick to your guns. There was a bit of worry, especially the title, *Highway to Hell*. They were a bit worried, especially from the American South as to whether it would be played. But we had said, 'You know this is what we called it and this is what we like,' and so we stuck to our guns. And funny enough, all the Southern states were the first ones to play it! And I suppose for Bon it probably was the peak of his career. The guy was full of life, and then he had the tragedy. When I think back in hindsight, he was a guy that I always knew was full of life."

24 THE TROOPER IRON MAIDEN

1463 points

from Piece of Mind (EMI '83)

Moving from the bombed-out cathedral into pitched street battle, *The Trooper* is an angst-ridden update on *Hallowed Be Thy Name* with Bruce urgently exhorting that time is of the essence, that the iron is hot, strike forth for America and conquer. As twin leads go (at least in the Maiden camp, one less emotionally valid than Thin Lizzy's), they don't get any better than *The Trooper* — Murray and Smith creating the sounds of death-impending WWII air battle, or conversely, The Wild Ride or perhaps The Four Horsemen of the Apocalypse (**The Nightcomers**?). *The Trooper* is also the classic bravado he-vocalist song of the early '80s metal wave, Bruce left alone to push all that air while we wait on tenterhooks for all those notes to be hit, rooting for the mini-man, applauding when this band on fire kicks in and kicks it home.

Bruce Dickinson on *The Trooper* . . .

"Yes, that was a vocal twister indeed. The crucial thing about *The Trooper* is that it starts off at one speed on the record and as we've played it over the years it's gotten progressively faster and faster and I've taken more chunks off the end of my tongue as my teeth have collided with it. But we've more or less got it down to a medium-paced gallop now, not the kind of off-the-clock sprint that it was earlier."

25 SMOKE ON THE WATER DEEP PURPLE

1460 points *from Machine Head (Warner '72)*

Methinks folks vote grudgingly for this one, because they believe it's simply required by the gods who made heavy metal, or if not the metal immortals, their custodians from upstate New York, Manowar, the circuitous absurd logic being that Eric Adams has got to be Ian Gillan's biggest fan in all of Valhalla. *Smoke on the Water*'s riff, after all, is the tantamount heavy-metal cliché, no competitors really, Ritchie unwittingly creating a stupid simple monster that stands up and sits down, repeatedly, on nothing more than your civic hall-variety folding steel chair. But people forget the woven funk of the verse, as well as its musical plot twists, Jon Lord giving the track spice, while Ian turns an inane (and probably in execution and event, quite boring) war story into some sort of life and death drama.

Ritchie Blackmore on *Smoke on the Water* . . .

"The first thing that comes to mind is that when we recorded *Smoke on the Water*, we got kicked out of the studio that we were in. Because it was a makeshift ballroom, because we were making too much noise and the police closed us down. So we had to get this other place, and the only place around was an old broken-down hotel. So the way we utilized the hotel is that we had the Rolling Stones truck mobile, which was stuck outside, put into the courtyard of this hotel and then the leads were run up the corridor. Well, they were through the reception, up the stairs, down the corridor, through a bedroom, then out onto a balcony, along the balcony, back through another bedroom, through a bathroom, through another bedroom, into a corridor, and that's where we were playing. So every time we would listen to a playback . . . normally, when you're in the studio, it's like, 'Come and hear that one and see what you think, lads,' every five minutes. With that, it was such a trick. And we had to walk along a balcony, and it was snowing. There was like a foot of snow. So you had to put your overcoat on to hear a playback, and walk, it was like fifteen minutes away. So after a while we'd just say, 'It's OK, Martin,' who was the producer, 'We believe you,' or we would hear it back through the cans because it was so far to walk. So that's how we recorded *Smoke on the Water*; it was very strange. It was freezing. There was no heating in this hotel. We were kind of blowing on our hands to try to warm them up."

26 BALLS TO THE WALL ACCEPT

1389 points *from Balls to the Wall (Lark '83)*

Balls to the Wall was considered at the time to be one of the few anthems to successfully borrow that simple intangible AC/DC had exploited to insane success in the low '80s. It is Accept disarmed, daring its fanbase to listen to the silence, the space between the dressy alchemical fireworks to which they'd become accustomed. Indeed *Balls to the Wall* is a classic of resolute, plodding metal, warm, reassuring guitar tones hanging over an unapologetically primary drum rhythm. Strapped with back-up vocals for miles, the song also contains one of the era's best meditative breaks, Udo whispering his rise-up exhortations before yet another round of that clarion chorus, which through the distortion, became stripped of any political implications, arriving at no more than a headbanger's complaint at the various things we all figured were complaint-worthy as young metal militia cheering on the general.

Udo Dirkschneider on *Balls to the Wall* . . .

"We had the hook line, 'balls to the wall,' which was in a book or something. Wolf or Stef came up with that and I came up with the melody. We had the idea that this song has to be against all the types of slavery in the world, that people have to start thinking that they won't be slaves, that they have to be free. So we had that idea, and then Stefan Kaufmann came up with the riff. It was a studio song, a studio creation, built up from the riff. In the beginning, no one knew how this song was going to turn out. One night I was alone with Stefan Kaufmann in the studio. I was really drunk (laughs) and I started singing in a different way, more like talking. And then the next morning, I said, 'Stefan and me can go to bed, and everyone else can listen to this stuff, and if you like it, OK, and if not, we have to think of something else.' And everybody came out and said, 'Yeah, that's it!'"

27 PEACE SELLS MEGADETH

1332 points *from Peace Sells . . . But Who's Buying? (Capitol '86)*

A fairly witty and self-deprecating lyric to this one, and what's more, the band are writing selflessly, simple, determined, workmanlike riffs, plodding to nowhere while Dave tells us about his unsavoury self. It's a well-loved Megadeth song though, because it's a welcome patch of open architecture amongst the band's wall of often unproductive speed. Plus it communicates, although the whole idea of the title and the chorus is completely disconnected from the verse, sort of tacked on as a fourth-quarter hurry-up offense, which just adds to the hapless charm of the thing, a charm which starts instantly the second Ellefson knocks off his disco intro.

Dave Ellefson on *Peace Sells . . .*

"Well, *Peace Sells,* it was back in January '86 I believe, Dave and I drove over to pick up our then drummer Gar Samuelson, and I remember it was kind of really rainy and Dave was just sitting there in silence in the car and he goes, 'You know, I've been thinking, what you think about this, "Peace sells but who's buying?"' and I'm like, 'That's pretty cool!' I didn't know what to say, but we got down to the studio and he picks up his guitar and he writes the riff and that was probably the quickest Megadeth song we'd ever written up to that point. It pretty much came together in one day, within one evening's rehearsal and that was it, it was done. And I remember the next day we were playing it, during the outro chorus, chiming in with the harmony, throwing this little vocal harmony on top and everybody is looking at me; they either think I'm completely losing my mind or they think it's really cool (laughs). And it was cool, Dave composed it, but it was one of those group moments where everything fell into place. It was like the song was there, it just had to come out."

28 RUN TO THE HILLS IRON MAIDEN

1321 points *from The Number of the Beast* (EMI '82)

Once more, a track from the endearing fan fave of Maiden albums scalps and yelps its way far up the list, hooves a' tumblin' and rumblin' while Harris and Nicko create a gallop that is out on the edge of collapse at any moment. If **The Number of the Beast**'s title track was melodically a light, slightly swishy twister on the band's breakthrough, *Run to the Hills* is even more so the record's guilty pleasure. Playing and ploying to the child within the man, it is about cowboys and Indians, which the track's low-budget Keystone video would reinforce. But even without the lyrics and the natty vid, the little melodic pirouettes at the end of each verse line and chorus line send this song into colouring book terrain (conversely, one can picture Cossacks doing the little kick foot crossed arms dance). Still, to my mind, *Run to the Hills* and *Gangland* are the weakest links on a rickety album. But this little warpaint and tomahawk shuffle obviously was taken to heart by many, perhaps also aided and abetted by the fact that it was the record's lead single, its biggest radio track. And we all know how radio and its communal spirit thereof can bring out the warm fuzzies.

Bruce Dickinson on *Run to the Hills*. . .

"*Run to the Hills* was the first track that we recorded together.

Actually, the whole album was recorded and mixed in five weeks, without a computer. There were no computers in those days. We had to break the board down halfway through because we had to record and mix a single, and go right back to square one and record the rest of the album. So that's probably one of the reasons *Run to the Hills* was a bit rushed."

29 YOU'VE GOT ANOTHER THING COMIN' JUDAS PRIEST

1317 points *from Screaming for Vengeance* (CBS '82)

Never underestimate the hypnotic Little Richard power of the rock 'n' roll two and four two-by-four. Priest did, until they saw the light and dimmed the light with *Living After Midnight* and their embarrassingly biggest hit *You've Got Another Thing Comin'*. Real stupid but real understandable, this track brought the primary-coloured love to what was a pretty heavy if boorish record, *You've Got Another Thing Comin'* stomping almost dirge-like through to an actorly, melodic, pre-chorus and then those, well . . . not exactly convincing words of warning coming from a band aiming to please with doughnuts. Basically, the band's Gene Simmons tribute, sweaty leathers, percussive retardation post-Peter Criss, listlessly listing and clogged brownish grey for miles.

Ian Hill on *You've Got Another Thing Comin'* . . .

"That was very much thrown together in the studio. We were mixing the album in Orlando, Florida and the album came up short. And the record company was screaming at us for a commercial type song, or something commercial for us, that they might be able to get on radio. And it very much took shape within an afternoon really (laughs). Although obviously it took a couple of days to get it put down. We got in there, started taking a few ideas around and that's what came out. It was very much a last minute thing."

30 HOLY DIVER DIO

1251 points

from Holy Diver (Warner '83)

Pompous, gothic, percussive and purposeful, *Holy Diver* is both the epic of its namesake album, as well as the debut-era track with the greatest throwback to Sabbath. Lyrically, it's Ronnie at his most malevolent and mischievous, the image reinforced with the album cover's fairly chilling and tasteless depiction of Murray doling out some punishment to a man of the cloth. And as with sister track *The Last in Line*, Vinny proves his mastery of the dirge, sparking the spaces with sparse but complexly placed accents, really pounding interest into a song that might pale with less impressive players.

Ronnie James Dio on *Holy Diver* . . .

"*Holy Diver* is, I guess, some form of religious song. It's about a saviour figure, like Christ, who is on another planet and has done the same as we know: God supposedly sacrificing his son for the sins of others. At this particular point, this Christ figure had done all that on this other world and now is going to another world to do the same thing, which could have been earth; it could have been anything. But the point was, the people in this first world were saying, 'Don't go down there. There are evil animals. There are tigers with stripes that are mean and there are all kinds of bad things. You're going to go down there and you're never going to come back again.' Its whole point was, gee, aren't people selfish? They just got through being saved by someone who died for their sins and now everything is OK in their world. But you won't let him go, because you're afraid that he won't always be there for you. What about other people in the universe? So again, it's a 'people are really weird' song (laughs). I don't think most people know what that song really is about. They have their own interpretation, which is cool to me, because I like to write songs that allow people to have their own judgments and make it their own song in their own special way. But that really is what the song is about."

John Dolmayan from System Of a Down
Iron Maiden — *Powerslave*
Slayer — *South of Heaven*
Fishbone — *Freddie's Dead*
Rush — *Hemispheres*
Led Zeppelin — *Misty Mountain Hop*
AC/DC — *Back in Black*
Deep Purple — *Space Truckin'*
Scorpions — *Holiday*
Metallica — *Whiplash*
Jimi Hendrix Experience — *Hey Joe*

31 FOR WHOM THE BELL TOLLS METALLICA

1244 points *from Ride the Lightning (Music for Nations '84)*

Perhaps this is Metallica's first great song, or at least the first one that wasn't doomed to slum it in the metal underground. *For Whom the Bell Tolls* was downright rock starry, daringly slow, stark come riff time, punctuated by lonely drum fills from Lars that sound like happy mistakes (especially the second one). It had atmosphere, heft, drama, indeed evoking images of war in slow motion, tanks and troops advancing inexorably on your indefensible position. Brilliant is as brilliant plods, and peppered throughout are breaks and bursts, slice-and-dice twin leads, and ultimately that boulder over the shoulder close that must be the soundtrack to the above imagined mercenary play-by-play. A sparkling, surprising patch of songwriting which, along with *Escape*, proves that the band could write better commercial slow songs on their second record than they were capable of through **Metallica** (The Black Album), **Load** and **Reload**.

James Hetfield on understanding Metallica . . .

> "People tend to overanalyze stuff too much. I sympathize a little bit, because I know it's got to be hard putting the two albums next to each other after five years of life that they have not lived with us. We've travelled the road but the fans have taken a Lear jet from that point to the present. We were on the road and we knew what was going on with us. It must be hard for them to accept change that drastic. For us it's not a change. It's so natural. There's no scheme, there's no plan. Things happen naturally and a lot of people worry so much about 'my Metallica.' It's very personal for a lot of people. If you're a Metallica fan, you follow us through thick and thin. Some of them might be really struggling to hang on. All they have to do is listen to the music and feel the honesty and integrity in it. That's what is Metallica. I think a lot of people understand that."

32 SHOUT AT THE DEVIL MÖTLEY CRÜE

1243 points *from Shout at the Devil (Elektra '83)*

Doomier, more decadent and somehow more uneasy in terms of basic sound, *Shout at the Devil* marked a second very distinct sound for the Crüe, the band leaving behind the youthful frenzy of the debut for this thick death shroud, distinguished by Tommy's dry, cardboard boxy drum sound and similarly hung, drawn and quartered guitars. The song fits perfectly the band's confused tangle of bubblegum in Satan's locks, galumphing along both dumb and dark, accessibly angled guitars stacked simply like heavy metal head-scratching Kiss circa **Creatures of the Night**, **Speak of the Devil**, **Talk of the Devil** (both Ozzy; same album), **Shout at the Devil**, and finally the original bee-boys Stryper with **To Hell with the Devil** . . . everybody was in on the coy Luciferian wordplay at the time.

Nikki Sixx on the satanic imagery of **Shout at the Devil** . . .

"I think that was more of the press taking something and running with it, you know? If you forget about the music for a minute, image-wise, by the time **Too Fast for Love** came out we had already evolved into doing this other thing, getting more macabre and theatrical, and *Shout at the Devil* was just a song, a political song at that. It had nothing to do with Satan. It was about Ronald Reagan, and that got twisted. We were just getting theatrical. It's cool, it was fine with me; it was our **Goat's Head Soup**."

33 FAST AS A SHARK ACCEPT

125 points

from Restless and Wild (Brain '82)

Bands had been this fast before, but perhaps not as thickly and gleefully heavy at the same time. *Fast as a Shark* (lyric interchangeable with *The Ripper*) went for the jugular, no frilly art rock maneuvering of the type you might find within fast Priest or Purple, just a rumbling pain pack of power set to thumping double bass drums (still a rarity at that time, save for Motörhead), topped with a vocal that was the perfect match for the track's apocalyptic landside. The song is a summit within the Accept catalogue, for everything before it, and indeed after it, never bit as hard. A true top-up to 11, *Fast as a Shark* continued but triple-underscored what is now a dependable metal tradition: opening a record with a white-out blitzkrieg, a hearty hello, the next wake-up wallop to eclipse this one coming with Metallica's formidable *Fight Fire with Fire* two years hence.

Udo Dirkschneider on *Fast as a Shark . . .*

"When we did this song, we weren't really thinking that we had to do this or that. It just came out, and what we did with *Fast as a Shark*, we were looking for an interesting beginning (laughs). That was the opening track for the **Restless and Wild** album and we were looking for something interesting to open up the whole album. Dieter Dierks is a very well-known name, the producer of Scorpions and he was also producing Accept. So Dieter Dierks' mother came up and she said, 'Yeah, what about if you start with a German folk song?' And I said, 'Yeah, uh-huh, let's have a listen.' She said, 'Yeah, I had this single, from when Dieter was twelve years old. He was singing together with a little girl, this German folk song.' So yeah, don't ask me why, but we said OK, this was interesting. There is that scream at the beginning, and it's something that is 'against.' It starts out very nice, but then she was very angry afterwards when we started scratching this record (laughs). So sometimes you do some kind of crazy thing and everybody was laughing at it at the beginning but now this has been like a trademark for a long time for Accept. And also, *Fast as a Shark*, a lot of people told me this, and I don't think Accept realized it, but people call it one of the first speed metal songs ever."

34 SABBATH BLOODY SABBATH BLACK SABBATH

1118 points *from Sabbath Bloody Sabbath (Warner '73)*

One of those ridiculously overloaded Sabbath lagwagons that may as well have featured Tony and Ozzy alone, *Sabbath Bloody Sabbath* finds Bill knocking the stuffing out of the song, battering the accents, pounding unconventionally the whole ball of rusted cables into the memory banks of a hopeless generation, simply because the year is 1973, and things are going to pot. Oz puts in one of his most harrowing, distressed vocal performances yet, and the bridge, or break, or first spade of earth, whatever that is, well, those are likely the most doomful, creepful seconds in an often fantastically dishevelled catalogue. And then the conclusion/concussion aches hits like whipping, recording guitar strings, once more Sabbath sailing convention right out the window, randomly, accidentally, fortuitously, brilliantly, finding something that would die on paper but somehow works horrifically but impressionably on tape.

Bill Ward on Geezer's lyric abilities . . .

> "One of my favourites is 'Bog blast all of you' on *Sabbath Bloody Sabbath*. It's just such a neat way of saying 'Screw you,' because he does it with such polite terminology. It absolutely got the point across. It's very difficult to pinpoint. Privately, and it's not very private anymore, but I've always referred to him as The Irish Poet. And I kind of romanticize like that when I think of him, because his descendency is Irish. Sometimes I see him as this kind of almost impish Irish vagabond writer/lyricist, which is a nice way of looking at him."

35 STAIRWAY TO HEAVEN LED ZEPPELIN

1065 points *from IV (Atlantic '71)*

When I started this project, I thought this song would win the whole enchilada, based on how it's always been the perennial (and cliché) victor of all those classic rock radio polls at New Year's. A certain line of thought might leave one obligated to place this classic gently in the number one slot. But time has marched onward, and folks who care about this stuff are both younger and heavier. This song is often consciously or unconsciously disqualified by certain voters as irrelevant or part of the larger rock world lite (and elite). But of course it's vaulted high nonetheless, *Stairway* being perhaps hard rock's most immortal, god-like composition, in base terms, an early power ballad, in slightly kinder terms, argument for Zeppelin as a prog rock band. Never been much of a fan myself, finding the lyric (and vocal) bloated, fuzzy and self-important, the mellow bits not nearly as sensual and sumptuous as say, *Going to California* or *Babe I'm Gonna Leave You*, nor the heavy bits nearly as remarkable or inventive as any half-dozen regal riffs off of

Physical Graffiti. Bit of a duff track really, filler; would have made a good B-side.

John Paul Jones on *Stairway to Heaven* . . .

> "I remember *Stairway to Heaven* was done kind of around the fire, a big fireplace, sitting around drinking cider. Page had a few things worked out on the guitar. He had these different sections and he was just playing them through and I remember picking up . . . I had brought all my recorders and my bits and pieces and I picked up the bass recorder and started playing that run-down with the guitar. Then Robert started jotting a few lyrics down. It was a very organic process, as most of our music was. Somebody would start something and somebody would follow, and it would turn into something else and you would sit down and work out what sections you've got and you'd put them together. It was all very easy, very relaxed."

36 ENTER SANDMAN METALLICA

1058 points

from Metallica (Elektra '91)

I've always considered this the next good radio rock song the band wrote after *For Whom the Bell Tolls* and *Escape*. But then the album took a crapper, as did the next two. *Enter Sandman* was an advance single from **Metallica**, better known as The Black Album, and it is an irresistible groovy rocker with a faux-evil riff and a primary-coloured, child's play lyric. Kirk's solo is annoying but Lars' trashy autopilot drumming is endearing to hear after such fuss and floss thus far in the career. A pivot track on a pivot album in the lifecycle of the band, one which surprisingly found critical praise and sales working in concert, *Enter Sandman* seemed designed to emanate metal experience rather than scream it with a bullhorn. To my mind it is no great shakes of a track, catchy but not godly, no real reinvention, but praiseworthy for its clarity and indeed its bravery to simply be a song. Needless to say, *Enter Sandman* broke it open for Metallica (12 million happy customers), simultaneously breaking the back of thrash which crawled back into the underground where it belonged and bonged.

Jason Newsted on *Enter Sandman* . . .

> "That was a tough one to do, because when it started to feel like it was going to be something, Bob was really adamant about me keeping things simple and thumping. He didn't want me to . . . like I did a few little things that were perhaps a little more Geezer-like in the earlier recordings, some of that regular kind of blues box stuff? I mean, in those sessions I learned so much, more in those 20 days than I learned probably in any 20 days. Just getting serious about how everything works, how sound actually works going to people's ears, you know what I mean? How the human ear hears shit, all these totally fundamental things that you would think could be so plain, but they really weren't."

37 STARGAZER RAINBOW

1041 points *from Rising (Polydor '76)*

As pioneering power metal epics go, only Zeppelin's *Kashmir* rubs epaulets with this strident astrological wizard rocker from Rainbow. Opening with a highly memorable drum film from the usually reticent Cozy Powell, the song thenceforth settles into its phase-shifting bulk. Ritchie and Ronnie are of entirely like minds, opening wide the book of secrets, taking us deep into a romanticized and ornate and magical past. Cozy plays conductor, bashing like Bonham an open, patient rhythm, while the rest of the band, significantly keyboardist Tony Carey and the Munich Philharmonic Orchestra, revisit materially and immaterially many *Kashmir* touchstones (please proceed to the ascending scale at the 4:38 mark). Perched as track one side two, *Stargazer* is a moody foil to a similarly lengthy and much speedier track, *Light in the Black*. Ritchie perhaps points to the importance of the former by sequencing the slow track at the pole position. In any event, *Stargazer* stands as the silent, wise and prescient monolith emanating instruction toward today's profuse power metal permutations. Priest, Zeppelin and Scorpions may all form part of the root system, but it is Rainbow and in particular *Stargazer* that embodies most quantifiable the mysteriously fanciful characteristics exploited so plainly and painfully all through today's beat to death with a broadsword Euro-metal scene.

Ronnie James Dio on **Rising** . . .

> "I was involved on the writing on all of them all the way through and I thought the first album blew the hell out of the other one. I thought the second one was amateurish and looking up people's asses, to tell you the truth. I thought the first album was populated with great songs, and the second album was nothing but an exercise on side B for Ritchie and Cozy to do what they eventually did in the live shows, which was to relegate us to go behind the amps and have drinks and Ritchie to play a solo on every song, which he did on *Stargazer* and *Light in the Black*, and for Cozy to be what he wanted to be, which was a drummer who plays all by himself."

38 HELLS BELLS
AC/DC

1003 points *from Back in Black (Atlantic '80)*

If *Highway to Hell* was misunderstood, then what we have here is the band's first spooky song, a successful attempt at a dark mood, ringed by ominous bells, soon to be a tiring live trademark of this basic band. But the appeal (!) of this song is the way it moves from the sludgy intro riff into a plush boogie recline for the verse, then back again, all a seamless bit of heavy fabric finery. Wot's the Hell? Who knows, life without Bon, perhaps. In any event, the track acts as a sonic sister to the album cover, much more synergistic to the message than the warm beer goggles rock elsewhere on this ten times platinum nation-state of a record.

Angus Young on acquiring Brian Johnson . . .

> "I remember the first time I had ever heard Brian's name was from Bon. Bon had mentioned that he had been in England once touring with a band and he had mentioned that Brian had been in a band called Geordie and Bon had said, 'Brian Johnson, he was a great rock 'n' roll singer in the style of Little Richard. And that was Bon's big idol, Little Richard. I think when he saw Brian at that time, to Bon it was, 'Well, he's a guy that knows what rock 'n' roll is all about.' He mentioned that to us in Australia. I suppose when we decided to continue, Brian was the first name that Malcolm and myself came up with, so we said we should see if we can find him. I never really compare them because they're both unique characters. Brian, at the time, had big shoes to fill. He's certainly done that and more so they both got their own unique characters but they both have similarities which in AC/DC we all share. All our backgrounds are pretty much the same; we all come from working-class families, we all have the wit that seems to sustain us when things are a bit tough."

39 THE LAST IN LINE DIO

972 points *from The Last in Line (Warner '84)*

Possibly the white hot apex of the classic Dio line-up's chemistry, *The Last In Line* rumbles with an authority that establishes Dio as a metal machine every bit as valid as Sabbath. Everybody works to stir the passionate brew, the result being a song driven by a formidable rhythm section — Bain and Appice in possession of both power and finesse, the song breathing deeply, blessed with seemingly infinite spaces in which Ronnie melodicizes mournfully. Viv's attack is measured, Zeppelin-esque, his flashy fills the icing on the cake. All told, what occurs is a slow song made interesting by neck-throttling performances, elocution through execution, a tough beast to wrangle and rope right.

Ronnie James Dio on *The Last in Line* . . .

"I write songs for people, how people feel about being lonely, for being pecked at for not being the greatest physical specimens on earth; things like that just happen. So this one for me describes people who persevere through all the stones and slings and arrows that are tossed at them. The last in line, that's usually where people like that are placed, the end of the line. But to me, just because you're at the end of the line doesn't mean that you can't succeed. And I usually find that the people who are willing to stay there at the end of the line will succeed."

40 SEASONS IN THE ABYSS SLAYER

971 points *from Seasons in the Abyss (Def American '90)*

Man, Slayer made speed and then Slayer undermined that position with their irresistible groove proposals, this panoramic record-closing epic humming along like a pop song compared to the thrash of old. But it's the kind of undeniable rhythm 'n' riff that translates live, allowing for a little fun Spinal Tap dance choreography on the part of a band that otherwise, let's face it, is very preoccupied with just trying to get it all done. *Seasons in the Abyss* is like *South of Heaven* with trees and hedges and birdbaths, a secluded garden cultivated with patient attention. The song is wound like a gold pocket watch, from a position of assassin-motionlessness to precision timekeeping, indeed even Araya singing calmly a disjointed phrase game of pain.

Tom Araya on *Seasons in the Abyss* . . .

"I remember when I came up with the first verse. I was reading a book by Stephen King, about a writer who had a dual personality. It deals with black crows, and it was about a writer who had a fictional character. Every time he would write about something, the murder would actually happen, what he wrote about actually came true. But the first verse, I got from this paragraph that was describing him holding up a knife, and how he was looking at the knife, and on the edge of the knife he could see his victim, that kind of thing. And that's how I came up with 'razor's edge etc.,' the first line of *Seasons in the Abyss*. But the main thing I remember about that is the video, which we filmed in Cairo, Egypt. We were there for nine days and filmed for nine days, and that alone was an experience. I really enjoyed my time there. I wish we could be free to travel there without any problems, because it's a really awesome place. Everyone should visit the pyramids at least once in their life."

41 BURN
DEEP PURPLE

960 points

from Burn (Warner '74)

The light is blinding on this album's undeniable showcase, *Burn*, containing no less than Ritchie's most note-dense and characteristic riff of the album, Ian Paice's opportunity to play lead drums like Keith Moon, and finally, the chance for the band's duelling lead vocalists (an embarrassment of riches), to play-off for decision of dominance. Everything else on what turns out to be a pensive album, pales in comparison as Deep Purple grudgingly compresses all the rock they are required by law to deliver, so the blues and funk can breathe and bloom and expand elsewhere, much to Ritchie's chagrin, the man eventually bounding off-screen to re-create the song's machine-gunning glory with Rainbow's *Light in the Black*.

Glenn Hughes on *Burn* . . .

"*Burn* was for that line-up of Deep Purple, what *Highway Star* was for the previous line-up. When we wrote the song, I realized that this song was going to become a trademark intro on tour and on the record. I knew it directly when we started to write the song. We just knew it was the one. There was no doubt that *Burn* was going to be the opening track as well as the opening track on the live show, which it was. To me it was a major song to be involved with. I had parts to sing as well and it was a really cool thing for me to get up there and sing to millions of people. So it was the opening of a big door for me."

42 COWBOYS FROM HELL PANTERA

947 points *from Cowboys from Hell (Atlantic '90)*

In direct, meticulously sustained fashion, *Cowboys from Hell* defined the dry, gated Dimebag sound better than any other sledge on the seminal album or any of this record's fine successors. Hot-stamp and stop-clocked, *Cowboys from Hell* is all angles, the band chopping metal into black and white, infinitely dense or unemotionally absent, Phil almost rap-roaring the new impressive glam-discarding Pantera credo, a two-fisted package which could not be ignored.

Vinnie Paul on *Cowboys from Hell . . .*

> "A staple. It would be like going to see Kiss and them not playing *Rock and Roll All Nite*. You gotta play it, you know? *Cowboys from Hell*, we've played at every show we've ever done. That's the one that started it for us. That's the one people know us by. It's our nickname, C.F.H., and it will always be part of the set. Same thing with *Walk*, it's always been part of the set, ever since **Vulgar** came out. Those two will always be in there no matter what we change. I remember when we wrote *Cowboys from Hell*, we all knew at that point in time that it was the very best song we'd ever written. It was pretty much a launching pad for the direction we took with our music from that point forward."

Vinnie Paul from Pantera
Judas Priest — *Metal Gods*
Black Sabbath — *Sweet Leaf*
Van Halen — *Outta Love*
Judas Priest — *Electric Eye*
Metallica — *Whiplash*
Led Zeppelin — *Immigrant Song*
Kiss — *Black Diamond*

Black Sabbath — *Neon Knights*
Black Sabbath — *Planet Caravan*
Slayer — *Raining Blood*

43 BEYOND THE REALMS OF DEATH JUDAS PRIEST

924 points *from Stained Class* (CBS '78)

Priest of course got dragged into court over this defiant epic (can art cause one to off oneself?), an emotionally devastating song poetically blurring the edges between intellectual and emotional withdrawal, autism, coma and suicide. Set to a haunting acoustic backtrack, Halford turns in a resigned, plainspeak, echo-plagued vocal performance, which becomes anguished come pounding chorus time. The riffs, once they arrive, resoundingly drive home the point that withdrawal is an irreversible choice, that volume will drown out all reservations. The culmination is a veritable guitar war, topped finally by Halford upon high.

Rob Halford on *Beyond the Realms of Death* . . .

> "I love that song because whenever I sing it, emotionally it takes me on a wonderful journey. I think about a lot of things when I sing that song. Obviously I think about my times with Priest. I also reflect on some of the unfortunate situations that happened with people in rock 'n' roll, to some extent the fans, people who have difficulties in life and for one reason or another, want to end their life in different ways. But also it's a song that has a lot of strength because it's talking about an individual surviving those difficult times."

44 SYMPTOM OF THE UNIVERSE
BLACK SABBATH

922 points *from Sabotage (Warner '75)*

It didn't work out in the history books this way, but *Symptom* should have replaced *Smoke on the Water* as the ultimate heavy metal riff, Iommi churning out a no-nonsense smudge of unapologetic evil that motors along, driven capably by one of Bill Ward's most maniacal performances. Lyrically, it's also a stunner, very poetic, very otherworldly, with hook-laden phrasing and druggy complexity at every linguistic turn. Its cocktail jazz back half derives from either genius, lunacy, or hallucination, Sabbath throwing up one of their kaleidoscopic surprises, the concept of these left turns becoming commonplace by the time **Sabotage** finishes presenting its full width and girth and mirth.

Bill Ward on *Symptom of the Universe . . .*

> "Well again, there is the fact that we actually show up with jazz parts. And that goes back to our roots where there were some jazz influences in our playing. But back then, as we do right now, the songs are a little bit unpredictable. So we never quite know. We try to make it a bit unusual for the listener. We have a similar thing going on right now where there are surprises and things aren't repetitive, little twists and turns. And *Symptom of the Universe* was one of those songs. In terms of my drum fills, it was just the appropriate thing to do. Tony and Geezer just hammered it out, and as soon as Ozzy's voice got on there and we got closer, it was just a natural thing to do. So I'm not aware that I had any preconceived notions. I just played it, I just played against wherever we were at the time."

45 SOUTH OF HEAVEN
SLAYER

911 points *from South of Heaven (Def Jam '88)*

Having combined, on **South of Heaven**'s predecessor **Reign in Blood**, the power of these guitars in concert with producer Rick Rubin, the war-beating backbone of Lombardo (the drum tornado), and the abstract concept of dynamics, Slayer set out to explore the many ways and means of heavy. *South of Heaven* opens the album of the same hellish title and delves straight into atmosphere, barely advancing, laying it on thick, moving like a mall-sized black pig that thenceforth begins a groovy pork leg dance, tossing off hair salons and sunglasses huts as it advances through the deep muddy wallow of a flooded ravine. Seems like a pro-choice anthem but then again, the next one looks to be pro-life, even though both wanna rock the apocalypse hard, fast and soon, please. Slayer-style. Well done. Burnt.

Dave Lombardo on *South of Heaven* . . .

> "*South of Heaven* is a song that, to me, was written in a way to conform to a kind of mainstream style, yet still retaining a cutting edge. It had choruses, you know, 'on and on south of Heaven' (sings it). That was very different for Slayer, because Slayer rarely used any of the titles in their songs. They did, but they didn't, not that often, and if they did, not in a very accessible way. **South of Heaven** was cool; that was an OK period. Then with **Seasons**, things started to go down. But **South of Heaven** was a good time. I really wasn't happy with the drum sound, or I should say with the overall sound, because they put the drums up front, which to me was like 'Oh man, what are you guys trying to do?' The mix wasn't quite all there. I mean, it was there, but it was not how **Reign in Blood** was. The drums were more upfront, in-your-face, which is great. Now that I look back at it I think wow, that's a real compliment to me."

46 RAINBOW IN THE DARK DIO

906 points *from Holy Diver (Warner '83)*

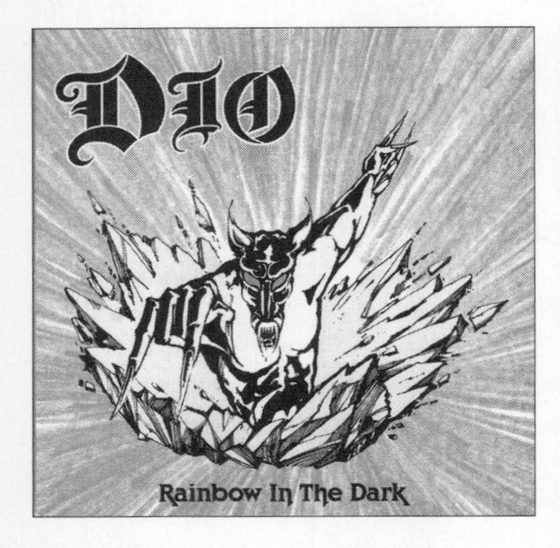

Somewhat derided both for being a hit and for featuring a wimpy but addictive Casio-level keyboard line, *Rainbow in the Dark* charmed people due to its straight-eight *Louie Louie* melody, as well as Vinny's stirring, propulsive drumming. It is also a free and easy Ronnie lyric, clearly discernible, ably and concretely addressing the themes for which Ronnie is known. Its construction is simple enough for radio and more importantly, the stage, where mud obscures fusspot rockers like *Stand up and Shout*. I'll never forget the surprise I felt hearing *Rainbow in the Dark* in a beer commercial. It was radio, granted, but it was still Dio. Bloody 'ell!

Ronnie James Dio on *Rainbow in the Dark* . . .

> "I don't know why it touched so many hearts but it did. I wanted to get rid of that song. I hated that song. I absolutely hated that song. In fact, I came real close to taking a razor blade to the tape! Everyone said, 'Please don't do that! That's a good one!' Luckily, they talked me out of it!"

47 DETROIT ROCK CITY KISS

881 points *from Destroyer (Casablanca '76)*

No surprise *Detroit Rock City* crashed way up our chart. It is the grand objet d'art on the only Kiss record that could (quizzically) be described the same way. Its chords are foreboding, matched perfectly with the simple yet chilling tale of twisted metal. **Destroyer** was one of those magical Beatles on Ed Sullivan albums for many a metalhead of a specific age, and the brilliant way this song opens the record — first eerie sound samples and then that thrilling military-snared wind-up — sets the tone for NDE tracks like *God of Thunder* and *Great Expectations*. And don't it groove, Paul singing black, Gene playing black (or is that Paul? Only Bill Aucoin would consider spilling the beans), even Peter shuffling resolutely through the song's airy, open spider crawl. The break is spooky and astonishingly more Lizzy-like than lizard-like. As well, the chorus soars with an authority Kiss would rarely carry again, and to be fair, would rarely attempt, purely by deliberate choice. The epic of the catalogue, and a rare Kiss song that glides lubricated heads held high above the band's usual burger barn BTO stomp.

Ace Frehley on *Detroit Rock City* . . .

> "We opened up the last tour with that. That's a real kick-ass song, a lot of fun. And it's basically Kiss' tribute to the second city that kind of gave us life. Obviously, New York was the first. But a lot of people in the early days thought we were from Detroit because we kind of broke out of Detroit. We were headlining in Detroit prior to headlining in a lot of other major marketplaces. But basically that song was inspired by the fact that Detroit gave us life. Working with Bob Ezrin was different, you know? He was kind of like a dictator. He had new ideas and some of it didn't always go with the flow of the way everybody thought things should go. But I think in retrospect, Bob had a lot more knowledge than we did at the time and we were wrong and he was right. Because that album stands the test of time."

48 WALK
PANTERA

877 points *from Vulgar Display of Power (Atlantic '92)*

One of those crystallizing moments in the invention of aggro rock from hardcore and metal's base elements, *Walk* pimp-rolls, jackboots and moshes all at once, Phil menacing with a violent, "Are you talking to me?" over one of the band's early stark rock boxes. The production is quintessential Pantera, and its strict pattern allows you to hear the mountains move within Dimebag's sonic six-string concoction. Endearing because it's clear, clean and credo.

Rex on **Vulgar Display of Power** . . .

> "I definitely think it's one of the key albums. I think **Cowboys** definitely turned some heads and then here comes **Vulgar Display of Power** and it definitely went and twisted peoples heads all the way around. It was different from anything anybody was doing at that time. I think a lot of it has to do with timing, but at the same time if you took those songs today and put them out . . . it still comes up with the songs. That's all there is to it and that's what we've always tried to do, to make the fucking song the best you can make the song. I think Pantera is Pantera. We've been kicking everybody's fucking ass for a long time."

49 CHILD IN TIME DEEP PURPLE

797 points *from In Rock (Warner '70)*

The only rule-breaker on an otherwise pioneeringly metallic album, *Child in Time* is first and foremost a vocal showcase for Ian Gillan, who gets to prove his mettle amidst virtual silence. It also is indicative of this band's support of an admirable rock quality in the '70s, this idea of no boundaries, no rules, and indeed no time limit. Whether crowds at the band's live shows appreciated this last character trait is up for debate, *Child in Time* being more like hot dog and bathroom break time, despite what rewritten history might espouse.

Ian Gillan on *Child in Time* . . .

> "*Child in Time* was a nick. We nicked it from a group called It's A Beautiful Day and they had a record called *Bombay Calling*. We played that and slowed it down. It was very fast and it was with a violin. So we were just impressed with that and we played in the studio, in the rehearsal room one day, and it just evolved out of a jam really."

Andre Matos from Angra
Iron Maiden — *Hallowed Be Thy Name*
Iron Maiden — *Wasted Years*
Manowar — *Mountains*
Judas Priest — *Painkiller*
Def Leppard — *Foolin'*
Saxon — *Power And The Glory*
Queensryche — *Walk In The Shadows*
Deep Purple — *Perfect Strangers*
Helloween — *Eagle Fly Free*
Whitesnake — *Still of the Night*

50 SEEK AND DESTROY METALLICA

768 points *from Kill 'Em All (Music for Nations '83)*

The most instantly hit-like of the four groovy songs on **Kill 'Em All** (other three being *The Four Horsemen*, *No Remorse* and *Jump in the Fire*), *Seek and Destroy* is sort of a cruising song for secret agents, y'know, James Bond on the prowl for Josie or one of her Pussycats. It is linear, patient, clean and pure of purpose. Plus ain't that the most magical guitar sound you've ever heard? It's the type that rock stars like Metallica and Bob Rock spend hours and days trying to get rid of. At 6:50, it's a bit long, but the revisitation of the main verse riff is never unwelcome because of its undeniable Tom Jones swing. What's more, Metallica find a cool way to wind it up, simply trying out a few more perfectly serviceable riffs, riffs so good, they could have been songs.

Lars Ulrich compares then with now . . .

> "We're less extreme in the way we're sitting in the musical landscape than we were in 1983. We are, obviously, a lot more embraced by the mainstream than we were. But millions of records later, the same things still fuel us. I'm more into the cre-

ative process than I used to be, and less into the endless mindlessness of touring than I used to be. Those are probably the main differences between now and back then. I don't think that anybody who was there in 1983 would get the same vibe as they do from **Load**. But that doesn't mean that we have to deliver anything else than what we want. Part of that vibe, which is a vibe that I've had myself a lot with bands that I was into, was that you are the only kid on the block who was into that type of thing. I certainly got that vibe with a Diamond Head or whatever, but I never got that vibe with an Iron Maiden because Iron Maiden was just so big and there was a guy next to me who knew who Iron Maiden was. So I think that what certainly has happened is we are one of those rare bands that, as we grow older, we don't let age not interfere with what we do. I mean that the way I said it. We don't let age not interfere with what we do. We don't pretend that doesn't happen, where as I think a lot of other hard rock bands do that. I think they try and suppress that. I think that one of the things I'm very psyched about, generally, is the fact that that happens. You draw different influences and inspirations than you did five years ago, ten years ago."

51 RUNNIN' WITH THE DEVIL VAN HALEN

758 points — *from Van Halen (Warner '78)*

Van Halen somehow absorbed all sorts of entertainment rules practised by few other bands. One was leave them wanting more, which is the whole premise of this coy debut album classic. *Runnin' with the Devil* was like the band's highly revered **Montrose** album slowed down, and it also made a case for Van Halen as a blues combo. Indeed — leap with me — it seems the entire history of American film, TV and music is embedded in this brown, unattractive song for squares in the '50s. It has a tired conformist lope that even Dave can't revive, even though he and his credo share centre Catskills stage. Of course this miasma of middle America thenceforth gets a pan-seared strafing from Eddie's guitar, the track elevated further by the simple chorus, a typically naïve schoolboy harmony back-up vocal by this band of unsuspecting rock saviours. And like I say, the whole incredulous plod becomes a seductive and ultimately sold exercise in restraint, the low confident hum on a kaleidoscopic but jumpy album, a weird rest spot that somehow takes you back to the golden age of television, Dave's childhood monkey-around training ground that was to cause the Dave we all still love.

Alex Van Halen on the timelessness of music . . .

> "One thing I learned from my first gig at 13 is that music transcends age; it doesn't have to be a certain way. I mean there are limits. I don't think a 29-year-old rocker has New Kids On The Block in his collection (laughs). But music seems to stand the test of time. Take Zeppelin for example. Much of it is as relevant today as the day it was written. It means one of two things: either they were ahead of their time, or music hasn't come too far since. I think it's a little bit of both. But what came of it is that heavy metal or hard rock is now a bona fide specific type of music style; there's really no need to change it. You can expand on it and go in different directions, but it's basically a beat with blues-based stuff played around. Applying this to us, I think the key to our longevity is very simple. We don't think about following trends or setting trends and we don't think about anything contrived. We just go with the flow. Why change something that doesn't need to be fixed? If you get contrived, you're playing a game; you're gambling, and we're not gamblers."

52 OVER THE MOUNTAIN
OZZY OSBOURNE

750 points *from Diary of a Madman (Jet/CBS '81)*

Thankfully heavier than anything off the debut, *Over the Mountain* rattles into scope view with a signature double bass drum triplet barrage before Rhoads slices us sinister with a forceful, purposeful riff topped by an equally deliberate Ozzy in an unusually metaphysical mood (I always thought Van Halen's *Mine All Mine* was some sort of bastard child of this track). Come chorus time, the vocal melodies and indeed Ozzy's lyric echoes and quotes old Sabbath tones. But it's the avalanche of drums matched blow for blow by the steely lurch of Rhoads that makes this metal monster shine blind.

Ozzy Osbourne on being labelled metal . . .

"With me, it's never good enough. I'm the most self-critical person you'd ever want to meet. In three months time, I'll listen to the latest record and say, 'Goddamn it, I knew I should have done that bit.' But I suppose that goes for us all. One of the things that really annoys me is the fact that I'm put under the bracket of heavy metal. And heavy metal, to me, stems from Poison to Bon Jovi to Metallica to Ozzy. If you look at it, there's no comparison. Anyone with long hair and guitars is heavy metal, which is very sad, as it's very restrictive on my behalf. My music is . . . Ozzy music. I suppose I was one of the forefathers of what you call this fucking heavy metal. And honestly I think that if it's good . . . you know, there's some of this music I hear and I think, 'Fuck, what the hell is that all about?' But somebody likes it, so what right do I have to say that this is radical stuff, that this stuff that goes nowhere quick and ends up nowhere quick, is not good? But I do think it goes for six months at a time in cycles."

53 CHILDREN OF THE GRAVE BLACK SABBATH

748 points *from Master of Reality (Warner '71)*

Set to what was at the time, the world's first clear-cutting rhythmic tour de forest, *Children of the Grave* is another of Sabbath's big finger-wavers, warning of an apocalypse, no future in '71, keep on warring and there will be dead children everywhere. It is of course the riff that makes *Communication Breakdown* look like a little girl's summer blouse, a smothering bulldozer of a sped up slo-mo blur that finds Iommi's guitar cursed and howling in amplified hell. Gallop on, wayward son.

Geezer Butler on discovering a career . . .

"Hell, we just thought we'd last two or three years and that would be it until we got real jobs. We weren't thinking like, you know, this is revolutionary music and it's going to be around for years. We just thought it was something to pass the time. But the lyrics, they're all the same theme aren't they (laughs)? *Children of the Grave* was about how if we don't watch how we're polluting the earth we're all going to end up dead."

54 DIARY OF A MADMAN OZZY OSBOURNE

736 points *from Diary of a Madman* (CBS '81)

Practising the progressive rock of conceptual Alice Cooper, Ozzy and his band go for baroque in the house of metal mirrors. *Diary of a Madman* is sad and creepy at once, stiffly channel-surfing between very electric guitars and soundtracky acoustic, all glazed with occasional strings and punctuated by military snare. The buried treasure within is a brief Rhoads break which just might be the man's best riff, an elaborate sequence of off-tones that is over before Ozzy's Satanic cult choir can say "boo!"

Ozzy Osbourne on depression . . .

"Every single day I would have the feeling that I was terrified of living, but so afraid of dying. Every single fuckin' day. For years and years and years, I lived my kind of hell. Then I look at somebody like Kurt Cobain and I couldn't be that bad. There's got to be a lower place than where I was. That's dreadful. When you wake up in the morning with that feeling, it's beyond shame, it's beyond fear, it's beyond anything else. You just don't fit in this world. You can't find a place to go. To carry those feelings away, you have to do exactly the same thing that got you there the night before. It's like a merry-go-round of madness. Then you've got to perform in front of people. In the end you're taking valium, tranquillizers, drugs and booze, and you've got the fear itself. I started to blackout. I started to fall to pieces. I'm still not normal right now. I still have to speak to people. I still have to take medication, but for different reasons now. I have to take antidepressants and whatnot."

55 ACES HIGH IRON MAIDEN

736 points

from Powerslave (EMI '84)

Aces High, flying on fumes. Third and arguably the last record of the world's love affair with Maiden, **Powerslave** contained a few tracks that seemed forced. *Aces High* was one of them, a frantic romp of kitchen-sink creative panic, the story, gratingly topical and lame, the metal, a tad rehashed and concentrically idiosyncratic. But it is beloved, placing quite high on our list, rocking briskly within a very golden period for this band and metal in general, perched deliberately at pole position on an album that was hyped to the hills, *Aces High* expected to carry the hype, even as other tracks (I can think of three) quietly took over the task as Eddie's ambassadors. To my mind, the chorus, already weak, seals the ring around the mental block with that modulation bit, the band searching for the key to more of the great bits that were all over **The Number of the Beast** and **Piece of Mind**, coming up not completely empty, but disconcertingly forced to mete out rations.

Adrian Smith on *Aces High* . . .

> "The first time we played that was in Jersey, where we used to rehearse, in the Channel Islands. It's a typical Iron Maiden song, one of Steve's better songs I think. It's really exciting and uptempo. It was like, yeah, if this is how this album is going, this is going to be a great album."

56 WHOLE LOTTA LOVE LED ZEPPELIN

727 points *from II (Atlantic '69)*

As if to underscore the idea that *Communication Breakdown* was no accident, or at minimum, that Zep weren't done with this boorish bit of debauch called heavy metal, the band fired up another eternal riff, a memorable one, if a bit brown and weakly recorded. But as is the case until **Physical Graffiti**, Zeppelin's form of hard rock is inextricably tangled up in the blues, Plant especially, even if this time the boys try out a bit of half-hearted psychedelia, crap really, but given their pact with Satan, trumpeted as state-of-the-art. Can you tell I'm sick of this song? That I've never been a fan? That I think the whole album is the biggest stinkeroo of the catalogue, tied with **Presence**?

57 BREAKING THE LAW JUDAS PRIEST

719 points *from British Steel (CBS '80)*

I thought for years Halfie was saying "Darryl was completely wasted . . . ," picturing Darryl to be Rob's idea of some American hesher dude likely to blow his alienated jaw off. And this song doesn't really work autobiographically anyway. Rob's just too well-assembled, confident and cocksure to be in any sort of crisis, too aristocratic to be breaking any non-bondage-related laws. In any event, this became the calling card of the band's new straight-forward radio rock style, brisk like a winterized slap in the face, melodic, thespian ("You don't know what it's like . . ."), slightly mischievous come chorus time, *Jailbreak*-breakout come break time (compare: you'll see).

Rob Halford on *Breaking the Law* . . .

"*Breaking the Law* is just one of the great metal songs of all rock 'n' roll. It will be as strong as it was when it was created in '80, '81, and here we are 20 years later playing that song at Rock In Rio, and all the people are singing it word for word. And it just says everything above what rock 'n' roll represents. It's a real high-energy, anarchic, gang-type number. It just brings everybody together because of what it talks about, namely that we go through our early stages in life and we feel that we are being made a lot of promises and then when those promises are broken, we react. And that's something I think everyone can relate to. It's a fun song too. It has a serious tone but it's a great, fun song to experience and I'm aware that when I play that song around the world it gets an incredible reaction."

58 STILL OF THE NIGHT WHITESNAKE

709 points *from Whitesnake (Geffen '87)*

Man, they don't make riffs with bigger meat chunks or thicker gravy than this John Sykes monster combobulator. *Still of the Night* renders the Moody/Marsden version of the band a distant, dim light bulb of a memory, tearing out theater seats as it works through its reoxygenated Led Zeppelin bloodlines. And boy, did "David Coverversion" suffer the slings and arrows for it, critics conveniently ignoring the fact that this was the only time in the canon (save for maybe *Slow an' Easy*) the band went there with any deliberation. Any other recognizable tweaks you could, and should, put down to shared influences.

David Coverdale on *Still of the Night* . . .

"*Still of the Night,* a quick scenario: many, many years ago I was going through my mother's attic in the north of England, and I was going through all these old work tapes from the Purple days. So I grabbed them and threw them in my bag and listened to them. A lot of it was crap, but it was very funny for me to hear the journey from the seeds of songs that became ultimate Purple staples. And I found a demo that Ritchie Blackmore had given me and I thought, well, that's an interesting riff. So I took that and changed it around completely to the point where it had absolutely nothing to do with the initial inspiration. But credit where credit is due. And then I presented my take on this riff to John Sykes, who put a great attitude on it and took it further as only he could. There is lot of Led Zeppelin comparison there, which I don't have a problem with, because Zeppelin was fucking marvellous and continues to resonate. But the huge influence on that is one of my favourite songs from my childhood, *Jailhouse Rock*, Elvis Presley, and another huge influence was the Jeff Beck Group, when Rod Stewart was singing with them. And part of the atmospheric thing was an inspiration from a track of his called *Rice Pudding*. I tell you, I've played that song all over the world and nobody had a problem with it other than Robert Plant (laughs). And of course a couple years later I have Page playing it, going, 'This is fucking hard!' That's what he said, but no, he played it great. But it was interesting watching him go, 'What are these fucking chords?!'"

59 AIN'T TALKIN' 'BOUT LOVE VAN HALEN

690 points *from Van Halen (Warner '78)*

Live, electric and Zeppelin-esque, *Ain't Talkin' 'Bout Love* wins and wins more based on a central charm: Eddie. The man's riff is brilliant, and the execution thereof, volatile, alone, and in no need of window dressing. While the verse does its business, Eddie is staccato and behaved, and when the chorus comes along, rather than write anew, he simply frizzes out the previous pattern into power chord madness, while a chorus of laddish voices holler o'ertop. Also solidifying the track is a selection of cymbals from Alex, who crashes and splashes with music-making joy when not riding the ride bell with giant-slaying groove. *Ain't Talkin' 'Bout Love* is also a prime example of Eddie's ability to pull off soloing and end of bar guitar fills without resorting to an underlying, supportive rhythm track. You listen along, and you go, 'My God, this could be four guys live,' just like select Zep rockers, just like early tub-thumpers from Sabbath.

Alex Van Halen on David Lee Roth . . .

"As a human being, you're supposed to forgive and forget and all that shit. I have no problem with that. But I ain't going out for dinner with him, I ain't gonna have a drink with him . . . I don't want to talk to him. There's nothing to talk about. And I'm speaking for all the members of the band. There was no falling out: the guy treated us like shit. We never really told the press what really happened — the motherfucker fired us. He was pissed off 'cause the band wasn't named after him. That was all that it boiled down to. He wanted to be the big cheese. He didn't like Ed getting more attention. That's why he fired Steve Vai. Now he records with one band in the studio, takes another out on the road . . . I mean, what the fuck's the point? I believe in karma; I don't wish bad on anybody and I don't care. My feeling is total ambivalence. It was a long time ago. You gotta remember, Ed wrote all the music. And isn't that what counts?"

60 ROCK AND ROLL ALL NITE
KISS

675 points *from Dressed to Kill (Casablanca '75)*

A glam anthem if there ever was one, *Rock and Roll All Nite* is immersed in chords that are the electric equivalent of a rock 'n' roll hot tub, all delirious, hot, cocooning and child-like. Once more, Kiss write a song that could only come from one other place, and that's Bachman Turner Overdrive, both bands sounding like a naive summation of an embarrassing roots lexicon, zinged and zipped almost accidentally into a cogent and accepting time and place. How to write a hit song seems to be the crowning motivation, a hit song for guys, a hit song with an out of date boogie-woogie core, surmising that Little Richard never goes out of date. And oy vey, what a chorus, a gang of romper room voices turning innocent and truly primary, an idea that is actually pretty debauched: if you rock and rolled all night and partied every day, even for a half week, you'd probably die a dramatic drug-flamed death. In fact, it's a pretty evil way to spend even a few days, much crazier than anything I've ever seen a black metal band do.

Ace Frehley on *Rock and Roll All Nite* . . .

"I remember recording *Rock and Roll All Nite* and party every day. I remember Neil Bogart and a whole bunch of people in the studio; basically they came in from the control room, and everybody just started singing the chorus toward the end. It was a lot of fun, kind of a special night."

61 2 MINUTES TO MIDNIGHT IRON MAIDEN

668 points

from Powerslave (EMI '84)

If one digs deep into the philosophy and nature and structure of all that came before it, one can, through the fog, work out on a good enough calculator, that *2 Minutes to Midnight* marked a new style for Maiden, eminently successful, almost accidental, rarely revisited, never as successfully. Its secret is two-fold. First, it is a bona fide riff rocker, or more accurately a riff rock 'n' roller. It is somehow less Maiden-like than the brunt of the catalogue, more participatory in the muckabout that was the NWOBHM. Second, Bruce really shines lyrically, writing poetically and obscurely about a complicated subject, one even more complicated when one ascribes to it different meanings, the "two minutes to midnight" concept proposed as encompassing many levels of apocalyptic concern. The charm of the rock 'n' roll is further enhanced by the song's ragged nature, Nick deep, in fact slouched, in the pocket, the band's chemistry at an all-time high. Ragged as well, is the meandering but mood-enhancing break that sounds extravagantly loitered like Van Halen before it picks up and drives head-on into that rock 'n' roll riff of Adrian's once again. An epic without the fatigue of one.

Adrian Smith on *2 Minutes to Midnight* . . .

"Well, that's basically a hard rock tune. People know me and that's what my thing is in the band, and it runs through to what I did with Psycho Motel. I'm guitar-oriented. That's where my writing goes. I was one of the first of us to get a little four-track, a multi-track sort of recorder and I was sitting in my hotel room in Jersey working on this riff and there was a banging on the door, and it was Bruce, because we had taken over the whole hotel to rehearse, and he's banging on my door and saying, 'Wow, what's that riff?' So I played him the music to it and he had a bunch of lyrics and he started singing and we had *2 Minutes To Midnight*. We wrote it in about 20 minutes (laughs)."

62 HELL AWAITS SLAYER

664 points *from Hell Awaits (Metal Blade '85)*

Hell, half the song is intro, or more like a series of intros, pretty damn good ones, starting with the demonic backwards incursions, a chilling effect from a band that didn't use many effects. The anticipation is great though, the band tribally pounding into yer head, the benefits of a life in metal before shattering the contemplative throb with a shower of flying glass, the song setting the tone for an album often remembered as speedier than it is. *Hell Awaits*, or specifically, the back white noise portion of it, is indeed built for speed, as the boys learn to create the idea of chaos through musical structures that are anything but.

Kerry King on *Hell Awaits* . . .

"I think that title came from when we used to flyer our own gigs, doing all the little clubs in Orange County. I remember some of our early flyers said, 'Evil has no boundaries, demons show no mercy,' like the first record. And then we started putting, 'Come see Slayer. Hell awaits.'"

63 LIGHTS OUT
UFO

658 points *from Lights Out (Chrysalis '77)*

Tense, dramatic and metallic, *Lights Out* found UFO firing on all cylinders, the song providing the heavy anchor of a surprisingly light album. The band's arresting Heep Purple-ness shone through, Paul Raymond's Hammond grind mind-melding with terse, angled runway chord patterns from Schenker. The song's sleeve-drawn ace is its switch to gallop come chorus time, a deepening of the song's urgency which also counter intuitively sweetens the atmosphere with live magic melody. Sister sledge (or opposing pillar) to *Rock Bottom*, the two tracks serving as the uncompromised speed metal bookends of all that happy rock 'n' roll in the gooey centre of the band's catalogue.

Michael Schenker on *Lights Out* . . .

> "Actually, that was also co-written with Pete. He had the main riff and then I wrote the rest of it. I remember being in the studio mixing and it was very exciting. It was the first album we did with a great producer. We did the three albums before with Leo Lyons and then that was our big step, doing the Lights out album with Ron Nevison. Everything just went up, like 100%. The songs were really good, and plus we had just found Paul Raymond so we had a very, very good chemistry between the producer and Paul and the band, etc. It was the most, how would you say, complete UFO album."

64 THE FOUR HORSEMEN
METALLICA

647 points *from Kill 'Em All (Music for Nations '83)*

Metallica demonstrate their songwriting skills, as well as James' quick right hand on one of **Kill 'Em All**'s four songs that don't thrash. Riffs are front and centre on these tracks, and indeed time stands still as the band tries them on for size, switching from denim to leather and back to denim again. There's a coy "blues" break in here reminiscent of Sabbath, but there's also a nice call and response that would be codified next record on *Creeping Death*. Once more, it's all about (and too much about) the riffs, Metallica finding a bunch of fresh ones here, enough to fill a seven-minute track with very little fat or tiring repetition.

Lars Ulrich on injecting more groove into his drumming in the '90s . . .

"This time around, I wanted to see if I could get the same energy and aggressiveness without having to hit that snare drum so often. As a drummer, I got a little bored. I've proved to everybody that I can play, but I don't feel that competitive anymore. There was a time when I felt that I really had to prove myself as a drummer. I think to a certain degree I did, but I don't feel like that right now. Right now I feel like kicking back and getting into more of what we're doing, than trying to prove myself as a drummer. It's a lot more of a relaxed and comfortable attitude just sitting back there and driving those songs without having to take control of them. It's a really fun way of playing drums right now by just sitting back and listening to these monster guitar riffs."

65 PULL ME UNDER DREAM THEATER

633 points *from Images and Words (Atco '92)*

Fresh, heavy, dynamic, Zeppelin-esque . . . *Pull Me Under* arrived at a time and place where prog metal was created more on a dare than anything else. All metal was dead, let alone the fussy, self-important stuff with goofy keyboard parts. But here it was, and doing well, Dream Theater opening new sections at will, circling back to that wide-angled chorus, practising some metal mayhem rare for this band of Berklee numismatists. Nu-prog in total, but taken in pieces, an efficient tour of the metal world as it existed across the major label landscape reaching back a good dozen years.

James LaBrie on *Pull Me Under* . . .

"I can remember when the song was being written and recorded. I mean, nobody knew at the time it was going to be something that would go through the roof and take off everywhere. But I do remember everybody being pretty psyched about the song. And everybody thought it was a pretty heavy song. And it started off just bein' released at college radio and then it just completely took off. It's a fun song but I guess it's lost a bit of excitement for us because we played it one billion times. Still in later years I think I'm going to be able to sit down and listen to it and appreciate it for what it was when it originally hit me."

66 HANGAR 18 MEGADETH

630 points *from Rust in Peace (Capitol '90)*

On what is an inspired, frenzied, event-filled album, *Hangar 18,* and more pointedly its opening three riffs, serve as the record's most communicative and sweet sequences. It is a track that manages brilliantly to combine metallic mystery with the tricky concept of hook. The high twin lead riff is uncharacteristic of Megadeth or anybody for that matter, and beat-wise, new boy Nick Menza is in the pocket rocking linear, later come solo time, locking into a metal funk with Dave Junior. Lyrically, the track is over and done with pretty quickly, Mustaine offering a short sliver of Roswellian text about government conspiracy, world order and preserved aliens, his brief treatise quickly covered up by artful thrash jamming that strives to make the song an instrumental despite offering the album's very best conventional song within less than half the front end.

Marty Friedman on *Hangar 18* . . .

"That song had, I think, the most edits I've ever seen in a song. I mean, that song changed form so many times. By the time we got it done, the whole floor of the studio was full of two-inch tape. It really started off to be much longer than that and got hacked up and came to be what it was, just by being chopped up so much. It really was an experience in editing. That was before ProTools. There were a lot of computers being used at the time, but not the way they are used now for editing. There was actually physical tape all over the floor and I remember coming in to cut guitars and I remember them having to clean up the floor because there was so much tape on it. It was insane."

Marty Friedman from Megadeth
Kiss — *Deuce*
Raven — *Faster Than the Speed of Light*
The Godz — *Gotta Keep a' Runnin'*
Sleep — *Jerusalem*
X-Japan — *Miscast*
Cheap Trick — *Auf Wiedersein*
Mahogany Rush — *World Anthem/Talkin' 'Bout a Feeling*
Black Sabbath — *Hole in the Sky*
Rammstein — *Ashes to Ashes*
The Donnas — *Skintight*

67 BATTERY METALLICA
615 points *from Master of Puppets (Electra '86)*

No great improvement really over say, *Trapped under Ice*, *Battery*'s advancements are in a slight upkick in intensity, wrapped in barbed wire by the better production values **Master of Puppets** harboured and cobbled over the already head-slamming **Ride the Lightning**. As well, this track seemed compact, thick as a brick, leading with purpose, an example of barely contained chaos, a bomb packed with bent nails. Surprisingly mature intro as well, through which one can envision tumbleweed, Clint and guns drawn in a swirl of dust. Would have set a nice tea table for *Ace of Spades*.

Lars Ulrich on old speed versus new speed . . .

"That's something that we've always felt. We realized that really early on, many years ago. Even this time around, I realize you can have a really fast guitar riff like on *Through the Never* or

Holier Than Thou, but you stick to a mid-tempo or fast drum thing, but not speed or a *Battery*-type thing. It still has that speed, energy and aggressiveness but it has a little more. It has a balance and a swing to it that I don't think our earlier faster songs had. Some of the songs have really fast guitar pieces, where five or six years ago I might have stuck a *Fight Fire with Fire* or *Battery*-type drumbeat on it, gallopy, out of control shit."

68 KILL THE KING RAINBOW

605 points *from Long Live Rock 'n' Roll (Polydor '78)*

There it was, a red ruby on a dunce cap, *Kill the King* being introduced this novel way, tearing it up via the otherwise dreary and oblong **On Stage** before the studio version would similarly blind its companions on **Long Live Rock 'n' Roll** nine months later. *Kill the King* was Rainbow's first lusty modern speed metal romp (*Light in the Black* was too dark for too long), claiming pedigree through *Burn* back to *Fireball*. Its dramatic intro sequence is a simple but musical Cozy Powell triumph after which Ronnie and Ritchie strike up white-knuckle battle for the throne. *Kill the King* would become the second unanimously defended set piece after *Stargazer* in the construction of power metal's base componentry. And it adds to the story by being modern, nimble and double bass aggressive, only *Gates of Babylon* on this third studio album reaching the same level of imagination and enthusiasm on what is a rather clunky and dated last hurrah for Ronnie within Rainbow.

Jimmy Bain on the ramp up to *Kill the King* and beyond . . .

"I like the first album. We had to learn a few songs and everything, but I think that the Rainbow **Rising** album was more of a band effort. I mean, the first album sounds like it gelled and the songs are good. I thought **Rising** was a little bit short in terms of tracks, but I really liked being involved with it. It had great potential and I would have liked to have been around a little longer because I had just started getting into writing with them on a couple of songs that didn't make it until the album after that, *Kill the King* for one. I was involved with the writing of that with Cozy. That was the first band thing that we did. But by the time that it came out, it was just Powell, Blackmore and Dio, but I was involved in it too. If I had been in the band I think, I would have gotten credit for it. But we were starting to do things like that. But unfortunately, I don't know, Ritchie would wake up one day and he wouldn't hear Rainbow on the radio, because they weren't playing anything as hard as that, and he would decide to change one of the musicians. When I got fired, I was in shock. I went over to see him and he really couldn't give me a reason why he got rid of me. He just sort of looked every which way but at me. I had gathered from that that he had made a decision and he had to stick by it. Because, you know, the management had got hold of me and fired me, and then I went to see him. I don't know if he had second thoughts about it, but that's what happened. I know they had a little bit of difficulty replacing me because the guy that they got didn't work out, a guy by the name of Mark Clarke. And they gave me a call, and I said, 'I don't really think so. After you got rid of me once, it would be quite easy to get rid of me again, so why should I bother?'"

69 INTO THE VOID
BLACK SABBATH

600 points *from Master of Reality (Warner '71)*

Into the Void is the patron saint of **Master of Reality**, the grand-père, the proud and silent central force around which showier tracks dance, prance and preen. Its opening riff is the unsung blob of Iommi's prodigious digits and when the rockets finally glow, it becomes one of those exciting pioneering tracks that incrementally reinvents a form of music Sabbath had already built and modestly improved upon roughly six times over by this point. Apocalyptic and leaden in its grand destruction (Ward is drowning amidst the electrocution), *Into the Void* is the band's ultimate if endearingly naïve metaphor for despairing drug escape, written by a nauseous and undernourished foursome soon to be well versed on the subject.

Bill Ward on *Into the Void . . .*

> "*Into the Void . . .* I wasn't aware that there was an influence from any other band. That was Black Sabbath at its absolute height, when it was absolutely coming alive. And at that point Geezer was writing really strongly and the band at that point was unbelievably tight. We were really becoming confident and we had just done a couple of world tours. That was a science fiction one about how we were all fed up at the time and wished we could just get into a rocket ship and blast off."

70 BLACK DOG LED ZEPPELIN

598 points

from IV *(Atlantic '71)*

One of the earliest pure metal riffs of all time, *Black Dog* (named for the black Labrador that wandered around Headley Grange, the recording locale for the album) built on the uneasy intelligence of *Good Times Bad Times* and more permanently *Out on the Tiles*, exploding like *Let There Be Rock* did all over preceding AC/DC albums, all pumped with electricity, announcing with an exclamation mark the completion of four earth-shattering albums in under three years. Heck, you could now even accuse Zep of being prog rock (everybody hangs around while Page finishes his bowl of notes), this band of world-beaters greedily laying claim to whatever musical subculture came their way. Trivia note: the track's stop/go structure took inspiration (at least on Pagey's part) from Fleetwood Mac's *Oh Well*, at the time, a much celebrated, uncharacteristic breakthrough in flash for the grinding, otherwise quite purist, blues unit.

John Paul Jones on *Black Dog . . .*

> "*Black Dog* I wrote on the train (laughs). I didn't have an instrument. I write them in my head. Literally, I didn't even have manuscript paper. I have a system my father taught me, where you just use numbers and pluses and minuses and you can write a melody down on anything. As long as you've got a pen and a piece of paper, you can write music. And I remember coming back, I think it was from Page's house, after rehearsal.

Yes, I remember, I was listening to one of the cuts off of **Electric Mud**, Muddy Waters, and there was a riff that they did that kept going around and round. You thought it was going to stop and it didn't. And I thought, it would be great to write a riff that just kind of went around and round (laughs). So I just sat down and as I said, I was in the train thinking about this, and sure enough, it popped into my head as these do. So I got it down quick so I wouldn't forget it. I didn't actually do the arrangement, if you know what I mean. The vocal arrangement kind of dictated how that went. It didn't seem that Robert wanted to sing actually over the riff, so it kind of made sense that he sang a bit, then we played the riff, then he sang a bit more. Then Page did the other half (sings it), and then Robert did his stuff over that. Most of the stuff we did worked that way. Somebody would bring in an idea and the whole band would work on the idea and then we would add bits to it. And eventually it would become something through sort of an organic process. Out of all the different elements would come the final song."

71 FIGHT FIRE WITH FIRE
METALLICA

592 points *from Ride the Lightning (Music for Nations '84)*

Of utmost importance, *Fight Fire with Fire* carried through on the threat of the debut **Kill 'Em All** and its stinging slap, Metallica focusing its might and its creative faculties on the fastest, heaviest speed metal to date, literally announcing the next plateau to which the heaviest must aspire. So *Fight Fire with Fire* was both the most vicious and the most complicated track on the most important metal album since **Sad Wings of Destiny** eight years earlier. Them are the lead boots to fill, and I can still remember how this sledge filled the room when the needle dropped on my original UK Music for Nations copy a week after its unveiling. Instantly the rules changed and instantly you knew this band was going to be big despite the challenging and extreme blur of the proposition.

Lars Ulrich on losing his double bass skills . . .

"Yeah sure. I don't deny anything. I'm certainly not as interested in playing double bass as I was. When you're less interested in it, you do it less often. You do it less often, you lose your touch a little bit. I bet you didn't think you'd get me to cough that up (laughs)."

72 FOR THOSE ABOUT TO ROCK (WE SALUTE YOU)
AC/DC

592 points *from For Those About to Rock We Salute You (Atlantic '81)*

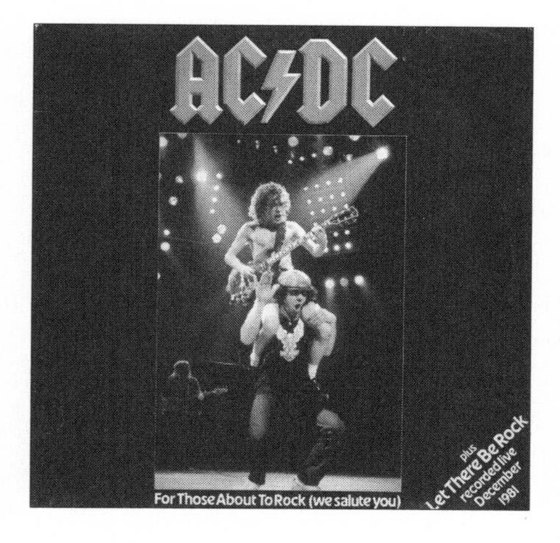

Providing the opportunity for the crowd to fire AC/DC's big guns, *For Those About to Rock* is built with expert pacing, beginning with a Son of bluesy *Back in Black* rumbling meander, then stopping for a little aerial bombardment before going to the double time major salute, one of AC/DC's tingly rivet-hearted moments, indeed, the reason for this song to live. The band find new ways to be subtly anti-commercial, namely and counterintuitively building a title track around a down-wound, deflated Sabbatherian plod. But when late in the anticipation game, the grand angles shine their potential through the magic of metal acceleration, all is forgiven and indeed forgotten.

Brian Johnson on lyrical inspiration . . .

"As Mal says, he just looks around at life; he sees it all around him. Sex is just one of the things he would draw on. It's just life all around you. I love it when people say these are sexist lyrics. Fuck it, we didn't invent sex."

73 YOU SHOOK ME ALL NIGHT LONG
AC/DC
589 points *from Back in Black (Atlantic '80)*

AC/DC's first massive hit helped push, along with *Hells Bells* and the title track, *Back in Black* into the top ten selling albums of all time. But the track is a somewhat alienating blend of feel-good pop and southern rock, the fey chick magnet song on an otherwise fairly grey album, a good example of the band's formula of a verse with spaces and a chorus with a torrential downpour of guitars, pushed to conclusion by Ruddy big cymbals. Brian Johnson's most rednecked vocal on a song about what else? Exercising the ol' Tom Jones.

Angus Young on the end of an era . . .

> "Bon just before he died, he'd come down with me and Mal. He got behind the kit and Mal said to him, 'Ah Bon, get on the drums, we need a drummer,' and that's what he loved. Bon wanted to be the drummer in the band. It was kind of funny; the first time we ever set down, here's this guy saying, 'I'm your new drummer.' Mal convinced him to sing, to get up to the front of the stage. Then he was there at the end again. The last you saw him, there he was behind the kit. He played the intro to one of the tracks. It turned out it wasn't one of the greatest songs, but the intro was great: *Let Me Put My Love into You*, just the intro of it before it goes into Mutt Lange territory. It was fuckin' good before then (laughs)! But yeah, me and Malcolm were working on material for what would be called **Back in Black**, and Bon walked in and sat behind the drums and started banging away and that was the last time we saw him. All I can really say is that Bon is still around and watching. He didn't want the band to split up or go into a period of mourning. He wanted us to build on the spirit he left behind."

74 RIME OF THE ANCIENT MARINER IRON MAIDEN

573 points *from Powerslave* (EMI '84)

The second coming of *Achilles' Last Stand, Rime of the Ancient Mariner* found Bruce ever so slightly at a *Losfer Words*, reduced to paraphrasing literature for a living. But it's a rollicking, rhythmic metal romp to which the tale is set, the band finding a way to hold the average punter's interest, at least until the boat creaks and groans under the weight of Steve Harris' lonely and ill-advised musical decisions (more like unadvised). But it all fits splendidly the Egyptian-toned musical motif of the album, in particular that of the title track.

Adrian Smith on *Rime of the Ancient Mariner* . . .

> "It was definitely a lot of work. Steve walked into the studio and said, 'I've got this song,' and he held the lyrics up and sort of let the paper go and it came down to the floor, you know what I mean? And so we had to get a . . . Bruce was doing the guide vocal, when we were rehearsing it, and we had to get something to pin the lyrics to so we could read them. And we found this huge stepladder and pinned the lyrics to the top of the ladder so they could hang down and you could see all the verses. We used to call it pyramid power."

75 BLACK METAL VENOM

567 points *from Black Metal (Neat '82)*

Black Metal locks then veers for the duration after a short, pleasant recording of Abaddon chainsawing the studio door (that screeching sound you hear is contact with steel bolts). The track is seminal early double-bass thrash, except the production values are so human and base, it comes off as inappropriately quick-picked punk, a sentiment enforced by the happy bits of soccer yobbo fish 'n' crisps melody sprinkled throughout. Cronos does a nice job of laying out the band's shock rock 'n' roll credo, unknowingly creating a huge well-defined genre of metal that would heartily adopt his tosser lark of a comment more than a decade later, and make it serious church-burning business indeed.

Cronos on the original idea for Venom . . .

"We didn't want to be any regular heavy metal band. Because basically, Venom came out of the big back end of the punk explosion in England. And we've always been basic rock fans, Deep Purple and Led Zeppelin and bands like that, but the thing for me was bands like Sex Pistols and The Damned, the real hardcore element. I really wanted to combine the two. I didn't want to be another Lynyrd Skynyrd or another fuckin' Journey or Boston. They were cool bands for what they do, but it wasn't what I wanted to do. I wanted to kind of look like them but a lot dirtier and swear a lot. So the Venom thing had to sort of fit into a new category. And we had to call it black metal because calling it heavy metal didn't describe it. We use to have this concept called 'heads down, meet you at the end.' And that's how we used to treat some of the songs. It was like, 'I don't where the fuck you are, but let's see if we can all stop at the same time.' (laughs)."

Cronos from Venom

Black Sabbath — *Sabbath Bloody Sabbath*
Status Quo — *Down Down*
Van Halen — *Atomic Punk*
AC/DC — *Jailbreak*
Judas Priest — *Screaming for Vengeance*
Queen — *Ogre Battle*
Thin Lizzy — *Bad Reputation*
Sex Pistols — *Anarchy in the UK*
Prodigy — *Smack My Bitch Up*
Rush — *2112*

76 BARK AT THE MOON
OZZY OSBOURNE

556 points *from Bark at the Moon (Epic '83)*

A silvery, sylvan slice of steel, *Bark at the Moon* finds Randy's replacement Jake E. Lee emulating Rhoads' ornate and quick picking. What's novel is that Lee is playing speed metal but the rest of the band locks onto an *I Don't Know/Crazy Train* zombie stomp. Lee's chorus lick is white fire, but the chorus is Ozzy's opportunity to kick back, Oz saving his breath for the hard-charging verses. A classic, however conceptually weak lyrically.

Jake E. Lee on leaving Ozzy's band . . .

"He asked me to. He fired me! He and I had a big argument two days earlier that had nothing to do with the band and the next thing I know my brother is calling me from the Rainbow Club telling me that he overheard the band saying that I was fired. So I phoned up Ozzy and he said, 'Yeah, you could say that' and that was it. After that I didn't feel like doing anything for awhile, so I took some time off and just worked on my cars. I hardly picked up my guitar all that summer. What will really help me and the band out is that I've got no restrictions now. Ozzy had an audience that expected a certain kind of sound and music and you had to keep yourself within the framework. Part of my playing now still reflects the way I performed in Ozzy, but now I can drift into different areas. Plus now I don't have to put on the clown outfits to perform. It's just great to wear what I get up in and play."

77 IMMIGRANT SONG LED ZEPPELIN

552 points

from III *(Atlantic '70)*

The first Viking metal song ever, *Immigrant Song* might also be the first smudge of gothic rock evidenced by Plant's exotic pre-Dio vocal melodies which turn an almost casual, incidental song into a quickly attacking then evaporating classic. *Immigrant Song* is also the opener on Zep III, the album's heaviest song and also its most immediate. Two other nice features: the tune's distorted elastic band intro and John Paul Jones' crazy-fingered bass line in the break, a section that also contains some of Plant's most acrobatic shrieks, the man fortunately getting it down on tape before he would surrender the top end of his range.

John Paul Jones on *Immigrant Song*'s legendary bass licks . . .

> "Yes, well, the first part is fairly easy (sings it), but then I decided to do these runs which are quite fast. But in fact, it's nowhere near as fast . . . I heard some bootlegs once. I'm not sure, did we used to start the show with it? But it was enormously fast, almost twice as fast! How we played that, I don't know. And we still made them swing. I remember, one funny thing. In the old days, black music was always taken at a much slower tempo, and it had that groove. And white groups used to speed up too much. Except for rock 'n' roll. Black rock 'n' roll, like Little Richard, was always really fast and I remember Little Richard quoted as saying that we used to speed them up so the white bands could never play them and swing at the same time (laughs). That was quite funny. But Zeppelin could play fast and swing at the same time."

78 KASHMIR
LED ZEPPELIN

550 points *from Physical Graffiti (Swan Song '75)*

A monumental feat (and a close second on my own list for a Zep track, next to *In My Time of Dying*), *Kashmir* is widely considered among the first five gothic metal tracks of all time, along with the flag-waver for Zeppelin as pioneering middle-eastern music incorporators, edging out a weakly arguably Deep Purple, but then quickly being tied or trumped by Rainbow, who re-wrote *Kashmir* twice on one side of **Rising**. It's a gorgeous, sensual, winding rock ride, framed on a simple, hypnotic riff and attendant beat, but then dressed with legendary orchestration. It builds slowly, layers ebbing and flowing, a measured urgency entering the mix as the journey grinds on through shape-shifting, phase-shifted desert heat. All performances are measured, reflected upon, Plant eventually cutting loose with some distant anguish as the song's concluding drift commences. Within the context of a breathtakingly event-filled record, *Kashmir* still manages to hold one's own, against short tracks, against similarly long tracks, due to its cohesive sustain, due to its dominant and remarkable idea, due to its unearthly creation of a new kind of rock music.

John Paul Jones on his contribution to *Kashmir* . . .

> "That was my orchestration, but it pretty much closely follows the guitar. That definitely was a Page thing."

79 KILLERS
IRON MAIDEN

532 points *from Killers (EMI '81)*

Both frantic and bombastic, *Killers* was an early Maiden experiment in progressive speed metal, still juiced with Di'Anno's hormonal punk charge, but stepping out with punctuated little breaks, complex transitions and dive-bomb guitar antics, all executed at speeds which at the time were considered unsafe. And it's cool how it adds to its namesake full-length's mature variety, *Killers* being the only track remotely like it on an album with many pioneering metallic alloys. Also a nice twist on the new NWOBHM gallop, the band creating a self-serious but resolute and ambitious link between *Running Free* and *Run to the Hills*.

Paul Di'Anno on *Killers* . . .

> "Well I remember, from the very first, there's a video, **Live at the Rainbow**, and the lyrics on that are completely different from what was on the record. Because I had about five minutes to make it up, otherwise it would have been instrumental. So I had to make it up before we went on stage (laughs). It's a bit stupid when you're playing in front of 3500 people and it's the first time you're ever doing a live recording. I think it took me two takes to get it right. The only problem we ever used to have recording-wise was basically Steve and his clacky bass guitar sound, where he doesn't use a pick (laughs). That was that and it went through nearly every bloody song. He never used a pick. I don't know if he does now, but he never did then. And with a Fender, you get the most amazing horrible clacky sound all the time. It was a nightmare."

Paul Di'Anno from Iron Maiden
Sex Pistols — Pretty Vacant
Ramones — Blitzkrieg Bop
Stiff Little Fingers — At the Edge
Gary Numan — Cars
Anti-Nowhere League — So What
Motörhead — Bomber
Sepultura — Refuse/Resist
Metallica — Don't Tread on Me
Ramones — Beat on the Brat
Trust — Antisocial

80 MR. CROWLEY OZZY OSBOURNE

531 points *from Blizzard of Ozz (Jet/CBS '80)*

An inflammatory bit of uneasily insightful Satanism for a man who likely barely knew what he was babbling at the time, *Mr. Crowley* sports creepy, sweetly melodic music to match its anguished, pleading, spiritually lost vocal. Rhoads' performance is signature Randy, raw, L.A.-overblown and steel-on-steel metallic, compressed and goaded into a song of many hooks. The effect is a churchy, regal song which manages to avoid gothic Rainbow-like clichés. The scariest of maybe four dark curtains obscuring Ozzy's first and last enigmatic, curious album.

Ozzy Osbourne on working with Randy Rhoads . . .

> "I can't really tell anybody what I want musically. I don't speak that language. I have a painting in my head and I usually have a problem getting that idea across to a producer or a band member. One of the things that I'll be forever indebted to Randy Rhoads for was that he was very patient with me. He'd sit with me and I would explain my thought pattern and he would work it out with me. It's like when Randy was alive and he came up with the solo for *I Don't Know* . . . when he came to me with that solo, I knew instantly that it was going to be great."

81 WAR ENSEMBLE SLAYER

527 points *from Seasons in the Abyss (Def American '90)*

Reprising the instant cold water shock of *Angel of Death, War Ensemble* is a speeding thrash attack that gets the heavy, heavy headbanger into the **Seasons** opus but quick. One instantly notices the quality of the drum sound, the stinging cymbals, the dry deadly thudding finality of the toms. Over Lombardo's apocalyptic gallop, King and Hanneman turn in an intricate riff which gets downright artistic during the song's triangular half-time war dance. Also, look for some trademark atonal, head-bursting, widdle-awry soloing near the song's exploding, information-overloading climax.

Tom Araya on *War Ensemble* . . .

> "I remember sitting in the hotel with Jeff and Jeff had partial verse and partial chorus ideas. I said, 'What are you writing a song about?' And he goes, 'It's about war, about strategy.' And I said, 'Well, I don't know anything about this shit. Do you have any of your books here with you?' Because he's into war. 'Do you have a book I can read that will give me a clue as to what it is you're trying to write here?' (laughs). And he grabs a book and says, 'Read this section right here.' So I read a chapter and it describes all about the insides of war, infiltrating, strategy, the whole idea. And Jeff had a better understanding of it. So I remember, him and I were living in hotel called the St. James Apartments while we were recording the album, and that was one song he had partially written and we sat down and I had read that, and then it was like, 'How about this?' 'That sounds cool!' 'Howabout this?' 'That sounds cool too.' So he and I collaborated on putting that song together. But I actually remember taking a book and reading it so I could get an understanding of the strategy of war and what it was he was trying to say. We had also heard that they used it in the Gulf War to scare the enemy (laughs). That's pretty cool."

Fernando Ribeiro from Moonspell
Black Sabbath — *Black Sabbath*
Iron Maiden — *Aces High*
Judas Priest — *Love Bites*
Bathory — *A Fine Day to Die*
Celtic Frost — *Circle of the Tyrants*
Root — *Aposiopesis*
Samael — *Baphomet's Throne*
Dio — *Holy Diver*
Type O Negative — *Black No. 1*
Morbid Angel — *Immortal Rites*

82 POWERSLAVE IRON MAIDEN

512 points *from Powerslave (EMI '84)*

Forced but forced into a sunlight where Maiden can tan to a golden brown, *Powerslave* was the glue of a disconcertingly unravelling album. It provided the Steve-steeped gallop we all wanted, the mid-paced groove, the twisty Middle Eastern melodies, and it also provided the lyrical companion for the album's front cover, the stage show, and little else. Lyrically, Bruce was, well, average, dipping (skimming) (skipping) into his history books, coming out with plainspeak and not the metaphorical poetics of say, a *2 Minutes to Midnight*. Still, the chorus redeems, drilling concentrically into a mercuric ebb and flow metal zone with its wide-angled riffing. The (coffee) break stinks, but then, don't most of them?

Adrian Smith on *Powerslave* . . .

"I'll tell you a great story about *Powerslave*. We were in the Bahamas, and like I say, we used to party a lot. I had been in the studio with Martin Birch and the engineer and we had finished the night before and we'd been working quite hard so we decided to have a little bit of relaxation if you know what I mean. Anyway, about five o'clock in the morning we were all kind of staggering around and I said, 'Look man, I've got to go to bed,' so I left, fully expecting to have the day off the next day. And then the phone rang at about two o'clock in the afternoon as it was Martin. He was the last person who I expected to hear from. And he was slurring, 'Come down to the studio and let's do some work.' And I thought, oh my God, no. So I went down to the studio and apparently he had been up drinking with Robert Palmer all night, because he lived next door to the studio. So Robert Palmer is sitting there in his dressing gown, and they were both drinking tequila and they wanted me to work and I was completely hungover and I felt like death and I was totally intimidated because Robert Palmer was there, big-name guy and I plugged my guitar in and I think I did the solo in *Powerslave*, my first take, I don't know how I did it, because I felt at death's door. And Robert Palmer was jumping up and down and really getting off on the track. It was bizarre. And then after that we went home and slept for a couple of days."

83 HALL OF THE MOUNTAIN KING
SAVATAGE

510 points *from Hall of the Mountain King (Atlantic '87)*

Criss Oliva (R.I.P.) instantly garners full attention with this track's opening noise-immersed riff, which is a cross between the band's **Sirens** songs and something Yngwie might do at a particularly belligerent moment. As the tune lunges forward, Savatage demonstrate their penchant for large thundering grooves, over which Jon Oliva turns in one of his most frightwigged performances, the apex being that closing authoritative restatement of foreboding, where the walls of the hall shake with the pounding drum power of Steve "Doc" Wacholz.

Jon Oliva on *Hall of the Mountain King* . . .

"That was a great track. That was a song I wrote with my brother Criss. That's the one we have to play every night. The thing I remember about it is this that it was the first time we ever did a heavy metal piece with orchestration, where we first used a full-blown orchestra, which is in that intro (sings it); that was our first venture into that area. So in a way, *Mountain King* was a very experimental track for us."

84 TAKE HOLD OF THE FLAME QUEENSRYCHE

509 points *from The Warning (Capitol '85)*

Probably the most easily accessible and discernibly metal track from a rapidly complicating band, *Take Hold of the Flame* was also the hyped first single. Still, the production was a bit annoying and the drums too busy, but man could that guy sing like a summer-frocked girl, Tate yelping out a lyric that had a bit of Ronnie's theme about it, romance with the seductive powers of evil, attraction to the dark side, or on a base real world level, the charms of mysterious malevolent womanhood, this whole vibe being a big part of metal's early to mid-'80s wave in general.

Michael Wilton on *Take Hold of the Flame . . .*

> "That's a song we recorded for **The Warning** in London and for me it brings back that whole recording sequence with James Guthrie, the producer, who did **The Wall**. It was a very memorable time being in England and living there and just ripping through these Marshalls and recording a great rock song."

Geoff Tate from Queensryche
Steppenwolf — *Born to Be Wild*
Jefferson Airplane — *Somebody to Love*
Cream — *White Room*
Black Sabbath — *Falling off the Edge of the World*
Alice In Chains — *Would?*
Pearl Jam — *Jeremy*
Pearl Jam — *Black*
Humble Pie — *I Don't Need no Doctor*
Aerosmith — *Seasons of Whither*
T Rex — *Bang a Gong*

85 ROOTS BLOODY ROOTS SEPULTURA

506 points *from Roots (Roadrunner '96)*

Arise kicked us squarely in the Slayers, but **Roots** — and this signature anthem from that album — invented both world metal and nu-metal and more directly, Soulfly. It's a juggernaut of abrasion and fairly pig-headed, but all the gravity and levity and significance of Ross Robinson took it into a football and cricket place of passports and ethnic cachet. And Max . . . well, this is a death metal vocal that crosses into sing-along.

Andreas Kisser on *Roots Bloody Roots* . . .

> "*Roots Bloody Roots* overall was such a great experience for everybody because we brought so much from the Brazilian music into it. We were working with the Indians and everything. *Roots Bloody Roots* was pretty much the first song we worked on. We were working in Phoenix at that time in the summer, which was really painful, but in a way it helped us to be pissed off about stuff and write something really deep. It was the first time we used really low tuning, a direct influence from Korn. Max really liked that kind of stuff. During these sessions we were playing the Deftones' first demo a lot, the Korn album. I was studying a lot of classical guitar, as I still am now, but at that time I was really deep into it, and doing it every day. I got more of my influence from that side of it, the arrangements and stuff. It's a pretty simple riff, and it started with that simple riff and grew in all directions. It's very special."

86 SCREAMING FOR VENGEANCE JUDAS PRIEST

505 points *from Screaming for Vengeance (CBS '82)*

Stuck stunned and a mite bit rudderless between *Rapid Fire* and *Freewheel Burning, Screaming for Vengeance* was one more shot from Priest's speed metal cannon, one more stitch of evidence proposing this band as the forefathers of the form. Still, it didn't sit well on this album of huge melodies and door-to-door solicitor platinum hooks, with even its pacemate *Electric Eye* sounding more purposeful and synergistic to the plain power chord summation of the record. But it demonstrates this band's desire to keep composing widdly riffs and for that, whole nations of Primal Fears and Narnias and Iron Saviors must be thankful.

Ian Hill on *Screaming for Vengeance . . .*

> "It's funny, because that is one of the tracks that Priest will be known for, although also *You've Got Another Thing Comin'*, because it was all over the radio at the time. But *Screaming* almost epitomizes Judas Priest with the speed and aggression. And that was very, very much worked on. That was planned for, that one. It was the key track on the album."

87 PHOTOGRAPH DEF LEPPARD

504 points *from Pyromania (Mercury '83)*

A watery track from a milky album, *Photograph* was **Pyromania**'s biggest hit, eroding the rampart between the fairly unarguably committed and vigorous hard rock status of L.A.'s first wave and the too slick kicks of the second wave, which would cause the year punk broke in America. It chugs but it's gay and fey, and those harmonies were as inhumanly constructed as they were chipmunk chirped.

Rick Allen on *Photograph . . .*

> "The original idea was a carryover from **High 'n' Dry**. And I think that was really Joe's obsession with Marilyn Monroe, and I guess

his frustration of not really ever being old enough to really know her or be around when she was at her peak. So yeah, that was Joe's obsession with Marilyn. I guess that's pretty natural for a red-blooded Englishman (laughs)."

88 NEON KNIGHTS BLACK SABBATH

504 points *from Heaven and Hell (Warner '80)*

Neon Knights works gloriously because it's a fast track, yet rhythmically and riffically still somehow from a simpler Sabbath time. As well, with Ronnie on board, there is a new treasure chest of vocal melodies. Ozzy never would have sung this verse, although I can hear in my head his pleading one-step-removed-from-streetperson bleat on the chorus. And what production — Martin Birch finding a whole new way to make Iommi heavy, adding brightness without losing heft. When Tony solos, it's like a friendly hot summer Top Gun ballet, all buoyant, optimistic. All told, it's a snap-happy track that is both new and daisy-fresh as well as timelessly rocked with Sabbatherian rhythm physics that are all about elevated weight, heavy things stored precariously on the top shelf. *Neon Knights* optimistically throws open the door to what will be a couple very successful years for the band. On paper, Iommi's riff simply isn't his, but with this production, this new voice, and a couple of old buds trundling behind him, Tony essentially glows. Up top, Ronnie also makes sure to put spring in his step, bestowing upon the world of metal his old-school goth values, here sweetening them for the masses. A few and far between jolly pirate pint-clinker from a band more accustomed to going "Boo!"

Bill Ward on *Neon Knights* . . .

"A very nice song, but that was quite a bad time for me. In that particular time in my life, I don't remember recording *Neon Knights* to be honest with you. I was still gone with feeling ill. That was me playing drums on the whole album, but I was blacked out. I was so ill that I don't recall playing the songs. *Neon Knights* felt a little bit light for me in comparison to some of the lyrics we had in the past. So lyrically, I thought it was nice and that it had some good melodies there definitely. But I thought hmmm, this is a little bit different. It kind of edged a little bit towards the mainstream more than what I'd been used to."

89 CEMETERY GATES PANTERA

495 points *from Vulgar Display of Power (Atlantic '92)*

Pretty wild hearing Phil singing like he was in Alice In Chains or something, but there he is crooning along to a Pantera power ballad. Elsewhere there's a sour goth Pantera riff and a shockingly ordinary rock 'n' roll verse that has Phil half-singing in Hetfield mode. For a seven-minute song, nothing much happens, *Cemetery Gates* containing fewer events than many future shorter songs would entail. But it stands as an anomaly, the band's attempt at guilty gilt funeral music, a rare slowing of a four-cornered blood pool that is usually frothed, roiling and jacked for beer.

Vinnie Paul on *Cemetery Gates* . . .

"Done it live a couple of times on a couple different tours. We've always, on this past tour, we've been using the mellow part on the front as a segue into *Fucking Hostile*. But for us, at this point in our careers, to play that song in its entirety, all seven minutes of it live, it's kind of a boring song to play live. We haven't really included it in the set. Although there are tons of fans that want to hear it. And I think it would just take a little more arm-twisting to get Phil to go with it. I think the rest of us might do it. It's possible you might hear it on this tour but it's not a song we really feel is made for the live setting. When we're writing music, we never think about formats. We never think about, is this going to work on MTV? Is this song four and a half minutes or is it 3:59, exactly what a radio station needs? We just start and wherever the song starts, wherever it goes and however it finishes is how it ends up. I mean, a song like *Primal Concrete Sledge* is only 2:13, and that's as long as it needed to be. It felt right, you know? And *Cemetery Gates* just ended up being a long song."

90 ROCK AND ROLL LED ZEPPELIN

492 points *from* IV *(Atlantic '71)*

One of the cornerstones with which Zeppelin built a metal reputation they didn't want, *Rock and Roll* is actually boogie rock showered with metal sparks — Pagey injecting the idea of riffing but never creating a framework you can touch, Ian Stewart invited along to add some Jerry Lee, reinforcing the boogie gala gaga of the thing. Of course, Plant is at the height of his game (re-creating this toon live soon became a chore, although it would persist as giddy gig opener until '75) and Bonham finds a way to make genius kissy-face through a deceptively simple snare and open high-hat pattern to set off the explosion, later percussively commenting on the carnage to close the show. Ergo, with one song (and aided doomfully in his quest by dying young), Bonzo becomes the first and last word in hard rock drumming.

John Paul Jones on *Rock and Roll* . . .

> "The lyrics might have been influenced by some old song, I don't know. The first I heard of it . . . I mean, basically Bonzo just started playing (laughs). He just started playing, and I think his drums were still out in the stairwell and it just kind of turned into an immediate jam. Robert, sometimes, just to get the song going, would use lyrics that he knew, and then he would change them; sometimes not (laughs)."

91 N.I.B. BLACK SABBATH

477 points *from Black Sabbath (Warner '70)*

Dreary Birmingham's version of *Smoke on the Water* — and hey, to be fair, its precursor by a long shot — *N.I.B.* is an often overlooked major metal milestone. Because, picture this, if Black Sabbath's debut is ground zero for metal, this song's Godzilla riff is ground zero on the album, the witchy microcosm of a whole new dark musical realm about to blow open. Surely, dribs, drabs, remnants and mistakes of metal precede Black Sabbath — **Black Sabbath**, but this record is the first self-aware comfy chair home of heavy, and *N.I.B.* is the fat pig eating chips staring at the telly (the title track is the grease-stained shag). It slashes, it burns, it slices, it's basically *Iron Man* on a brisk autumnal walk. Indeed, there are no unapologetic riff rockers this pure of purpose back into the previous decade, so, er, be thankful, 'cos metal is borne.

Bill Ward on *N.I.B.* . . .

> "*N.I.B.* is kind of a famous song. That's the one we threw together in Switzerland in 1968; actually. *N.I.B.* is named after me. The guys nicknamed me Nibby. I mean, Tony still calls me Nib to this day. It came out of a session, a time when we were doing a lot of opium (laughs). And we were all high and everything and for some reason through the hallucinogenics of it all, Geezer and Ozzy thought I looked like the top of a pen, you know? A pen nib. And they totally got lost behind the idea of that, cracking up. And it just stuck. And it's been it for the last 30-odd years. But I think it's just a real good hard rock song. I like Ozzy's lines. The 'oh yeah''s showed up. That was kind of the stamp of approval on that one."

92 I WANNA BE SOMEBODY
W.A.S.P.

475 points *from W.A.S.P. (Capitol '84)*

Peering down the dark alley of the first wave of the L.A. glam, one first encountered Crüe, followed further into the mess of trash cans by W.A.S.P.. There one heard Blackie Lawless screeching and crowing a capitalist credo over a moderate speed metal riff. What Blackie wanted to be was somebody nasty, loud, decadent in a significant performance art way, even if none of us noticed the artiste behind the codpiece. The track drove squarely toward a chorus that wouldn't be out of place on a

Twisted Sister album, all set to a swinging deliberate drum rhythm that was the groove foil to Chris Holmes' reigned-in staccato riffery.

Blackie Lawless on *I Wanna Be Somebody . . .*

"I heard that VH1 was doing the top 100 or top 50 songs of all time and that was No. 21 or 22. Musically I never thought it was one of the strongest songs that we did but I understand the sentiment, and the sentiment is what pushed me in the first place to do the song. Because I really thought that there's got to be a lot of people who feel like that. It's a very simple idea, one that had not been said before but I'm sure a lot of people were thinking it. To me I've always thought that a song title, or an idea of a song was probably worth as much if not more than the song itself. If it's a sentiment that people can latch onto, I think that's real important."

93 ROCK YOU LIKE A HURRICANE SCORPIONS

474 points *from Love at First Sting (Mercury '84)*

I still remember the magic, excitement and mystique shooting like fireworks all over the radio when this song was launched as a pre-release single. Everybody felt **Love at First Sting** couldn't help but be the band's long-suffered breakthrough album, set up wonderfully by the chromium octane of **Blackout**. Little did we know *Rock You Like a Hurricane* would be this watery, vanilla-washed record's most innovative track, and maybe its second or third heaviest. The guitar sound is gorgeous, and the way the intro builds is resplendent metal drama, before the bottom falls out for that stealth-breath verse, which was both melodically brave and a forbearer of simpler times to come. But the song's magic lies in its two big hooks, both the verse and the chorus being remarkable radio rock, and both managing to sound pop and metal at the same time, aiding and abetting the rise of pop metal as it would exist in the late '80s.

Rudolf Schenker on *Rock You Like a Hurricane . . .*

"I remember composing the song and coming to the rehearsal

room and playing around with it. The melody was there, everything was there, and Klaus came up and said, 'Rock you like a hurricane' and I said immediately, 'Yes, oh great, that's a great line.' And people said, 'No, hurricane isn't strong enough, it has to be even faster!' And we said, 'No, no, it's the perfect situation.' I'll tell you one thing, the music and even 'Rock you like a hurricane' goes together; you can't do it better. You could easily throw it out because you don't think it fits together. Some people have different minds about the hurricane. Some people think it must be faster, some people think it has to be more crazy. But I think the lyrics, especially the little bit of, what do you call, double meaning lyrics, give the whole thing a kind of sexual hurricane."

94 LIVE WIRE MÖTLEY CRÜE

473 points *from Too Fast for Love (Elektra '81)*

Compressed, grinding, but still furtive and fast, *Live Wire* is a sound of the times. Crüe were the glam punks of the new metal moon over L.A., and this song was a dense chaotic rat's nest of frayed nerves, announcing the waves of hedonism to come over the next decade. Vince is a little flat, but Tommy saves the day, already practising endearing cheeseball excess on that combat-ready whack of his. As an opener, it's perfect, dirty, shocking, irascible, one of the few deliberately metal tracks on an album stuffed with happy mistakes.

Nikki Sixx on whether hard drugs entered their lives before the first album . . .

> "Hard drugs? Not like that. Although even when we were doing our first session, during *Live Wire*, Vince was shooting cocaine, because he had a rich girlfriend who was a drug dealer, Lovey. She's dead now. She got stabbed 60 times in a drug deal. Dead."

95 REVELATIONS IRON MAIDEN

463 points *from Piece of Mind (EMI '83)*

Lyrically, Bruce is quite arty here, ahead of his time really, *Revelations* being a better match for **Powerslave** or **Seventh Son**. But no matter, his pan-mysticism adequately captures the idea of *Revelations,* Bruce mixing Christian and Egyptian imagery in a song that lumbers then packs its bags and runs off. Look for the brilliant Thin Lizzy soloing at the five-minute mark, as the band jams towards the final wind-down and mellow outro. A bit of a statement sticking a ponderous seven minuter at track two, but then again, *Revelations* rocks deceptively hard much of the time. Surveying the album as a whole, this track serves variously as anchor, money pit, layaway, dark smudge, and early rest spot before the long, inspired haul ahead.

Bruce Dickinson on *Revelations* . . .

> "Well, I was deep into reading all my Aleister Crowley books then and I was major into Egypt and everything else, pyramids, and I just got a big grab bag in of all the imagery I could find and glued it all together along with the lyrics of an English hymn for the intro and the outro."

96 ROCK BOTTOM UFO

461 points *from Phenomenon (Chrysalis '74)*

Absolutely dominating everything on UFO's tentative wake-up album, *Rock Bottom* is a surprise bit of note-dense speed metal, Schenker's impressive calling card, a song every bit as slick and modern as your favourite white-knuckle Deep Purple raves. And to push it through mere metal status into the epic zone, the band explore their newfound Anglo-Euro synthesis with intelligent gothic chapters, Michael's yearning Germanic melodies working in concert with the band's rough, raw and charmingly accidental English space rock predilections. Grand with big collisions and even bigger aspirations.

Michael Schenker on *Rock Bottom* . . .

"*Rock Bottom* is a good one. We were all in the studio and Phil was reading the paper and we were just desperately trying to find something really good. So we were all jamming, jamming, jamming and then I started that riff, *Rock Bottom*, and then Phil jumped up and yelled, 'That's it!' Funny. But writing in general, there's not too much to it. Writing songs, I'm just being myself. I practise and that's when I find something to work on. Usually the songs that I write are all by accident. When I practise, I bump into something I like and I put it on a cassette. They are usually ten seconds of pieces, and then when it's time to make the record, I listen to those pieces and whatever inspires me most, I take that and turn it into songs. And then when I finish the instrumental parts, I give that part to the singer and then he does the rest. So it's not really so much like, 'I met this girl and I wanted to write a song about her,' or something like that. Everything I do, it's really all musical."

97 2112
RUSH

457 points

from 2112 (Anthem '76)

Certainly *2112* is one of the better hard rock concept pieces both musically and lyrically. The band is sprightly in its theme changes, heavy often, fresh, a little jazzy, the perfect context for the concise tale of a future time and space where music is outlawed, yet where lo and behold, a guitar has been found. This aural garden's rock anthem is of course *The Temples of Syrinx*, which splashes and crashes into view after a vast instrumental workout called *Overture*. Onward and inward, five more movements burst optimistically forth, Rush maintaining the drama through metal highs and Floydian lows, the whole situation getting tense and heroic for *Grande Finale* which explodes in an Orwellian burst of metal skronk, a fitting close to a well-paced and always entertaining suite of songs.

Geddy Lee on dusting off *2112* for the **Different Stages** live album . . .

"We changed a bit of the emphasis and changed the tuning of

the song a little bit to give it a heavier feel. But other than that it's a fairly accurate reinterpretation of it, 22 years later (laughs). I was really pleased with the way that it came out. It was really a lot more fun to play live than I ever thought it would be."

98 METAL HEALTH (BANG YOUR HEAD) QUIET RIOT

454 points *from Metal Health* (CBS '83)

After a career of embarrassing fits and starts, Quiet Riot hit with this bad pun of a song, the anthemic centrepiece of an album pockmarked with sour holdover glam and smothering speed metal. *Metal Health* is the anvil touched with AC/DC's magic wand (the stalking verse, the drum-beat) livened by Kevin Dubrow's leonine call to arms which frankly sounded hollow out of his yap: he sold Dubrow the vocalist, but he didn't sell his allegiance to metal. And heck, with our crap bar band Torque, this was our final encore, the definition of what a bar band was in 1984, "bang your head" being about as direct an order as one could give to MTV's new metal masses.

Frankie Banali on *Metal Health* . . .

"Before we actually started doing national tours and we were just playing around Hollywood, especially around 1982, that song was the epitome of what Quiet Riot was about at that point in time. And the song basically came about two ways. Number one, just a real steady meat and potatoes drum groove. But there was a song that Carlos had, in a band he had prior to Quiet Riot called Snow, and the song was actually called *No More Beers* (laughs). So from humble beginnings (laughs). . . . So he had that riff and Kevin started working with him on it, and the actual idea for 'bang your head' actually came up from Randy Rhoads, because Randy was over in England and already playing with Ozzy, and he had called up Kevin, and he said to Kevin, 'You're not going to believe this, man. Kids over here, they come to the shows, they have cardboard guitars and makeup, and they are, you know, banging their heads.' And it was a term that was already being used in England. And Kevin thought that that was a nice key phrase. And I think the idea of *Metal Health,* the actual wording, came from an ad that he had heard. I think it might have even been a Def Leppard radio ad for some show that they were doing. But the actual metal health wording had nothing to do with a Def Leppard song or lyric. I don't want anybody to think we got it from Def Leppard (laughs)."

Frankie Banali from Quiet Riot
Led Zeppelin — *Kashmir*
Black Sabbath — *Black Sabbath*
Ozzy Osbourne — *I Don't Know*
AC/DC — *Back in Black*
Quiet Riot — *Metal Health (Bang Your Head)*
Dio — *The Last in Line*
Van Halen — *Running with the Devil*
Judas Priest — *Electric Eye*
W.A.S.P. — *The Headless Children*
Ted Nugent — *Stranglehold*

99 LIVING AFTER MIDNIGHT JUDAS PRIEST

453 points *from British Steel (CBS '80)*

Ah yes, the track that painted over the band's complex metallic coppers and deep regal blues in garish square primaries. *Living After Midnight* was the stinging pop metal slap on a record that deliberately simplified, deliberately sold out. The verse still rocked but the chorus, man, that's pretty much Bay City Rollers with distortion petals. The track however ingratiates itself into your memory circuits, working as planned, becoming an unbecoming instant hit, Halford playing man on the prowl with growling aplomb.

Ian Hill on *Living After Midnight* . . .

"Again, we were expected to do a commercial track. And Rob had this great lyric, living after midnight. And it just fell into place. It was one of those things. It was one of those tracks that was worked on with an eye to being commercial and radio-friendly, and it turned out to be a very popular track. It's still in the set today (laughs). That's one of the tracks you can't drop. People will go to the live show expecting to hear that and if you don't play it, they'll walk away disappointed."

100 ROUND AND ROUND
RATT

451 points *from Out of the Cellar (Atlantic '84)*

You could rightly snicker at the music of other metal upstarts of the MTV age, but not these boys, Ratt trumping Quiet Riot, Twisted Sister, Bon Jovi and even the concurrent cereal bowl versions of Priest, Scorpions and Helix, with tight interesting songs rumbled streetwise with competitive melodic fire. *Round and Round* was the best of them, an obvious hit, textured through with guitars that slithered like Joe Perry, topped with a vocal from a (then skinny) man who still had some brain cells left. Their clothes were another matter.

Bobby Blotzer on *Round and Round* . . .

"I just remember, when we were writing that tune, that was probably around spring of '83 and we were rehearsing in Redondo Beach, at this place called Music Works. It was a guitar store that had a rehearsal room in the back. I was stoked because I was getting the guys to drive up from Hollywood, whereas I was always driving to Hollywood to rehearse, and this was in Redondo Beach, which was my hometown, so that was cool. As dumb as that might sound (laughs), that's my biggest memory of that, not having to drive to Hollywood. Then of course, the song taking off, and rapidly. I mean, we did our first show April 9th of '84 in Colorado Springs, and by May we were playing huge gigs, and by June and July, the thing was a smash. And I don't know how the thing went that quick. Normally it takes a lot longer than that. Felt good though, that's all I can say. And thank God for that song, and thanks to my partners for writing it."

101 FEAR OF THE DARK IRON MAIDEN

447 points *from Fear of the Dark* (EMI '92)

Maiden's true *Mother Russia*, or somehow its muse-dead panic of an update to *Run to the Hills*, *Fear of the Dark* eked out a draw with its hooligan wind me up. Embarrassing all around, lyrically, musically, production-wise, it nevertheless was a direct look at hook, at least come chorus time. One could see the bleachers shake as drooling idiots bounced up and down — the only possible outcome of success at the blood collar game being a collapse thereof and a twisted death with an eternity of spooky dark. Somewhere about the 380th song in which Steve bullies, ruses, cajoles, ingratiates his way into a role where bass simply should not be, Bruce matches witless wits with him in coming up with a stupid lyric designed for seven-year-olds.

Bruce Dickinson on *Fear of the Dark* . . .

"*Fear of the Dark* again, was one of those stand-out tracks on the album, very atmospheric, a great live track to do and one that is very satisfying to sing vocally, because it's a really full-bodied kind of vocal."

102 BLACKOUT SCORPIONS

446 points *from Blackout (Mercury '82)*

Alas, *Blackout* is widely believed by diehards to be the last great metal song these fallen Germans ever wrote, and it is undoubtedly pure tuneful genius. Dierks' production is superb, with highly electric guitar tones precisely stacked so you could hear every brilliant Schenker riff, drums the epitome of slick no-nonsense metal and the whole thing just cruising along on a plane reserved for stars with guitars.

Rudolph Schenker on *Blackout* . . .

"That's a good story (laughs). I remember we had a party with K. K. and Glenn from Judas Priest and there were also the guys there, for a while, from Def Leppard. K. K. and Glenn gave me a drink, and it was beer, and I was, 'No, no, you have to have the right mix: whiskey, beer, and then wine on top of it.' And they're like what!? And I was, 'Yes, come on.' And we were going heavily drunk and we had a good time. And I think K.K. had the idea, 'Hey, let's go to the Def Leppard guys.' Because we were in Cleveland, the Cleveland Hall, and next door was the hotel, so we went to the Def Leppard guys and they were watching television. They were very young in these days. This was 1980 I think. Def Leppard, Judas Priest and Scorpions in Cleveland. So I saw them watching TV and I put my drink into the television (laughs). And the whole television went 'poof!' And this was the situation and I said, 'OK, we have to leave, we have to go now.' But anyway, it became so crazy, and the next morning I wake up in my hotel room. And I said, 'What's happening?' I went to Herman and he wasn't there, he wasn't at the party, and said, 'Hey, I'll tell you what, it was crazy last night. I remember to this point and this point' and he said, 'You know what you had? You had a blackout.' And I said, 'Blackout?' And then he said, 'Hey, you know, that's a great title for an album.' And because of this kind of special party, I went back home and said I think I have to write song, the music, because Klaus was writing most of the lyrics. So I sat at home and made the song and then went to Klaus and he came up with the lyrics and then we had it."

103 WHIPLASH METALLICA

444 points *from Kill 'Em All (Music for Nations '83)*

Maybe this album as a whole didn't rewrite the rules the resounding way **Ride the Lightning** did, but on a micro level, this particular song did. Thrash just got faster, tighter and magically more vicious, Metallica tightening their grip with a sickening fatalist final creak that builds on something started with *Fireball* and *Exciter*. *Whiplash* was a statement, edged with the malnutrition of punk, a direct spike to the pumping heart, carving away everything that didn't look like a metal elephant. And even if Slayer motored along the same track, Metallica loomed larger and louder and wider doing it.

Lars Ulrich on Metallica's development . . .

"Making records, studio shit, writing songs and all that crap, whether you want to realize it or not, it's a learning experience. You can sit there when you're 19 and write a song and say, 'This is God's gift to the fucking universe,' but you've got to keep an open mind, and you've got to keep being receptive to new ideas. The main thing is that we've learned not to suppress any ideas or instincts that we have about anything that we do. You always have to give shit a chance. If it's an idea that comes from inside your head or inside your heart and soul, then it is you. You should never be afraid to let that come out. Over the last few years, we've learned not to come out that way. I'm not one that believes greatly in fate or anything, but I try to never tell myself when I have a thought that it shouldn't be let out. We've learned to write better songs, know our way around a recording studio, and to let shit happen and not stand in the way of letting the shit happen the way it does. There are places on some of our past records when it sounds a little forced, like we're trying to prove ourselves as musicians."

104 UNCHAINED
VAN HALEN

435 points *from Fair Warning (Warner '81)*

People instantly loved this song because it tricked you into thinking it was a regular riff rocker like most of the gleeful debut and dense 4/4 II. But that quickly proved erroneous once Dave started singing and Eddie began wondering and wandering. And then there's the odd time signatures of the pre-chorus before that burning free riff comes back and makes everything happy once again for people who spent more of their Grade 12 money on their car stereo than they paid for the whole car. A great example of the dangerous new Van Halen barely held together with chicken wire, forcing us to listen attentively, for we have become brief, occasional and more than you notice, experimental.

Michael Anthony on lyrics . . .

> "Our more recent lyrics are a lot more serious without being serious to the point where you're trying to preach. We're not politicians or religious people. Unless it's something we feel really strongly about, we just as soon leave all that heavy stuff to bands that like to do that sort of thing."

105 DOCTOR, DOCTOR
UFO

434 points *from Phenomenon (Chrysalis '74)*

Previously dolts, UFO smacked themselves smart with the acquisition of the agile and loony Michael Schenker, who quickly writes his signature track, *Doctor, Doctor* galloping along to a smart symphony of celluloid riffs and rhythms and sing-songy Schenker solo licks (the word "lick" was made for odd musical moments like these). Doesn't really have a chorus, but that recurring break (let's call it that) is classic goth metal courtier curtsy pomp fascism, the spot where Yngwie becomes possible by way of Michael and Ritchie before him.

Pete Way on *Doctor, Doctor* . . .

"That was one of the very first things we did, I think. When it first came out in Europe, I think it sold about ten copies as a single. When we came back with **Strangers in the Night**, when that record became big, suddenly all the songs we'd been doing for a long time became very popular songs. And *Doctor, Doctor* became very much an anthem and it still is. I mean, it already was popular, for the 2000 or 3000 people who would come see us every night. But it wasn't until **Strangers**, when we were playing the bigger places in America; for instance, in Chicago, I think there were about 14,000 at that show. It's that type of song that gets them going; it's an audience song. So it's funny, it was a rediscovered song, but it was always popular."

106 WASTED YEARS IRON MAIDEN

434 points *from Somewhere in Time* (EMI *'86)*

Yes, indeed, and most fans would agree. But this track unintentionally held a mirror to the band's ugly mug-faced mugs and saw that it was true. And it reflected wistfully, passionately, melodically, with a poignant spot of insight that made the tune one of the only uncontrived bits of actual art on **Somewhere in Time**. Its verse is one of the band's increasingly three-legged awkward moments, but *Wasted Years* is in possession of a pre-chorus and chorus that is chaotic but connecting, Bruce truly selling the sentiment, perhaps in the back of his mind taking note of the wear and tear of fame and fame's hotel to limo to gig to hotel to airport mental and physical scarring that could conceivably (we wouldn't know) cause a rock star to lament these last 48 months (just ask Sabbath). A loveable tangle of a song.

Bruce Dickinson on *Wasted Years* . . .

"*Wasted Years* was written very much in the middle of the time when we were on the road so much that there was a certain sense of irony about that song. Because when Adrian wrote that lyric, I think he was, along with all of us, sitting there on the road going, well, this is great. And there are some people that would cut their limb off to do this full-time. But boy, there are some days when we really feel we could do with a break (laughs)."

107 OVERKILL MOTÖRHEAD

433 points *from Overkill (Bronze '79)*

Overkill is basically an improvement on *Motörhead* on its way to perfecting the form with *Ace of Spades*. But the form, a rudimentary pioneering gesture at inventing thrash metal, is a bit suspect and simple, uneventful riffery packed like a sore tooth with punk. But hey, credit is due, the whole of this album still pre-dating the NWOBHM, Motörhead nefariously and with stubble, helping to cause Venom and later Metallica, with a rough-shot violence frighteningly boozy for its time. And the song itself is a lightning rod, a metaphor for the band's daring dirt in its most aggro form.

Fast Eddie Clarke on *Overkill* . . .

"Well, *Overkill* is really down to Phil. We were going into rehearsals and we were just starting to do well. We had just gotten a deal to do a second album, the **Overkill** album, so we were quite excited. And when we went into rehearsals, Phil had gotten a new drum kit at this point with the double kick. So he's sitting there showing his kit off doing his fast double bass, like at the beginning of *Overkill*, and he says, 'Why can't we do a song like this?' So he's fucking thundering away on the drums. Because you know, he's always speeding; he was kind of a bit like that. So he's thumping away at this beat, and I started playing and then Lemmy started with his 'grr' bass sound, so I joined in and went 'grr,' together all in E. And that was it, the birth of the song. And then once again, we did our usual thing. We rocked on with it for awhile and then we started to give it a bit of shape.

I said, 'Here, let's do that there and let's do that here.' And then Lemmy stuck the lyrics on it. Lemmy always did the lyrics. It was his department. He was a very good songwriter. And I've always believed the singer's got to write his own lyrics because he's got to sing them."

108 THE RIPPER JUDAS PRIEST

431 points *from Sad Wings of Destiny (Gull '76)*

Damn, throw their horsehide keesters into the Rock 'n' Roll Hall of Fame for that blood-curdling serial *Killer Queen* intro alone. And then put them on the stud-encrusted metal throne therein for that brilliant fast break, a symphony of singing guitars and operatic Halford highs that duel 'til you drool. And all this happens within a compact and immensely catchy few minutes, the band building the track like a '30s Hollywood talkie, Halford at his most thespian, the band stalking then chasing prey through the dark rain of London. Ends with as much killing class as it begins. Nasty surprises all around.

Ian Hill on the **Sad Wings Of Destiny** sessions . . .

"I think we really had our own sound by then, and we just got on and did it. The first album, we had a tiny budget and the second album we did as well. I mean, we were on the night shift. We would work from dusk 'til dawn because that's when the cheapest hours in the studio were (laughs). We would sleep outside in the van during the day and that was the scene that was going on with those two albums. But the major difference on the second album is that the production was much, much better. **Rocka Rolla**, the material was fine — there was nothing wrong with that — it was just poorly put down. It was funny because Roger Bain, he had just come off . . . he was just producing Black Sabbath and we thought, 'Oh god, we're onto a winner here!' But it just didn't sound good. It just didn't come across at all; no dynamics, nothing. The record company, Gull, were looking upon us as their meal ticket. I think they were hoping that we were going to make the record company big rather than the other way around. And they did try hard. You can't knock the effort that they did put in but they just didn't have the financial clout to make it happen. When you have to record overnight (laughs) . . . I mean, you're young and you just do it because you want your album up there on the shelf. But when you think back with what you put up with, I don't think people would do it today (laughs)."

109 QUEEN OF THE REICH QUEENSRYCHE

430 points *from Queensryche (EMI '83)*

In essence, Queensryche had instantly improved metal's lot with this one song, cleaning up on Maiden, significantly reinventing power metal for the first time since **Stained Class**, even if the band would spin its wheels through two more records before its next revelation, **Operation: Mindcrime**. But *Queen of the Reich* produced the impossible vocals of Geoff Tate, creating a musical template for Helloween, a crystallized actualization of Northwest rock that otherwise thrashed about through Metal Church, Culprit, Wild Dogs and TKO. Tight, galloping, groovy, and very, very high, *Queen of the Reich* was accomplished and confident like no new metal currently proposed other then say Mercyful Fate's **Melissa**, a world away in every other way. Also significantly, it gave notice that America wasn't going to leave castle rock to countries that actually had castles.

Michael Wilton on *Queen of the Reich* . . .

"That's a song that Chris came up with. He had this riff and I just said, 'Let's just rat this thing out,' let's get a really nasty guitar tone and play it fast and have Geoff sing these crazy lyrics (laughs). That was done at the Triad Studios in Redmond and we just use these Marshalls, and Tube Screamer stomp boxes. It was a very eye-opening experience because it was the first time we'd ever been in a real studio, so it was a big learning experience as well as a huge level of excitement. And Geoff's vocals, you know, you hear that opening scream. What was that one Deep Purple song? I won't go there (laughs). It was just, 'Come on Geoff, let's show your muscle here, let's show your range,' and boy, he had it! (laughs). But the lyrics are all silly, fantasy-oriented. So I think it's just the emotion and the delivery that Geoff put into it that really made it something heavy and exciting. And for us it was like, 'That is so cool; it'll never get played on the radio!' And look what happened, it was all over the radio and we're like, 'What!?' We were all 21 years old. I mean, influence-wise, it was either listening to the British metal invasion or listening to pop music. And we didn't want to do to Top 40 candy-ass pop music. We wanted to do heavy hardcore metal with lots of riffs (laughs)."

110 HELL BENT FOR LEATHER JUDAS PRIEST

429 points *from Killing Machine* (CBS '78)

Pointing the way toward the coming invention of Metallica, *Hell Bent for Leather* thickens Priest's speed metal experimentation, kicked off by the high screech of *Exciter* and *Call for the Priest* before it. This note-dense brethren to those is however shorter, more angry and a bit cheeky and gay. As well, its roar is throatier, its guitar gutsier and its sense of song more purposeful, like it's watching the clock, again, guardedly and nervously predicting the voraciously metal-munching motivations of a stereo hi-fi combo called Metallica.

K.K. Downing on Rob Halford and his sexual orientation . . .

"In the artistic world, sexuality means absolutely fuck all. If you have an artistic temperament, you have an understanding about a lot of things. And it's just been there from day one. We've done so much travelling and roughing it. Jesus Christ, we used to sleep in the back of the van in Norway and Sweden and Germany, and we used to clean our teeth all together in the fucking snow. We were all doing the same thing and it just wasn't an entity, know what I mean?"

Adrian Erlandsson from Cradle Of Filth
Judas Priest — *You've Got Another Thing Comin'*
Iron Maiden — *Killers*
Iron Maiden — *Aces High*
Saxon — *Princess of the Night*
Defiance — *Insomnia*
Forbidden — *March into Fire*
Slayer — *Die by the Sword*
Slayer — *Hell Awaits*
Judas Priest — *Freewheel Burning*
Manowar — *Metal Daze*

111 MOUTH FOR WAR PANTERA

428 points *from Vulgar Display of Power (Atlantic '92)*

It's amazing to see a band strengthen and solidify such a cold steel new direction for metal, especially at a time when the genre's battered corpse was being dragged around by the new hard alternative of grunge. **Vulgar** did that, and its opening salvo *Mouth for War* finds the band abstractly comfortable in this parched place. The groove is massive, smeared like red mud, slow but loud like an airplane hangar testing the latest people movers. Dime is the metal master, stuffing this three-speed wind chamber with riffs not paralleled in projection since Metallica's **Kill 'Em All**.

Phil Anselmo on *Mouth for War* . . .

> "I actually wrote the initial riff. Kick-ass song and once again, very anthemic. The anthemic style is in full force there. Whenever we play that live, people are really receptive and they respect the song for what it was. It was the first track you heard from a record that is still to this day, a lot of people's favourite Pantera record."

112 FLYING HIGH AGAIN OZZY OSBOURNE

428 points *from Diary of a Madman (Jet/CBS '81)*

A dear grandmotherly song to many, this was the **Diary of a Madman** track that had most in common with the debut album, more happy rock 'n' roll, autobiographical, disarming, almost relaxing. And it moved at a swelling, swirling pace that allowed Randy Rhoads to show his quick mind in quicksand, his ability to texture and turn a non-event into a strafing original metal anthem that feels like something off of Zep's **Presence**. It's almost fallible to the point of filler, yet at minimum, crowd-connect inclusive, Ozzy beginning his long conversation with his fans about falling and getting back up.

Bob Daisley on *Flying High Again* . . .

"I'll tell you a story about *Flying High Again*. My mother's family is from England and they immigrated to Australia and I was born in Sydney. When I was in Sydney as a teenager I was in a band. We went to the country to do a gig. This was in the '60s and we were all dressed in our flower power gear. We had on fringed jackets, flowery shirts and little square glasses. We must have looked really freaky to the country people. I used to have a station wagon with a Marshall stack in it and I was loading my gear in after the gig and this county looking guy came up to me and said 'Are you going back down to the smoke tonight? Are you going back to the city?' I said yeah. To him people in the city must have been weird and all on drugs because he said 'Are you going to be flying high again in Sydney town?' That stuck in my head. When I was writing the lyrics for *Flying High Again* I was doing a bit of coke with Ozzy and I thought, 'Here I am flying high again.' I was doing a bit of coke, not that I was really into it but I did a bit from time to time, and that guy's voice came back to me and I thought, 'Fuck, that is a good title.' But for that album it was Lee Kerslake, Randy and myself. A lot of times Ozzy wasn't there as he either had hangovers or he was off to see his family. He was there for some of it but the main bulk of it was the three of us. Lee came up with several of the vocal melodies for that album. I know he came up with the vocal melody for *Flying High Again*. He used to have a microphone at the side of his drums. He would sing along just to have somebody to sing while we put the songs together."

113 SYMPHONY OF DESTRUCTION MEGADETH

428 points *from Countdown to Extinction (Capitol '92)*

I still consider *Symphony of Destruction* the most expertly assembled metal song of the '90s. It was a deserving smash hit, stuffing the memory banks of all it touched with four or five (double, durable, adorable) platinum hooks. Each power chord, each vocal, each synchronized accent, succeeds in creating grooves as canyon-gorged as the best from AC/DC, while the sparing but thirst-quenching guitary bits speak to a lasting thrash education subsumed to, but patiently present within, Megadeth's new songwriting skills. And that riff . . . it is the stark star of metal through the eons, a certain illuminating type of metal, the kind that elicits a barely contained smirk in the listener, who then imagines a similar smirk in its creators, one that betrays an instant excitement that this somehow points to a true abstract objective Platonic ideal of art, one that suddenly makes the rest of the material sausage-ground through the sessions seem belaboured and ordinary.

Dave Ellefson on *Symphony of Destruction* . . .

"The writing of the songs for **Countdown to Extinction** happened in two sessions and *Symphony* came out of the second one. We were working at a rehearsal studio in North Hollywood. We worked for a while and then we would run outside and shoot hoops, play Pig or whatever. And after about 20 minutes we would come back inside and write songs. Right as we came in and Dave picked up the guitar was usually the moment of brilliance when a whole new riff would come up, and that's when *Symphony* happened. And I just remember how it developed between the stops and the riffs and then the ascending bass line during the chorus, and again, that was just one of those magical songs that came together really quickly, but when it happened, we just felt there was greatness that was going to come from that song."

114 TOM SAWYER RUSH

423 points *from Moving Pictures (Anthem '81)*

After thirty years, *Tom Sawyer* is still Rush's most recognized track, additionally occupying the pole position of the band's best-regarded album. *Tom Sawyer* is a masterful yet enigmatic and playful treatise on mankind at the hands of master Max Webster lyricist Pye Dubois. Musically the song finds a way to maintain interest while being very slow, the listener psyched and sucked into its vortex by Geddy Lee's droning synth effect, Peart's quick hi-hat pattern and Pye's elegant, tantalizing, tingly wordplay. As well, there's the drama of the breaks, Peart's air drum heaven fills culminating in critical mass toward the final slightly sinister chords.

Alex Lifeson on getting it just right . . .

"We are very meticulous in our preparation. Neil and I are both Virgos. We're always too anal about how we prepare ourselves. Everything is very orderly. We've reached a point in our career that we can take our time for just purely financial reasons. At the same time, you impose certain demands and restrictions upon yourself."

Fuzz from Disturbed
Rush — *The Spirit of Radio*
Rush — *Tom Sawyer*
Triumph — *Fight the Good Fight*
Tool — *Aenima*
Molly Hatchet — *Flirtin' with Disaster*
Yngwie Malmsteen — *Far Beyond the Sun*
Iron Maiden — *Can I Play with Madness*
Godsmack — *Awake*
Pantera — *Walk*
Pantera — *Fucking Hostile*

115 A DANGEROUS MEETING MERCYFUL FATE

422 points *from Don't Break the Oath (Roadrunner '84)*

Already way better than anybody else (except maybe Savatage, Queensryche and Metallica) by the time of their second album, Mercyful Fate continued to sharpen their machine-tooled steel by writing shorter and more focused songs. *A Dangerous Meeting* kicked off **Don't Break the Oath** by killing seven people that would dare mess with the powers of Hell. The riff is elegant and mesmerizing, backed by a superior locked groove and excellent production. It is an instantly hooky song, yet it is progressive and very dark. As well, King's vocal melodies are arguably the best of his career, surreptitiously snaking their way through the black twin lead poisoning of Denner and Shermann. And the concluding moments are sheer terror, King simply and unemotionally laying out the fate of the seven doomed interlopers. Originally recorded with different lyrics as *Death Kiss* (King offers a different story; see below), which was a little more rock 'n' roll, a little less venomous, less Crossroads-culpable.

King Diamond on *A Dangerous Meeting* . . .

"Yeah, that's another one I love playing live. That originated with the band Brats, which turned into Mercyful Fate. Some of those songs were integrated and changed in the rehearsal room. *A*

Dangerous Meeting was called *Walking Back to Hell* before that and had a few riffs that were different in it. A lot of things happened that way. We were rehearsing four times a week and that's where we developed the whole sound. But at that time, there was also a certain immaturity because it was a struggle to get anything past Hank musically. Which isn't the case anymore. We all grew up and learned things and we have none of the stupid fights anymore in either of the bands. But back then it was, 'Yeah, well, that works pretty well, but I have this song here!' But the way it started was, we would play those songs live, and people would say, 'God man, why is that song not out!?' And it's like, 'Well, it was already written at the time of **Melissa**.' 'No way! You should have put that on the album!' 'Yeah, well, we didn't.' Then it was like, it had to be there on **Don't Break the Oath**."

116 WRATHCHILD IRON MAIDEN

415 points

from Killers (EMI '81)

Maiden's debut wasn't exactly a fluke, but let's face it, *Wrathchild* was the first sophisticated arrangement of the band's long creative career. Less punky and more proto-power, the track served as a metaphor for the new first-class direction which would drive Di'Anno away. Drama, pathos, a classic bass line, militaristic punctuation marks, even built-in crowd participation . . . all crossed paths to work up a determined critical mass without forgetting hooks and without blathering on forever, a particular crutch of Steve's writing in the Bruce years.

Paul Di'Anno on *Wrathchild* . . .

"I'll tell you what, and I don't want to sound bigheaded, but I don't do more than two or three takes, because if you don't get it right in that time, you shouldn't be doing it at all (laughs). I think that took about one take, but someone might contradict me on that. The lyrics were all down to Steve on that one."

117 POWER AND THE GLORY SAXON

414 points *from Power and the Glory (Carrere ’83)*

If past anthems were to have you thinking about clunky, clanking motorcycles, *Power and the Glory* sliced the sky like a fighter jet. This was the work of a band at the height of their game, driven deep into gleaming metal heavens by a new drummer and new producer who together created grooves that we thought this awkward rockscrabble band was too white to own. Highly strung, screeched and confident, *Power and the Glory* found all of Saxon’s ragtag disparate hodgepodge tube lines crossing at the station of the metal cross. And even if lyrically it was another fist-pumped paean to the solidarity of the metal minions, it operated from a position of strength, Biff’s armies already having heeded the call, even if most preferred to open their wallets for Iron Maiden and Def Leppard versus this suspiciously old-looking bunch of fish and crisp wankers.

Nigel Glockler on *Power and the Glory* . . .

> “*Power and the Glory* was written up in Suffolk during the Falklands War. In fact, a lot of that whole album was. We’d come back from the rehearsal studio — it was a barn — and the conflict was on TV every night. Biff and I are really into documentaries about WW2, in fact any conflict throughout history. We’re into the same films and books about it as well. **Cross of Iron** and **The Blue Max** are two faves — hence the “raise your glasses high” lyric. Once one has an idea about the subject matter, and the basic song idea has a rough structure, then you

start honing things down. I can't remember who came up with the basic riff, but it ends up with a lot of jamming, getting parts and grooves sorted out, etc."

118 TYRANT JUDAS PRIEST

414 points *from Sad Wings of Destiny (Gull '76)*

Tyrant is the agitated heart of **Sad Wings of Destiny**, its rolling rock, its critical mass, the overbearing character of the album, a zipped-up winter jacket that impatiently says "let's get on with it then." *Ripper* is as carnal, but this one is perhaps the most ambitious in terms of plotting a career. Sinewy twin leads thrust and parry with an exacting Halford, who seems to be playing the role of typecast Nazi officer or at minimum, some cruel bureaucrat at the motor vehicle registry office. As he lays down the way it's going to be, the band pressurize and cook towards an inevitable, sorrow-tinged conclusion. No surprise that *Tyrant* is still a staple of the live set, indeed the protein of the show.

Rob Halford on *Tyrant* . . .

"I love *Tyrant* simply because of its class and style and approach in its lyrics. It's an area that I want to re-explore actually. It just talks about the fact that in the world there are these tyrannical figures in life that control and terrorize people. It's a combination of fantasy and reality but I love the musical composition because it's a real roller coaster. There are twists and turns and a lot of information and a lot of musical directions happening within that one moment."

119 I WANT OUT HELLOWEEN

413 points *from Keeper of the Seven Keys Part II (Noise '88)*

Folks glommed onto this one fast because of its spaces, its hanging chords, its easily dissectable, Accept-able arrangement. Then there's that chorus, punctuated anthemically by a sentiment with which any teenage metalhead can easily relate. But I was never crazy about this album's *de rigeur* '80s production, its brash and cold drum sound undermining a song that could have grooved much better. Look for the cool prog metal break, where Michael Kiske works his Geoff Tate-able pipes along with a nice backing vocal arrangement.

Kai Hansen on *I Want out* . . .

> "*I Want out* is really a song that describes the personal situation at the time in Helloween when the chemistry was already falling apart and when I already had the thought of leaving as it was all getting too much around me and I thought, if I can't go on with the whole thing, what shall I do? And it all came down to this basic feeling: I want to get out of this situation. I want out of here. So this song was really emotional. It really came from the heart. Looking back, it's of course a bit ridiculous to release an album with a song that says I want to fucking get out of this band (laughs). And the album was a really big success, but already there were a lot of negative vibes, so it has a really strong meaning for me."

Kai Hansen from Helloween
Queen — *Tie Your Mother Down*
Motörhead — *Bomber*

Sex Pistols — *God Save the Queen*
Judas Priest — *Exciter*
Iron Maiden — *Killers*
Holocaust — *Heavy Metal Mania*
Ramones — *Beat on the Brat*
Rainbow — *Kill the King*
UFO — *Love to Love*
Deep Purple — *Child in Time*

120 CIRCLE OF THE TYRANTS CELTIC FROST

413 points *from To Mega Therion (Noise '85)*

Demonstrative of many Celtic Frost traits, *Circle of the Tyrants* is a fan favourite due to its multiple speeds, allowing for judicious moshing at all cycles. It is also uniquely untuneful and hapless and jagged, almost punky, shocked full of Venom-mouse energy. Therefore, it is modestly proggy, blessed (cursed?) with a break that invites all the headbangers to chill for a minute and do that mindless swaying thing (y'know, where everyone realizes how tired they are and that they have to go to work in seven hours) until the boys thrash out again for Tom's buried alive guitar solo. Trivia note: clear and crushing in its original mix (see the Noise '99 reissue of **Morbid Tales**), boozy and Bathory for the official **To Mega Therion** album.

Tom Warrior on the band's legacy . . .

> "We have often wondered whether the public has ever fully comprehended what Celtic Frost was all about and perhaps more poignantly, what we tried to arouse and how impassioned we felt about it. That is a very difficult question to answer. Is it really true, am I a legend? Or is all we ever did massively overrated? I was involved far too closely and passionately to know what our actual legacy is. And I still am. If it's true that we moved more than the average band, it leaves us flattered, as I said before. All we ever wanted was to improve on the basis of our previous work. As absurd as it sounds, the limitations imposed

by the industry made it sometimes necessary to have a lot of guts to actually go and develop in such a way. That hardened us and made us even fresher and bolder. Such freshness didn't always result in sensible albums, as everyone familiar with the band knows. On the other hand sometimes it made us create the things that now people rate as legendary. But we are not legends. We are just a bunch of curious guys."

121 WHOLE LOTTA ROSIE
AC/DC

409 points *from Let There Be Rock (Atlantic '77)*

Whole Lotta Rosie is **Let There Be Rock**'s link to AC/DC's pub rock past, a spot of '50s rock amidst a batch of songs trying to turn and burn the band into an overseas phenom, courting most notably England. But like the whole album, it is cow-prodded with a torrent of electricity and a neck-knocking racket of guitars, pounding and bounding it out of its retro-rocker past, wrapping Quo in newly-minted barbed wire, turning crusty boogie into spun gold, all the while scratching its back, bumming a smoke and waiting for the bus as the band's most casually written song from '77 or later.

Angus Young on pressure to become more commercial . . .

"The guy that was managing us wanted a pop sanitized band. It was kind of weird; he was a quick buck merchant and the buck went his way. We were poorly educated but we did know a little bit about math. He wanted everything his way. He said to me, Malcolm and Bon, 'You guys should look like millionaires' and Malcolm said, ' Well, then you should fuckin' pay us like millionaires!'" He used to say that I should be in the back, because the little girls wouldn't like to see me, nose running, my hair all over and me snarling at the audience. At that time I said, 'Listen buddy, I'm playing for the whole audience, not to entertain a couple of girls with autograph books. I get up there and play guitar. Who gives a shit if I have acne?' How much Brady Bunch bullshit can you take? An audience is not easily fooled. The women with the 'Give me flowers, give me a big house' — at the end of the day they end up running off with the friggin' gardener because he's a man! But we just wanted to have fun. The big kick for us was to play anywhere there was a rock audience. That was always our big thrill. It was great to walk in and have all these odds against you. Malcolm always said to our manager, 'I dropped out of school to be in a rock 'n' roll band and now you want me to be nice?!'"

Aaron Stainthorpe from My Dying Bride
Motörhead — *Ace of Spades*
Iron Maiden — *Run to the Hills*
Celtic Frost — *Rex Irae (Requiem)*
Bathory — *13 Candles*
Artillery — *Terror Squad*
Iron Maiden — *Rime of the Ancient Mariner*
Slayer — *Raining Blood*
AC/DC — *Hells Bells*
Candlemass — *Samarithan*
Candlemass — *A Sorcerer's Pledge*

122 RIDE THE LIGHTNING METALLICA

401 points *from Ride the Lightning (Music for Nations '84)*

There must have been three-mile smiles on the faces of Metallica after the knowledge that *Fight Fire with Fire* would be **Ride the Lightning**'s track one, side one, and that this multi-tasking title track would follow quick on its heels. It is a pairing that would shake the foundations of the metal world, this sophisticated second track demonstrating the band's new talent and vision at a wider selection of speeds than track one. *Ride the Lightning*'s slow yet rhythmically complex verse riff would also be a blighted demonstration of dry smothering power that predicts the rise of Pantera almost a decade later, Metallica setting upon tones that would leave the competition gasping for air.

James Hetfield on bettering oneself . . .

> "I don't think we were content bein' down there. There are some bands who are fine with it. They love what they do and they don't like change; they're afraid of it. They just want what they are doing; that's fine. We got some bug up our asses that makes us want to go, 'We've done that, let's do something else, I'm bored, let's go somewhere.' We've had that hunger since day one. That mixed with a total, pure, from the heart honesty. This is what we're doing. We aren't candy-coating nothing. We're not putting a cloud in front of you; we're not trying to fool anyone. We're playing music for ourselves and if you like it, then that's good. If you can't please yourself, it's near impossible to please other people."

123 LOOKS THAT KILL MÖTLEY CRÜE

399 points *from Shout at the Devil (Elektra '83)*

Looks That Kill was all attitude, and it absolutely had to be, given a riff that on paper is an all too well travelled, vanilla-white pop metal construct built by and for lesser bands. But Tommy drives it gravely and heavily, wading through production values that sound like the dens of iniquity this track haunted for years through every cover band slinking the circuit. But there's a craftiness there, because what we find is that the band is holding back all their metal acumen for the chorus, which rocks smarter and well, kind of British. As a package however, the track is still an extremely simplistic headbanger, existing on junk food, cheap drugs and the sheer squalor emanating from the pores of this band over the course of two brilliantly brain-damaged records.

Nikki Sixx on the early days . . .

> "Our thing was a direct rebellion against what was going on in Los Angeles. The thing is, when this band got together, every-

body in the band looked the way they looked. It wasn't like, after we came out, it was, 'Let's look like this.' It was just four guys that had the same passion and they looked like that. It became something that people talked about more than the music. And we were like, 'I've always looked like this, what's the problem? What's the big deal?'"

124 PHANTOM OF THE OPERA IRON MAIDEN

399 points *from Iron Maiden* (EMI '80)

Like the title track, *Phantom of the Opera* starts with a left field widdle — Steve, of course, wedged in as part of this one — before the band spreads its dank, doomy, prog rock raven wings. The song goes many places, the band on a mission from 'Arry, adding to the world's library of speed metal, but also adding to the sparse shelves of epic metal, stacking part upon part, really driving home the point with percussive punch, before diving back into the verse and a final vocal Zorro Z from the gamely, gangly thugchild at the mike.

Paul Di'Anno on *Phantom of the Opera* . . .

> "That's another one of Steve's. Now that one did take a bit of time because it's a bloody nightmare to sing. It's bad enough live, but to get it dead on for an actual recording, I think I had to do that one three times or so. If I said less, I'd probably be lying (laughs)."

125 DANTE'S INFERNO ICED EARTH

398 points *from Burnt Offerings (Century Media '95)*

Toiling away during the dark days for his love it/hate it label, Jon Schaffer made a series of hopeful albums, records produced during an era when people constantly pontificated whether metal was going to make a quick bounce-back return. Never happened, but that didn't stop Jon from honing his dark, thrashy power metal sound before that bane term existed. *Dante's Inferno* fits the bill perfectly, sounding almost like melodic, accessible Death crossed with **Justice**-era Metallica and the darkest thoughts of Steve Harris, Schaffer providing a wealth of gloomy traditional precision to feed your bitter, undergrounded, bombast-imbibing soul.

Jon Schaffer on *Dante's Inferno* . . .

"Well, God, I bought that book. I have a copy of that that is 100 years old now. I bought it at a flea market in I believe late '92, after the European **Stormrider** tour. I was at this flee market and I saw this book, and it just really drew me to it from across that little section. And I picked it up and I really felt, 'Man, I'm really going to get something great out of this thing.' I just felt it immediately. So I bought the book, spent like a hundred bucks on the thing and that was a lot of money for me. It was a big, big risk. But I really believed I was going to get something special out of it. It was very hard to read. I ended up spending two or three years writing that song, not all at once certainly. I worked on it here and there. But I had set in my mind pretty much immediately after getting that book that I was going to write a song that was going to be the biggest epic that we had ever done, and hopefully the biggest metal epic that had been done to date by anybody. And the big challenge for me was to write a song that was between 15 and 20 minutes, which is what I decided, that wasn't going to feel like 15 or 20 minutes. It would have to stay interesting enough, minus all the musician masturbation and bullshit that so many bands do when they do a big epic song. Now I'm not talking Maiden, because Steve has always been a great songwriter. But you hear a lot of bands, like prog rock bands that really don't get to any point. They're just jamming. And some people really enjoy that — that's cool — but I don't. To me when I hear that stuff, it feels like 15 or 20 minutes. So it was a big challenge to make sure there were enough hooks and enough interest that people didn't get tired of it. And I think I accomplished that. When I look back at the **Burnt Offerings** album, which is my least favourite record, that is this song for sure that is the highlight."

126 TORNADO OF SOULS MEGADETH

397 points *from Rust in Peace (Capitol '90)*

A deep album track on a record full of sustained overflowing electricity, *Tornado of Souls* is a surprise dark horse way up the list. It is a belligerently punky or at least Anthrax-tinged combat rocker with a chorus that reaches out. But like much of the rest of the album, things take a turn for the reverse, the song becoming a passionate melodic thrash for its deadly conclusion, metal conquering and coddling the damaged narrator who is resolute in snuffing the life out of his two-legged obstacles.

Marty Friedman on *Tornado of Souls* . . .

> "That seems to be one of the tunes if I do a guitar clinic or seminar, people always ask me to play the guitar solo in that one. I guess it's a long solo, maybe that's why. That's when I really felt like I was in the band, when we were cutting that and I nailed the solo. Mustaine came in, and he hadn't heard me playing any of it. He just came in and listened to it when it was done and he didn't say anything. He just shook my hand and he had this look on his face just like, dude, right on. And I was like, pretty cool. But to me, I was much happier with some of the other work I had done on **Rust in Peace**, but I guess that's the one that stuck with most people."

127 THE MOB RULES BLACK SABBATH

397 points *from Mob Rules (Warner '81)*

As testimony to the creative depth of the uneasy shotgun marriage between Dio and Sabbath, *The Mob Rules* is one of those always interesting accidents of melody to which Iommi haphazardly, intermittently casts glances. Dio attacks much like this song's storyline over a thick percussive rumble, the track announcing the album with a brisk pace and relentless force unusual for Sabbath, ravenous from all four corners, to the pertinent point, point being that this album will have greater shockwave complications than its classier but less self-aware predecessor.

Ronnie James Dio on the post-**Mob Rules** break-up of the band . . .

> "That was a time when we had a lot of success, via the **Heaven and Hell** album and the **Mob Rules** album. Life had changed for the guys, going from not being successful to being very successful again. And once you get to that point, all the temptations come out, and there were a lot of conditions. And I think that clouded a lot of intelligence on their parts too. When we reformed and did the **Dehumanizer** album, both Tony and Geezer came to Vinny and I and said, 'Look, we're sorry that we let this happen.' And you know, thank you for the humble apology, but it didn't quite wash it all away for me, because I had always been a person concerned with the group and the band, never with myself, although maybe being accused of that, because of having a bit of a higher profile than the rest. But my feeling was always you know, 'us against the world, let's do a great job, and whatever you want me to do, I'll do.' But like I say, some egos and the success factor got in the way and it just spelled the end at that time. It's stupid and sad, but that's the way it was, and life went on. And maybe I should thank them because I have had a nice career with Dio. But as I say, the guys owned up, 12 years later when we did the other album. They were certainly wrong and very sorry about what happened."

128 THE SENTINEL JUDAS PRIEST

391 points *from Defenders of the Faith* (CBS '84)

Scarred by a turgid recording, *The Sentinel* nevertheless projects a regal omnipotent sense of melody that hearkens back to Priest's hallowed religious classics, evoking a sobbing metal resignation that darkens this record's otherwise slightly scrambling tracks. The lyric is moderately ambitious, a storyboard about some kind of supernatural good versus evil street battle which is ultimately resolved by no more than "rows of throwing knives."

Ian Hill on *The Sentinel* . . .

> "*The Sentinel* has always been an epic, yeah. It's one of my favourite songs as well, and until very recently it's been included in the live set. And I think in fact, we've just only recently dropped it. It's a great, exciting track and it's a bit of the show-piece for Ken as well."

129 BORN TO BE WILD STEPPENWOLF

388 points *from Steppenwolf* (RCA '68)

Folks pontificate whether the term heavy metal came from **Naked Lunch** by William Burroughs, some rock critic (I forget which one now; not Lester I don't think, maybe Metal Mike Saunders) or from this song's "heavy metal thunder." In any event, *Born to Be Wild* is seminal original metal, from a band not usually prone to such things, John Kay having the voice for it, but his band . . . well, it was mostly Doors-y psychedelia. But this song, whether by accident, hook or by crook, got to the point immediately with its instantly recognizable slashing power chords, perhaps the most universally understood hard rock intro, golding to the silver of *Purple Haze* and the bronze tie between *Smoke on the Water* and *Whole Lotta Love*. And like, "born to be wild". . . what better sticker slogan for your heavy metal bumper?

130 REVOLUTION CALLING QUEENSRYCHE

384 points *from Operation: Mindcrime* (EMI '88)

A true rock epiphany, *Revolution Calling* opens wide after two named intros and one of its own, building, lifting, harmonizing, before a surprisingly simple anti-climactic riff. But then this red carpet introduction to an album called the best progressive metal concept record of all time continues, through the deft mind manipulation of the hopeful pre-chorus strapped to the rocket of an ecstatic chorus. *Revolution Calling* instantly rounded the troops, this wayward band and their fans, exploding in all directions in an explosive call to arms. It is the clearest, cleanest moment of an often difficult album, and indeed the first time in the band's career that we see the purpose of all those cooks in the kitchen.

Michael Wilton on *Revolution Calling* . . .

> "That was a great time in the band's career. We were all working together in Scott's basement, just throwing cassettes in, riffing, building songs. That was one of the first songs we wrote for that album. There are about three or four songs that Chris and I came in with and that was one of them. And I think that one came together pretty quick."

Michael Wilton from Queensryche
Judas Priest — *Dissident Aggressor*
Iron Maiden — *Murders in the Rue Morgue*
Judas Priest — *Beyond the Realms of Death*
UFO — *This Kid's/Between the Walls*
Iron Maiden — *Phantom of the Opera*
Jimi Hendrix Experience — *Are You Experienced?*
Tool — *Hooker with a Penis*
Led Zeppelin — *Black Dog*
Metallica — *For Whom the Bell Tolls*
Ozzy Osbourne — *Diary of a Madman*

131 DISPOSABLE HEROES METALLICA

379 points *from Master of Puppets (Elektra '86)*

Sweet soul sister to *Master of Puppets*, and perhaps a bridge between *For Whom the Bell Tolls* and *One*, *Disposable Heroes* is an "album track," one of those sturdy sentinels with much substance but little of the spotlight. It is quite an addictive track, mid-moshing then furiously thrashing, then collapsing back into a memorable cruise-ready chorus and various jammy, meandering, unnecessary breaks. But *Disposable Heroes* stays close to the plot, making it another example of a long Metallica song that gets that way by repeatedly revisiting the particular track's five or six viable riff constructs.

Lars Ulrich on broadening his tastes . . .

"I've always been one to explore and check different things out. I remember very clearly at one point around 1993, 1994, I got really bored with hard rock and metal in general and started getting into many different things that I thought I would never get into, like British pop music. There's probably some correlation between wanting to be a better songwriter and getting into a lot of different music. Have I lost touch? I don't think I've lost touch with anything. I've chosen to remove myself from certain things in my life very much on purpose and I don't think you can call that losing touch. I find that as you become more popular and everybody wants a piece of you, you have more and more things on your plate. You choose and you narrow what you want to do with your time. I find that you treasure the time when you are by yourself. You do the things you want to do for yourself and by yourself. You have to choose certain other things more selectively. I find that I spend, for instance, a lot less time exploring music now than listening to stuff that I know I like. I choose to do these things. I choose not to listen to a lot of hard rock music anymore. It's not that I'm losing touch. It's just that I'm not that interested in it. If I want to listen to hard rock, I know that I can put on the ten best hard rock CDs that were ever made and I know exactly where they are. I know that if there was something that came out in 1996 to rival that, I know people around me would tell me what it was and I wouldn't have to sit and spend time searching for it."

132 ORION METALLICA

376 points *from Master of Puppets (Electra '86)*

Same position, length and purpose as *Call of Ktulu* on **Ride the Lightning**, yet *Orion* lays back a bit, presaging future sparse moods within the band, Lars especially working out his signature staggered style of the band's second steam. *Orion*'s main riff without a doubt sticks in the head, with its soundtracky advancing melodies, its plot-line march. But man, that middle baroque bluesy piece is a snorefest, the track somewhat redeemed by the new theme that marches us out. All told, a patient, rock starry indulgence much less eventful than its inspired predecessor.

James Hetfield on festivals like Lollapalooza . . .

> "It's not like we're ruining anything. We've done festivals in Europe since day one that are exactly like that. We played a European festival where we went on after Peter Gabriel, Lenny Kravitz and Neil Young. Those festivals exist all the time and it's not something different for us. People overanalyze us. The thing about the Lollapalooza stuff is that we're kinda hated again. I like that."

133 FUCKING HOSTILE PANTERA

375 points *from Vulgar Display of Power (Atlantic '92)*

This track was a vortex for the stark new credo of the ass-kicking Phil version of Pantera that the Texan tornadoes were loudly imposing upon the metal community. Not since the blurred average of Metallica's first two albums had metal seen an intensification like this, Phil, Dime, Vinnie and Rex combining hardcore and death metal with pure rage on top of aggro-anthems that invoked the sweet science of a nuclear plant. A shocking blast from a man and a band with a plan.

Vinnie Paul on *Fucking Hostile* . . .

> "*Fucking Hostile* is just a good, up-tempo thrash song. We felt that it really hit home with a lot of people with what Philip had to say with the lyrics and everything and still to this day, it's a great one to play live. And when that part comes around that says, 'Fucking hostile,' the whole crowd says it, man."

134 YOUTH GONE WILD SKID ROW

374 points *from Skid Row (Atlantic '89)*

Baz gets indignant (surly?) when snapped in the same cosmetics case as Poison, but the first album, man, it ain't that much of a stretch. Oh sure, they scowl and call themselves Skid Row, their jeans are ripped, their piercings pierced, but *Youth Gone Wild* is a Kiss song, replete with big chorus and an equally convertible-blasted pre-chorus, dramatic lost generation verses . . . assert your malcontent along with pointy boots. One also hears a fair bit of Ratt in there, which marks an elevated level of sophistication and guitarismo, so we'll now suspend the jibes and maybe even forgive those crowd participation "woah's" that close off this new burger and fries generation anthem.

Dave "Snake" Sabo on *Youth Gone Wild* . . .

> "We just wanted to express our rebelliousness. When you're growing up, your rebelliousness comes from different places. You're slighted in school because you're different or the outcast or you're not socially adaptable. We've all gone through our own trials and tribulations of being persecuted for how we look or our belief systems. And we felt that when we had gotten together, we had all gone through many similar situations where we were outcasts from the mainstream and that song was a reflection of those feelings."

135 GATES OF BABYLON RAINBOW

374 points *from Long Live Rock 'n' Roll (Polydor '78)*

Camel stacked high with all of Ritchie's and Ronnie's rugs, candles and incense, Rainbow set out for *Kashmir*, creating their third epic (preceded by *Stargazer* and *Light in the Black*), a tight, taught, Tull-trolled bit of castle rock popcorn on a harsh, unforgiving record, the coldest yet from a cold band. *Gates of Babylon* is the result of a professional working relationship that would soon sour, and is Rainbow's most pronounced manifestation of why this relationship was able to hold for three studio albums — the reason being simply that both men had a passion for the same exotic metal climes, Ritchie delivering through his guitar, Ronnie, through his voice and words.

Ronnie James Dio on *Gates of Babylon* . . .

> "We were in France at the time. I know we wrote it in the studio, in the chateau in France where we did that album. I remember that because the middle bit we worked on with our then keyboard player, David Stone. David was in France with us at the time. The song itself, I just wanted it to be really dark. Because it was so eastern in nature right away, to write to it was not so much simple, but it led me to where I needed to go. It was just hard to find what I was going to use as a title for this very, very eastern song. There were so many choices. But perhaps some of them were a little too silly, too jolly, too stupid. But this seemed to work really well. I remember looking at a map when we were writing the song. I was in my room looking at an old map of the Middle East, and saw Babylon and thought, well, there you go."

136 HALLOWEEN
HELLOWEEN

373 points *from Keeper of the Seven Keys Part 1 (Noise '87)*

Halloween is 13 minutes of blazing post-Maiden mania, the train of a track getting right to the point, rocking hard into the underground, Kiske and band scorching a pre-power metal path into the spirit of October 31st. Perhaps the most thorough, direct and obvious paean to the night of the pumpkin, *Halloween* talks about trick or treating, Charlie Brown and Linus, ending with a horror scenario more appropriate to the context of metal, that knock at the door that reveals evil, "the snake," and a subsequent slip into another dimension. As tongue in cheek as the whole loony cartoony Helloween image, it's songs like this that imbued the band with a self-deprecating lightheartedness that could only bring them closer to their fans.

Kai Hansen on *Halloween* . . .

> "*Halloween* was a song that really took a while to write. It started just with the intro riff, and then we jammed around with that a bit, and all the rest I wrote together with good old Ingo, the old Helloween drummer, in the rehearsals room, over a time period of about four weeks. And this song became more and more of a masterpiece, a really big thing where everything was fitting. And it was a song where I definitely wrote the vocal lines for Michael Kiske's voice. Always, with every part I had his voice in mind. And that was different from before; it was a very good experience writing this song."

137 HAMMER SMASHED FACE
CANNIBAL CORPSE

369 points *from Tomb of the Mutilated (Metal Blade '92)*

Framed here and there (he says vaguely) like *Raining Blood, Hammer Smashed Face* contains all of death metal's attractive dynamic shifts stuffed red, raw and bleeding into one action-packed package. It projects through the band's difficult catalogue because it's blessed and butchered with a number of speeds, as well as empty spots in which one can contemplate the horror. Melody also meekly ekes out, but in essence, this isn't one of the band's more songly songs.

Jack Owen on *Hammer Smashed Face* . . .

> "Alex wrote the majority of that and I think he was in an angry mood when he wrote it. So the main thing was have just this kind of pounding intro, just like pounding somebody's head in (laughs) and the title came about. We were back in Buffalo then, we were having problems with the band, problems with the scene, so I think it came out of an angry mood."

138 MOTHER DANZIG

367 points *from Danzig (Def American '88)*

Strictly speaking, the version everybody voted for as the best Danzig song is from the live EP, Danzig catching one of those baffling industry breaks over which he still shakes his head. Verily, this is a lame version of a filler track — he knows it, I'm saying it — but it just stuck, sucking sheep over the cliff, wallets flapping in the wind shear. Pretty embarrassing track, sort of AC/DC meets scrappy hair metal, riff straight from a sparsely attended mall at the edge of a boring town, chorus slightly redeemable because of its slight acceleration, which inexplicably takes over verse #2, the band sounding like they just want to get it over with.

Glenn Danzig on *Mother* . . .

> "Well, of course now, it's almost like a rallying cry for angry, disassociated people. Because of course when it came out on the first Danzig record, MTV refused to play it because they were freaked out by the video and about the PMRC. It was very taboo at that time; they didn't really want to discuss it. And then later on, because of all the constant touring, Danzig became a band that was selling out major venues with no radio airplay or support from any major distribution chain, because we had no MTV airplay; we had nothing. We just went out on the road and took

it to the people and that's how that song eventually appeared on an EP that had some live tracks on it. Then it blew up on radio and even MTV couldn't stop it, which of course, they tried, by not playing it. But eventually even they had to play it. Then the weeding out process began. You kind of filter out all these people who just knew *Mother* but didn't know what the band was about, so that's what took place after that. What we have now are people where they hear that song and it just makes them go out of their minds. It's their rallying cry for everything they're angry about, everything they feel they have no say about. That's what it means to me, and when we do it live, the whole place just erupts. There's this aggression being released, all this frustration that they deal with every day."

Greg Strzempka from Raging Slab
Deep Purple — *Burn*
Humble Pie — *Stone Cold Fever*
Led Zeppelin — *Dancing Days*
Rose Tattoo — *Rock 'n' Roll Outlaw*
Budgie — *Whiskey River*
Accept — *Fast as a Shark*
Van Halen — *Beautiful Girls*
Rush — *Bastille Day*
Focus — *Hocus Pocus*
AC/DC — *Night Prowler*

139 EYES OF A STRANGER QUEENSRYCHE

366 points *from Operation: Mindcrime (EMI '88)*

Eyes of a Stranger is like a big ribbon-wrapped metaphor for, or microcosm of, the swellegant **Operation: Mindcrime** album. Its opening tones recall Floyd's *Welcome to the Machine* and then we get swimming

Maiden circa the bloated mid-years. And as with many of this album's emotional touchstones, there's a nice build to and follow through a moderately memorable chorus. As well, the track is a prog-percussive tour de force, recalling an earlier era in Queensryche's history when time stood still and drum clinics were studied with eagle-eyed envy.

Michael Wilton on *Eyes of a Stranger . . .*

"*Eyes of a Stranger* to me, is a great live song. It has a monster riff in it, and what I remember most is doing the video for it because it was a time when we were low on sales and just basing everything on touring, being a touring rock band. And then MTV started playing hard rock and that song garnered us a little spot and the next thing you know we were on the Metallica tour, which was a big springboard for us."

140 SWEET LEAF BLACK SABBATH

362 points *from Master of Reality (Warner '71)*

Sure thing, Sabbath are the grandpappies of metal, but it really did take two full albums before the foggy, hormonal backwash of the band's youth would drip from their torsos and seep into the storm sewers. *Sweet Leaf* subsequently announced with a hair-raising pre-**Exorcist** hacking English cough that the metal has to come to a boil, let the games begin. When *Sweet Leaf* kicks in, one witnesses simultaneously the invention of stoner rock and the heaviest guitar sound yet barely contained on black wax. Everything spells doom, Ozzy's anguished sweet nothings to weed, Tony's audible fret noise, Geezer adding to the pronounced wallow, Bill just following the chords with a jazzy disinterested groove, the only anti-approach that could possibly work. The song hangs forlornly on a masterful riff which must be destroyed and is, as the song eventually and inevitably lets go like a blue exhale, an untied balloon let fly, a reel-to-reel tape unthreaded.

Bill Ward on *Sweet Leaf . . .*

"We were in Wales; I remember when we wrote that. And I think it was either Geezer or Ozzy, when they first came up with that lyric, 'When I first met you I didn't realize,' and I realized it was about having a relationship with marijuana. And I thought, you know, this is fucking incredible. Now, it just seems to me that it's a great song, but at the time it was like, man, this is real hardcore, because back then it was hardcore, to be talking about a relationship with oneself getting high. It was basically us saying, 'Hey, we stand up for marijuana,' which was what we were doing back then. And then we did *Snowblind*, which again was like putting a seal of approval on yet another drug. Which, in hindsight now I can look back and go, I mean, I'm certainly not ashamed of it because we went through that, we did that. But as you know, I'm an addict as well, so in my life now that is something that is absolutely discouraged. But back then when I was going through it, it was like 'yeah.'"

141 AM I EVIL? DIAMOND HEAD

359 points *from Lightning to the Nations (Happy Face '80)*

Judging by this sinister doom classic, the answer is yes, the rest of the catalogue, no. But this is also the most immediately influential of the band's grand statements (of which there are about ten over the four record catalogue), most rife and riddled with the band's inept charm, this one surprisingly competent with its two-speed verse riff. Although besides that, little else happens, save for the cliché luke-milk OTT fast break. And its primary coloured blueprint is almost forgiven when heavy lids drop and bob back into that avalanched plod that so deftly caught Metallica's attention and then in '01, Megadeth's.

142 WAKE UP DEAD MEGADETH

358 points *from Peace Sells . . . But Who's Buying? (Capitol '86)*

Vaulting way up our list, *Wake up Dead* has made quite an impression, perhaps based on its placement as track one, side one on one of the band's most beloved albums, perhaps due to its hurried, impatient illogic, the track holding one's attention by switching gears before the fan becomes complacent with its direction. It's practically an anti-song, the listener forced to stamp out brushfires as Dave croaks out a hilarious absentee lyric. But if the track houses a mumbled sentiment that may not be one of Dave's gleaming literary achievements, musically, it's a series of events that lead the band down unpredictable prog pathways, none of them making much sense, but perhaps conjuring longevity because of it.

Dave Mustaine on *Wake up Dead* . . .

> "*Wake up Dead* was written about me cheating on a girl I was living with because I needed a place to stay and I needed someone to feed me. But the girl I really loved was the one I was cheating with, and thank God David Ellefson had a van. I would sneak downstairs into the parking lot of the apartment and I'd have sex with this girl and then I'd take those miniature bottles of vodka and splash that on my face and say I'd been out drinking with the boys and I'd come home. I mean, that's alcohol abuse right there. So I'd come up, and most of the time I would just flop in bed, but every once in a while I would have to do an encore performance and it was a little bit harder, if you know what I mean."

143 PARADISE CITY GUNS N' ROSES

355 points *from Appetite for Destruction (Geffen '87)*

Just off the bus and pining to get back on, Axl expresses the same sort of ambivalence for his impending junk food, junk culture and junk corruption as he addresses on *Welcome to the Jungle*, all sets to swirling Aerosmith riffs that knock the stuffing out of the clean version of Joe Perry. *Paradise City*'s seduction lies within its power surges, its pregnant pauses blown up by bursts of trepanning guitars, its actual jostling of correct time. Ends with a little Catskills soft-shoe, Axl raving aimlessly as the band furiously aims to entertain in earnest. Trivia note: Tracii Guns from L.A. Guns, who of course was once in GN'R and is the Guns in the name (gasp) told me that he and Izzy were just sitting around listening to *Zero the Hero* off of Sabbath's **Born Again**, and Izzy made a remark with respect to what a great riff it was, and a song became born, right there, again. Go compare. Neat, huh?

Duff McKagan on *Paradise City* . . .

> "I'd written the chorus for that one right when I moved to L.A., so it was before the band. I was living in this shithole. In 1984, after the Olympics, all the police had basically left Hollywood and it turned into this cesspool. The police and the city had come in and cleaned it up for the summer Olympics and once that was over, they just left. And for awhile, it was just kind of a shithole. It's come back now, like every place has. You can walk through downtown Detroit now without a problem, whereas ten years ago or maybe more, you wouldn't have walked in certain places. So I lived in this apartment and *Paradise City* was written about an imaginary place that I wasn't in at that point."

144 NO MORE TEARS OZZY OSBOURNE

353 points *from No More Tears (Sony '91)*

Unusually emotionally harrowing for Oz this deep into rock aristocracy, *No More Tears* is best remembered for that bobbing bass line and its borderline misogynist sobbing video (sister slice: The Cars' *Drive*). Ultimately it's a sort of churchy song, somewhere between Sunday service and wake. Patience is the name of the game as the band gets down to the grey business of doing time, building to a coagulated dry-eyed close that emulates death.

Zakk Wylde on *No More Tears* . . .

> "Well, Mike started off with the bass and we just all kind of joined in. Randy started playing drums and then John put that keyboard intro and then I put in the slide thing. It all kind of happened at once. And then we stop playing and Mike kept doing the thing with Ozzy, a kind of a question and answer type thing, where Ozzy sang a line and then I did the riff. The piano bit in the middle, I ended up writing when we were down at A&M. We didn't have that. We didn't have any of the middle section so I came up with that and we stuck it in there and then I wrote the guitar solo section, and then we were all done, man. All the guitar work on that track is just one guitar. I remember I wanted to double the guitars. The guys were playing John Madden football at the time. And that solo I did was just one take and I said, 'Oh man, I could probably get a better one. Let's do another one,' and they're all like, 'Dude, it's fucking fine and anyway, we're fuckin'. . . we've got the playoffs going on right now.' So they were playing video games and saying, 'Dude, it's fucking fine, just fuckin' leave it.' And I was always like man, I wish I would have doubled it, but that's the way it was. The Madden was fuckin' more important than the record (laughs)."

Zakk Wylde from the Ozzy Osbourne band
Ozzy Osbourne — *Diary of a Madman*
AC/DC — *Back in Black*

AC/DC — *Hells Bells*
Black Sabbath — *Into the Void*
Black Sabbath — *Sabbath Bloody Sabbath*
Jimi Hendrix Experience — *Purple Haze*
Led Zeppelin — *Heartbreaker*
Led Zeppelin — *When the Levee Breaks*
Ozzy Osbourne — *I Don't Know*
Van Halen — *Eruption*

145 SAILS OF CHARON SCORPIONS

351 points *from Taken by Force* (RCA *'79)*

The last bullfighting gasp of the classic creative Roth era, *Sails of Charon* is a flavourful flamenco metal classic, scorched by the hot winds of a Roth solo that thenceforth collapses into a verse of pure metal drama. It is the highlight of a tug and pull album, a metaphor and a catch basin for a band overblessed with metal ideas forged well outside the normal modus operandi of the biz.

Ulrich Roth on the end of an era . . .

> "Well, it was inevitable that I leave, because my time in the Scorpions was a little bit like an apprenticeship, in terms of regarding the whole music scene, the whole business, touring, making records. And I did enjoy it very much, but only for the first four years. And then in the last year I became very, very dissatisfied. It was like a growing dissatisfaction because of the direction the band was taking, which was more and more alien to the direction that I wanted to go in. The band had its own framework which we basically established ourselves. Some of the things I wanted to do would have completely split this framework. For instance, at the time that we did **Taken by Force**, by that time I was already writing things like *Earthquake* and *Sundown*. And I could never have played *Earthquake* in the Scorpions. So for me there was no alternative. It was a necessary step and we parted on very good terms, and that's the way it had to be."

146 JUMP VAN HALEN

350 points

from 1984 (Warner '84)

Shocked the hell out of me at the time, I'll tell you that, Van Halen sadistically casting *Jump* out as a pre-launch single, the band ballsy and audacious enough to try please their axe-adoring throngs (or everyone: they wanted the world) with a stark, retarded, crudely-fashioned synth line for a verse. But it all worked out, and how could it not with these four do-no-wrong cocksures telling America what's good for them? And did we get told, Eddie further inciting revolution with a synth solo equally nonsensical to the verse. Perhaps as diversion, Dave regales us with his buoyant autobiographical outlook, his "might as well jump" serving as both an invitation to submit to the pure, simple fun of Eddie's synth line or perhaps the suggestion that jumping is an appropriate suicide solution response.

Alex Van Halen on the pressure to write a hit . . .

> "I think in the beginning, we had so many people around us, and the band had 'x' amount of music it was capable of and 'those' people wanted us to have a hit. So not to point a finger — it wasn't Ed, me or Michael — but 'another' wanted us to try anything — just have a hit, which I think is just complete garbage. Total fuckin' shit! But in all fairness, since we were a different band, and all of us were getting along pretty well then, we said, 'OK if you really want to do this shit we'll give it a crack.' Thus came out stuff like *Dancin' in the Streets*. Hey, some people may like that song — God bless you — but I thought it sucked! The music was great, but why did he have to put other lyrics to

it? We could've called it anything we wanted to! It was so radically different from the original. The point I'm getting to is that there are a number of people involved in a band, and you're not always going to be in the same direction, so things split up."

147 FLIGHT OF ICARUS IRON MAIDEN

349 points

from Piece of Mind (EMI '83)

From what is arguably Maiden's best all-around album, *Flight of Icarus* is perhaps the best-written track therein, logical, well-reasoned, rich with melody, measured in delivery of its charms. One of those charms is the leading, ponderous frame on which it's built, the band valiantly persevering with less and modulations, Bruce and his sense of drama being the key performance, Nicko as well holding responsibly the fort. And quite an impenetrable and impervious fortress it is.

Bruce Dickinson on *Flight of Icarus* . . .

> "Me and Steve had a stand-up row in the studio about the tempo of that song. He still, to this day, hates it and thinks that the studio version was way too slow. I, of course, disagree (laughs). I basically said look, it's my song, and this is how it should be played."

148 FREEWHEEL BURNING JUDAS PRIEST

346 points *from Defenders of the Faith* (CBS '84)

It was a bit of a headscratcher why Priest followed up a very successful fence-straddler of an album and its low IQ single with a heavier, thicker, faster album, and this heavier, thicker, faster track as a single. *Freewheel Burning* is a bracing vehicle for Halford as both schoolmarm rapping your hand with a yardstick and rapid fire balls-out belter. As well, the twin leads are on fire, even if a big wet hose is turned on them through the smothered, synthetic production job and Dave Holland's poor fast drumming. Still, it was a brave exercise in commercial suicide, and suicide it was, even if the patient experienced a slow painful repose as it searched half-heartedly through two more declining albums for a pulse before taking its last **Painkiller**.

Ian Hill on *Freewheel Burning* . . .

> "It's a typical Priest track, fast, aggressive. We had gone through a phase. There's a program over here called 'Top Of The Pops,' and we call it our Top Of The Pops phase, where you're on the local commercial TV station. I don't know, we just wanted to get away from that and wanted to head into a heavier, contemporary direction, at least superficially. I mean, we've always been that way but people were trying to portray us as something we weren't at one time. That's one of the reasons we thought, well, OK, instead of making a video for the most obviously commercial one, the ballad or whatever, we'll go ahead and do one with our other dimension (laughs)."

149 SINNER JUDAS PRIEST

346 points *from Sin after Sin* (CBS '77)

One of those steady anchors of a frenetic, kinetic album, *Sinner* is the mid-flow glue between the down-wound or experimentally beatless, and the record's speed. Still, the copacetic verse gives way to a lot of action, first bit of battle being a truly doomy chorus, next being the song's swirly repeating vocals and attendant snaky breaky riffs: cathedral rock extraordinaire, the later reaches of the song beckoning you beneath into the catacombs like *Victim of Changes* one record back. It's actually a platform for a lot of Halford, a lot of Simon Philips, and a blustery bit of guitar noise, way more than you bargained for, like sin itself.

Ian Hill on *Sinner* . . .

> "Yeah, that's another epic song, a production piece. There are two or three different solo parts in it, intricate rhythm parts. It was a very involved track to put down. And it's another one we played on stage for a long time."

150 WHERE EAGLES DARE IRON MAIDEN

346 points *from Piece of Mind* (EMI '83)

This one is Nicko's track, a rite of passage for aspiring drummers in metal's heady heyday. *Where Eagles Dare* is almost a bigger anthem than *The Trooper*, just this rhythmic invasion that announces Maiden's presence on the scene with crescendo after crescendo, until you're deafened by the blast. The cool thing about the track is that the band just takes off, forgetting any responsibilities toward song, just digging into a tangent that imprints your circuits forever. Production, power, rumbling confidence, synchronicity . . . this track found Maiden firing upon all cylinders, really this record being the first time you could check off all the cylinders, even if many of them worked equally well on other records.

Bruce Dickinson on *Where Eagles Dare* . . .

"I remember that quite vividly, because first of all, I was a huge fan of the movie, we all were. And secondly, there's a drum part on it which, I mean, I know a bit about drumming, I'm not a great drummer, but I know a great part when I see one. And Nicko wanted to use a double bass drum and we wouldn't let him (laughs) and he did the whole thing with a single bass drum, and he still does and still refuses to use double bass drums. Because after playing that bit with a single bass drum pedal, he's like, 'No, that's it, I'm going to use a single bass drum pedal. Everybody else is going to have to catch up.'"

151 NO ONE LIKE YOU SCORPIONS

345 points *from Blackout (Mercury '83)*

Memories are happy when the soundtrack is a hit record. Here Scorpions, through the Americanization of Dieter, Rudolf and Matthias stumble upon car stereo manna. *No One Like You* is a supercharged power ballad with purpose, spaces a' plenty then a cha-ching clang of unchained power chords, anointed by a most delightful guitar solo and all the silliness of a power ballad but with a melting metal chorus. Of course it's all an accident (think Colonel Klink), but one can hear Queen, UFO and especially Foreigner within the tones, melodies and the three steps to wallop. One of those crafty hit factory songs, pinned to the breastplate by that penetrating two times exhilarating high note come solo time.

Rudolph Schenker on *No One Like You* . . .

"*No One Like You* is a very interesting story because I composed the song already four years before the song was released. I always played it to the guys and I never got the reactions until one time I played it for Matthias and he was saying, 'Hey, that's great,' and I said, 'I know, but you have to convince Klaus,' who said, 'Yes, it's good, not bad.' But he started to write lyrics and then we went into the studio and we created this arrangement."

152 METROPOLIS — PART I
DREAM THEATER

345 points *from Images and Words (Atco '92)*

Virtually an instant success due to a vacuum in the highly unfashionable world of prog metal, or more distinctly, a dearth of bands doing this with major label backing, Dream Theater cracked their knuckles with this kitchen-sink think tank, combining *de rigeur* world beat drumming with odd time signatures, crazy note-dense playing and an unflinching sense of drama. It was everything long-haired clinic-attending, instructional video-buying metal technicians could want, which meant it was a bit much to swallow, a bit self-evident, a bit prog-aseptic and not very prog-eccentric. But after many years, the track is another Dream Theater staple, significantly from the album that is the near unanimous choice of fans, inevitably, forever.

James LaBrie on *Metropolis — Part I . . .*

> "Oh boy, that's a pretty sick song. I think that was basically our way of showing that this is an incredibly progressive band and that everybody knows their instruments very well. And it allowed me to be very dynamic vocally. It's just a song that wherever we are in the world playing, and we pull that out, people just go crazy and we really appreciate that. It's like our progressive signature. And you can tell how powerful that song is to us because when we released **Scenes from a Memory**, there was *Metropolis — Part II*. So it was an important song for us just to show where we were coming from, what we truly stand for."

Lajon and John from Sevendust
Black Sabbath — *War Pigs*
Kiss — *Detroit Rock City*
Pantera — *Mouth for War*
Led Zeppelin — *Immigrant Song*

Thin Lizzy — *The Boys are Back in Town*
Jimi Hendrix Experience — *Foxy Lady*
Sex Pistols — *Anarchy in the UK*
Black Flag — *My War*
Ted Nugent — *Free for All*
Bad Company — *Bad Company*

153 TOYS IN THE ATTIC AEROSMITH

344 points *from Toys in the Attic (Columbia '75)*

Riding ripsaw on one of Joe Perry's best bad-ass riffs, *Toys in the Attic* is one of the first couple dozen speed metal songs ever. And characteristic of a brisk bit of six-string alchemy, the song veers and careens, tripping here and there. In fact it's an early example of the band's top-drawer writing, the band redlining it with panache, adding at will, parts safety-checked to Boeing standards.

Steven Tyler on anger in his lyrics . . .

> "I'd say I'm pissed off that I let drugs take me down. I'm pissed off that we had to crawl out of the ashes and be safe. I'm pissed off that I love some of the songs the people call wimpy fuckin' ballads. I love ballads. In my heart I'm a romantic. If they only knew what I get off on. I think that's all the angst that you go through being an artist; I have to be able to feel good enough to lend the family parrot to the town crier and let everybody know, and take my lumps as far as what they saw on my sheets the night before."

154 SUICIDE SOLUTION OZZY OSBOURNE

343 points *from Blizzard of Ozz (Jet/CBS '80)*

Heaving, lurching and grimly driving toward an ethereal and aimless end, *Suicide Solution* was this album's most conventional metal track (followed by *Steal Away* and *I Don't Know*, I guess), fairly Sabbatherian, raw, and oddly framed by a linear rhythm section watching their watches. The publicity nightmare that would be Ozzy's colourful life saw spark first with this track. The lyric was written by Bob Daisley as a warning to Oz who had been famously drinking himself to death, alcohol being the suicide solution. But of course the track was misinterpreted as saying, 'Hey, kill yourself already,' and Oz got dragged through the courts on that basis. Whatever your interpretation, *Suicide Solution* has endured as the catalogue's top example of Ozzy identifying — connecting deeply and depressively — with his fans and their collectively shared life-threatening trials and tribulations.

Ozzy on drink and drugs . . .

> "I was drinking excessively on and off for years. And I woke up one morning after doing a lot of cocaine and a case of beer. I didn't feel particularly hung over or shitty, and I just looked in the mirror and something clicked. Maybe I'll go back and drink again; I hope I don't. I've found a therapist that I'm really happy with. I'll be 43 years of age this birthday and I've just done it all. It wasn't working the same way it did years ago. I wouldn't say that I'm on the wagon though. What got me for awhile in rock 'n' roll is that everyone who decided to get clean and sober was telling everyone else in the world to do so also. Fuck that, man! If you want to go and drink a six-pack, that's your business. I don't give shit. I just chose not to drink anymore. I'm not a fuckin' flag-waver. I'm not a Salvation Army member. I'm not saying don't do it because you're going to do it anyway if you want to do it. To just make a statement like, 'I ain't never going to drink again' is complete and utter bullshit because again is infinity. To say 'I ain't gonna drink today' is 24 hours, and more realistic. And I woke up today saying, I ain't gonna drink today, or do drugs, except for the ones prescribed to me by my therapist . . . which is about time I took one."

155 EXCITER JUDAS PRIEST

336 points *from Stained Class* (CBS '78)

Sounds tame and even simple after 25 extra years of canal-splitting ear itch, but at the time, *Exciter* was quietly rewriting the rules of heavy metal, establishing a new speed plateau, offering a rare double bass drum barrage at unsafe velocities. Of course, it was all clean and strangely quiet, the band providing a behaved backdrop for Rob to stretch his lungs. Like much of **Sin after Sin**, this track has an eerie religious quality, Halford playing Spanish Inquisition, obfuscating with big words, announcing the arrival of either God, Devil, alien, or just some cool fireworks guy who's good at flying. Simultaneously sermonizing and searing.

Rob Halford on working in the studio . . .

> "I'm dead easy-going, I'll tell you. But if you make the slightest fuck-up, I have a really short temper. And if you get one of my looks (laughs), I only have to look at people and they go, 'Oh fuck' and that's enough. But I'm pretty reasonable in the studio. I do have my prima donna moments, but they are directed at myself. If I can't get right what I have to get right, I get really pissed off at myself. Because I can't understand, all these years later, why I can't get a note right. I hear the playback and I go, 'That fucking sucks, why can't I do it?' That's just another fault of mine. But that's directed at me. But yeah, I've got an ego. I've got what I feel is an important positive ego. I'm OK with people as long as they do what needs to be done. And I think that's the minimum you can ask of this environment because there are a lot of responsibilities involved. I don't like to let people down and I like to give them the best."

156 ACHILLES LAST STAND LED ZEPPELIN

335 points *from Presence (Swan Song '76)*

Led Zeppelin's last epic, more like. In fact few would even grant them that, many clock-watchers deciding that the band had run out of ideas on **Physical Graffiti**, a layer of curmudgeons even stunting and stopping one back from that. But here they were trying, and many were pleased, *Achilles Last Stand* being a made-to-order fan track, long, purposeful, progressive, percussively heavy, lyrically grand, cheap-laugh-Middle-Eastern-mystical of riff. Plant sounds drained and wafer-thin but the frothy wave of the decent pop combo behind him carries our nasal minstrel through a long, loud, bashing, winding Moroccan-smoked slog which is the "hail metal dude" track on an otherwise deflated, world-weary, yearning album.

John Paul Jones on not getting a credit on *Achilles Last Stand* . . .

> "Well, yes. I didn't get a writer's credit on that one, did I? I mean, think of it with a different bassline (laughs). It would be very different. And again, is that arrangement or a composition? I don't think, especially in that case, it was reflected in the credit. But again, you know, same with Bonzo's stuff. Is his contribution reflected in the credit? I don't know if it is. It probably would have been fairer to split it much more evenly. The credits were kind of a default."

157 SOBER TOOL

332 points *from Undertow (BMG '93)*

A sick, depraved bit of progressive grunge from a band that just gets scarier with each passing year, *Sober* makes good use of Maynard's dual vocal attack, his neuron-misfiring switch from catatonia to raving paranoia. Musically, you get the same vibe, calm before the storm and then fierce fire-filled winds, all recorded in earth-shaking hi-fidelity by Sylvia Massey. With Tool, it's disaffectedly arbitrary picking a key track, but

Sober is more or less conventional as well as insidiously, corruptingly hooky, and its angles square the listener firmly within the crosshairs of a band that sounds not so much angry as morally incinerated and subsequently detached and way past cynical.

158 DEUCE KISS

332 points *from Kiss (Casablanca '74)*

Hard to listen to any of the debut album in hard rock (?) context. It exists in a weird non-music Slade-meets-Mountain trip-state that, after hearing the whole album fresh again today, leaves me highly curious at what the critics at the time called this stuff. But *Deuce* sort of breaks through into a surified hard rock, stomping sinister, delivering something akin to diabolus in musica compared to the album's recurrent fruity tasting yoghurt boogie. I mean, there are riffs here, a few of them, from a band precious and stingy in their riff ruffage, or at least demure, until the next album, **Hotter than Hell**, on which this tar pond of a song belongs.

Ace Frehley on *Deuce* . . .

> "*Deuce* has an interesting history. It was the first Kiss song I ever heard, when I auditioned for Kiss. I was the last person to join the band. So that was the first song I heard. Paul, Gene and Peter performed it for me when I was auditioning, and they said, 'Here's the song,' and I played a guitar solo to it and two weeks later they hired me. And to this day, it's still one of my favourite Kiss songs."

159 I LOVE IT LOUD KISS

330 points *from Creatures of the Night (Mercury '81)*

After three albums of doofus drift, we were glad to hear Gene tell us lies like this. But we excused him and thanked him for somehow pulling the mess out of the fire, beginning a string of three albums that are next wave fan faves. This track was a direct Manowar-mongering statement that threatened your woofers and found a way to bring the band back to the anthemic ambitions of *Detroit Rock City*. I dunno, it just feels venerable, like a cross between Zeppelin and Sabbath and Kiss and Ted Nugent, and I don't say that too often (er, never), especially about bands with doddering dunderheads for drummers and "Dating Game" stand-ins for guitarists.

Gene Simmons on the critics . . .

> "Today, we're on the cover of all the magazines. The critics have always been our enemy because of the self-appointed, self-anointed, holier-than-thou approach they take. Even though they rarely have credentials, never went to school, never studied journalism and have no ethics, they have the point of view that their opinion is more important than ours. They are a bane to society, a completely worthless form of life as we know it on this planet."

160 CHILDREN OF THE SEA BLACK SABBATH

327 points *from Heaven and Hell (Warner '80)*

Stumbling, bumbling and rumbling like shaggy old heavy metal, *Children of the Sea* corrected for an album which, at least at the time, was suspiciously considered too slick and noticeably missing the appropriate nutcase at the hambone microphone. It is also one of arguably three epics on the album, from a band who had forgotten how to write them, now invigoratingly better for the acquisition of a singer who really knew no other way. Plus Geezer gets to free-form and fill and filibuster a bit, playing with old-school bass wank values on a song in no hurry to serve, please or resolve.

Bill Ward on *Children of the Sea* . . .

> "Geezer had been our most prominent lyricist within Sabbath and Ronnie was now writing lyrics. A lot of the themes I'd been used to had changed. I wasn't totally in touch with Ronnie's lyrics. I could appreciate *Children of the Sea* though, which is a favourite of mine. It's a blues-based song; Tony and I just played blues behind it because that's basically what it is."

161 AMONG THE LIVING ANTHRAX

327 points *from Among the Living (Island '87)*

More of an SOD song than an Anthrax song, *Among the Living* was a hyper bit of technically elevated punk, Anthrax bum-rushing the guitars from a number of angles, seemingly at random stripping the gears for the next righteous riff. Some of Belladonna's vocal melodies are questionably sour (particularly the last verse), but all is forgiven when that 1-and-3 verse march grinds into the concrete for a chorus that was capably known to incite mayhem in the pit.

Charlie Benante on *Among the Living* . . .

> "I remember writing *Among the Living* and I remember the state

of mind I was in at the time. I was still living at home and I still had my room there since I was younger. And it was like all these years of accumulating everything just packed into that one room. And I remember just sitting there with my little Marshall Mini-stack and my guitar and my tape recorder just writing riffs. And I would leave a tape in the recorder all the time, because if I got inspired I would just, boom, click it and just write what I was feeling. And I remember really feeling that the whole hardcore music and metal thing was coming to fruition, with the SOD record and DRI who were totally coming into the metal scene. And I just remember being inspired by that whole thing, and the thing we created, how **Spreading the Disease** was kind of going off into that next level. That was the album before **Among the Living**. And I just had this kind of hardcore mentality at the time, writing things that were very fast, but with a metal feel to them. And that's how *Among the Living* came about. And Scott took the song . . . he was really into Stephen King at the time so he took the idea from a Stephen King book, **The Stand**."

162 HELTER SKELTER BEATLES

326 points *from The Beatles (Apple '68)*

Like Queen or Zeppelin creating metal, or even in a sense Deep Purple, given both Ian and Roger's irascibility at the term, the Beatles seemed to parachute in, make impressive gains, then leave satiated. Granted, big difference; unlike the above, the Beatles only wrote one metal song. But bloody 'ell, it was a clanging crusher of an attempt, all the more inspired given its psych-era vintage. Just proves what we all know: one band was ever this prescient and visionary, maybe two, if you count Zeppelin (and I'd like to). I mean damn, *Helter Skelter* is not only metal, it's a pretty smart arrangement thereof, more like doom versus the paint-by-numbers accidents of contemporaries who were doing little more than bulking up pre-psych garage band riffs.

Dryden Mitchell from Alien Ant Farm
Scorpions — *Rock You Like a Hurricane*
Bad Brains — *Secret '77*
AC/DC — *Back in Black*
Black Sabbath — *Paranoid*
Yes — *Roundabout*
Pixies — *Velouria*
Papa Roach — *Last Resort*
Rush — *Tom Sawyer*
Mötley Crüe — *Red Hot*
Beatles — *Helter Skelter*

163 INDIANS ANTHRAX

320 points

from Among the Living (Island '87)

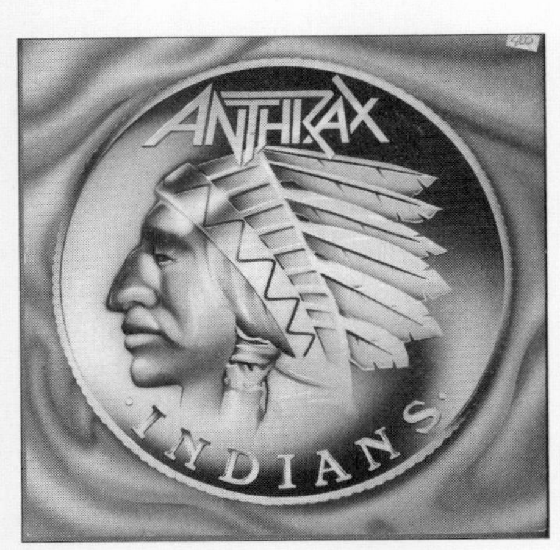

Unleashed like Lizzy meets Maiden, or to speak modern, the Geronimo metal of Soundgarden, *Indians* is a frantic frenetic mix of combat-booted hardcore, thrash and the band's signature meal-sized mid-mosh. It's cool how the lyric is positive, clear and socially responsible (beats the hell outta *Run to the Hills*), Anthrax unafraid to wade into this type of material, backed with the might of their urban concrete thrash. Grim, workmanlike, but all worth it once the delayed chorus breaks through; that is, if you ignore the brutal, atonal, gutless solo section.

Charlie Benante on *Indians* . . .

"The thing about *Indians* that I remember, we would get a lot of letters from kids on Indian reservations saying thank you so much for recognizing us. And when we would play shows, we would get a lot of Indian kids coming to the shows, just saying thank you, thank you. It was very strange for us, coming from New York; we never, ever dealt with something like that first hand. And here we were, and we just had this idea. It's very strange to me, because how it evolved, the social commentary, wasn't the initial idea. To be honest, the song actually started because of an **F-Troop** episode."

164 SWEET CHILD O' MINE GUNS N' ROSES

319 points *from Appetite for Destruction (Geffen '87)*

Instantly recognized for Slash's ambulance siren lead, *Sweet Child O' Mine* was a little southern rock light relief on an album chock-full of corporate punk rock. Axl turns out to be a good country singer, and the band, whether by accident or skill, turn out to be good arrangers and stackers of parts. Monster hit for the band of course, and in fact, a nice direction that would pave the way for *November Rain* and *Don't Cry*. Plus by some definitions, it rocks. *Sweet Child O' Mine* floats along with considerable verve, accentuated and punctuated by a combative rhythm section that we find can drive even the most hayseed of numbers.

Duff McKagan on *Sweet Child O' Mine* . . .

"That's written about Axl's girlfriend at the time, ex-wife. I'll tell you something about that song. We wrote the song really as a joke. Axl was serious about the lyrics, but we were like, 'A ballad?! Come on.' So you know that beginning guitar riff? It was absolutely written as a joke, at first. It was meant to sound funny. If you listen to it, it's goofy. But like everything at that point for us, it worked (laughs). Everything worked. But it was really written as a goofy . . . like a circus riff, because nobody wanted to do this thing."

165 SWORDS AND TEQUILA
RIOT

317 points *from Fire Down Under (Capitol '81)*

It's proud, steely, cutting-edge metal like this that left folks perplexed that Riot didn't break big. The obvious evident blue-collar face of American metal, this was surface rock lovable for that surface alone, **British Steel** versus **Stained Class**, **Mob Rules** versus **Sabotage**, Riot versus Aerosmith. And that surface was polished and produced smooth for stadium rock consumption. *Swords and Tequila* was also blessed with a chorus that took you higher.

Mark Reale on the Riot sound . . .

> "Basically the whole style just came from the fact that there was just this amalgam of influences we had. I was heavily influenced by Ronnie Montrose and that first Montrose record, that whole high energy kind of approach. We used to go see them in concert. And that was the model I had in my head. I was also into the European bands like Deep Purple, Rainbow, so from my end it was the heavy guitar thing. Guy Speranza was more into bands like Thin Lizzy, more of a pop thing. And when it came together, Riot is pretty much what came out. You had this very guitar-driven music with this melodic vocal on top. So we were pretty much just feeling our way through on the first two records. I don't think it was until **Fire Down Under** that we pretty much nailed our sound."

166 (DON'T FEAR) THE REAPER
BLUE ÖYSTER CULT

317 points *from Agents of Fortune (Columbia '76)*

There's the whole story about how Blue Öyster Cult lyricist and conceptual man Sandy Pearlman thinks The Byrds were some fancy-pants manifestation of heavy metal. Well, here he sees the plan in action — Buck Dharma writing the mellowest song in four albums, a very Byrdsy track about love and the ultimate commitment (death), an epic that had the rough and cynical New York crowd up in arms crying sell-out. The reason this kind of departure happened is that the band members were each given the latest four-track machines prior to writing **Agents of Fortune**, so BÖC were able to multi-track and bring in songs that reflected their individual natures more definitively versus the old "boys will be boys in the band house" collaborative method. This one's all Buck — Buck's innocence with a dagger vocals and Buck's velvet hammer guitar work gliding and sliding and meshing toward the inevitable doomful, devil with a lollipop conclusion.

Al Bouchard on *(Don't Fear) the Reaper* . . .

> "Donald, I would have to say is not very generous as a person but he can surprise you sometimes. He's incredibly talented. Anything he does seems to be without any effort whatsoever, and he can be very funny. He's very witty, he has a great sense of humour and that's it. He's a pretty interesting person I would have to say, and yes, *(Don't Fear) The Reaper* was a pretty interesting piece of work. It was a folk song, the most un-BÖC-like thing we had ever done. It felt profound and touched something. We each spend most of our lives trying not to fear the end, and *Reaper* addressed that fear. But yes, *Reaper* marked a better sense of 'Yeah, okay, we really are doing this. We are professionals.' There was this book I lost some years ago that best describes our fans' fascination with us. Best translated, it means 'pleasure from fear.' If you know that you can return to a normal world, there's a pleasure that comes from playing with darkness. It's part escapism, part survival from confrontation. To stare at evil somehow makes it safer."

167 I'M EIGHTEEN ALICE COOPER

314 points *from Love It to Death (Warner '71)*

From an older, simpler hard rock time, *I'm Eighteen* nevertheless remains one of metal's great teen alienation anthems, almost poignant, definitely brooding, insightful, while using few words. To boot, it's one of rock's original power ballads in the modern sense of the term, plodding, pushing, if not pounding, while darkly melodic. Plus you can't fault the somewhat hapless musicality of it: a) this band didn't have chops and b) **Love It to Death** came out in 1971, a year after metal's arguably official start date and a year before the form would solidify and become comfortable and almost commonplace with **Machine Head** and **Vol 4**.

Alice Cooper on *I'm Eighteen* . . .

> "*Eighteen* was just a riff we used to jam to, to warm up. I remember when we first started to do *Eighteen*, it was in Detroit. We used to rehearse in this dump and everybody had a bottle of Boone's Farm Apple Wine. It was just the worst, I mean, I don't think it's ever seen anything except chemicals. And we'd all have a bottle of that and that was just the chord progression (sings it), and it was a good riff for everybody to warm up and jam a little bit on. Bob Ezrin kept hearing that and he kept saying, 'You know, that's really a good riff.' He'd listen to us rehearse and he'd say, 'Let's make something out of that.' It's one of those things that I would like to say, it was during the war, the end of the war, and there was always that controversy of 'I'm a boy, I'm a man.' I can go get killed for my country but I can't buy a beer. So *Eighteen* was that juxtaposition of being both. And then, when it sounded like a complaint, then it turns the corner. It says 'I'm eighteen, I've got angst, I don't know what I am, I don't know if I'm a boy or a man, and I like it!' And that was the selling point of it. It was the fact that instead of 'I hate it,' it was 'I'm eighteen and I like it.' And everybody related to that and said, 'Yeah, I dig being screwed up.'"

168 DREAM ON AEROSMITH

314 points *from Aerosmith (Columbia '73)*

Some call this the first power ballad, and folks might have a point (hey, what about *I'm Eighteen* or *Child In Time*?), but it's a creaky drafty one, understandable given that in '73 there was no rulebook yet. And it's a little proggy for Aerosmith, and a little dour, more of a Dio lyric and melody. Joe Perry has some signature guitar lines that everybody remembers and Tyler mirrors Ozzy in that his vocals on the debut are lower down the dustpipe than on all later albums. Always leaves me spiritually dissipated and not so much spiritually drained, more like craning around to see if the ennui valve is leaking.

Steven Tyler on the early days . . .

> "I may be retarded, but it doesn't feel like 20 years since we got together in Boston. The last thing I can remember is sitting around trying to figure out where we wanted to have a band, not the name of the band, but where! Figuring we should go from New Hampshire to Boston to play the college scene, instead of going to New York — being backstage and seeing the girls with tits from Hell and skirts up to their earlobes. It feels like yesterday. It seems like yesterday when I was pissed off that *Dream On* wasn't recognized until the third album, instead of the first. Maybe that's keeping my wheels of youth spinning. All the better because I have enough to write about for the next 20 years."

169 EASY LIVIN' URIAH HEEP

313 points *from Demons and Wizards (Bronze '72)*

Commendable in that it is vaguely an early form of speed metal, definitely really heavy, and melodically mournful, tuneful and complex, *Easy Livin'* is also Heep's most famous song from a long, eventful but often arid and repulsive catalogue. And it manages all these innovations in a very compact timeframe — Heep building inspirationally massive, weather-impermeable walls of guitars, cathedrals of Jon Lordian keyboards from doppelgänger Ken Hensley, and a fierce little goth breakdown before falling back into its strange Lee Kerslake shuffle, the drums very interestingly overwhelmed by the dense throb of the house-painted guitars and keyboards.

Ken Hensley on *Easy Livin'* . . .

> "Up until that point, **Demons and Wizards**, we'd really concentrated on the European market, and it was *Easy Livin'* that first got us into the American charts, opening up a new phase in our career. It is a song that I think typifies Heep's early commercial success; simple, straightforward, powerful and with a lyric that is not hard to relate to! I still perform it and enjoy it, perhaps more than the audience does."

170 LET THERE BE ROCK
AC/DC

312 points *from Let There Be Rock (Atlantic '77)*

The Baptist revival punk rock version of *Baby Please Don't Go, Let There Be Rock* is a gangly, jangly mess of snarly guitars, which drop away for Bon to deliver his sermon, pattering Book Of Loud in hand, finger-tapping the royal throne somewhere between James Brown and Jerry Lee. Angus gets to stretch as well, throw switch electrified, solos digging into the showman past of why the guitar had to exist in the first place. Six glorious minutes of rock history pounding forward on the muddy boots of an inexorable march, punctuated by axe attacks, which periodically dissipate to the critical mass of Bon's engaging tale of finger pickin'. Ends with a near infinite firestorm of atom-smashing juice.

Angus Young on the release schedule for **Let There Be Rock** . . .

> "It was because we had played most of Europe; we had played most of Britain and a lot of other countries around that area. We came to America the first time in '77, and at the time they had released our first album, **High Voltage**, and what they had done was taken our first two Australian releases (**High Voltage**, 1974

and **T.N.T.**, 1975) and put them together. They had signed us in '76, so our record company felt if they put a combination of those two records together, it would be a good introduction. That's how that came about. Then we released the album **Dirty Deeds** for the European side of the world. We had just finished recording **Let There Be Rock**, so the North Americans said, 'We want what's current, so we'll have **Let There Be Rock**.' It was a bit strange, but they felt they wanted the current thing and they felt that was great because they knew we were going to be touring in the summer for the first time, so they wanted a good strong introduction. And for us, it was a good thing too because we were very proud of the **Let There Be Rock** album, especially Malcolm and myself, because for the first time we could really feature the guitars."

171 DENIM AND LEATHER SAXON

311 points *from Denim and Leather (Career '81)*

Likely stumbling onto it by accident, Saxon quickly cornered the market on band as fan-to-fan identification, Biff and his balding boffers standing shoulder to patched shoulder with the throngs making the NWOBHM into a phenomenon. *Denim and Leather* was a typically uninspired old hat riff for the boys, but Biff lifts it out of the bins with his grandma vocals and his lyric about how metal (even metal this hungover on a grey English Sunday morning) is gonna save the world from lesser, poseur forms of music.

Biff Byford on *Denim and Leather* . . .

"The actual title is from an Alice Cooper song called *From the Inside*, from a fabulous album of the same name. And on it there is a lyric that says "denim and leather." But obviously there has been denim and leather before (laughs). But it just twinged a chord in my head and when we got a chance to write a song. I was looking to write a song about our audience in the '80s to that point, which is the longest two years anybody has ever spent basically. From 1980 to 1982, we had three albums out in two years. It was crazy really, cramming four years worth of life into that. Anyway, that's another story (laughs). But I wanted to write a song about our fans and *Denim and Leather* fit the bill, really. We had a big competition in a magazine at the time; I think it was **Sounds**. That was the forerunner of **Kerrang!** Metal got so big in the '80s, they had to have a separate magazine. So we had this competition and 7000 or 8000 people wrote in. I can't remember what the question was, probably something dumb like, 'What was my name?' Anyway, the winners got to come to the studio to record the track with us. So the singing on the end of the original *Denim and Leather* is actually fans in the studio, about 30 or 40 of them."

Biff Byford from Saxon
AC/DC — *Highway to Hell*
Van Halen — *Runnin' with the Devil*
Black Sabbath — *Sabbath Bloody Sabbath*
Rush — *The Spirit of Radio*
Metallica — *Enter Sandman*
Deep Purple — *Highway Star*
Pink Floyd — *Money*
Judas Priest — *Breaking the Law*
Iron Maiden — *The Number of the Beast*
Led Zeppelin — *Stairway to Heaven*

172 EMERALD THIN LIZZY

310 points *from Jailbreak (Vertigo '76)*

Emerald is the proud power metal anchor of an album that is quite varied and not all that heavy, save for this track, *Jailbreak* and *Warrior*. But what a fighting machine this one be, Downey driving it high, long and far, his ride cymbal the clarion call of a song dancing on the top shelf of groove. The breaks are also classic, first the sparked metal bit (unpack yer air drums?), then those pre-**Black Rose** heritage sounds, followed by duelling solos afire. Mythic, legendary battlefield rock, swords clashing, axes hammering away at a signature sound.

Scott Gorham on the Thin Lizzy treadmill . . .

> "I think I matured more as a guitar player when I left Thin Lizzy. Let me take that back. I grew up being in the band. I guess I was 20 years old when I joined. As a person and as a musician I grew up a hell of a lot. As soon as *The Boys Are Back in Town* hit it was total chaos. This chaos surrounded our lives all the time, just because of the massive touring and then you're slammed into the recording studio, and you're off on another tour. You never really got to sit down and see how you were doing as a musician. It was only after I left Thin Lizzy that I thought about the way I was playing. I really didn't like the way I was playing at all, so I sat down and really tried to improve."

173 OUTLAW
RIOT

306 points *from Fire Down Under (Capitol '81)*

Expansive, immediate, drenched in electricity, *Outlaw* is one of Riot's grooviest songs, blessed with stacked, mid-paced power chords which sweeten come chorus time before that crescendo-courting full stop. Its magic is in its dramatic spaces, through which the underrated Guy Speranza sings a time-honoured desperado tale replayed visually on the cover of Motörhead's **Ace of Spades**. Alone, the riff is simple and unremarkable, but with this power and this production, it blossoms into a proud monolith of classic American steel.

Mark Reale on pressures to go commercial . . .

> "We were on Capitol at the time, and they wanted us to go in a very commercial direction, and we'd made a feeble attempt at that in rehearsals. We began to record some tracks that Capitol

wanted us to do that were pretty much horrendous. And of course midway through the recording we decided, the hell with this. And we knew what was happening at the time in Europe with the New Wave of British Heavy Metal, and we just said the hell with this, and went on to record what became **Fire Down Under**. Of course, when Capitol got it, they were really pissed. And that's why we left them."

174 HEARTWORK CARCASS

306 points *from Heartwork (Earache/Sony '94)*

Beloved by scowling, angry metal folk scrounging the underground for spare change, Carcass evolved into an innovative mix of intelligent Maiden riffs, groovy grindcore, pre-Swede semi-death vocals and thick, impressive guitar tones. *Heartwork* contains all of the above, the production acumen of Colin Richardson turning the song and album into a thick, vitamin-fortified stew, the resulting package way ahead of its time. Carcass' fate was thereafter sealed, forever cast as the acceptable face of grind Napalm refused to become, the link between English eccentricity and the death 'n' roll of Entombed, the anchor and the anvil of extreme metal.

Michael Amott on *Heartwork* . . .

"That's one I wrote together with Bill. We actually played that one live a lot on tours before the album was recorded. So that was one we felt really good about from the word go, so we just incorporated it into the live set and played it for about a year before we put it down on tape. It's quite funny, because I remember us playing in Israel in '93 or '92. It's quite weird, because there was a song by Kreator called *People of the Lie*, and the chorus to *Heartwork* was kind of similar and people thought we were playing that, when we were in Israel. Which was kind of confusing, because the whole front row was singing along to this Kreator track (laughs). But there was really no influence. But it's got a sort of harmonized blast beat-type riff in the intro. It's pretty cool. It's one of my favourite Carcass songs."

175 ERUPTION VAN HALEN

305 points

from Van Halen (Warner '78)

Not highly indicative of the oblique, almost anti-social style Eddie is known for, *Eruption* nevertheless captured the abstract media hound idea of an Eddie Van Halen, announcing loudly the arrival of the new guitar god. It's remarkable that this man and band had the guts to put a true guitar solo on their first album, but such was the bravado of the new California breed who would dominate metal for the next two big waves, roughly centered on 1983 and 1989. This track attacks immediately as well as offering patented hammer-ons, soon to be every mullet's chick-pulling party trick. But it's not the tone Eddie would adopt two records hence, and in total it is an all-out blitz, lacking the crazy legs, 'round-the-back tunefulness of future solos. Still, it made a huge impression, causing many an aspiring axeman to crack his knuckles, hunker down (skip Friday night with the boys), woodshed (skip Saturday too), and together one and all (but jealously guarding personal sleights of hand), invent shred.

Alex Van Halen on Eddie's guitar work . . .

> "I remember originally when a lot of guys began playing Eddie's lyrics. He had very mixed emotions. On one hand he was flattered, and on another he felt he had been infringed upon with something that was very private to him. He felt his trademark, or the way he was identifiable, was being ripped off. But then after awhile, he realized how public he was and that anyone could do anything they wanted to do with it."

176 ORGASMATRON MOTÖRHEAD

305 points *from Orgasmatron* (GWR *'86)*

It's kind of sad, but *Orgasmatron* — great chomping rock ride that it is — stood out partially due to its weak rockscrabble competition on Motörhead's ill-regarded late '80s/early '90s output. But like I say, it's a bruiser, bolstered by a steel backbone, its riff determined, mud-caked and sleep-deprived, Lemmy's vocal fully battle-worn and war-mongered. The lyric reminds me a bit of the character sketch technique used for *(We Are) The Roadcrew*, even if this is anything but lighting truss lighthearted. Lemmy shines as a wordsmith cynical at mankind and its indiscriminate bloodthirsty motivations, the man ready to blow the whole mess up. Ably and famously covered by Sepultura, who prove that the track, with its monotone, monochrome, metronome grind, is a borderline death metal classic.

Lemmy on *Orgasmatron* . . .

> "Well, people have been telling me all about Woody Allen ever since I wrote it but I didn't know about that. I mean, I saw the movie but I didn't take it in consciously; maybe it's subconscious, I don't know. I just thought of all the alternatives to orgasm, which are war, politics and religion. You don't have to come, just give praise to the Lord (laughs)."

177 CAT SCRATCH FEVER TED NUGENT

304 points *from Cat Scratch Fever (Epic '77)*

One in a long, time-honoured tradition of ludicrously simple riffs sent chart-high, *Cat Scratch Fever* likely got that way through the inaccessible, abstract and unspoken panache with which Ted commandeered its central riff. As well, Tom Werman found a way to thin and minimalize the production of the thing so that it could conquer our tinny radios, if not our heavy, blasting boat-ballast home hi-fi's. Ted's vocal is a wisecrack of the whip, and it has to be, given that when he's signing, the riff drops into an anaemic hard-ish rock standby boogie. No matter, that freight train returns come chorus time, modestly metalling up the place again, as Ted croons a tune to the love that keeps on giving.

Ted Nugent on *Cat Scratch Fever* . . .

> "A perfect example, may I dare, of what a musician who is driven by the music and who virtually in absolute terms craves to play and create and wallow and celebrate the musical ideas that he collaborates on, especially in an optimum setting that the virtuosos bring to my musical campfire. Again, if you examine the musicians who performed with me on that, I give them great credit. It was a rhythm section of unbelievable blackness. We don't have any white influences. Rob De La Grange on the bass guitar and Cliff Davies on the drums on that session brought a thumping, pummelling, grinding, grunting, snorting rhythm and blues spirit to those tracks that is exactly what I envisioned when I came up with it. It's just a classic jam lick turned into a wonderful, musical rock 'n' roll statement and again I attribute a lot of that to the rhythm section that Cliff and Rob brought to bear, executing my musical vision."

Ted Nugent

Moby Grape — *Omaha*
Lonnie Mack — *Suzie Q*
Yardbirds — *Train Kept a Rollin'*
James Brown — *I Feel Good*
Wayne Cochran — *Going Back to Miami*
Jimi Hendrix Experience — *Are You Experienced?*
Rolling Stones — *Little Red Rooster*
Red Hot Chili Peppers — *Give It Away*
Aerosmith — *Toys in the Attic*
Ted Nugent — *Cat Scratch Fever*

178 MURDERS IN THE RUE MORGUE IRON MAIDEN

301 points

from Killers (EMI '81)

My favourite track from a maligned album, *Murders in the Rue Morgue* is a dark horse that has proven its lasting power, no doubt in large part due to its saccharine verse melody, its punk verve, and the progressive and jaunty flair of its many parts. Cool how its switches gears so much, as well grooving multi-tiered, Di'Anno proving himself a consummate deliver of tales, the band fired up, fast but well within control, confident of bigger stages to come.

Paul Di'Anno on *Murders in the Rue Morgue* . . .

> "That one was a nightmare, another three-take job (laughs), three or four. I really didn't like that album much at all, to be honest. I thought we were changing and not for the better. I suppose in a way we were, because it was getting more polished and a little, how should I put it, less aggressive. It was getting a bit too intricate for me. I like it rough and ready (laughs)."

Coby Dick from Papa Roach

Joan Jett — *I Love Rock 'n' Roll*
Faith No More — *The Gentle Art of Making Enemies*
Social Distortion — *Down on the World Again*
Refused — *New Noise*
Alien Ant Farm — *Sticks and Stones*
Guns N' Roses — *Welcome to the Jungle*
Metallica — *One*
Aerosmith — *Sweet Emotion*
Pixies — *Gouge Away*
Jane's Addiction — *Mountain Song*

179 BOHEMIAN RHAPSODY QUEEN

300 points *from A Night at the Opera* (EMI '75)

Colour me loaded, but on some objective level, I thought *Bohemian Rhapsody* (as well as *Stairway to Heaven*) should and would vault way further up our list. Maybe it's because both these tracks belong to the greater music world than that perimetered and guarded by self-respecting metalheads. In any event, no one would argue the genius of this track, its ornate, go-for-baroque creative expulsions drugging the listener with dizzying possibilities. Queen broke through, after a slow build to this destiny, the path already rarefied, this discovery arriving beyond the pale. Even the conventional parts gathered in clusters would have made for songs more impressionable than almost anything in Zeppelin's catalogue. The melodies could rival those of the Beatles, the metal workout, most notably its springy verve, is prescient of Eddie Van Halen, and the opera . . . well, that took courage, or at least panache, or at least a lot of time. The end result: *Bohemian Rhapsody* is a song that couldn't help but be a unanimous smash, even if some of the love was degradably derived from its novelty and comedy.

Brian May on longevity . . .

> "Longevity? Staying together is rule No. 1. If you stay together, you stand a lot better chance of doing well. Internally, it's good for you, because you learn to appreciate each other and you get to use a balance of talents if you're lucky, with different people taking care of different areas. And if you're lucky, which we were, you have four different people who write different material. So we had a big sifting process throughout our career which I feel gives us more strength than if we had only one writer throughout the whole career of the band. Externally, it makes a difference because of the identification thing. People know the band and know it's the same four people who were in there in the '70s and '80s so they relate and understand what we're all about. They don't have the confusion of following different people going in and out of the band. I guess there aren't that many bands that have stayed together intact for as long as we have, are there? Maybe Slade? (laughs)."

180 ARISE SEPULTURA

299 points *from Arise (Roadrunner '91)*

An old thrash classic, *Arise* combines a love of Slayer with the incendiary nature of hardcore and the unique happenstance of its creators hailing from a far-off elsewhere. The lyric ambiguously combines terrorism and the idea of a more thorough apocalypse. But the main point one should take away is the idea that neither the lyric nor Max's elocution thereof sound like the non-Anglo dross of the Sep clone countrymates who were still stuck back home. Full participation in the muck of American death touring had already resulted in worthy product that somehow retained an exotic urgent worldliness that would work diligently in the background as Sepultura worked towards their best album **Roots**.

Andreas Kisser on **Arise** . . .

> "**Arise** was after doing the **Beneath the Remains** tour, where we toured for the first time outside of Brazil. We were in such high spirits and the record label was really confident in the band and we had a manager, Gloria, working with us. All the conditions were right. It was just a bigger step from **Beneath the Remains**. *Arise* is a very powerful song today that we still play a lot in our set. A lot of Sepultura fans think that is our best album, and it's a very special song all over the world. The influence is pretty much Slayer."

181 HAIL AND KILL MANOWAR

299 points *from Kings of Metal (Atlantic '88)*

Quite cool seeing a track from what is widely considered an unremarkable mid-years record zooming into the number one slot for Manowar,

Hail and Kill rocking mid-paced and melodic, Eric really selling it with one of his more directly confrontational, truly histrionic and Halloweenie vocals. The chorus is a scream, but the song really lives on its sturdy, almost melancholic and Metallica-like melody lines. And it's long but not built like a long song, so you really get to live with its patient freight train pacing.

Eric Adams on *Hail and Kill* . . .

> "I remember a little bit about that one. I remember when we were doing the end, when we decided to have the crowd do it, the 'hail hail, hail and kill' thing. We thought, well, let's just wait and do that live. I knew it was going to be one of those songs that was going to go over great live and it does."

182 DAMAGE INC. METALLICA

298 points *from Master of Puppets (Elektra '86)*

Compressing vice-like *Master of Puppets* with opening partner-in-grime *Battery, Damage Inc.* proved that this destined band could still thrash like *Whiplash* and *Trapped Under Ice.* But *Damage Inc.* is a little boring, a little comfortable, a little post-punk post-denim, a little self-aware and embarrassed, presaging Anthrax and that band's self-deprecation and insecurities. Then again the song's compact battle plan also seems to say that Metallica can thrash with four hands tied behind their backs, the song moving with hilarious speed and precision like no punks would dare.

Lars Ulrich on fame . . .

> "I think they were pretty good at maintaining an intimacy with our audience. Every kind of gig you have to approach differently. I think were getting a feel of how to take care of an arena without sounding snobby about it. We still like to go back and play club shows. What I don't like about arenas is the sameness every day. When you play 45 cement arenas around North America, you

find it difficult to tell them apart. I think it's all down to your attitude too. I don't consider ourselves much different than what we've been before in terms of our relationship with our fans. The numbers are bigger. I think sometimes people make that stuff up in their minds a little saying, 'Now the band is too big and inaccessible.' We're just as easy to get hold of as we've always been. Most of our fans have a really relaxed approach to us because we're easy-going people. With us it's like, 'Here are the drunken slobs from Metallica again!' It's a pretty relaxed thing and we feel pretty good about that."

183 GUTTER BALLET SAVATAGE

295 points *from Gutter Ballet (Atlantic '90)*

OK, so it starts slow, goes into *Eye of the Tiger*, then some sort of thespian AOR thing that is pretty unexpected from these vicious delicious rockers. But *Gutter Ballet* masked a new painterly actorly ruefulness for Savatage. Sorta reminds me of Angel's *The Tower* in epic scope, unironically baked by a second nature metal band with a penchant for Queen ballads. And it is a grand update and what's more, it is one of the band's memorable choruses of very few within the prog years.

Jon Oliva on *Gutter Ballet* . . .

"*Gutter Ballet* was a huge experimental track for us, because that was not only the song that brought in the piano as a main instrument in the band, but it was also the beginning of the concept ideas. *Gutter Ballet* was originally part of the **Streets** story. And Paul had originally wanted to make **Gutter Ballet** a concept album, but I at the time was too chicken to do it (laughs). And I said, well, let's just do a couple of songs and see how it feels on the record. So we did *Gutter Ballet* and *When the Crowds Are Gone* which were part of the same thing. So that was a very experimental and important part of the band's career."

Jon Oliva from Savatage
Black Sabbath — *War Pigs*
Deep Purple — *Highway Star*
Deep Purple — *Smoke On The Water*
Led Zeppelin — *Kashmir*
Rush — *2112*
Black Sabbath — *Heaven and Hell*
Motörhead — *Ace of Spades*
Venom — *Welcome to Hell*
Metallica — *Seek and Destroy*
Queen — *Bohemian Rhapsody*

184 NOVEMBER RAIN GUNS N' ROSES

294 points *from Use Your Illusion (Geffen '91)*

A river swollen to a depth of importance thrust upon this lucky and unlucky band, *November Rain* features Axl in full diva mode, indulging his inner Elton John, Slash gamely searching out a place as Joe Perry-esque guitar hero valiantly trying to sound and look cool covered in sap. But oddly, it's pretty visceral, convincing and emotionally torrid for a power ballad, no doubt rendered so by the avalanche of baggage surrounding it and its creators. Still, its successfully efficient sprawl reveals a band with a bench depth far beyond the malnourished creators of **Appetite**'s sanitized sleaze.

Duff McKagan on *November Rain* . . .

> "That's a song that Axl had this piano riff for. And it took years to get that song out. It was never done and finally we had to kind of battle to get it done for the **Illusions** record. That last part where it all of a sudden goes into that outro riff, was going to be another song and it just kind of got thrown in there. The rest is kind of history. Axl was getting into ballads. I don't know, I think

hindsight is what it is. I think if we would have stayed away from ballads and just been this rock band, the legacy would have been a bit more hardcore. But, it's what it is. We became who we became. We were a certified pop band at that point, after *November Rain*."

185 SCHOOL'S OUT ALICE COOPER

293 points *from School's Out (Warner '72)*

Way heavier in people's heads than the actual swimmery post-psyche swing of the thing sounds in actuality, *School's Out* is a schizophrenic little dearie with bits of garage rock, metal and prog, all delivered with unravelling charm perched on the tricycle wheels of a bouncy bass line. The military march of the chorus really hits home though, although man, what a bunch of dated sounds, Alice succeeding by sounding retro in '72, radio-friendly through use of handmade tools, edge taken off by a back-gaggle of actual school kids. But all this wouldn't exist without that pendulum of a riff, and for that, the song is firmly an early metal cornerstone.

Alice Cooper on *School's Out* . . .

"I would say that *School's Out* was . . . you know, when you're writing a song, and there's a momentum in the song where you know that it's a hit. At times, very apparent, other times not, where you write the song and you say, 'Oh, this is a really good song,' then all of a sudden it falls off the album and it's a hit and you go, 'Oh, great.' *School's Out* was designed to be a hit. It was designed to be an anthem. And it was designed to appeal to every single person in the world because everybody has sat through school on that last three minutes before school is out. The longest three minutes of the year is that last three minutes on May 30th or whatever it is. So I said, if we can capture the joy of the kids screaming, knowing they have three months off of school, well, that will be a big hit."

186 SWEET EMOTION AEROSMITH

290 points *from Toys in the Attic (Columbia '75)*

Whether it be the spirit of the '70s, the raw talent, or the superman drugs, Aerosmith by this point were writing in a hallowed zone, *Sweet Emotion* taking a half-dozen new hard rock liberties, that puffy cloud bass line, chorus at the front, the roller coaster break and above all, the boxing ring back end, meeting at the crossroads for a song that was a hit-bound happy meal and a seven course dinner all at once. And Tyler's lyric knows it, the good-for-nothing punk sounding smarmy and smart while his band sparks up their rainbow of colours behind him. A compressed version of an adventuresome album.

Steven Tyler on the creative spark . . .

> "I've never done that before, said, 'Let's write a song about a rock in my shoe.' It was always after the fact; Joe would come up with a lick, and I would go off on a scat and I'd pick words out of my scat. Somebody once said, 'If you write something every day . . .' — which includes writing something, something, something a hundred times — 'as long as you write, you're gonna get better as a writer.' And it never dawned on me to just try to capture in a song what kind of feelings were going down that day."

187 SMELLS LIKE TEEN SPIRIT NIRVANA

289 points *from Nevermind (Sub Pop/Geffen '91)*

Just like punk in '77, this new style (already a good three years old by the time inquiring minds swung to **Nevermind**), was metal without solos, as well as metal with oddly foreign melodies, as well as metal with slightly angrier vocals. Fact is, *Smells Like Teen Spirit* rocked, thanks to Dave

Grohl's cymbal-smashing groove, thanks to grunge's ever-evidenced eye on the Sabs. *Smells Like Teen Spirit* was grunge pop though, if not grunge lite, and it was recorded cleaner than past kicks at the cat, so in it went, into every happy home that consumed rock products. Nirvana buzzed in the most inspiring of possible ways, bubbling up from the underground, art all the way, and of course way past, through darker albums and even the suicide . . . art all the way. This track was of course the anthem of the times (close second: Pearl Jam's *Jeremy*), and it likely stuck in the craw because its verse riff gave delicate ears a pause for tingly refreshment, painting a world of blissful, light disenchantment before we could all live dangerously, come majestic metal chorus time, through those darn ungrateful kids and their oh so nasty punk rock guitars.

Dave Grohl on *Smells Like Teen Spirit* . . .

> "Well, that song came from a jam that we had. We used to practice in this shed behind some guy's house and it stemmed from one of the jams we had back there. And we knew we wanted it to be on the album, but there were other songs that I thought would be the big song on the record. We played a show at a place called the OK Hotel, before going down to Los Angeles to record, and we did the show on like a week's notice, just so we could make gas money to drive down to make the record. And we played that song and it was the first time we ever played it in front of people and people really went off to it. And I don't know if it was the new dynamic we were experiencing or were experimenting with, or if it was just the rhythm of the song or what it was. But people seemed to react to it. And you know, I like the song a lot, but I never thought it would do what it did."

188 WELCOME TO MY NIGHTMARE ALICE COOPER

288 points *from Welcome to My Nightmare (Warner '75)*

The last of the golden era records, **Welcome to My Nightmare** opened with this tangle of confused signals, Alice for the first time going upscale on production and arrangements, perhaps catching a whiff of the different worlds to which his new Hollywood friends were attuned. The song's a funky near-disco morass of a mess, a strange choice of genre given the lyric, and the first uneasy inkling that this isn't so much about being a band of rock pigs making rebellious songs for teenagers anymore. Same thing would gradually happen to Kiss from '78 through the low '80s.

Alice Cooper on *Welcome to My Nightmare* . . .

"*Welcome to My Nightmare* was just the absolute, the theme for that whole album. It's a play on *Welcome to My Dreams*; there's an old song (sings it). Well *Welcome to My Nightmare* was saying, here it is, we're going there, we're going to go to this nightmare. A nice little play on words. And actually, it was pretty jazzy, and that was the Ezrin touch in that. My idea was that in the beginning of that, all the parts were very dark and Doors-y, Alice-y and Doors-y combined. But when it came to the end of that song, it really just took off into a whole horns and jazz and rock kinda funky thing. But it still stays creepy. I mean, that's Bob Ezrin."

189 YOU CAN'T KILL ROCK AND ROLL OZZY OSBOURNE

287 points *from Diary of a Madman (Jet/CBS '81)*

Power ballad, southern rock ballad, confessional, song about rockin'. . . *You Can't Kill Rock and Roll* is really Ozzy collapsing like a tumbled ice cream cone for a fireside chat, the man stating the here and now, trying to predict his inevitably absurd future. It's a long tough slog, kinda like a bloated hard-wheezing Sabbath song from **Never Say Die**. The heavy part sports one of Rhoads' worst riffs and the metal part's just eerie Ozzy, a dark horse of a melody that touches something but stays on the surface. Crazy long fade on it too, one punctuated by Rhoads screeching away atonally over bad drumming and lost bass playing from a band who did many great things but could rarely groove.

Ozzy Osborne on performing live . . .

"I don't want to fake it. You get me as you find me. Sometimes I'm shit, and sometimes I'm good. I like it when I'm good, and I hate it when I'm shit. All I can do is give what I can give. If it's good, it's good. If it's bad, it's bad. I'm just trying to play music that makes me happy. There's not a feeling on this planet like getting off a stage feeling that you've accomplished what you set out to accomplish. And there's no feeling on this planet like getting off a stage having let not only yourself down, letting down the people who paid money to see you. I have a responsibility to go on that stage and give the best performance I can each night."

190 BLACK DIAMOND KISS

287 points

from Kiss (Casablanca '74)

Less self-aware and therefore more emotionally destructive than its flashier Satan spawn *Detroit Rock City*, *Black Diamond* was sung by a thug, so you knew that whole "out on the streets" vibe had some dirt to it. As well, the song forces you into the seat of dark drama with that death-shrouded intro, Kiss knitting a lull cardigan in your head and then hitting with chords too big to control, so they don't. Peter's voice is great. They should have utilized it more regularly, and the whole song perks and struts along like the early American A-grade metal anthem that it is. Great close too, Kiss once more placing an ambitious fire in the iron, staining a part of the canvas that rarely saw activity, except, as we all found out, in the hidden machinations of this middle-rifted band of exaggerated characters.

Peter Criss on the band's fragile chemistry . . .

"It's amazing. Doc McGhee put it so well. He said, 'You can go up to each one of us, ask us the same question and get four different answers meaning the same thing.' That is so well put, because we are so different, each one of us, immensely, with everything. But we'll put on the makeup and hit the stage and we are all one. It's ridiculous. There's this magic we've had since way back in 1972, when we were rehearsing in our loft on 23rd Street, freezing our buns off and trying to scrounge up enough money for a train ride to rehearsals. There is definitely something there that I've seen and felt on many nights. Then after the show, we'll get back into our street clothes and we'll head off in opposite directions. It's strange."

191 SPEED KING DEEP PURPLE

186 points *from In Rock (Warner '70)*

If Deep Purple found a way to lose by inches as metal history progressed, you have to give them credit for creating hot steel like *Speed King* as far back as 1970, summoning a level of pioneering proficiency Zeppelin couldn't touch and Sabbath couldn't care. And somehow, with Ritchie throwing up a castle in the time it took your hard rock fan to light up a bowl, Deep Purple actually found a way to be both jazzy and classical, carrying one last lone good vestige of the '60s into **In Rock**, the world's first modern metal album.

Ian Gillan on *Speed King* . . .

"That was originally called *Kneel and Pray*, which had another meaning altogether."

192 EAGLE FLY FREE HELLOWEEN

285 points *from Keeper of the Seven Keys Part II (Noise '88)*

Creating their best material during a strange time for metal, well after the first big wave and just before the second (which would seriously lack a European dimension), Helloween found themselves quite alone with their Euro speed franchise. *Eagle Fly Free*, in retrospect is one of power metals building blocks, many of which originate with Helloween's material from the two **Keeper** albums. Insanely fast and just as fluffy and sweet, *Eagle Fly Free* is almost too ornate and singsongy for American tastes, a strange effect that persists to this day, with power metal's most robust sales happening in Europe, Japan and South America.

Michael Weikath on the origins of Helloween's need for speed . . .

> "I think Rainbow were way ahead with speed and the double-bass approach. We're not influenced by those speed and thrash bands of the '80s. In fact, I think this is just a continuation of Rainbow, Deep Purple, UFO and even Led Zeppelin. Most of the other speed metal bands from the '80s lacked melody. They didn't create structures or even songs. Speed metal was always very primitive to me."

193 CAUGHT IN A MOSH ANTHRAX

285 points *from Among the Living (Island '87)*

Capturing the overactive brain spasms of Anthrax on full-throttle, *Caught in a Mosh* was almost a parody of the band's punk metal conundrum. Or sod that, it was just good fun. Insanely fast, ripped and zipped with the spirit of hardcore, and featuring vocals that sound like a Three Stooges routine, *Caught in a Mosh* is a blur of high-science playing skills applied forcefully to thrashy, under-appreciated street music for Neanderthals. Speed metal's version of William Burroughs' cut and paste routine; the back-switching, bareback results in anything but routine.

Charlie Benante on *Caught in a Mosh* . . .

> "*Caught in a Mosh* is probably the best story. We were on the **Spreading the Disease** tour, playing Denver and the show was just totally out of control; kids were going absolutely apeshit. A kid jumped on stage and as he was jumping off, he dragged a whole pedal board into the pit with him, and our guitar tech, Art Ring had to jump in after this kid and get it. As he jumped in, he got turned around and boom, landed right on his back. He got pulled out and everything and after the show we were sitting backstage and he was pretty hurt and he's like, 'Oh dude, I got caught in a mosh.' Ding!"

194 DON'T TALK TO STRANGERS DIO

284 points

from Holy Diver (Warner '83)

One of Dio's uneasy morality tales, *Don't Talk to Strangers* is notable for its dual personality, its sobbing, resigned slow sections, strafed with a deliciously gothic set of Viv riffs propelled by the groovy craft of barrel-chested soul drummer Vinny Appice: a classic performance from the golden era line-up. It's cool how the band strips your gears at the end, forcing you to adjust to their attacks and retreats before the final triumphant march into . . . misanthropy?

Ronnie James Dio on *Don't Talk to Strangers* . . .

> "That was the second of the songs I wrote before we had a band, going into **Holy Diver**. I wrote *Holy Diver* first and I wrote *Don't Talk to Strangers* second. Those two songs are the ones we presented to Vivian when we auditioned Viv; we showed him those songs, and that was the beginning of the whole shebang really. At the time I was writing it, it was a difficult time. I wasn't in a band yet, and I hadn't put this band together yet. I just went out and wrote those things, really for future reference. When there was a band, there would be some songs to start with. So it was a difficult time in terms of, what's going to happen next? It was about how people promise you the world and then just . . . bend over, here it comes. So that's what it was about, the idea that strangers can be devilish if you let them; beware of what's going on. I kind of put myself in that place a little bit, being one of the strangers as well, just for a turn in the lyric, and not because I felt I was one of those evil guys."

Christian Olde Wolbers from Fear Factory
Suicidal Tendencies — *Institutionalized*
Faith No More — *Surprise! You're Dead!*

Metallica — *Master of Puppets*
Killing Joke — *Love Like Blood*
Rage Against the Machine — *Killing in the Name*
Black Sabbath — *War Pigs*
Sepultura — *Chaos A.D.*
Bad Brains — *I Against I*
Black Flag — *Damaged*
Metallica — *Motorbreath*

195 18 AND LIFE SKID ROW

282 points *from Skid Row (Atlantic '89)*

A powerful power ballad forged in the days thereof, *18 and Life* had all the drama of America's metal mullets gone pie-eyed, delivered in dark detail by hair metal's consummate vocalist. Baz had the talent, looks, both good and bad rock star qualities, and he carried this fairly average musical track on an album full of nondescript musical tracks. Still, it was a convincing hair extension of Alice's *I'm Eighteen* and its take on teen alienation — it, along with the more representative *Youth Gone Wild* and *Piece of Me* — pushed Skid Row to stardom with what would be their only bad album of three.

Dave "Snake" Sabo on *18 and Life* . . .

"I was working in a music store in Tom's River, New Jersey, which is where Rachel and I had met and I had these chords and whatnot that I would fool around with in the music store and I said to Rachel, 'I've got this idea for a song.' Originally it was supposed to be about my brother who went to Viet Nam, and his name was Rick, but we couldn't just grasp that at the time. We couldn't wrap our heads around that particular story line. Whether it was too close to me and I couldn't contribute . . . I don't know why. So we just came up with this fictitious story based on true to life events. Once again, a lot of the lyrics come from Rachel and he just has a way of making certain situations very poetic, and yet have a strong message and an ability to connect with the audience. And that song in particular just seemed to connect because people have seen friends go through that situation. So it was a pretty universal conjoining of band and fan."

196 SOMETHING WICKED (TRILOGY) ICED EARTH

282 points

from Something Wicked This Way Comes (Century Media '98)

Much more Maiden-like than Jon's other legendary epic *Dante's Inferno, Something Wicked* is 20 minutes of aliens vs. ancient drama, the trilogy (*1. Prophecy; 2. Birth of the Wicked; 3. The Coming Curse*) building and often ebbing hypnotically like *Rime of the Ancient Mariner* (proceed to middle of *The Coming Curse*!). But as usual, Schaffer tries to keep the silvery, shivery, sylvan metal flowing, much of the trilogy moving like malevolent power metal seemingly forged hundreds of years ago. Matt Barlow by this point is becoming the star of the band, dead serious in his serious stance, long red hair flaming forth from any given Iced Earth live love-in, his voice a scythe.

Jon Schaffer on *The Coming Curse* . . .

> "*The Coming Curse* is the ending to my little teaser to the *Something Wicked* story. On that record that was probably my favourite song. *Watching over Me* is in some ways my favourite because it is so personal, but *The Coming Curse* was the climax, if you will, of the *Something Wicked* trilogy. I can't get too far into the story because there is so much more to come on that. To me it was the darkest song on the record no doubt and it was the most evil and the most intense. It's one of my favourites still."

197 VOODOO CHILD (SLIGHT RETURN) JIMI HENDRIX EXPERIENCE

282 points *from Electric Ladyland (Reprise '68)*

More indicative of the mountain of magic sparking through Jimi's fingers than the trampled and travelled *Purple Haze*, *Voodoo Child* sounds like a man and band unreal, Jimi's guitar gushing and surging like a waterfall of electricity, captured amidst production values that contain all the admirable warm wallow of the '60s sound, but none of the dry screech of competing records at the time. It is progressive rock before there was such a thing, metal before there was such a thing, and an early, understated form of shred before there was such a thing. In terms of specific legacies, *Voodoo Child* contains the man's most celebrated example of guitar and voice in unison, people often forgetting what a first-rate vocalist Jimi was, and it also contains Jimi's ability to make electric blues that was far more interesting and ornate than anything Cream could dare muster. Arguably (and in my opinion) this is Jimi's masterpiece track, a composition that made the boldest case for this man as something from another time and exotic space.

Matt and Mike from Vision of Disorder
Black Sabbath — *Into the Void*
Soundgarden — *Jesus Christ Pose*
Sepultura — *Roots Bloody Roots*
The Beatles — *Helter Skelter*
King's X — *Dogman*
Led Zeppelin — *Immigrant Song*
Judas Priest — *Electric Eye*
AC/DC — *TNT*
Metallica — *Master of Puppets*
Megadeth — *Holy Wars . . . The Punishment Due*

198 BLACKENED METALLICA

280 points *from ... And Justice for All (Elektra '88)*

When Lars whacks that lonely snare, you know you're in for a fresh kind of Metallica album, *Blackened* thenceforth scurrying out into harsh light, epitomizing the compressed, difficult cyborgian thrash of **... And Justice for All**. To be sure, *Blackened* is a thrasher in the spirit of *Whiplash*, *Damage Inc.* and *Battery*, but it rings foreign, mechanical and oddly unheavy, more about the dry cold logic of riff than neck-wrecking. And of course, it veers off into all sorts of pointless pretty parts, some of them forecasting the droopy doom of the Black Album, most of it just showing off, best bragging bit being the mathematical mindgames and trick signatures briefly thrown at the main (Slayer-esque) riff.

Jason Newsted on *Blackened* ...

> "James and I were in my apartment in San Pablo, California, a little apartment I lived in when I first got the gig with Metallica. He came over and I had a four-track machine in my room, in the bedroom actually (laughs). And there was a Damage Inc. poster right over that thing. I remember that, so I was pretty much into it, you know? And I came up with that original riff, that really fast, kind of off-kilter thing. And then he caught on to that and I know we taped it that day on the four-track, the main bits of it. And then I think we went to One On One Studio in West Hollywood. We were in between producers. It was really a weird time. We hadn't been into that fancy of a studio before. There were a lot of distractions in Los Angeles, I remember that. I went in with the assistant engineer, Toby Wright, who has come to fame now recording Alice in Chains and stuff like that. I remember Toby and I recording in a room, nobody else around. It's different from any of the other sessions we did with Metallica. I had never been into a studio like that. The only way I had ever recorded was the way we recorded with Flotsam. Four days and $1000 or whatever, 'Ready? Go!' And then we did the **Garage Days** record the same way, where it was six days and we just pounded it out. And I thought, that's how it went. Whatever you play is what you get. There was no ProTools back then or whatever, fixing shit. We just played it. So then it came time to make the **Justice** record. And for that one, there was no other

producer guy or anything was in the room. Toby was just the assistant guy then. So we did that together, very simple, with the same rig that I recorded the Flotsam album with. So it was really simple shit."

199 COME TO THE SABBATH MERCYFUL FATE

280 points *from Don't Break the Oath (Roadrunner '84)*

Come to the Sabbath is the last track of a two-album show of force from a band of disturbing intelligence, Mercyful Fate set to explode and become a thing of hushed tones before reforming nine years later as mere mortals. As a career closer, *Come to the Sabbath* loses its grip on reality much like the debut's *Satan's Fall*. But the random riffs are more inspired, and they come and leave quicker. Indeed once it flares out, the lasting memory is of King's uncharacteristically emotional invitation at the beginning of the intelligent mess/mass, King perhaps grasping the double-edged sword, evoking both the tragic, empty sorrow and the triumphant majesty of being a Satanist. But ultimately, the song unravels due to the speed shifts and key changes, Mercyful Fate seemingly bent on cataloguing as many Hank Shermann riffs as they can before he leaves Lucifer's domain for happier metal hill and dale.

King Diamond on *Come to the Sabbath* . . .

"Another classic, of course. That was the first song that I wrote for the band. These were written already when we did the **Melissa** album. When it came time to record **Don't Break the Oath**, we had a better budget and about 18 days in the studio. I think you can hear the extra attention on that album too. I wouldn't say it's a better album songwriting-wise, but it was a development, staying within the Mercyful Fate frame. We used different instruments to create a heavy mood and my voice developed as well."

200 PRACTISE WHAT YOU PREACH TESTAMENT

278 points *from Practise What You Preach (Megaforce '89)*

Practise What You Preach featured Testament participating wide-eyed in a higher stakes world, where heavy music of a slightly lighter variety was selling like hotcakes, and there was a chance that Chuck 'n' Eric could be kings of the dark side. Ergo, this title track and its mid-mosh hardcore stomp, the band sounding like a cross between old Metallica and new Anthrax, production from somewhere in the Exodus zone, vocal melodies straight from Hetfield's little black book.

Eric Peterson on **Practise What You Preach** . . .

> "That was a great era for Testament. Things really came together for the band. The record was actually recorded live, excluding the vocals, so it was a good feeling to all be in a room just looking at each other. The only problem was our headphones kept falling off. It was a great vibe and a raunchy sound. I'm not crazy about the production, but the song is very solid. It really shows Testament's commercial side of songwriting, mixing that with a little bit of heaviness."

201 BLACK NO. 1 TYPE O NEGATIVE

276 points *from Bloody Kisses (Roadrunner '93)*

Simultaneously a happy car crash of a celebration of goth culture, *Black No. 1* points a laughing finger at the look, Pete sounding attracted and embarrassed by the baggage building up around the band. *Black No. 1* was pretty accessible compared to past rin tin dins, but beneath its plainspeak lyrics and mid-4/4 rock pulse, there are progressive moments, the song taking on new directions late in the game, Type O clutching and coddling the one thing they crave the most: freedom, freedom to unravel, freedom to occupy a good chunk of your time with a presentation that is a tangle of parodies on top of ironies.

Pete Steele on the Type O sound . . .

"If I had to pigeon-hole it, either junk rock, which I really like because we just take a bunch of things that are old and worn-out and throw them all together and make something out of it. If I had to come up with something a bit more contemporary, I'd say gothadelic might be close enough. Lyrically, it's nothing spiritual. I don't believe that I have a soul or a spirit. I consider myself 240 pounds of chemicals, that's it. I am here by chance. Anything that happens to me is just a case of being thrust into chaos, and I happen to be there while it happens. There is no God, there is no Satan, there is nothing. After death, you will know the same thing you knew before conception, which is just a beautiful, black, furry sleep."

202 PANAMA VAN HALEN

275 points

from 1984 (Warner '84)

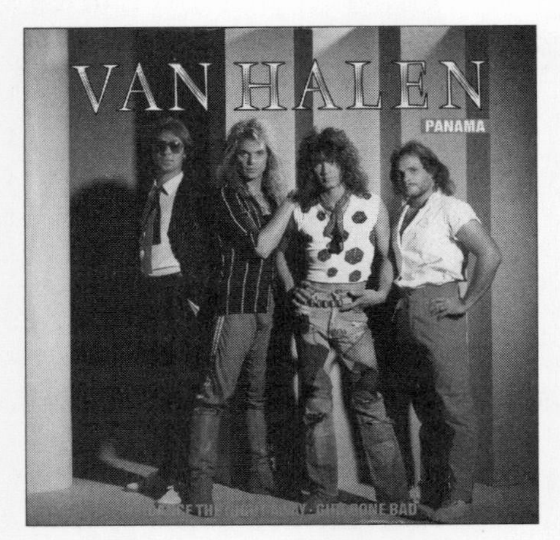

Proof that the most inconsequential premise can sell if you are Van Halen and if you are Van Halen making videos, *Panama* was a rock stomp completely devoid of brains, planning, elbow grease, Hell, even production. Nothing but net. But that windy whiff is money in the bank if it's Diamond Dave providing the play-by-play. So there he does and is, while Alex and Michael pound like a headache, behind a lark of a guitar that's more soundcheck than bodycheck. Fun in a bottle I guess, Atlas shrugged.

Michael Anthony on the Van Halen method . . .

"It's just us being ourselves, plain and simple. All the way from what we look like to what we play. We just play and write from the heart, and we jump on no fashion or trend bandwagons. I feel that's what's kept us popular for all this time. People know what to expect, which is just four knuckleheads who like to jam (laughs)."

203 PURPLE HAZE JIMI HENDRIX EXPERIENCE

275 points *from Are You Experienced? (Reprise '67)*

I'm surprised *Purple Haze* isn't vaulted higher on our chart, given its status as pretty much the most immediately riff-wrapped hard rocker from what is arguably the first heavy metal artist. I mean, outside of Hendrix, all you had was Cream or The Who making this much noise, not counting less significant worker ants and their experiments and mistakes. But Hendrix vanquished Clapton as a guitar hero, *Purple Haze* immediately staking new turf with its opening caterwaul mechanics before relaxing into its loud still somewhat psychedelically dated metallic funk, punctuated of course by one of the greatest full stops in rock 'n' roll.

204 RESTLESS AND WILD ACCEPT

275 points *from Restless and Wild (Brain '82)*

A reassertion of the top-flight metal song skills exhibited on **Breaker**, *Restless and Wild* is a song of many glorious parts, all driven by Stefan Kaufmann's drum grooves and simple, effective fills at every break, verse, pre-chorus and chorus curve. It is a broken English series of various nomadic vignettes, a sympathetic bookend to the sentiments in *Balls to the Wall*, and Udo's vocal positively bubbles to the top and then laps over the side, the rhythm section pushing the jolly chain-smoker from mumbles towards blood-curdling screams come climactic chorus time. A worthy album anchor oddly situated at track two but so comfortably at home at whatever port it may call. There was no stopping this band after an album and anthem this carnal and clarion. Udo stalks then attacks on what is a brilliantly paced bit of deceptively simple mainstream metal, Accept grabbing and shaking violently that space between smart Priest and dumb Priest, and then tipping the cart into a meat-eating metal grinder with the shoving shoulder of engineer Michael Wagener, who on the strength and integrity of this album, will be tapped for a looming classic called **All for One** by irrepressible punk metallists Raven.

Udo Dirkschneider on *Restless and Wild* . . .

> "Don't laugh (laughs), but we were thinking that the whole rhythm of this song is like you're riding a horse (laughs). It was also, in a way, strange. That was the era, the time. Restless and wild. That was the whole situation of the band. We were restless and wild, always wanting to do something. And that was the whole meaning of the song."

Mike Watt from Firehose

Black Sabbath — *Supernaut*
The Who — *Young Man's Blues*
Black Flag — *My War*
The Stooges — *Down on the Street*
The Stooges — *T.V. Eye*
Mott the Hoople — *Walking with a Mountain*
Blue Öyster Cult — *The Red & the Black*
Blue Öyster Cult — *Hot Rails to Hell*
Motörhead — *Ace of Spades*
Slayer — *Mandatory Suicide*

205 DEAD EMBRYONIC CELLS SEPULTURA

273 points *from Arise (Roadrunner '91)*

Probably the most instantaneous, communicative and mainstream track from the band so far, *Dead Embryonic Cells* is a multi-speed hardcore with melodic echoes of Sabbath. The main riff is fairly sophisticated, like prime Anthrax, and there's a one-and-three speed metal breakdown that almost blasts. The general theme is not being asked to be born, but mixed in ambiguously is a laundry list of other complaints, including war, terrorism, biotechnology, and finally the mere inconvenience of dying. Musically, the track's charm is one attributable to the band as a whole, the undisciplined and anarchic drone of Max's riffs (a drone that is now a staple of nu-metal) coupled with the man's grandfatherly bark, which contains just enough accent to sound isolated and eccentric.

Max Cavalera on *Dead Embryonic Cells . . .*

> "*Dead Embryonic Cells*, my best memory is, after we did the video, there was an MTV party in California, and we were invited because we won some award in Brazil. So they flew us to that and James Hetfield was there and he complimented us on that video and I was speechless for the next half an hour. I didn't talk much; I was kind of like in a coma (laughs). I came out of it eventually (laughs). I'm such a huge Metallica fan, and then when James said that, I was like, 'You know we exist!?' I was thinking, 'He knows who we are!'"

206 THE BEAUTIFUL PEOPLE MARILYN MANSON

272 points *from Antichrist Superstar (Interscope/MCA '96)*

The Beautiful People turns out to be the lightning rod for the Marilyn Manson experience as far as this poll goes, the ghoulish one's next ranking coming in at a paltry 59 points. And it's no surprise, the song being his/their biggest hit, its hook being its hobbling, militaristic beat and its repetitive chorus which is a classic "us vs. them" mutterance backed up synergistically by the graphic ugliness of this band, one that tries studiously and meticulously to look like mutants grown like mould under forgotten rocks. Are they metal? See 'em live and they may as well be, wot with all those jagged guitars and frightwig visuals. The alienation is also a bonus, Marilyn succeeding in creating oneness with the teenage dispossessed. On a material level, Manson, along with Rob Zombie, is one of the few bands still melding industrial and metal to commercial success, and in the minute characteristic department, Manson (and this short slash of a song) is one of the prime examples of the whisper/shout school of metal vocalists, an effect used to pad wallets bigger and fatter within today's nu-metal cash grab sweepstakes.

Marilyn Manson on his themes . . .

> "Marilyn Manson as an entity is a true product of America. Parents realize that they're losing grasp of their youth, and they want to take it back. Yet it's too late. You made this monster and you have to deal with it. And if you don't raise your kids, someone like me is going to. That terrifies them because this is the most horrible thing that can happen, for someone like me to put something in a child's mind. However the most dangerous thing I have to offer America's youth is individuality and freethinking. A lot of my lyrics are obtained from my childhood, from people I've met along the way, experiences that I've had. I just relate these things with music so that other people will be able to relate to them also. Yet most people will have to find their own interpretation of the lyrics. I just try to be honest. That's why our lyrics are something more raw than what people might expect."

207 TERRITORY SEPULTURA

266 points *from Arise (Roadrunner '91)*

Exploding to life through an exotic patch of percussion from Igor, *Territory* collapses into a mournful hypnotic plod evoking the miserably predictable and inexorably accumulating grime crimes of zestful corrupt regimes. The track offers many surprises, including more percussion, an astonishingly Crimsonian guitar solo, jazzy breaks, inspired use of splashy cymbals and well . . . that's enough from a Brazilian death metal band, innit? Look for the wondrously inexplicable bit of thrash meditation tacked to the end of the song, a half-minute of grinding groove designed perhaps to prove that there is no design, only chaos.

Max Cavalera on *Territory* . . .

> "*Territory* is a really interesting song, especially with what's going on today, the whole Palestine/Israel fight. We were thinking about things like that even back in those days and that's what's in the news everyday now. The more I watch that, the more I think how ahead of the times that song was. Nobody was writing about things like that at that time, man. And we ended up going to Israel and filming a video for *Territory*, where there are scenes of me and the band mingling with Bedouins on the side of the road, and on the other hand, us walking in the Masada, mingling with Jewish people. It was really interesting, controversial in a way to do something like that at that time. I don't think a band would go there and do a video now; it would be kind of scary (laughs)."

208 WELCOME HOME (SANITARIUM) METALLICA

266 points *from Master of Puppets (Elektra '85)*

They figured they'd write *Fade to Black* again and here it is, *Welcome Home* opening with the same tentative soundcheck balladry before finding an ornate chorus riff and then a very cool uptempo scraper come break time. This track is a big part of people clueing to the **Master/Ride** pairings, the albums coming out quite similar in nuts and bolts componentry. *Welcome Home* contains no surprises, but enough meat to vault it well onto our chart.

209 THE ZOO SCORPIONS

263 points *from Animal Magnetism (Mercury '80)*

Proving their ability to forge heavy metal successfully from a myriad of ingredients, Scorpions compose this lead weight of a track that is both ominously slow and melodically accessible. The key is Klaus' Berlin burlesque vocal melody, which is forced to carry the song inexorably forward. The band join him a the beer-drinking round table for the swingin' chorus, one which brightens the song considerably, before we drop back down into the tantalizing, tempting murk of the Sabbatherian verse riff. Bookends the title track wonderfully, on an album with many uptempo shots at the American charts.

Rudolph Schenker on *The Zoo . . .*

> "I remember it was the first time as a rock band in America, and the management was based in New York, Leber Krebs, and they said to us, 'We have a good friend here, and he will show you the interesting parts of New York.' And he took us out and said, 'Here's this, here's this, and this street here, this is The Zoo.' And we said, 'What, The Zoo?!' 'Yeah, they call it The Zoo because it's crazy here.' Then I remember sitting somewhere in the Midwest and picked up the guitar and it was one of the only songs which I wrote on the road. I was watching television and there was a warning, what do you call it, a twister, a tornado warning and I was like (sings the riff) and I made the whole thing in around 20 minutes. And I came into the dressing room and said, 'Klaus, here, I have to play you something' and he said, 'Hey, you know what that reminds me a little bit of? The street, The Zoo' and we went back home and Klaus wrote the lyrics."

210 SAD BUT TRUE METALLICA

262 points *from Metallica (Elektra '91)*

Can't help but picture Spinal Tap breaking out of their pods when confronted with the flashing scabbards of *Sad but True*'s opening chords. But then the song lurches into a successful execution of Metallica's new Keep It Simple Stupid attitude, curiously pausing and pontificating for a few bars before illogically switching gears for a third time as James raps over a thick black Sabbath smoke. Lars gets to really reach back into percussive childhood, turning in practically nothing, which is exactly what is required. The result is a song so annoyingly Green Day memorable, that it is surely this 12 million selling album's prime example of seductive, subconscious melodic imprinting over the concrete self-evidence of fusspot substance.

Jason Newsted on *Sad but True* . . .

> "That's another album and that's a whole different planet. That was a few years after I joined and however many hundred shows later, and quite a few things learned. It's a simple song, yeah, but not necessarily so simple to execute, to make it so. At the time anyway, I didn't think so. First time with Bob Rock as a producer. First time in the hot seat, as it were. You're right under his microscope, right there in the room with him, with everything that you. . . every little scratch of a pick or any of that stuff. You know what I mean? So that was very interesting in itself. To actually have the down-tuning though, to have a nice bass that was sounding so thick and felt so good under my hands, and good headphones that worked, you know, taped into my head . . . I could do whatever I wanted to and it was just there, shaking my whole body. I would always have a subwoofer that I would keep my foot propped up on, so the vibrations would shake all through my bones. I didn't have to have it that loud in the room, but just have the subbies on that you don't really hear, but that you only feel; just have it coming up through my boots. Lately when I do it, I just take my shoes off so it's coming up right through my feet, have my feet right on the sub, stick it up right like that, yeah!"

211 WILD CHILD W.A.S.P.

257 points *from The Last Command (Capitol '85)*

Pretty effeminate way to open a W.A.S.P. album, *Wild Child* sounding like some sort of romantic pre-hair love letter, considerably restrained, which kind of works a seductive underwater magic come chorus-time, Blackie weaving an impassioned melody around those falsetto "you"s. I guess this was meant to be some sort of chart-bounding production piece (check out the sound effects brush-stroking the solo break), a ploy for serious rock god status. Of course, the next track is called *Ballcrusher*, so there you go, even if once again, the production is downright timid.

Blackie Lawless on *Wild Child* . . .

> "Most of *Wild Child* was written really before W.A.S.P. ever got a record deal. It wasn't titled. It didn't have a title until the day I actually sang the vocals. Because I didn't think *Wild Child* was that great of a title. So I just waited and waited and waited until I just couldn't wait anymore. And I mean, I was driving to the studio, knowing I was doing the vocal track that day and I was like 'OK, man, you gotta make a move' (laughs). What are we going to do? So that's what that ended up being. Originally, I was going to give the song to Nikki, to let Mötley Crüe do it, but we knew Vince couldn't sing it, because of the range of it, so I kept it. And good thing for us that we did."

212 5 MINUTES ALONE PANTERA

252 points *from Far Beyond Driven (Atlantic '94)*

5 Minutes Alone gives new meaning to the term rhythm guitar, Dime scraping bone dry this exercise in mechanical, inhuman machine rock,

Pantera gleefully running a rusted contraption without oil just to see when it will explode like shrapnel. It is a gorgeous metal moment in history, the album's catchiest and indeed rappiest hip-hopped-up track, Phil getting to ride Dime's sub-strata thump with an equally hoarse course of action. But the chorus redeems with an earth-moving groove that hides a hint of Joe Perry beneath the rage, a smoky blues haze, Dime creating an endearing old rock dimension to what is otherwise all stoic friction.

Vinnie Paul on *5 Minutes Alone* . . .

> "*5 Minutes Alone* is a song we wrote about one of the first lawsuits that we've ever gotten into. We were opening up for Megadeth at Pine Knob in Detroit and it was one of the best shows I think we've ever had. There was this one kid in the front row standing there flipping Philip off the entire time. And after about four songs Phil got sick of it and called out to the kid to stick it up his ass and at that time about 15 people in the crowd jumped the kid and pretty much beat the living shit out of him. And his dad called up our management one day during the process of this lawsuit and was blowing all this shit up about how he wanted to kick Phil's ass and one of his lines was if you just give me five minutes alone with that Phil Anselmo I'll tear that fucking punk up, you know? And Phil came up with the term, 'No, you give me five minutes alone with your ass,' so that's where that song came from."

213 THE TOXIC WALTZ EXODUS

252 points *from Fabulous Disaster (Combat '89)*

By this point, Exodus were beating a dead horse within a larger metal genre that rewarded every horse at least with a carrot and maybe an apple. *The Toxic Waltz* recalls Anthrax the most, the unattractive novelty component, albeit with massive production values and a mosh within a song about moshing that is pure gutsy, grinding groove. Steve Sousa belts out a tale in the time-honoured tradition of dance-describing songs, only this time there's blood in the pit. Lotsa words, sorta funny, slammin' riff.

Tom Hunting on *The Toxic Waltz* . . .

"Actually, I have to dedicate that title to a friend of mine, James, who is dead now. I believe it was my brother's bachelor party and we were extremely high (laughs), standing around the next day and everyone was hungover and the sun was like, 'urr,' beating down on us and he was just rambling on and rambling on, like drunk, passed out in the corner, and he came up with that phrase. He's like, 'Man, this is definitely a toxic waltz we're dancing,' or some shit like that."

214 FAIRIES WEAR BOOTS BLACK SABBATH

252 points *from Paranoid (Warner '70)*

One of the reasons we should perhaps not worship the **Paranoid** album as much as we do, *Fairies Wear Boots* rattles like a clanging empty milk can, seemingly slapdashed together — music and lysergic lyric — like some sort of doom blues jam by guys with a limited musical vocabulary and a slightly more optimistic drug budget. But there are elements of magic in Sabbatherian spontaneity, all wrapped in the complicated temporal happenstance of this being some of the earliest forged metal, for better or worse. The "better" lies in the loud power trio aspects of these arrangements and movements; the "worse" lies in the stark stupidity and tastelessness of the way these movements are stacked together.

Bill Ward on *Fairies Wear Boots* . . .

"That one, like *N.I.B.*, and some of the really early Sabbath stuff, was done at the Aston Community Center. I think the idea did come from the thing that was going on at the time between the Mods and the Rockers, which was a big thing back then. And I think it originally might have been aimed towards the skinheads. But again it was Geezer and Ozzy who put the lyric together. And it's very much an early Sabbath feel, a '67, early '68 feel in the sense of the jazz and again really no solid sense of time. We kind of just clumped my drums around Geezer and Tony really (laughs). Every time we do that song I can never play the same thing twice. Every time we go on stage it's always different. So we keep making these different versions of *Fairies Wear Boots*. It's probably pretty close but every night I never know what I'm going to do. It's usually quite close to what I had played the night before but I'm never quite sure until I'm actually doing it because it's based on wherever I am physically and wherever I am mentally at the moment; I don't base it on any level of criteria. I don't have that. I seem to be lacking in whatever it is you have to have to get it perfect or whatever every night."

215 METAL DAZE MANOWAR

249 points *from Battle Hymns (EMI '82)*

The first of many paeans to the music called steel, *Metal Daze* really evokes the band's '70s roots like few other in the catalogue. The verse riff is mainstream, meat and potatoes U.S. metal, one could picture coming out of any New York borough, and the chorus is almost southern rock in its well-wishing singalongs. But you can feel the excitement, Manowar endearing in their direct, unadorned enthusiasm for metal like no other band at the time save for Saxon. Ultimately, it is a consummate regular guy, crack-a-beer party track from a band that would become fully caught up in being bulgy Manowar starting with the very next record.

Eric Adams on *Metal Daze* . . .

"Yeah, that was great. When we recorded *Metal Daze*, we grabbed everybody. I remember we were trying to make the fans be part of the show. So *Metal Daze* was the first anthem we came out with. And every album since has always had an anthem. And we went out into the street. We were in Miami at the time. So we went out to the beaches and grabbed any hot bitches we could find, and some true brothers that were drinking with us during the day and brought them into the studio with us at night when we recorded. Nighttime is the right time, brother. That's when we record. And we had everybody in the studio at night partying down, half-naked, and we all sang that part, and we had a fucking ball doing it, it was great."

216 I DON'T KNOW OZZY OSBOURNE

247 points

from Blizzard of Ozz (Jet/CBS '80)

Track one, side one of a remarkable, some say improbable career, *I Don't Know* establishes the strangely grounded and sparse pop metal sound that only Randy Rhoads could have produced, although much of the credit could also go to this set of Daisley, Kerslake and the Oz, each with their distinct styles. I've always twinned this track with *Crazy Train* (and I'm surprised *Crazy Train* got #4 with 2940 points and *I Don't Know* couldn't muster a tenth the marks), both being angular, almost disco-thumping songs with impassioned pre-choruses and choruses to darken the oddly danceable verse sections. As well, part of *I Don't Know*'s charm is this biographical trait Oz instantly built then maintained, the idea that he is perplexed by everything.

Bob Daisley on *I Don't Know* . . .

> "OK, well, when I first started working with Ozzy, he used to tell me stories about when he was in Black Sabbath. Because Black Sabbath was considered an occult band and that sort of thing, people used to tend to ask them questions and think that they knew answers to things that other people didn't know. You know, what's really going to happen to the world? And I just wrote that song about that sort of situation. And that's why it's, 'Don't ask me, I don't know' (laughs). It was fairly simple. And the middle section, 'It's not how you play the game, it's if you win or lose'. . . what I meant is that it doesn't really matter what your philosophy is, if it's something positive and you're winning from it, you know, then that's a good thing. It was a kind of a philosophical song as well. It's up to you. Don't look to other people. It's a bit like in **Life of Brian**, the Monty Python film, when he says, 'You don't need to follow anybody! You don't need to follow me. You're all individuals.' One guy puts his hand up and says, 'I'm not!' That's what that song was about, just Ozzy's situation in Black Sabbath and people just asking him what's really going to happen."

217 EVIL
MERCYFUL FATE

246 points *from Melissa (Roadrunner '83)*

Not since **Sad Wings of Destiny** did an album of such otherworldly perfection simply drop and methodically infect. *Evil* is the crack-opening track on the debut album, and Mercyful Fate put on an immediately seductive show. The production is organic yet faultless, the groove, one of the band's best to this day twenty years later, King's intentions clear through a nasty low growl punctuated by piercing cries. And even though the track packs in a lot of events in under five minutes, it all makes perfect dramatic sense, lifting, descending, revisiting themes, Fate instantly creating a dark corner of the metal game that would always be theirs and theirs alone, this idea of elegant progressive black metal using all the most intelligent manoeuvres from traditional British metal.

King Diamond on *Evil* . . .

> "*Evil* is definitely trademark Mercyful Fate. It was the first song you ever heard if you bought something from us, the regular stuff anyway, the first album, **Melissa**. It's the first song on the album — right in your face — and it's a great sing-along song, and that has always meant a lot to both us as a band, and the fans. You can see it in the response when you're playing it."

218 (WE ARE) THE ROADCREW
MOTÖRHEAD

245 points *from Ace of Spades (Bronze '80)*

This always struck me as one of those Maiden on Sesame Street numbers, line by lining a job description awkwardly, as if there was any rock 'n' roll way to do it. But it's an inspiring direct title, supported by Lemmy selling the song over a pounding one and three jackhammer, punctuated with a memorable full-stop train wreck. Not sure how sincere Lemmy is about supporting the load-in lackies, but at least for this moment you believe the hails (and after all, Lemmy himself was once a roadie for Hendrix).

Fast Eddie Clarke on *(We Are) the Road Crew . . .*

> "By the time we got to this stage, **Ace of Spades**, **No Sleep** era, the road crew had obviously been through thick and thin with us. We had been through quite a lot together, Europe and all that. And they had joined up when we weren't doing so well. So they were more like friends, you know what I mean? We were like a team. And they prided themselves on what they did; they fancied themselves as one of the best road crews around. And there was a lot of talk that they were a good road crew. We had our guy called Mick Murphy. He was kind of our minder; he was a real tough nut. He had to be really. There was a time, when he first got involved, there was a really big . . . no, I'm not going to go into that; fuck it (laughs). But just because of that, we just wanted to do something that was a thanks to the road crew. So we bumbled about with a riff for it. Lemmy didn't have too much trouble with the lyrics. The lyrics are quite basic. We just sat down in the rehearsal room and banged out a riff and then just tidied it up a bit. We didn't really write our songs in depth. We just kind of jammed them out, you know?"

219 A QUESTION OF HEAVEN ICED EARTH

245 points *from The Dark Saga (Century Media '98)*

Death denied, heaven denied, love denied . . . all answers are elusive in this mournful closing track that begins like a power ballad and then turns uneasily but peacefully metallic. Angels sing and guitar singe, as Barlow, ever the thespian, digs into the part of man on three brinks. Bell well rung, does the bell toll for thee? As the track winds down, you never find out as limbo beckons and Schaffer turns in a gorgeous, understated solo over doomy Maiden chords which eventually are accompanied by more beautifully dovetailed female vocals.

Jon Schaffer on his listening habits . . .

"I listen to mostly non-metal stuff. If it's metal, it's usually old stuff, when we're partying or whatever, feeling a little kooky and want to go back to my childhood (laughs). I listen to Celtic guitar, classical, new age shit. But I'm not even that big of a music fan to be honest with you. I don't really sit around and listen to music. I don't watch TV either. My form of entertainment, most of the time is working the band. But if I do get free time, I build horror and sci-fi model kits, comic book characters, vinyl kits, hand paint them and stuff, plus read books, comic books. But most of the time, I'll have music on in the background, as a kind of medium there. But I don't intensely sit down and listen to it much anymore."

Jon Schaffer from Iced Earth
Judas Priest — *The Sentinel*
Blue Öyster Cult — *Cities on Flame (With Rock 'n' Roll)*
Iron Maiden — *Hallowed Be Thy Name*
Iron Maiden — *The Number of the Beast*
Black Sabbath — *Black Sabbath*
AC/DC — *It's a Long Way to the Top*
Kiss — *Creatures of the Night*
Alice Cooper — *Halo of Flies*
Alice Cooper — *Ballad of Dwight Fry*
Metallica — *Fade to Black*

220 I AM THE LAW ANTHRAX

244 points *from Among the Living (Island '87)*

A headbanging example of Anthrax's ability to take cinder block riffs and make catchy songs, *I Am the Law* documents the band's love for comic culture, something that would eventually cartoonize the band much to the chagrin of metal purists. Oscillating between mid-mosh groove, double time and firebrand thrashpunk, the track is one of those meat and potatoes working man pillars of the catalogue, hardcore made palatable, really quite S.O.D. in its grim, grey methodical lunchbucket measures.

Charlie Benante on *I Am the Law* . . .

> "I had this monster riff. That's what we used to call it, this monster riff and that was the riff to *I Am the Law*. We were on tour again in Europe, **Spreading the Disease**, and at soundchecks I would always play this and we would try to build it. And when people would hear the riff, they would say, 'Dude, that sounds like Godzilla,' you know, stomping through New York. And we were really heavily into the comic book scene at that time, especially Judge Dredd, which was a comic book from England, big, big, big character there. And that inspired us to write a song about him."

221 WOULD? ALICE IN CHAINS

243 points *from Dirt (Sony '92)*

On a record full of riff-mad metal highs and mucous-clogged lows, *Would?* straddles both camps capably, riding a tribal, Zeppelin-esque verse, exotic and swimmingly quicksanded before bursting into the rock 'n' rollsy chorus. The end of the song also ends the record with a climactic question over a musical track unrelated to the rest of the song. Lyrically, Cantrell is sparse and barely communicating, coming up with one of his many cryptic drug poems, perfectly suited to Staley's mentally anguished yet detached and jaded drone tones.

Layne Staley on stage wardrobe . . .

> "We really don't come up with ideas, we just do things. People have to understand, we just do things. We don't think of them at all. I just bought a suit and thought, 'Fuck it, this looks good, I'm going to wear it tonight.' I started wearing the suit in Toronto. But sometimes I wear the suit, sometimes I wear shorts, some-

times I wear jeans. You know, whatever I put on after I get out of the shower is what I put on for the gig. I don't feel any pressure at all. I just do whatever I do. If I had to do a gig right now, I'd wear what I'm wearing right now. I'm not one who is big on image. Like, I go to the mall, I'm shopping, I'm buying clothes, I see some red Manic Panic hair dye and I go, 'Give me that too.' It's that quick. It's not thought up or thought of. It's not, 'Hey I'm going to change and become this redhead guy and that's my new thing.'"

222 PRINCESS OF THE DAWN ACCEPT

241 points

from Restless and Wild (Brain '82)

Featuring the most garbled and confusing cut and paste fantasy metal lyric you're likely to read (suggestion: don't; just listen) *Princess of the Dawn* is a hypnotic, sophisticated track for its restraint alone, the band locking onto a mysterious riff and then following it like a night train through exotic terrain. Its guitar solo, and indeed the foreboding build towards it, is pure metal magic, extremely musical, resolving, gothic, event-packed, elliptical, a symphony of good guitary taste, once more inexorably strapped to that determined riff. Then, after a few silly cult-called chants, the song simply vanishes.

Udo Dirkschneider on *Princess of the Dawn* . . .

"Ooh, strange song. Wolf came up with the riff. He said, 'I have a really stupid riff, but it's interesting.' This was a song that after a couple of weeks in the studio we said, 'Oh no, this isn't interesting, and maybe we won't use this.' We weren't coming up with any good ideas. There was just this riff there and we said, 'This is too boring.' And then we said OK, let's do the lyrics first, which are like a Cinderella story. And then we worked on it during the whole production of the **Restless and Wild** album and the song became more and more interesting. It was a real studio creation. And then we said, let's put this song as the last song on the album and we'll see what happens, and it turned out to be a real classic Accept song in the end. You never know, sometimes all you have is a boring guitar riff, and then somehow you end up with a real classic."

223 COLD SWEAT THIN LIZZY

239 points *from Thunder and Lightning (Vertigo '83)*

Well, it ain't these short snappers on the swansong, fortresses impermeable to sympathy and production and the sly charm that arrangement can cause? *Cold Sweat* is a crude Thin Lizzy environment, but maybe it matches the crashed state of affairs that is the band at this point, less linear than on autopilot, loud without reason, screaming in a vacuum, a battle waged by John Sykes who becomes new blood for an incompatible recipient.

Scott Gorham on **Thunder and Lightning** . . .

"That was another problem. We thought we were losing and beating our heads against the wall because there weren't enough people that were actually getting what we were doing. That floored Phil especially, because he absolutely was Thin Lizzy all the way. I think what should have happened was that we should have given it a rest for a year and then maybe thought about coming back. I was too far gone at that point to think in those terms, so it never got said. Phil kept getting worse and worse, deeper and deeper into the drug thing until finally his body couldn't take it any longer and he died."

224 DIRTY DEEDS DONE DIRT CHEAP
AC/DC

239 points *from Dirty Deeds Done Dirt Cheap (Atlantic '75)*

How dare they actually waste time recording such a small empty song? This was the cheek of AC/DC or for that matter punk rock, which was to break one year hence. *Dirty Deeds* played the whole dropout trick: let the singer sing over a bit of a beat and then hit 'em with what you've got, even if the effect of these tame and simple power chords come chorus time are more of a fey and feigned glancing blow on the way to the bar for more courage juice. Even still, you believe Bon when he tugs your earlobe with the assurance that he can take care of your little problem and it won't cost much. Devilish ditty built out of scrap lumber and razor wire.

Malcolm Young on landing a great job . . .

> "I think it gets back to our starting days again. Working for a couple of bucks a week. Working our butts off, getting covered in oil and all that shit that goes with it, and when we got to play club gigs, luckily enough, we thought this is it! We don't have to work. 'Angus, we can make 50 bucks a week each here, we can survive without a day job.' That was our big plan (laughs). So everything outside of a club gig is a bonus to us. We made it 25 years ago as far as we're concerned."

225 PRINCESS OF THE NIGHT
SAXON

237 points *from Denim and Leather (Carrere '81)*

Plane, motorbike, ocean freighter, steam train, mail truck . . . your guess is as good as mine. But Biff often fondly recalls the track's beat of metal motion, *Princess of the Night* parking proud as a sort of minimalist melodic speed metal, precise, quickly picked, packed with payoffs, one of which is a jumped-up boogie passage which serves as a platform for Saxon's meat and potatoes soloing style, a tired, cawing screech to match the band's photo shoot attire. In any event, *Princess of the Night* marked a slight elevation in song construction for the band, an eye to pacing, the measured placement of mini events, aspirations past the clubs towards fulminations of what might translate at Donington.

Biff Byford on *Princess of the Night* . . .

"*Princess of the Night* on that album is classic, a classic metal song. The idea of *Princess of the Night*, I mean, all of my lyrics are pretty much from my childhood or based on experiences or history, which again, is usually from my childhood, Dallas and things. *Princess of the Night* is about a steam train. When I was a boy, I used to watch the steam trains come over the viaduct near where I lived. At night, they used to light up all the sky with all the fire and everything. And that was going to be *Wheels of Steel* but actually *Princess of the Night* was better. The train was called Princess Elizabeth basically. Millions of people think that song is about a girl but it's actually not. But you know, people can think what they want to. It's up to them."

226 COMMUNICATION BREAKDOWN LED ZEPPELIN

235 points *from Led Zeppelin (Atlantic '69)*

Zep could never claim first heavy metal album, but they could arguably claim first metal song, a stronger argument to be made for first metal song by a band widely (though very superficially) called heavy metal. *Communication Breakdown*, with its no-nonsense machine gun between the numbers riff, is that song, a short shocker with one purpose: to rock you like a hurricane. Nearly one of many innovations the band would conjure then abandon with a royal wave of the hand, heavy metal seems to be impatiently proven here, or efficiently covered off, check-listed, before the band becomes tired with its tiring self-evidence, moving on to more important business.

John Paul Jones on Led Zeppelin's early days . . .

"We didn't move into a style. I think we kind of created it. And if you would have asked me in 1969, as people did, what sort of band I was in, I would have said a progressive rock band. But then that became to mean something else. There you go banging up against categories again. That came to means something else entirely. And then it was just sort of like blues rock, because the band was quite blues-orientated. And it was just the style, the way the members of the band played together. But in terms of actual riffs, well, anything with notes (laughs), lots of notes, like *Black Dog, Good Times Bad Times* . . . those were my riffs. And anything that was kind of lurchy and chordy, were Page's riffs. That's how you tell them apart."

Chris Goss from Masters of Reality
Led Zeppelin — *Hots on for Nowhere*
Nirvana — *Heart-Shaped Box*
Jr. Walker and the All Stars — *Shotgun*
Kyuss — *Green Machine*
Marilyn Manson — *The Beautiful People*
David Bowie — *Ashes to Ashes*
Led Zeppelin — *For Your Life*
Yes — *And You and I*
Led Zeppelin — *Rock and Roll*
Jimi Hendrix Experience — *Manic Depression*

227 IRON MAIDEN IRON MAIDEN

235 points

from Iron Maiden (EMI '80)

Trying harder and writing weirder likely had a bit to do with Iron Maiden's success, and the opening twin lead of this one is certainly weird, the song thenceforth hep-hepping into a double time build, after which we relax into the brisk, exciting new style of dark metal that is the domain of a select dozen or so NWOBHM documents. But the regular fish-and-crisp yobbos in the band buy us a pint with that shamelessly glam chorus, making the world right, happy and glee-twee, comforting and commiserating with the jean jacket armies who need a little comforting right now, given that many of them got into this smoke-filled pit o' perdition with fake ID's. An ever so slightly bright, all-inclusive headbang, positioned well at the end of what is a creepy album, sending us stumbling off to the tube station with a few more tape-trading friends than we had going in.

Paul Di'Anno on *Iron Maiden* . . .

"I did like that one actually. That was one of the songs that actually got me to join up with Maiden. Because they had the song before me, when they had already worked with two other singers. I went to see them one night. I'd been offered the job. And I went to see them play, and me and my mate, actually the guy who became the drum tech for Maiden, we was best friends at school, we walked out on Maiden twice. We thought they were absolutely garbage. But that was the one song that I actually thought was any good (laughs)."

228 GYPSY URIAH HEEP

234 points *from Very 'Eavy Very 'Umble (Warner '70)*

I've always meekly (and it seems weekly) cited Heep's first album as one of the first metal albums proper (along with **In Rock**, **Black Sabbath** and **Paranoid**, all spawned in 1970). And *Gypsy* is its stomping behemoth, even if *Bird of Prey* was both more modern and more metal. *Gypsy* in fact has a Sabbath vibe and melody, with overt Deep Purple toolings, especially the manic, panicked, nightmarish keyboard work of Ken Hensley. Great production as well, hi-fived up against anything in the '70s let alone in 1970, and Sir David Byron, well, he manages to evoke the literary escape of the original Byron with this stirring, timeless tale of forbidden seduction (when's the last time you were whipped by her father?).

Mick Box on the Uriah Heep legacy . . .

"We just played hard progressive rock. The term 'heavy metal' was invented way after us, Sabbath or Deep Purple were successful. Heavy metal was just a journalistic pigeonhole. I think we were the first band to use five-part harmony in a very effective way. Prior to us it was the Beach Boys which was very soft and sweet. We gave it an edge. We were once called 'the Beach Boys of heavy metal.' We always had comparisons to Deep Purple, but my stock answer was that they only had one singer and we have five. We are very proud of our legacy and what we are producing today but if you have your family and they are all healthy, this is all you could wish for."

229 YOU CAN'T BRING ME DOWN SUICIDAL TENDENCIES

229 points *from Lights . . . Camera . . . Revolution* (CBS '90)

At the height of their game, snatching punk and metal babies off the street in equal doses, Suicidal blasted off with this ugly bit of vicious guitar thrash set to a surprisingly picket fence with rickets beat. Muir was exalted and proposed as the mini Rollins for a couple of years there and the sentiments he's hollering here fit the bulging bill, Muir stamping his credo with a boastful rhythm that is trash talkin' but not quite the skate-faced Anthrax hip-hop found elsewhere in the catalogue. Great riff though, uptown metal strapping itself around your coffee pot like Megadeth circa **Rust in Peace**.

Rocky George on success and integrity . . .

"It's really weird cause I never really expected to be where we are. It wasn't in my mind ten years ago and each year that goes by, it keeps getting better. A lot of perception has changed over time and musically people's tastes have changed and we've changed too. I'm totally different than I was back then in a lot of ways. People see that we have a lot of integrity and feel good that we've had this following for a long time. I'm just so disgusted with people: some people are just spineless pussies. They do everything for the wrong reasons; they're scared about what everyone has to say. I'm sick of these people and I know they ain't going anywhere. Sometimes there's just no other way to say shit. But remember, it's not only what you say, but you have to listen and you have to listen with your eyes too."

230 MISSISSIPPI QUEEN MOUNTAIN

229 points *from Climbing! (Windfall '70)*

As a kid, without really thinking about it, I used to find *Mississippi Queen* and *Saturday Night Special* interchangeable. And I guess both were early, metal, accidental metal, and metal so heavy they had trouble walking. *Mississippi Queen* even had trouble breathing, smothered by both an oppressive guitar riff and guitar sound, its intro lick one of the purest electric epiphanies of its age. All told, the song is written in an old dreary traditional style (think Cream, Savoy Brown, Humble Pie, Cactus, Free), but by hook or by crook, everybody in the tactical trio just rocked their bad selves out of the thing, and what we ended up with was the one song that Leslie West's been riding for 30 years.

Leslie West on *Mississippi Queen* . . .

"You know, VH1 just had this thing called the 100 Greatest Hard Rock Bands of All Time. Sammy Hagar said that Mountain was the first American heavy metal group. That made me feel great. I wrote that tune in my apartment with Corky. The funny thing was that Corky had that song with another group. It was a disco song. I said that I had a great idea for a riff and some chords. We went into the studio and we needed a count off. Felix told him to count it off and to use the cowbell. That is how that started and ended! It was 2:16 of a freight train."

231 STAND UP AND SHOUT
DIO

227 points *from Holy Diver (Warner '83)*

Given the recent pasts of Bain and Viv, it's unsurprising that *Stand up and Shout* is both a tribute to tracks like *Kill the King* and the exploding NWOBHM. It is the album's OTT rocker, its flashpot, a cage for Viv to shake, a playpen in which he paces with menace. Ronnie manages to weave mysterious spells within the lyric simultaneously with metaphors concerning the playing of live music, and all is well in the hall tonight. *Stand up and Shout* is also an expert launching bad for the precision percussion rockets of Vinny Appice, the man, on this pacemaker racer of a track, bestowing upon the world some of the most memorable and air-drummable fills ever known to man.

Ronnie James Dio on *Stand up and Shout* . . .

> "That was an interesting story. Jimmy Bain and Vivian Campbell went back to England after we had completed the album. But *Stand up and Shout* was only a backing track. So after they left, I had to write melody and lyrics for it. So they had never heard the song before, and we sent them over a copy of it. It turned out to be that album's real anthem."

232 WHITE ROOM
CREAM

226 points *from Wheels of Fire (Polydor '68)*

Volume and fuzz, as well as a crude duct-taping of the blues to some imagined new rumble . . . that's pretty much why Cream made an impression on our list. Coughed up by the British blues invasion, Cream were psychedelic hippie superstars with a rock god guitarist, inflatable egos all-around, big, big amps and at least a handful of pre-Zep precepts. *White Room* didn't extend as fully a hand to Sabbath as, for example, *Sunshine of your Love*, but at least it went places making noise. Not much more than that, really; just the new concept of the power trio accidentally forming within and without the confines of a previously uniform and uniformed music biz. Key performances: Jack Bruce's ethereal lead vocal and Ginger's busy, stumpy, frumpy Flintstone drumming. Overrated performance: Clapton's thin, meandering wah-wah fuzz solos.

Jack Bruce on *White Room* . . .

"*White Room* is a difficult one. The lyrics started out, I think, they had something to do with selling fridges to Eskimos, and then it became something about a bicycle tour of France and then ended up *White Room*, yes. In terms of psychedelia, yeah, the Beatles were pretty late in that, and pretty lame as well. The Stones were even lamer, let's face it. But we were the real thing. We were kind of, of our time, and our time was '67, really. That was the high spot of the band's career, going to the Fillmore and the Summer of Love and all that. Yeah, we were definitely out there before they were."

233 LOVE TO LOVE
UFO

225 points *from Lights Out (Chrysalis '77)*

The most Queen-like morsel of this consistently Queen-like track is the opening guitar wash which finds the band loading up on the studio trickery before a simple gong ends the shenanigans. What follows is a gorgeous and artistic bit of **Exorcist** piano bolstered by lush guitar arrangements and finally strings; all told, a fine, ambitious arsenal of intros to what is the band's most beloved epic. The oncoming verse is equally aesthete, the band turning in a Baroque string-swirled waltz, uncommonly morose for UFO, before the song returns to the dark apocalyptic march of its intro sequences, more verses and eventually a southern rock-styled blazeout with entirely new riffs, Michael electric and carnal overtop like his life depended on it.

Pete Way on *Love to Love* . . .

"I like doing it live; I think it's a great song. It was interesting; Michael would come up with the melody and I guess we jammed around the melody and we put the sort of hard front thing in, which now reminds me of Metallica or something like that, then into that melody thing. I really enjoy doing it because it's got so much scope, so much depth. I don't think there is so much of a Queen influence on it, really, but, I don't know . . . we recorded it in London (laughs). Funny enough, I think Michael has that tone that Brian May gets, but I wouldn't say that it is so much like Queen. I think at that time we took a lot of care with our songwriting, although I guess we've always done that. Ron Nevison was a big part of putting things together, although having said that, we jammed a lot of the stuff. We'd take certain elements of our songs and play through them; we're always open to things. And also, Paul Raymond's keyboards had a lot of special things about them."

234 MAN ON THE SILVER MOUNTAIN RAINBOW

224 points *from Ritchie Blackmore's Rainbow (Polydor '75)*

This venerable power metal anthem is the most characteristically Rainbow-pointed track on the wobbled debut, exhibiting the chemistry that Ronnie and Ritchie would solidify on **Rising** and **Long Live Rock 'n' Roll**. Yet *Man on the Silver Mountain* is sluggish, unadorned and not all that gothic, sort of *All Right Now* crossed with *Gates of Babylon*, in effect more functional fortification than cathedral. Its riff is almost a modest update on *Smoke on the Water*'s simple hook, exhibiting unremarkable yet dependable solid footing, Ritchie plodding along perfectly in step with an almost weary Ronnie. The thick old oak of wizard rock.

Ritchie Blackmore on *Man on the Silver Mountain* . . .

"We did the drums on that one in three edits, because we had a good friend of ours playing drums, Gary Driscoll, and he was a very funny drummer. We would be recording and he would often just stop. And we would say, 'Why did you stop?' And he would go, 'Well, I thought someone told me to stop through the headphones.' And we'd go, 'Well no, nobody told you to stop,' so we would carry on playing. The next time . . . he was one of these drummers who moved around a lot and his headphones would start to come off as he was playing, and it was hilarious to watch him trying to keep his headphones on, on his head and balanced, when he was playing the drums. Of course he failed every time, because halfway through the song, his headphones would come off and crash onto the cymbals and we'd have to stop again. So it was really hilarious how we got through that song."

235 BEYOND THE BLACK METAL CHURCH

224 points *from Metal Church (Ground Zero '84)*

Epic, lusty and crunching at once, *Beyond the Black* is evidence of this band's riff mastery early on, demonstrating an ability to compete somewhere between Metallica, Mercyful Fate, Yngwie, Fates Warning, Exodus, and Seattle homers like Culprit and Queensryche. Quite proggy with dark acoustic moments, *Beyond the Black* is fantasy rock pure of headbanging spirit, pounding mid-paced and rhythmic, drenched in old definition goth, lacerated by a speed metal break that retains the previous medieval tones even while David Wayne is screaming his head off. Ultimately the song points to exciting possibilities for the future of American metal, the idea that crushing uncompromising post-NWOBHM gloom tones could in fact go mainstream.

David Wayne on his witchcraft past . . .

"Well, to be honest with you, I was what you would call a practising crafter, or to be more blunt, I enjoyed the practice of witchcraft. I had fun with that stuff; I'm not going to lie about it. It was like a drug to me. I had quite a collection of herbs, tinctures, powders; I had an extensive library, on what some people would call the dark arts. And I was miserable, I wasn't very happy with it. And I'm not going to beat anybody over the head with the Bible or whatever, because I think people need to make their own decisions, be they bad or be they good. Because I for one, when I was having my little forays, and sexual mores, I certainly didn't listen to anybody. I've always had to go to the school of hard knocks. And I had to do that with my crafting."

236 SIN CITY
AC/DC

224 points *from Powerage (Atlantic '78)*

Just off the Highway to Hell, *Sin City* is a serious place, plunked at side one, track one, the band's first big dark rocker amidst a catalogue that so far has been designed for spitball battles in detention room. Panoramic, wide, dramatic and climatic, *Sin City* is AC/DC's first statement of quiet confidence stuck quivering on an album that otherwise is up to the usual beer-goggled shenanigans.

Angus Young on the loss of Bon Scott . . .

> "I think it's just something that is part of you. It's like you lost someone close to you, in your family, or a very close friend. You always got that feeling they're there but you just, I suppose, miss them in the physical sense. There's always memories that keep coming back to you, and it doesn't matter what the situation is. You could be travelling, you could be relaxing somewhere, or going to play or being in the studio, there's always something that reminds you."

237 ANGEL WITCH
ANGEL WITCH

223 points *from Angel Witch (Bronze '80)*

Angel Witch (the album; one of the hallowed, seminal NWOBM documents) opened with Heybourne's first-ever written song, *Angel Witch* having been penned when Kevin was a mere tyke of 16 or 17. A classic opener, *Angel Witch* rolled off the forked tongue with a corker of a melody, cranked with a heavy metal rumble that possessed the crux character set of all those 7" singles flowing out of the NWOBHM. As well, Kevin's voice was a perfect match for the mystique of the music, naïve, almost hurt. The man could really sell fear. It is a sweet bit of seductive melody before the album cracks open with storm clouds that would darken and dampen the entire genre that would unfold over the next three years.

Kevin Heybourne on *Angel Witch* . . .

> "The basic premise of the rhythm is something like the one from the band Pink Fairies. I think the song was *Chambermaid.* It was something like 'she took me to a room and hit me with a broom'; it kind has the same rhythm and the same chord progression. The Baphomet picture for the single, the goat thing, we got that from the Tate Gallery in London, same place as the album cover painting. We had to get the rights from the gallery to use the transparency for the album cover. I originally I saw it in a book by Dennis Wheatley. I've always been interested in that stuff but I've never taken it seriously. I see religion as religion is, you know what I mean? I think it can be just as bad as Satanism. But I mean we were just into the old Hammer horror films. It's just imagination and fantasy. I thought, you know, a lot of bands sing about love and stuff like that, real issues, and I just wanted to get away from that, do pure fantasy. A lot of people out there want to hear that, you know?"

Kevin Heybourne from Angel Witch

Black Sabbath — *Hole in the Sky*
Megadeth — *Holy Wars . . . The Punishment Due*
Metallica — *Dyers Eve*
Rush — *Xanadu*
Megadeth — *Take No Prisoners*
Pariah — *The Brotherhood*
Alice In Chains — *Angry Chair*
Thin Lizzy — *Bad Reputation*
Judas Priest — *Victim of Changes*
Black Sabbath — *Symptom of the Universe*

238 JAILBREAK THIN LIZZY

221 points *from Jailbreak (Vertigo '76)*

Hard to think of a better James Bond riff than that one (*Secret Agent Man*?), especially with Phil's hushed warnings about a particularly eventful night to come. The mystique of the song is in its spaces, some of which Phil fills with cautious yet threatening thespian aplomb. And for once in a song, the break is truly just that, the culmination of the gangland ruse, sirens wailing, shapes flashing in the night, a successful execution thereof which might result in the reunions and new unions celebrated in *The Boys Are Back in Town*.

Scott Gorham on ambition . . .

> "There was just this love of what we were doing and where we were going. We felt we were a band that didn't really sound like anyone else out there. Maybe that was a commercial death. We weren't following the norm. We weren't absolutely radio-friendly. Phil and I had the same kind of sense of humour. We had started this thing, so we were going to finish this thing. We were going to be the best rock band in the world. It was all that kind of attitude. If you can't keep up with us then move over and let someone else in. We liked calling ourselves the Thin Lizzy juggernaut."

239 A CHANGE OF SEASONS DREAM THEATER

221 points *from A Change of Seasons (Eastwest '95)*

The fabled progger to end all proggers. Or so we thought, Dream Theater returning in '99 with an even more elaborate and elongated concept called **Scenes from a Memory**. In any event, *A Change of Seasons* contains all sorts of Dream Theater trademarks, main constant being big, blustery, busy, almost tribal heavy parts, often touched with a bit of castle rock, LaBrie always actorly and dead-serious about his role as storyteller extraordinaire. Like *Metropolis — Part 1* and Marillion before it, the band is aware of bases to be covered, Dream Theater more or less checklisting through a rainbow of emotions and motions, arriving at a definition of progressive metal that is a composite of the patchy history before it.

James LaBrie on *A Change of Seasons . . .*

> "Oh boy, well, there you're getting into an epic song. That was a song that was around for a while and then finally we took the time to sit down and put it all together and arrange it properly and make a 23-minute song out of it. It was exciting to do because everybody back then . . . it was released in 1995, but even when we were out on the **Images and Words** tour, and the **Awake** tour especially, we had tons of people saying, 'You know, we've heard about this 20, 22-minute song you have in the works.' And we would be like, 'Well it's just an idea we have at this point; we haven't sat down and made it complete yet.' So we knew after the **Awake** album we had to sit down and do something with it. And it's a really cool song for us to play live because there are just so many different sections to it and it's moody and it really is epic."

240 DREAMING NEON BLACK NEVERMORE

220 points *from Dreaming Neon Black (Century Media '99)*

Within Nevermore's smothering, battering guitar-drunk canon, everybody remembers the quiet moments in this plush, gorgeous, dark, mostly acoustic track, specifically the shining harmonized "nothing" before an appropriately swampy metal dirgeness ensues. It is a haunting, Floyd-like title track with deep dark memorable memories, high-quality arrangements, and above all, a multi-dimensional vocal performance from Warrel that is brilliantly thespian. The plot twists are legion, the playing first-rate and for a truly progressive track, it all makes sense by the end, Nevermore managing to tie up all the musical loose strings, even if the literary mystery of the drowning death within remains.

Warrel Dane on **Dreaming Neon Black** . . .

"The record tells a simple story about a guy who goes quietly mad, after losing a woman who was very close to him, not knowing what happened to her, not having closure, having nightmares about her being drowned, horrible feelings about his own self-weakness, blaming himself, and then eventually blaming God and denouncing God. For me it was more of a challenge in terms of writing lyrics based around emotion, because I'd never really done that before. The story has some basis in reality, but it's been embellished a little bit. I don't kill myself at the end of my story (laughs). It's not an overblown concept like most concept albums. It's more of an enclosed very simple story, something that I think a lot of people can relate to just because it is really emotional."

241 FOOLIN' DEF LEPPARD

220 points *from Pyromania (Mercury '83)*

Foolin' was actually an example of the specific advantages such a huge commercial sound could bring to bear to the right track. A classic whisper to roar rocker, *Foolin'* stayed interesting during the mellow part, given all that hi-fidelity, and then exploded into chivalrous epic nether-zones come that wide-angled metal chorus. Sure, the vocals sounded machine-tooled beyond the warm wet circles of rock 'n' roll, but combined with that firestorm of quite sinister guitars, it was almost the epiphany of the album. And in umbrella terms, the song found a way to be metal, or at least dark, while on paper it was nothing more than a glorified prototype power ballad.

Joe Elliott on *Foolin'* . . .

"*Foolin'*, when we wrote the lyrics, that was definitely a nod to *My Generation*, the stuttering F bit (sings it). We kept throwing things out there, 'We want it to sound like The Who!' and they were like, 'No you don't, but you can do this.' And it was like bringing all the bits in. 'You can't make a record that sounds like

1964.' It was the idea that nobody had stuttered since Bachman Turner Overdrive. And then even when we did that, I specifically remember, on the *ooh* part of the *foolin'*, they brought into it massive amounts of vibrato to sound like singers. It had to be screamed, it had to be terrorist-like (laughs), but at the same time it had to have a quality to it that was alien to what everybody else was doing. So it was totally a unique sound."

242 ALISON HELL ANNIHILATOR

219 points *from Alice in Hell (Roadrunner '90)*

Central track on the band's most beloved album, *Alison Hell* is fraught with all sorts of unnecessary wankery, including (count 'em) five intros, with the worst bit of faux-prog puff being the ballerina/falsetto break, which has got to be the absolute pinnacle of Jeff Waters' Spinal Tapfoolery. But (almost) all is forgiven due to the one-two punch of the song's sterling silver verse riff and attendant chorus slam. Standing back, one can see how Waters is in creation of a classy, stadium rock thrash akin to nothing out there, save for Megadeth. High standards from the inside, with notoriously high standards demanded of his players, Waters instantly established Annihilator as a professional and serious metal force worthy of the pretty healthy sales and video play that briefly ensued.

Jeff Waters on *Alison Hell* . . .

"That's definitely the song that kicked Annihilator's career into the metal 'big leagues.' It's the song off the record that had a wide variety of styles all in one song. My catchy, or annoying, high voice in the chorus, Rampage's growly, mischievous vocals, the bass intro and the solo sections are the highlights of that one. It's one of those rare gems that comes along very infrequently in a songwriter's life span."

Jeff Waters from Annihilator
AC/DC — *Back in Black*
AC/DC — *Hells Bells*
AC/DC — *Highway to Hell*
Kiss — *Detroit Rock City*
Judas Priest — *The Sentinel*
Iron Maiden — *Hallowed Be Thy Name*
Judas Priest — *Electric Eye*
Judas Priest — *Victim of Changes*
Slayer — *Angel of Death*
Metallica — *Master of Puppets*

243 ATOMIC PUNK VAN HALEN

218 points *from Van Halen (Warner '78)*

One of the band's darker, more metallic numbers, *Atomic Punk* somehow reprises the overdriven cosmic heft of *Space Station #5* while talking back the word punk from those who would dare make bad English music. Simply another example of a band on a plane past the last, *Atomic Punk* served as a reminder that buried beneath the debut album's recurring light-hearted merry-go-round buffoonery, there are real jungle cats with sharp teeth. Nowhere on the album is Eddie more black and blue and note-dense than on *Atomic Punk*, the song ripping a strip more in keeping with the Teutonic works of Uli Roth than those of wiseacre-fer-miles David Roth.

Alex Van Halen on keeping it natural . . .

> "I think the best way to describe the whole big picture is that when you go to play, and try to be creative, it's just down the how you feel at the time. I wouldn't say it was easy, but to write something for a specific purpose — 'we're going to write a hit' — can become very mechanical. So we don't do that. We feel that every little mechanical process in the way of us can hamper our flow. We just play what we like. We genuinely like what we do and we like to keep it interesting for ourselves. And this boils down to the fact that we are not really any different from our audience."

244 STRANGLEHOLD TED NUGENT

218 points *from Ted Nugent (Epic '75)*

Odd that the two lonesome Ted tracks that would crack our poll, live or die on big steel mill riffs that howl through the night shift, belching the smoke that means paid mortgages for the working man. But of course, *Stranglehold* is an oddity, being interminably long and just as slow, skulking and shoulder-bulking like a patient jungle cat, patient but not willing to enter the night's slumber hungry. What develops over time is essentially a dark and doomy blues epic, not unlike an efficient *Dazed and Confused,* Holmes crooning all soulful, Grange and Davies locking hypnotically, Ted's Gibson Byrdland moaning, advancing, fading, driving towards well-planned, methodically realized conclusions.

Ted Nugent on *Stranglehold* . . .

> "In the case of *Stranglehold,* the incredible, soulful, Aretha Franklin-like vocals that Derek St. Holmes brought to the lyrics was every songwriter's dream. So I take plenty of credit for those mystical moments, but I give a gargantuan salute to my collaborators. There's a grinding, absolute musical homage that we paid to our rhythm and blues motivators. Really, if you really pay attention, and get past the intensity of the playing itself, there is a James Brown, Wilson Pickett, Sam & Dave, Chuck Berry grunt factor that really spurred us forward. Those moments, they just reek of that dynamic, even when we play them in the year 2001. So when you hear the performance, the fire has not waned one spit. I just get . . . it's just hysterical."

245 WORKING MAN RUSH

217 points

from Rush (Anthem '74)

Working Man features Alex Lifeson's first and last Black Sabbath riff, Alex mournfully unravelling a weighty tapestry that slows everybody down, allowing the time and space for Geddy to get oddly bluesy with his legendary shrill shriek. Great idea too, the lyric showing empathy like BTO's *Blue Collar* and Skynyrd's *Simple Man*, Rush going the extra mile and extolling the virtues of cold beer. Later in the track, Sabbath is invoked once again with a jammy and raw power trio break, nicely placed and quite necessary given the song's epic yet slothful heave.

Geddy Lee on the band's formative years . . .

> "Well, it has to do more with the period than anything. Alex and I were already starting to write more complex stuff, and part of what wasn't working with our first drummer was the fact that he was more of a rock purist, and Alex and I wanted to play more complex stuff. And Neil coming into the band was a kind of confirming final piece of the puzzle. That was very much where he was at. He liked to play things that were very difficult to play, and that was the direction Alex and I were moving in. It had a very catalytic effect."

246 HAIR OF THE DOG NAZARETH

217 points

from Hair of the Dog (A&M '75)

My vote for best use of cowbell by drunken Scots, *Hair of the Dog* is a surprising bit of hi-fidelity modern metal for 1975. No surprise it was a hit. That rhythm is pure rock in blood infectious, plus the chorus sez "son of a bitch," a bit of good-natured cursing for controversy. A winner from start to finish, the song's got a fancy sailor's knot of the riff, which ties tight for tall power chords come chorus time, the song's moment of truth, Dan McCafferty driving the point home with his signature paint-peeling roar, one that fellow Scot Brian Johnson would ride to monster fame five years later.

Dan McCafferty on the band's reputation for alcohol consumption . . .

> "We are fond of a jar or two. It has been known for alcohol to cross our lips (laughs). But drug problems, no. Because I think, again, having families and stuff like that, the little man in the back of your head goes 'you do it and you die.' It just never appealed to us."

247 THE SIGN OF THE SOUTHERN CROSS BLACK SABBATH

217 points *from Mob Rules (Warner '81)*

Tony is dangerously riding the line of self-parody on this riff, but it's not all his fault. He positions himself closed by injecting the situation with game and gamy gothic, then gets prodded further through a lame lyric delivered by a vocal presence that is flowing robe wizardry personified. Still, the atmospheric verse recalls favourably *Heaven and Hell* and Vinny Appice exhibits his greatest glory, his ability to marble slow material with massive, memorably rhythmic fills. No one pushes air like Vinny, and without him, this song might have bogged badly. Although to be fair, a version with Bill Ward might ring with an air of authenticity missing within this manufactured version of the band.

Ronnie James Dio on *The Sign of the Southern Cross* . . .

> "I love that song; I think it's a great song. That's a song everybody always mentions when you talk about that album. I've always loved that title. When I was a trumpet player when I was a little kid, there was a song called *The Southern Cross*. And I did a little research into it. The Southern Cross is very Australian-related as well. But I just loved the idea of the Southern Cross. So when it came time to write a track, we needed something that was going to be a little more *Heaven and Hell*-ish, and that was the title we put to it. And I remember it was a lot of fun to write."

Silenoz from Dimmu Borgir
Dio — *Rainbow in the Dark*
W.A.S.P. — *Wild Child*
Judas Priest — *Metal Gods*
Saxon — *747 (Strangers in the Night)*
Iron Maiden — *Powerslave*
Darkthrone — *Ablaze in the Northern Sky*
Black Sabbath — *Devil and Daughter*
Napalm Death — *Suffer the Children*
Exodus — *Piranha*
Agent Steel — *Agents of Steel*

248 DISSIDENT AGGRESSOR JUDAS PRIEST

215 points

from Sin After Sin (CBS '77)

Insane, incinerating progressive metal, *Dissident Aggressor* makes the catalogue to come a comedy of errors. This was a band operating at the creative fringes of metal — hell, of progressive rock — Simon Phillips and his splash crashes being a big part of the song's intellectual thrust, Phillips making you think it's something other than 4/4 tome when it's not. The song's intro is one of the most dramatic in metal, Halford piercing the air with one of his patented Metal God screams before Phillips and his toms count us in. The verse riff is massive, like a fog, and once Priest collapse into the chorus, the contrast in grooves is glorious. Depressing, for it is the likes of *Exciter*, *Victim of Changes* and most pertinently *Dissident Aggressor* that offer a glimpse at what was lost with the ensuing simplistics of **British Steel** and beyond.

Rob Halford on the band's methodologies . . .

> "There was always friction in Priest. There was always that there. Everybody wanted to do everything else. I would have liked, in Priest, to go in the direction of a band like Queen for example. If you really sit down and have a complete understanding of the mind and the music of Judas Priest, it's very much in that kind of Queen-like approach. You can do anything.

Anything. I mean, just look at what Judas Priest has done, the different kinds of music that we created. It's remarkable, really. I think a lot of people miss that. They just look at it from album to album. But if you look at the diversity and all the adventures that Priest had, it's remarkable. I don't think there's ever been, or will ever be, another metal band that can make those kinds of things happen, and make them stick."

249 TRAPPED UNDER ICE METALLICA

214 points *from Ride the Lightning (Music for Nations '84)*

Along with *Creeping Death*, *Trapped under Ice* was the throwback track, the pure thrasher, no fancy stuff, none of that confusing slowing down. Of course already, given the talent in the band and this album's brilliant, eccentric production, *Trapped under Ice* is state-of-the-art thrash, tight as a drum, an improvement over anything on **Kill 'Em All**, with one stroke of the pen, better than Exodus. It is **Ride the Lightning**'s anchor to purity, although granted, at the time, no one complained about the band's increasing sophistication the way they did with the Black Album and **Load**.

Lars Ulrich on fame . . .

"I'm fucking more hungry. I want to get this shit to as many people as possible. I'm more vibed and enthusiastic then I can ever remember being before. It's got nothing to do with how many thousands of square feet my house is, or how fucking fast my car can drive. I'm not doing anything different with my money than any other 27-year-old kid would do with a shitload of money. One of the bizarre things that happens when you sell records is that they start giving you all this money. We're more comfortable, but it doesn't have shit to do with how we play or anything else. Our feet are firmly on the ground."

250 SATAN'S FALL
MERCYFUL FATE

214 points *from Melissa (Roadrunner '83)*

A crooked finger invites the listener into this labyrinth of a track, victim unaware that the instant bouncy rock song of the first minute will evaporate into hellish witch cackles and Crimsonian guitar runs, followed by eight more minutes of progressive metal madness. In essence, it's a fairly jumbled pancake stack of riffs, one after another, taking you through the catacombs, 666 left and right zigs and zags resulting in death by maze. The only nod to normalcy is that the opening riff returns after an eternity away and makes a perfunctory bow as the band performs a rare jammy rock 'n' roll star closing wind-up note. Verdict: the band's worst dozen riffs lined up and shot.

King Diamond on *Satan's Fall* . . .

> "That one is really fun playing live, because you just get thrown all over the place. Of course, it's so long that you have to get around, but you certainly do in that one. There's all kinds of music in that one song. It so great, but at the same time so heavy. It's got everything that you know Mercyful Fate for."

251 STONE COLD CRAZY
QUEEN

212 points *from Sheer Heart Attack (EMI '74)*

When Queen broke huddle and made metal mayhem, they were on fire. *Stone Cold Crazy* is such a sneak attack, Queen creating a short, shocking thrash update on *Black Dog* and by extension, *Oh Well*, shutting down for the vocal then exploding like a pistol shot to the face. And its insanity is intensified by the surging production of the thing, electricity with angry, unpredictable free will, Taylor on crack, May bouncing checks with his pence pick. A brilliant and smug set of brief manoeuvres, *Stone Cold Crazy* is as long as it needs to be, over and out impatiently with a faux-spontaneous mind change of a lurching chord.

Brian May on his trusty axe . . .

"I'm still using the same guitar that my dad and I built years ago. It's made out of pieces of a fireplace and a table, junk that was laying around. It's well looked after, and if I ever lost it, it would be a great blow. I use it 95% of the time everywhere, except for acoustic stuff. It has a wide range of tones within itself, which gives it its different tones. Everyone has a sound in their head that they try to get close to, and I feel lucky that I have mine. Basically my sound is just a lucky combination of my guitar and amplifier. I used to call my guitar tone a splotter tone; it's warm, like a voice, but it also has that edge to it which gives it that articulation. To me, the guitar is the most expressive instrument ever invented in the world. And that's why kids still pick them up. They may be taught the piano or violin, but on their own time, for pleasure, they pick up the guitar. The reason is it just does that to you. It gets out your anger, your tears; it's that kind instrument. This may sound stupid, but it just makes that great big fat noise that does something for me, and for others."

252 DAZED AND CONFUSED LED ZEPPELIN

212 points *from Led Zeppelin (Atlantic '69)*

Dazed and Confused is the sight and sound and crackly airborne electricity of an impossible Soviet cargo plane horrifically listing. It is the unfathomable stretch of grey sky where the hard blues of the late '60s turn into the doom of Black Sabbath's ground zero album one, track one. One could argue (and that wouldn't be me) that Zep — I is the first metal album of all time, led by this mournful witch with cancer wallow, as well as *How Many More Times*, *Communication Breakdown* and *Good Times Bad Times*. If it doesn't bore you to tears, you may take pleasure in the individual performances, not so much Page or Jones, but Robert in full throttle peak fitness shriek and Bonham, with his bar-ending upendings, relentlessly inventive and vice versa, maybe rock's most interesting practitioner at the decade's crusty crux outside of Keith Moon. Legend has it that live, this song would go on for days and on rare occasions, weeks,

Peter Grant snapping off crisp thousand-dollar bills to promoters who would have to cancel and/or postpone and rebook three or four nights worth of stadium acts while Page sawed and scratched his way through significant chunks of the city's upcoming entertainment schedule.

253 RUST IN PEACE . . . POLARIS MEGADETH

211 points *from Rust in Peace (Capitol '90)*

If you weren't drained by the time you got to this ghoulish little two-fister, you were rewarded by a catchy swingtime thrash riff which by the time *Polaris* comes around, has accelerated into a classic thrash romp that musically takes you to that agitated place where nuclear missiles might be launched out of petulance, ego and revenge . . . damn the consequences, damn the torpedoes. As with much of the album, this final track finds Megadeth blessed with an embarrassment of riff riches, all of which get used, perhaps incongruously. But hey, with guitars that sweetly sinewy, you want to grab all you can, the listener brought into the factuality that this album is as much about good riffs as it is about good songs.

Marty Friedman on *Rust in Peace* . . .

> "I thought that was going to be the song that broke us into the mainstream of the world. I thought that was the best riff that we had, and our producer Mike Clink also thought so. And Mike Clink, at that time had just finished **Appetite for Destruction** from Guns N' Roses, and it was the biggest rock album of all time as far as I was concerned. And when he thought we were going to be huge because of that riff and *Rust in Peace*, I got all excited, because I agreed. And it turned out to be a sleeper and nobody really picked up on it. But I always thought it was a classic Megadeth riff."

254 ABIGAIL KING DIAMOND

211 points *from Abigail (Roadrunner '87)*

The evil beating coronary crux of King Diamond's unsavoury tale of adultery, pregnancy, possession and spikes, *Abigail* is a trademark King song full of creepy high vocals, incongruous riffs that give way to horror metal grooviness, and at its heart, a half-time grind driven by clear, stinging singing from King Corpsepaint and clarion ride cymbal from tech wizard Mikkey Dee, now long-time basher with Motörhead. Pretty progressive come twin solo time as well, LaRocque and Denner howling in the night, perhaps freaked out and looking for freedom from Devilman's ghoulish otherworld vision.

King Diamondon *Abigail* . . .

> "Yes, I do like that one. There are some things in there that are very difficult to sing live, where, depending on where in the set it is, if it's towards the end of the set where you're pretty pumped out of energy, when there isn't much there, it's tough, because some of those notes are so extremely high. That's one thing I've learned about that song. We are still playing it of course, and I love playing it, still today; definitely one of the King Diamond milestones."

255 HOLE IN THE SKY BLACK SABBATH

211 points *from Sabotage (Warner '75)*

Possibly the most goddamn Black Sabbath song of the whole Black Sabbath catalogue, *Hole in the Sky* rocks positively and gravely lead-poisoned with the original line-up's unspeakable chemistry, here more of a smoking, blood-red chemical cocktail given the manic mental breakdowns plaguing the band by 1975. Ozzy lets loose with one of his most powerful, confident vocals, white-knuckling his unique pipes through (like a lance; never over) a formidably authoritative power swell from Tony, Geezer and Bill. Tony . . . well, the riff is godly, mountain-moving stuff, and so is his freight train of a guitar sound, but look deep, and you will find one of his most musical solos until say, *Turn up the Night,* not many years, but a lifetime later.

Bill Ward on *Hole in the Sky* . . .

> "I love the 'dish ran away with the spoon' line; again, some of these lyrics, I can't remember them. *Hole in the Sky* is great to play. It's a tough one for a drummer because you want to push ahead but you have to lay back. That one is really behind the beat. So that one is kind of tricky. You've got to drive it hard but you've got to keep relaxed on it, otherwise you'll blow the track."

256 DESERT PLAINS JUDAS PRIEST

210 points *from Point of Entry (CBS '81)*

Here's a measured level-headed mid-metal rocker that seems like the mean median average from this blue/grey album. And speaking of visuals, the tale seems to relate an approximation of the album cover, Halford low-key/low-volume crooning a white line fever lyric about grinding through the desert on a motorcycle (full moon rising to sunrise), the culmination being a burning rubber screech to a halt after which the main character collapses into the waiting arms of his love interest. Except the front cover inexplicably features an infinite ream of computer paper, which gets more confusing butted up against the enigmatic album title. Musically, the track lives and dies on a strong rhythmic backbone, because Halford is distant, even laconic, and the guitars simply lay down bisecting and trisecting angles, even the track's solos possessing an aimless wandering quality.

Ian Hill on the **Point of Entry** sessions . . .

> "That was the first one we recorded in Ibiza, Spain. There's lots of distractions, I don't know about influences (laughs). We spent most of the time on the beach or in nightclubs or driving motorcycles through the mountains. It was great fun. But maybe that influenced us (laughs). With that album, it wasn't so much pres-

sure to be more commercial. We always had artistic license or artistic rights where if we didn't want to do something, we didn't have to. But these people do know their business. If they come to us and say, 'Listen, I don't think there's anything on here that's going to get you onto rock radio. How about trying this?' We'll obviously listen and pay attention to that. It was only ever suggestions."

257 CHEMICAL WARFARE
SLAYER

209 points *from Haunting the Chapel (Metal Blade '84)*

Everything's fast, fast, fast on this one except the main riff, which is a strangely sing-songy and simple contraption, over which Araya has chosen his finest Cronos upchuck. Long, dense, speedy and ultimately smothering, *Chemical Warfare* benefits from a recording that is actually more powerful and bassier than that of the follow-up album **Hell Awaits**. Closes with a choking blanket of sound that so poetically captures the main thrust of the (dashed-off?) lyric.

Dave Lombardo on *Chemical Warfare* . . .

"Another classic. Everybody tells me things like that. Even my own band members in Fantomas talk to me about it, tell me how great that song was. It was just fun. That whole era, that whole time, was just really interesting for me."

258 BATTLE HYMN
MANOWAR

207 points *from Battle Hymns (EMI '82)*

A closer that offers a glimpse of the Valhalla-booted valour that is to come, the bombast that is to be, and the bikes and broads that belong with the territory, *Battle Hymn* is a sort of loud Viking ballad, galloping but not swiftly, the band advancing through smoky hill and dale to the sound of Joey's buzzing bass and a choir of leather angels backing Eric's every word with violent deed. It is almost laughably over the top, especially with the debut's clanky production values, but the formula will be explored time and time again over the next twenty years, will much more powerful results.

Eric Adams on *Battle Hymn* . . .

> "The quiet part in the middle, when we recorded that, I'm laying down all these tracks because it's my first album and I wanted to sing, I wanted to do harmonies with myself, all this crap, so I'm throwing all these parts down, having a great time doing it, and then I go back home. I'm done with my parts and I go home. And Joey is mixing down the album, and he calls me back. I mean, I'm home for a few hours, from Florida to New York. So the phone rings and Joey goes, 'Brother, you fucked up one note.' And I'm 'Why, what do you mean?' 'You know the slow part in *Battle Hymn*? It sounds like you're a little flat on one note, brother.' I had to fly all the way back down to sing one fucking note. I'll never forget this; I flew in, the airport right to the studio, I sang the one note, right back to the airport and back home (laughs). It was fucked up (laughs), but I mean, that just shows you how we are. It has to be right. This is going to be around when we're not, and that's how we feel about any project we do."

259 HEADING OUT TO THE HIGHWAY JUDAS PRIEST

207 points *from Point of Entry* (CBS '81)

Sister song to *Breaking the Law* (and I do mean sister, little sister with asthma), *Heading out to the Highway* yearns similarly for escape at roughly the same speed-reading. But this girl's saddled with responsibility, anchoring an album which for the most part is a wallflower compared to the harder stupidity of **British Steel**. Once more, Sir Robert sounds all Broadway, relating a tale that is more or less Alice's *Eighteen* with resolution. This new vanilla wafer Priest however didn't last, fan uproar and low sales pushing the band into note-dense realms and subsequently stadiums come 1982.

Glenn Tipton on longevity . . .

> "We've weathered the storm as you know on many occasions. There was the death and thrash era and the punk era, and Priest have been all through these and we've had to just grin and bear it, bite our lip and sit in there and survive and we've always come out of it stronger. I think it gives us the determination to do that. It's like all these rumours now. OK, we'll just bite our lip and let it all be said and at the end of it our album will be the answer to that. People know we can deliver live now and it's a great thing to see. I don't think resurgence — I think maybe re-emergence is a better term. Metal has always been there and classic metal is always going to be in demand. This sort of silent majority out there that just want metal, true metal back. We've always been ambassadors for that and flown the flag and it's great that's emerging again and we'll go out and do our bit for it next year."

260 WHEN THE LEVEE BREAKS LED ZEPPELIN

205 points *from IV (Atlantic '71)*

Thundering, throbbing, reverberating blues is just one of the many things Zeppelin excelled at, and *When the Levee Breaks* is a good example of how their chemistry conspired to form something that was so compelling, it was considered base or flash by purists at the time, this one completely transforming an old Memphis Minnie tune into a juggernaut of new blues will. Plant adopts a low haunting hum and distant harmonica cuts angles in what is otherwise a mercifully smothering pillow. But it is Bonham with his ham hock shuffle that forms the most innovative performance on the track, his legendary and now much-sampled sound captured by random experiment in the boomy hallway at Headley Grange, the old mansion where the album was recorded. But like I say, innovation is taboo with respect to the blues, so Zeppelin never garnered the respect in this field from those who manned the genre's ivory towers.

John Paul Jones on *When the Levee Breaks* . . .

> "Headley Grange was a big cold, damp house (laughs). You had very large rooms which were very echoey. You had a big stairwell which was even more echoey. The sound on *When the Levee Breaks* happened because Bonzo was so loud in the room we were playing in - because it had these hardwood floors - that we pushed his set out into the hall (laughs), into the stairwell, because the sound was smashing around all over the place. And we just stuck a couple of mikes up and got this huge drum sound. So things like that came by accident. And you'd have amplifiers in the cupboards and amplifiers outside in the garden but it was quite good fun."

261 DR. FEELGOOD MÖTLEY CRÜE

204 points *from Dr. Feelgood (Elektra '89)*

Man, one of my favourite live moments of all time was watching this song explode — track one — live at Massey Hall in Toronto, late '90s reunion with Vince. That massive heavy metal factory floor shuffle, the guitar-polluted extra bars before the verse starts . . . it's a classic moment from a band with many classic moments, although many not this objectively well-written. Recording next door to Aerosmith might have had something to do with the tune's Perry-esque riff, but then again, Crüe had been plowing this field since *City Boy Blues*. Deeper in, there's more percussive brilliance, stops and starts, fits and starts, air drum moments, pure hair metal mania, Crüe writing some of their grooviest stripper rock in years, Bob Rock brightening the band's prospects through an element of discipline missing from past booze-throughs.

Nikki Sixx on the tour after the **Dr. Feelgood** tour . . .

> "For us it was the fact that we had been touring for another 13

months, but the demand was out there to have the band go tour again. We had just done about 15 shows in Europe, and everybody was like, 'You guys want to go headline festivals?' And we are like, 'No we want to play in the middle.' 'You want to play in the middle?!' And we were like, 'Who is out there?' And they'd say 'AC/DC or Metallica, but you guys aren't going to open for AC/DC or Metallica, you are bigger than them right now.' And we said, 'No we want to play in the middle; we want to play for 60 minutes.' And it all came back to this conversation I had with our old manager in like '82, '83 when we were starting to get pretty hefty, pretty big, and we were like, really cocky saying, 'Why don't you go and get Ted Nugent or Aerosmith and have them open for us?' and they could have. And he was like, 'You don't want to do that.' And I was like, 'Why?' And he said, 'I've seen that before. A new band with like two hit singles has a band like Aerosmith open for them who has like 15 years of history and you only give them 60 minutes, they will blow you off the stage every time.' So we took that concept and opened for Metallica and AC/DC and played 60 minutes in front of 150,000 people at night. Slammed!!! How are you going to keep up with a hot rod that only has to run a quarter mile and everybody else has to do two hours? So we went out there, slammed, kicked ass, and went home and took a break. It was a good thing and it was a lot of fun. But then it all blew up after that (laughs). Probably because we were so fried, and that's a big part of why."

262 SEVENTH SON OF A SEVENTH SON
IRON MAIDEN

204 points *from Seventh Son of a Seventh Son (EMI '88)*

On an album full of poncy intros, this track adds another one, which switches illogically and erratically into a three-legged rhythm unsuccessful due to the album's hurried and harried production. The chorus somewhat sticks due to Bruce's linguistic acrobatics and the title trackness of it all, and somewhere amidst the stumblebum nature of the track, there's an iota and an inkling of a **Piece of Mind** vibe. At the four-minute mark, the boys decide to shoehorn in another intro or warm-up exercise or scales lesson, whatever that is . . . hotdog break maybe, and for those with better taste, a race for the exit turnstiles once Bruce starts talking.

Adrian Smith on Maiden's patented twin leads . . .

> "We actually used to work separately. Dave would go in for a couple of days and do some solos, do some guitar lines and then I would go in and do my solos and put the harmony to what he'd done. And if it was Steve's song, Steve would be there, but both of us were in there, just making sure it's what he wanted. He's very meticulous about his stuff, you know."

263 ONLY ANTHRAX

204 points

from Sound of White Noise (Elektra '93)

Re-energized with a new vocalist and a fetching new album, Anthrax found a way to marry the dirty, ponderous heft of the new metal realities with traditional heavy metal values, even if tracks like *Only* bore little resemblance to the mickey moshes of old. *Only* is a majestic number that spreads, culminating in a groovy slo-mo double bass chorus, made royal and career-inspired by a passionate melody and John Bush's tough but still rangeful vocal acumen.

Charlie Benante on *Only* . . .

> "Only was the first song written for the **Sound of White Noise** record. I just had the song from start to finish, the music. And I knew it was catchy on its own. And John Bush came into the band at that point and that was the first song we wrote with him. When I play that song,

what I think about the most is how exciting a time it was and how it was all new again, coming together; it was really exciting."

Charlie Benante from Anthrax
Led Zeppelin — *The Song Remains the Same*
Kiss — *Deuce*
Judas Priest — *Rapid Fire*
Motörhead — *Ace of Spades*
Iron Maiden — *Hallowed Be Thy Name*
Black Sabbath — *Symptom of the Universe*
UFO — *Lights Out*
AC/DC — *Whole Lotta Rosie*
Sex Pistols — *God Save the Queen*
Anthrax — *I Am the Law*

264 KICK OUT THE JAMS
MC5
203 points *from Kick out the Jams (Elektra '68)*

Other songs by this transitory, transient band smelled more like the new metal, but *Kick out the Jams* got to the point quick, one and three-ing on boisterous chords, somewhere between James Brown, The Kinks and a Detroit heavy metal accident. So yeah, through three records of scattered brain waves and armed psychedelic conflict, this is ground zero for the band's legacy, kicking off the key album at the key live show, everybody keyed up at once, a rare convergence within this buzzed crash pad of hawkdoves.

265 GOD SAVE THE QUEEN SEX PISTOLS

202 points *from Never Mind the Bollocks, Here's the Sex Pistols (Virgin '77)*

A big hit given its flamethrowing sentiment craw-cawed by snot man at the apex of a recessionary and violent Britain, *God Save the Queen* might also have been accepted (really, commercially, it never really was), due to its quite sweet and melodic riff, the happiest on the record save maybe for *Seventeen* and/or *Anarchy*. But there's a sense of triumphant uplift in the track as well, especially come those cloudbursting "No future's." In metal context, the song became the most widely covered amongst headbanging bands eager to show their street cred, and really, the whole album, with its clean multi-multi-tracked guitars was basically a metal album without solos, fronted by a voice that was politely tolerated, given the steaming riffery below whatever it was that pencil-armed punk was on about.

266 CRAZY NIGHTS LOUDNESS

202 points *from Thunder in the East (Atco '85)*

You know the one, "lock and load crazy nights . . . ," it's very catchy, representing a dumbing down of the band that brought you the exalted **Disillusion** album, Loudness riding a vibe not unlike Priest and Accept to moderate success at this most fertile and rewarding time for metal. If you politely ignored the lyrics, what you got with this song and the album in general, was top flight stadium metal that was both weighty and melodic, a hard balance made easier through Max Norman's full-bodied production. No question, Takasaki had the riffs, even if he had become less esoteric, cerebral and well, foreign.

Akira Takasaki on the band's '01 reunion . . .

"I think my guitar style is always changing. As I get older it becomes more emotional and spiritual. I don't want to play in an old style; I always want to make a new style of playing. There really isn't one type of playing that I prefer. There are many styles that I can choose from, even from one song to the next if I want. It was much better now than when we were working together 15 years ago. I think the reason the band worked so well is because we did separate things and learned more about ourselves. Coming back together was like coming back to family. We really enjoyed being with each other and that made a big difference in the end, I think."

267 LET IT GO DEF LEPPARD

202 points *from High 'n' Dry (Mercury '81)*

'Twas a time when the Leps were actually well regarded by serious music fans, and that time peaked when they were the sprightly young British improvement on AC/DC, swinging and singing anthems like *Let It Go* and *High 'n' Dry*. But if AC/DC be a dim yet allowable comparative, you'd also have to look at vague inclinations towards Priest, UFO and that nebulous blob called American hard rock. Plus you would think the infectious enthusiasm from a few dozen NWOBHM contemporaries might have also had an effect on what was seen as the most careerist contingent to leap from the fish and chips and three pints fray. In any event, one couldn't deny the energetic, youthful hard rock glee emanating from this track, or from the half-dozen rewrites turned in by halfway through **Pyromania**, end stop, crash, delete.

Joe Elliott on *Let It Go* . . .

"*Let It Go* actually started out as a different song. We actually played *Let It Go* at the Reading Festival in 1980 under the name of *When the Rain Falls* or something crap like that, with one of these melancholic lyrics, 'Looking out the window on a Sunday morning.' And it was twice as fast as we ended up putting it on the record. And Mutt said, 'No, this has got to lope. We've got to slow this down, slow it right down, so those chords actually stand out more.' And we completely tore the vocal to pieces. I just sat back and listened to him start making noises over the top of it, and I was saying, 'I don't get this.' Because that was my first ever sit-in on a rewrite. I was like, hang on, we've just taken a song, and we've taken it to bits. We'd never done that. We'd actually rewritten songs, but never so rapidly and so well, and not with an outsider who was like, this guy knows what he's doing. It was like, 'Woah.' And I remember it being a lot of, 'This is bullshit; he can't do this with our art!' Until you realize a day and a half later that, 'Hell, it's way better, isn't it?' We'd all be nudging each other going, 'Great, isn't it?' (laughs)."

268 ANIMAL (FUCK LIKE A BEAST) W.A.S.P.

201 points

from Animal (Fuck Like a Beast) 12" *(Music for Nations '84)*

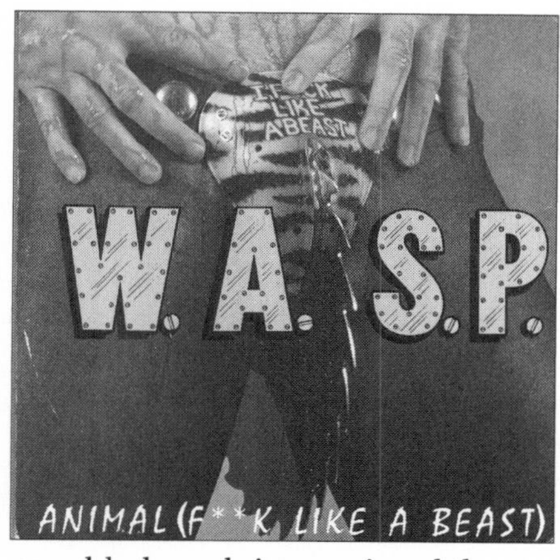

Released months before the debut album and then not even included on it, *Animal* is a pretty dim lightbulb in the W.A.S.P. canon, a rock by numbers riff recorded like crud, elevated by Blackie's paint-stripping vocals and one of those characteristically old school melodic choruses Blackie pulls from his complicated, long in the tooth past. A bit of a nasty title there, which, combined with the man's circular saw-blade codpiece, primed the pumps of controversy once Blackie got up and rode his Kiss from Hell act into the history books.

Blackie Lawless on *Animal (Fuck Like a Beast)* . . .

"Boy, the epitome of arrogance. That's what that was (laughs). The person who wrote that definitely believed that when they were writing it (laughs). Let's put it that way. Arrogance in big bold letters."

269 GODZILLA BLUE ÖYSTER CULT

201 points *from Spectres (Columbia '77)*

Sabbath gave us *Iron Man* in '70, Edgar Winter followed with *Frankenstein* in '72, and now BÖC, with panache to spare, crown the town with *Godzilla*. Buck has never laid down stupid heavy metal so smartly, *Godzilla* joining the ranks of the aforementioned, as well as *Smoke on the Water* and *Man on the Silver Mountain* as songs that celebrate cleanly and crisply the idea of riff. Of course BÖC, the intellectualizing cadre that they are, can only joke about it, and *Godzilla* delivers both musical and lyrical zingers, this big lizard more likely to gumshoe through skyscrapers than treat the process like work. Trivia notes: the riff was apparently partly inspired by a song called *Go Go Gorilla*, with Joe Bouchard's bass solo deemed a tribute to Stanley Clarke; on tour, Albert Bouchard donned a Godzilla mask between strobe flashes during his drum solo. Eric Bloom's Japanese rant translates roughly as, "Attention, emergency news! Attention, emergency news! Godzilla is going toward the Ginza area! Immediately escape, catch up, find shelter please!" Eric, to do the song justice, underwent an intensive 60-hour course in Japanese prior to the band's '79 tour.

Eric Bloom on learning Japanese . . .

> "Well, I was a language major in college. I always wanted to learn Japanese. So when we were going to go on tour, '78, '79, I went to the Berlitz School and took 20 or 30 intensive Japanese lessons. So when I got there, the funny thing was, is I get to Japan and I sat down with a guy from Sony Records who was Japanese American, and I started practising some stuff with him and he goes, 'Everyone's going to laugh at you for saying that stuff.' And I go, 'What do you mean?' And he goes, 'Well, that's like school Japanese. Nobody talks like that.' So I wanted to wring their necks for teaching me all the wrong stuff (laughs). So I had to sit down with him and phonetically learn a few good things like, 'How y'all doing?!'"

270 AFTER FOREVER BLACK SABBATH

201 points *from Master of Reality (Warner '71)*

Scoff if ye mite, but I figure *Sweet Leaf, Lord of this World, Children of the Grave, Into the Void* and *After Forever* got riffs afire that make anything and everything on the first two albums hide behind momma's summer frock. And of the four **Master** blasters, *After Forever* speaks of metal victory with the greatest authority, sod-busting through the history of music, bulldozing, er, Bob Dylan. Geezer and Tony just overwhelm poor Bill, who can only hold the fort as the string-clangers plow a wide berth for . . . God! But it's not all power chords. There's the obligatory solo jam, as well as that airy heavenly bit, again, Sabbath going to their substantial left field for some rock out of the box.

Geezer Butler on *After Forever* . . .

> "That was the Christian song wasn't it? We had a lot of Satanists and Jesus freaks and everybody showing up at the gigs and it was just a reaction to all this wild religious stuff at the time, all this peace and love. I have a very open mind. I was raised a strict Roman Catholic but I am very tolerant of other people's religions. Believe what you believe; I don't like preaching to anybody and that song just says that once you get to the end, are you going to be prepared for what you find? Have you lived a good life?"

271 IRON FIST MOTÖRHEAD

200 points *from Iron Fist (Bronze '84)*

Proving that residual, recycled, backdraft, jet stream, tailwind Motörhead is still a worthy exercise in spitting nails, here comes *Iron Fist*, Lemmy and crew trying to force a bush league version of *Overkill* and *Ace of Spades* into punters' keepers bins. Typical post-punk, low man's thrash, typically vague war theme, typical of an album that was quickly exposed for what it was: rehash.

Fast Eddie Clarke on *Iron Fist* . . .

> I kind of give that one to Lem a little bit. See, we'd been in rehearsal; I can remember this actually. We'd sit there and we'd be trying to write a tune. And Lemmy would go, 'OK, let's do one like this' (sings the Iron Fist riff), you see what I mean? And that's how that one came about. So he started doing that, and I remember coming in with it and Phil just started playing the drums, and once again we jammed off on it, and then we made the shape up later. By **Iron Fist** we were getting a little bit dry on ideas. They weren't coming so easily. We were having to work harder and also we were being more picky about them, you know? We were kind of finding fault with everything. It must be the same for all bands. It just gets a bit tricky when you've done four albums. You start scrutinizing everything and you start disallowing things because you don't want to piss the fans off. 'We can't do this, we can't do that,' and then at the end of the fucking day you've shot yourself up the ass. It made **Iron Fist** a difficult album to do."

272 THIS LOVE PANTERA

199 points *from Vulgar Display of Power (Atlantic '92)*

Power ballad with a capitol nine-inch spike, *This Love* explodes like no ungodly metal sledge on earth, Phil crooning ominously then loudly announcing the arrival of the full band concept, after which the boys seem to accelerate things with a real heavy accelerant, nudging the love until puncture wounds litter the corpse. The break is a prime bit of Dimebag dementia, first note-dense and then brain-dead, brilliantly sparse and caustic, before things mellow down again with a doob and a tumbler of head-warming battery acid. A final metal slash and a whole new break-style riff ensue before a return to two earlier themes puts pennies on yer eyes.

Phil Anselmo on *This Love* . . .

> "**Vulgar Display of Power** was the first Pantera record that really, really signified what Pantera truly is. That to me was the first album that kind of cemented the Pantera sound. And *This Love* was a major player in helping to do that. It's very, very, extremely anthemic, and definitely a song where the crowd wants to get involved, in a live situation obviously. What we did - and this has been borrowed by so many bands today - basically what we did was that the verses were done in a melodic-type mellow, mellow way and then through dynamics, we kick into the fucking chorus and it hits very, very hard. And I see so many bands today using that same fucking formula. It's kind of incredible, you know? They build up, build up, build up, here comes the chorus . . . wow! And then they're all on their pogo sticks, you know and clown outfits from Kmart. But you know, man? To us, when we were writing that back then, it was just a matter of basically writing a good song. And what mattered was how that chorus hit. And when the chorus hit, it was a fucking sledgehammer. So that made us very happy."

273 THE WRIT BLACK SABBATH

199 points *from Sabotage (Warner '75)*

If there's a tangled rat's nest of black cord in the tragic Sabbath tale, *The Writ* might as well be it, God forbid. By this point, it was all coming to a psychotic frothy hydra head, the band reduced to writing devastating epic odes to bad management. *The Writ* may singlehandedly have caused My Dying Bride, establishing a new reverse plateau for slow and grand, stomping wearily but with great emotional impact. It is perhaps the dark central hole of the Sabbath trajectory, a creative triumph amidst floundering utility, a crown of thorns, the king of downers, not so much a fire, but a pit of embers.

Geezer Butler on *The Writ* . . .

> "That was written about our management at the time and how we were just all fed up with everything, recording with a room full of lawyers. . . . Ozzy came up with those lyrics and I thought they were really good. But it was just this whole situation with everybody suing everybody else. We just wanted out of it. And like *The Writ*, *Megalomania* was also written about the management and record company people in general. It was so long because we couldn't figure out how to end the song. We just kept coming up with parts that were going to be new songs, but then we figured they would fit so we used them."

274 HERE I GO AGAIN WHITESNAKE

198 points *from Whitesnake (Geffen '87)*

Rode rough, put away, then pulled out again and polished for the smash **Whitesnake** album (called **1987** in jolly ol' England, with all sorts of performance and mix alterations), *Here I Go Again* is that rarest of rarities: a power ballad that is actually soulful. Perhaps it's its pedigree, its creation by a bunch of grizzled blues and funk veterans, but whatever the case, it's a passionate unfolding of events, culminating in that big redemptive silver lining of a chorus (pumping fist in one hand, foisted lighter in t'other), one that celebrates Kiss and the Stones and the Kinks and Mott the Hoople all at once. It has a flaw though, a verse that is purely a miserable grocery shopping melody. Yet I can still celebrate the song because it is so much more than just this verse.

David Coverdale on *Here I Go Again . . .*

"*Here I Go Again* I wrote many, many years ago in Portugal, before people in America heard it in '87 or whatever, and it was actually about the breakup of my first marriage. I wrote that in 1980, '81, so that's pretty old. It's interesting. That turned into a huge anthem, fist punching the air stuff, which is interesting because it isn't that kind of theme. But whatever. I've had enough people talk to me or write to me and say how helpful or beneficial the song was to them in a particular crisis in their lives. And that to me, as a writer, is success, when you can connect like that. And that was a problem I had with Whitesnake. A lot of the stuff was becoming so overtly pompous, catering to big rock stadium scenarios. You'd get the sentiment of the song in the beginning and then the group would explode in and I was just riding the gods of electricity, let alone trying to put any sort of emotional content into it."

Neil Murray from Whitesnake

Bon Jovi — *Livin' on a Prayer*
Van Halen — *Jump*
Journey — *Don't Stop Believin'*
AC/DC — *Back in Black*
Cream — *I Feel Free*
Thin Lizzy — *Don't Believe a Word*
Led Zeppelin — *Communication Breakdown*
Jimi Hendrix Experience — *Voodoo Child*
Black Sabbath — *Black Sabbath*
Free — *Mr. Big*

275 MELISSA KING DIAMOND

196 points *from Melissa (Roadrunner '83)*

Even more chilling than its preceding six tracks because it's quiet enough to let the evil seep through, *Melissa* is like a mournful ballad to Baphomet, King delivering the intro vocal in a voice that actually sounds human. But Fate can't contain themselves, adding ornate, heavy passages until it's some sort of progressive Satanic metal journey through the mind of a man who has lost his beloved at the stake. For some reason, as befits the parallel of both the albums at large, I've always equated the melancholy of this with *Epitaph* off of **Sad Wings of Destiny**, both songs, cozy bits on albums of howling, unearthly metal acumen.

King Diamond on *Melissa* . . .

> "We tried playing it live back in the early days, and we couldn't pull it off very well. We decided it wasn't a good song to play live. So we didn't play it live until not that long ago. It was four or five years ago that we tried it for the first time and we thought, 'Wow, this is pretty cool!' We figured, why don't we do it as a total surprise to the audience on this next tour? It was just at one little gig in a bar back in Copenhagen that we had tried it out and said, 'Oops, not good.' But it worked so well. People were so surprised because they'd never heard it played before."

276 WE'RE NOT GONNA TAKE IT TWISTED SISTER

195 points *from Stay Hungry (Atlantic '84)*

There's something so New York about this one, Twisted Sister turning in a rough but friendly stack of tried and tired chords and then selling you like a $2000 vacuum cleaner on their brilliance. It's Kiss all over again, pure hook, no trickery, a lyric that kicks you out of bed and into the rats, cats and dogs race, drums pounding like the night before and the morning after, drill sergeant Dee meaning well, which is why it works. Few bands would dare chords that sugary, but then not many had a sweet tooth for the toy store colours of rock like these sheep-suited wolves. Last laugh was on you, as Twisted became the unit-shifting bane of organized censor folk, despite ironically being the nice guys on the rock block.

Mark Mendoza on *We're Not Gonna Take It . . .*

> "I don't think there's one producer who has done Twisted Sister in the studio justice. None of them were interested in what the band sounded like live and what we did. They just came in and said I'm going to produce this and they hear their own sound. Because I'm a producer also, I kind of look at it both ways. You have to find out what a band is like when they're not in the studio. You can't take them too far from what they are. Now Tom Werman didn't want to do *We're Not Gonna Take It.* He heard it and he said there's just no way you guys are doing this. He actually didn't want most of those songs on the record. He wanted us to do songs from other bands, get other writers; we fought with him to the point where we may not have recorded that album. Although he's a good guy and we got along with him well, I don't think his production qualities were right for us. It's not a great sounding record. I think it's wimpy; it sounds small. Twisted Sister live was huge, monstrous. And these guys never saw us do anything live. But I mean, Dee and I really argued with him. I remember battling it out. He was so-so with *I Wanna Rock* but he hated *We're Not Gonna Take It.* With *We're Not Gonna Take It,* Dee came to me and said I have this killer song. Dee is not a good guitar player and usually when he wrote a song he would come to me first and say write chords around this. And he sung this incredible melody line, so I put some chords around it and it came together in like 20 minutes, the whole song, done."

Mark Mendoza from Twisted Sister
Montrose — *Rock the Nation*
Black Sabbath — *The Mob Rules*
Black Sabbath — *Heaven and Hell*
AC/DC — *For Those About to Rock (We Salute You)*
AC/DC — *Back in Black*

Cactus — *Long Tall Sally*
Mountain — *Nantucket Sleighride*
Black Sabbath — *Sabbath Bloody Sabbath*
Motörhead — *Ace of Spades*
Black Sabbath — *Snowblind*

277 INNER SELF SEPULTURA

195 points *from Beneath the Remains (Roadrunner '89)*

Even way back, Sepultura had discovered the atmosphere attainable from letting a simple riff sink in, *Inner Self* beginning with many variations on a simple theme, Igor left to his devices while the band chugged its way deep into your fleshy bits. As well, the track is quite ambitious, offering many speeds from Anthrax mid-mosh to speed metal with only a vestige of the band's earlier thrash vision. Plus check out the watery pre-Meshuggah guitar textures, the Seps deciding here and now that they were going to break out of Brazil and compete on a higher intellectual plane.

Andreas Kisser on *Inner Self* . . .

> "We were in Brazil; we had just finished wrecking our practice pad. It was all falling apart and we destroyed the place that was there. It was really fun, but difficult to put back. At the same time it was really nice to have a contract to put our stuff out worldwide. At that time Sepultura was really influenced by Metallica's **. . . And Justice For All**, that kind of that vibe."

278 THE WIZARD BLACK SABBATH

194 points *from Black Sabbath (Warner '70)*

Breaking rules immediately and admirably, Sabbath embark on one of their demon blues numbers, Bill Ward getting to belly-and-gut "push" another song, the way he sucked in and exhaled Black Sabbath (he explains this often, but no one ever knows what the hell he's talking about). *The Wizard* is actually a fairly thorny and perilous song, a deconstructed bit of oddball efficiency sent gee-gaw by Ozzy's hill and dale harmonica ramblings. And lyrically, Sabbath are staking their turf, conjuring paranormal people to cast spells and aspersions, surprisingly relatively virgin turf at the time for rock 'n' roll lyric ritin'.

Bill Ward on *The Wizard* . . .

> "That was a real sod to figure out. There are a lot of movements, just like *Symptom of the Universe*. So doing that live, way back when, because we don't do either of those songs now unfortunately. But being on stage in the middle of a tour, those songs are really quite, not difficult, but you had to be pretty physical to be able to play both those songs, especially *The Wizard* because it actually doesn't stop for the drummer from the beginning to the end. There's no actual time, so I'm actually just pushing it through with all the different rolls and things like that from top to bottom (laughs)."

279 DEAD SKIN MASK SLAYER

193 points *from Seasons in the Abyss (Def American '90)*

Here's one of Slayer's more open architecture songs, Lombardo just bashing a vigilant backbeat, the axemen hanging up a few chords, Araya ghoulish in one of his low-key monotones, getting inside the mind of a serial killer. When there is a riff however (more or less an intro or set-up), it's one of Slayer's best, and the song also contains an insane amount of frantic soloing, especially given the track's hypnotic drip.

Tom Araya on *Dead Skin Mask* . . .

"I wanted to have people talking in the background, maybe the people Ed Gein had killed. We had a friend of ours go in and we tried different techniques. We didn't use an effect. We tried different things to make his voice go up and sound like a little kid. I sat there and I told him, 'You are little kid, you're not happy, and you don't want to play anymore. You want out and you're pissed off.' When anyone first hears it, I ask them if they looked behind their back when they heard the little voice. It's more of a thriller. The voice represents a child which is basically him. He couldn't tell fantasy from reality."

280 DOMINATION PANTERA

193 points *from Cowboys from Hell (Atlantic '90)*

Featuring one of Phil's cut and pasted to red ribbons of whip scars lyrics, *Domination* is more or less a vehicle for "Diamond" Darrell's inspirational riffs, which collide often and at all speeds with the power and pregnant pauses of Vinnie Paul's percussion in a sort of gear-shifting soundcheck mode. It is much less a song, more of a collage, a storehouse of heavy water and spent nuclear fuel, a place where one can wallow in and be contaminated by the band's newly invented unbending metal. And again, what Phil says makes no sense whatsoever, unless taken in haiku-sized bites.

Vinnie Paul on *Domination* . . .

"*Domination* . . . at the front of that everybody thinks it says, 'Bart stinks like a motherfucker!' and all that stuff. I was really pumped up and we had just gone out to dinner and I came back and everybody said, 'All right, let's get a cut on *Domination*' and I went back there and I was fired up and I just said, 'First take like a motherfucker!' and we just kicked into it. For years and years there have been numerous things on the internet about what I said or what it was. It's funny. I've tried to clarify it but still to this day there's rumours and stuff floating around about it."

281 THE GREEN MANALISHI (WITH THE TWO-PRONGED CROWN)
JUDAS PRIEST
193 points *from Hell Bent for Leather (Columbia '79)*

Providing good solid red earth to an album that is so much about sky-high fireworks, this pounding cover was not part of the original English version of the album, which also featured slightly different cover art and was called **Killing Machine**. Although there are other slow songs on the album, this is the most straightforward and Sabbatherian, completely un-Mac just like *Diamonds and Rust* wasn't so Joan Baez. Halford turns in a low, measured performance to match the song's ponderous night-creep, K.K. and Glenn backing him up with thick, billowy chords that you could just tell were gonna loosen fillings once the pyrotechnic pair unleashed them on stage.

Glenn Tipton on *The Green Manalishi (With the Two-Pronged Crown)* . . .

> "It was a song we liked, you know? Peter Green has always been a bit of a hero to me anyway, a great white English blues guitar player and a great songwriter. I don't know whether I suggested it. In fact, I don't think I did. But it would have been one of us, as opposed to *Diamonds and Rust* which I think was suggested by the record company, and then we kicked it around."

282 LIMELIGHT
RUSH
191 points *from Moving Pictures (Anthem '81)*

Closer to the Heart, The Spirit of Radio, Limelight . . . these are connecting emotional songs from a band usually concerned with cold prog metal logic. Of the three, *Limelight* is the messiest, the liveliest, perhaps the one most likely to follow out of a power trio's frame-distressed U-Haul.

Swooping and swirling, youthful and debonair, *Limelight* finds a way to work in the calculator rock and Peart's beyond-busy tom fills as if they added to the songfulness of things (rarely elsewhere the case), the band, arguably at their peak, capturing, housing and feeding the optimism and ambition of young prog-aspiring pups who themselves wished to find and live the limelight life. Full cathedrals of melodies fuel that desire, and by track's end, Rush reward the attentive student with a grand finale charged with electricity and punctuated with prog power acrobatics.

Alex Lifeson on touring . . .

> "Touring is still fun. I think we learned that from the last two or three tours, for me primarily the last tour, how to do it and not make it feel like work. We got to the point where touring itself was work. There's a great labour of love in the studio where making records requires so much concentration and effort, but none of us would ever consider it as hard work because we really love doing it and it's very rewarding. Touring has always been the really tough thing. You get really tired of touring very quickly. It's incredibly boring. Granted, the two hours you're on stage is very exciting, but the 22 hours that you have to wait to get on stage can be really tedious, and that's when you really feel that it's work. Certainly in the early days it's exciting. It's a dream come true. You live for every second up there. But after so many years, it's really not quite the same."

283 RESURRECTION HALFORD

191 points *from Resurrection (Sanctuary '00)*

The Metal God was welcomed back with open arms when he decided to make his safe but solid '00 comeback album reflecting the efficient chromium steel of classic Priest. Title track *Resurrection* is also the opener as well as an autobiographical but history-rewriting kicker-in of metal doors. Frankly, the lyric ain't all that ambitious, but as usual, Halford attacks it with semi-ironic might, his new cronies instantly impressing the listener with their passionate grooves, right from the opening drum fill and attendant guitar squeals 'n' peals.

Rob Halford on *Resurrection* . . .

> "Well, I'm talking about a lot of personal stuff which I've never done before. Directly. I've always used language in a kind of an ambiguous way, innuendo, smokescreen language in my metal stuff over the years. But this is the first time I've walked up to the mike and said, 'I'm digging deep inside my soul to bring myself out of this goddamn hole.' That's pretty brutal, life is on the line stuff. So that was a challenge. Roy Z said, 'What are you going to write about?' And I said, 'Gee, I don't know. I've got to find something to say.' So he said, 'Just tell them about what's been going on in your life.' And I go, 'It's as easy as that?' And he said, 'Yeah, it's as easy as that.' And he got it right."

Mike Chlasciak from Halford
Judas Priest — *Electric Eye*
Judas Priest — *Painkiller*
Whitesnake — *Here I Go Again*
Warlock — *All We Are*
Primal Fear — *Church of Blood*
Accept — *Balls to the Wall*
Judas Priest — *You've Got Another Thing Comin'*
Dio — *Lock up the Wolves*
Deep Purple — *Burn*
Dio — *The Last in Line*

284 EPIC
FAITH NO MORE

191 points *from The Real Thing (Slash/Warner '89)*

All the bits and scraps that one could call rap metal before this state-of-the-art rocket ship of an anthem . . . well, they were either novelty songs or pleasant accidents, or not metal, or jokey and hokey, or kind of flopped onto tape in a casual manner. But even if *Epic* fit this fresh new hybrid perfectly, the band from whence it sprung would not, writing any number of aerial ballets in any number of directions, with perhaps the old Chuck version of the band, maybe, just maybe rapping a little more. So yeah, *Epic* is funk metal or rap metal or something to that effect, brilliantly and widely recorded, performed sizzling hot, miked up with a guy who more than anything, was road-testing one of his many versatile characters for the turbulent terrorist music that he would make through the rest of the ignored **Faith No More** albums as well as the truly avant-garde visions beyond.

Billy Gould on breaking with *Epic* . . .

> "We were the first band, from an industry perspective to make them realize that a weird band can get to the top of the charts, and that it'll still work. I think the industry became less rigid when we broke through. It definitely helped out a lot of bands, and has given them an opportunity. What we did wasn't planned; it just happened. We just felt that if we kept our heads together, everything would be alright. But 18 months touring was a long time; we were becoming numb. Toward the end we were pretty much happy to be done. I took a year off and I wasn't bored one day. It was the first time I'd ever had money and it was amazing, a major head trip."

285 HEARTBREAKER
LED ZEPPELIN

188 points *from II (Atlantic '69)*

Here's an example of Zeppelin's ability to stick a big ol' ornery polecat of a riff in a barrel and bang it around, end result being lots of shrieking but also soft muffled bumps up against the insides. So prattles and ambles *Heartbreaker*, hard and nasty for the blues, benign, round and dated for metal. Of course this flurry of mixed metaphors is further underscored by the fact that the song is practically defined by bass guitar as well as bassy guitar and bass drums. In fact it's just a big ol' dull headache.

286 MEGALOMANIA BLACK SABBATH

188 points

from Sabotage (Warner '75)

While *The Writ* ruined *Kashmir*'s day, *Megalomania* did the same disservice to *In My Time of Dying*, Sabbath blowtorching Zeppelin's idyllic daisy patch, winning the battle of '75, and doing it with half the amount of vinyl. So *Megalomania* is Sabbath's long journey into night, 11 minutes of metronomic metal pain, recurring bouts of rifling riffery, swirling cavalcades of tormented soundscaping. Ozzy delivers a performance that is one of his most riveting, aided by random foghorn technology, but so drenched with doom, the frills become unnecessary window dressing. Conclusions are inevitable after 11 ethereal minutes, but these conclusions are widely textured, complex and abstract like the song's musical and lyrical signals. One is left drained by the drive towards nothingness, and Sabbath, definitely worse for wear by journey's end, ultimately found themselves more mentally traumatized than any voyeuristic, art-demanding outsider could ever sustain without similar serious brain damage.

Bill Ward on *Megalomania* . . .

> "I don't know sometimes; I think *Megalomania* and *The Writ* are intertwined. *Megalomania* was about greed or coveting; that's at least what I interpret from the song. And then *The Writ* is kind of like the coveter or the greedy person or whatever; the end result was *The Writ*, if you like. They are kind of in the same family. But they are very different songs musically. Fantastic guitars, and I think the band sounded pretty hot on both of those songs. I liked Tony's solo in *Megalomania*. So I enjoyed very much putting a

very straight beat to it. It was like one of the only times I got the opportunity to do a very straight beat for a number of bars (laughs). So that was kind of cool."

287 DON'T BELIEVE A WORD THIN LIZZY

187 points *from Johnny the Fox (Vertigo '76)*

Within a modest 2:18, Thin Lizzy weave an elegant tapestry of guitars, placing their legendary tones over a boogie backbeat blessed with jazzy finesse. The twin leads are integral to the song, front row and centre, duelling with wandering angular chords, while o'ertop, Phil sings a mournful, hollow paean to a rock star's lack of moral fortitude. It is one of his great tragic lyrics revolving around weakness, a pair-able parable with *Got to Give It Up* or *Dear Lord*, sung with ache, over and out the door before you know it.

Scott Gorham on the impact of Phil's death . . .

"I think a lot of people started looking in the mirror after that happened. The thing with Phil was that people looked at him as the Mike Tyson of rock 'n' roll. This guy could take more drugs, stay up late, play more gigs, do more interviews. Like Mike Tyson, Phil got knocked out. But people actually saw that and they thought, 'If it can happen to this guy, it can easily happen to me.' There was a whole slew of people around at the time who took a double-take at their own life and eased off. In my case, that was one of the reasons why I wanted to quit because I had to get better. The last time I saw Phil was three weeks before he died and at that point I was actually clean for about a year. He was still hard at it. It's down to determination more than anything else. I wanted desperately out of that drug scene to save my ass."

288 GRINDER JUDAS PRIEST

186 points *from British Steel (CBS '80)*

Part of the new fat-farming program, *Grinder* is a deadly accurate and self-evident spot of simple metal on a simpleton record. But it works so well, rocking back and forth block-headed like Accept, dropping a stone for a fortified chorus of scraping doom before notching back up for another hummable, umbrella-swinging verse. Nice vocal phrasings as well from our man at the mike, Halford playing dominatrix, barking out pronouncements, carving himself a career with accessible song-smith songs.

K.K. Downing on the break with Rob Halford . . .

> "All I have to say about it is since Rob left the band in '92, a lot of people asked us why he left, expecting us to know. A lot of people expect us to know why he left the band. Well, I think any intelligent person, if they thought about it, they wouldn't even bother asking the question. They know. And now it's been confirmed. I don't have to say any more than that really. It's that simple. The fact that anybody wants that license of freedom, to be who they want to be, to surround themselves with people they want to, after such a long period of time, that's the answer. We can only surmise. We never really got a reason why he left. But his sexuality being that persuasion, being surrounded in this heterosexual environment for so long, it's kind of understandable. He probably got to a certain age, 40 years of age, which roughly he was, and said it's time to be with the people I want, who I feel more comfortable with. Simple as that."

289 BLINDED BY FEAR AT THE GATES

186 points *from Slaughter of the Soul (Earache '95)*

Ah yes, if At The Gates could only have a nickel for all the times they've been namechecked by bands and critics as one of the originators of today's creative and populous Swedish thrash scene. But throw this on, and it sounds eerily fresh, *Blinded by Fear* being smartly, perfectly recorded melodic thrashing speedy death, strafed with a touch of Entombed's attitude, but too razor-sharp and vicious to be called anything but something that didn't exist yet, outside of their own — let's face it — pretty much ignored world. Breaking up has never been so good for business, or at least reputation through a judicious, simplified rewriting of history.

Tomas Lindberg on the **Slaughter of the Soul** album . . .

> "We didn't want to sound like a death thrash band. We wanted the vocals to be pronounced well so you could hear them. It was such a relaxing environment when we did **Slaughter of the Soul**. We tried to not try too hard to be original because I think when you try to be original, you just end up being pretentious. You can't fake originality. We just said 'let's just do it and it will come naturally.' We wanted to write songs that were straightforward, hard-hitting and to the point. Every song is in your face in mere moments. We were searching for the right sound. On **Terminal Spirit Disease**, we kind of got closer to it and on **Slaughter of the Soul**, we actually found it. In a way, we tried to show people that you don't have to slow down or get all these weird instruments, like various singers or get all atmospheric, to be original. That's what we tried to show with the melodic parts in it. We could still be brutal and could progress in death metal without losing the brutality and aggression."

Jensen and Jonas from The Haunted
Black Sabbath — *The Sign of the Southern Cross*
Accept — *Fast as a Shark*
Judas Priest — *Victim of Changes*

Rush — *Xanadu*
Exodus — *Lessons in Violence*
AC/DC — *Riff Raff*
Motörhead — *Overkill*
Possessed — *Death Metal*
Ozzy Osbourne — *Diary of a Madman*
Thin Lizzy — *Emerald*

290 747 (STRANGERS IN THE NIGHT) SAXON

185 points *from Wheels of Steel (Carrere '80)*

Proving Saxon could write pop songs better when they weren't forced into it, *747* is a rocksy rollser built on a variation of the whole *Louie Louie, Hang on Sloopy, Since You Been Gone, Rainbow in the Dark* school of hooks. But the chorus takes a moody mellow twist, very sophisticated for Saxon at this point. Biff is in classic storyteller mood and really gets the listener involved, providing some cool, slightly agitated vocal phrasings against the straight-eight AC/DC riffing of his meat and potato backline.

Biff Byford on *747 (Strangers in the Night)* . . .

> "*747* is like two songs really, running together. It's a song about a power cut in New York that happened in the '60s I think, maybe the '70s, and there was a plane coming in to land and obviously couldn't land. The lights went off and there was a big panic. It didn't crash; it just went off somewhere else. And there were a lot of people trapped in lifts and actually a lot of relationships that happened due to that power outage. I've got two songs really. I've got one about strangers meeting in the dark and one about a plane coming down to land and it's all going on at the same time basically. I was watching a documentary on it. The guitar lick came loosely from *Hold the Line* by Toto. It's nothing like it, but there's a small influence there."

291 SUITE SISTER MARY QUEENSRYCHE

185 points

from Operation: Mindcrime (EMI '88)

Building like a cross between Alice Cooper, Pink Floyd and Marillion (or more accurately, Alice Cooper, Roger Waters and Fish), *Suite Sister Mary* is, at 10:39, the tough slog portion of the **Operation: Mindcrime** album, made no less difficult by the moody mellow weaves and the convoluted time signatures. The riffs are plentiful and sophisticated, but well-buried 'neath the story and all those drums and churchy choirs, as the band quite surprisingly go on forever without really rocking out.

Geoff Tate on *Suite Sister Mary* . . .

> "Recently we recorded *Suite Sister Mary* again for the live album. And we recorded with Pamela Moore singing the part of Sister Mary and it's really fun to do. It's a tough song to sing live but the crowd really likes it. The audience really appreciates that song. But at the time, we really didn't think about the length. We were just pretty much into this story, trying to get this story across from an audio standpoint. We had this really spooky piece of music and we had the idea and the concept and the lyrics and the melody, and we were in an all-out hunt to find the right voice for Mary. Pamela's name came up in conversation one night over dinner. And we started thinking about it, describing her sound to Peter, and he said, 'Well, let's fly her out.' So we got on the phone that night and called her and she flew out the next day. None of us knew her. We had met her a couple times around town, but we never knew her. She's sung in a lot of different bands around the Seattle area. She's had a couple of records out on small independent record labels, and we felt she just had the voice of the character. It's kind of a rough, raspy voice and she could sing it because she could feel the part. And she did. She came in and she just nailed it. She's really just a wonderful singer."

292 SCREAMING IN THE NIGHT
KROKUS

185 points *from Headhunter (Arista '83)*

A rare successful serious moment for this band of beer bottle breakers, *Screaming in the Night* also arrives on the Swiss quintet's most sophisticated album. The track is a dirty power ballad odyssey, hypnotically plodding through a doomy blues towards a warm, communicative twin lead break and then a hooky but morose chorus that works as contemplative, soul-fade moment amongst 1983's happy heavy circumstances, and indeed, the rest of this fireworked album. A rare bit of creative inspiration for the mellow metal song in general, coming from a band that usually sticks to numbskull, thumbnail, chainmail rock.

293 METAL HEART
ACCEPT

185 points *from Metal Heart (Portrait '85)*

Steely, focused, lofty and proud, *Metal Heart* was *Balls to the Wall* Part II in that it became an anthem squarely about the high-minded pursuit of all things metal. It treated the headbanger's domain as something upper-crust, rocking with deft authority over a riff that would make Ritchie Blackmore quiver in his elf boots and leprechaun hat. Its rhythm contained a gem of a hiccup, further implying that this was smart stuff. And then Wolf tears off a few classical music quotes and man, aren't we all going to the ball dressed to the nines? I was never too fond of that chorus, which slummed it next to the gleaming aerial cruise of Wolf's verse music, but all told, it's a minor complaint given the chromium airtight sum of the song's precision-tooled parts.

Udo Dirkschneider on *Metal Heart* . . .

> "I remember when we did that song, the lyrics were already there, the whole story of, 'We've got the metal heart, the real metal heart.' And there are also the lyrics about computers ruling the world in 1999. In the beginning, we didn't have that classical middle part. It was just a normal song, and then one night Wolf came in and put the leads in there and we said, 'Yes, this is now interesting.'"

294 BONDED BY BLOOD EXODUS

184 points *from Bonded by Blood (Combat '85)*

Hard to believe but the hype behind this Bay area band's pro-thrash debut had them neck and neckbrace with Metallica and Anthrax. And it wasn't hard to see why, with this album and this title track moshing forth and frothy with controlled aggression, with its hardcore anti-vibes and a vocalist in Paul Baloff who was a nasty blast of venom. But ultimately it was the guitars of Hunolt and Holt (that's them on the cover) that packed the punch, aided by the record's surging production values and that razor-tied build-up to and through the chorus, which lurches full stop with one of early thrash's early, er, bonding moments.

Tom Hunting on *Bonded by Blood* . . .

> "This is really dumb, but *Bonded by Blood*, there used to be a television show called **Grizzly Adams**, back in the day when we were little kids. And there was an Indian dude on there and when he wanted to be good buddies with someone, he would cut his thumb open and they would be bonded by blood. Lyrically on the rest of the album it was like, 'Look, we're singing about Satan in the most grotesque way!' (laughs). But *Bonded by Blood* was more a theme like, 'Who is playing at Ruthie's? We don't give a shit, we're going anyway!' Because it's going to be cool. It was a

hangout and a lot of bands from San Francisco were playing in the East Bay at Ruthie's. It was a scene and it was a different time, and I feel fortunate to have been able to grow up in it. I don't think a kid in his late teens would have the same kinds of options anymore. Clubs get closed, everything is really tight."

295 SNOWBLIND BLACK SABBATH

183 points *from Vol 4 (Warner '72)*

A prime example of Tony's ability to write monster riffs that basically drag everybody else along, *Snowblind* is one of those phenomenal metal bulldozers that makes you smile at this band's chin-first audacity. Ward is the track's boiler room however (despite the elephant gun to his drums) and without Martin Birch's bright black and blue production hue, the thing would collapse in a tangle of rusted cogs, fenders and zigzagged rebar. Bonus bump off the mirror: when it's not hitting you in the head with a ham, *Snowblind* is perhaps one of Tony's most elegant blues excursions.

Bill Ward on *Snowblind* . . .

> "That was our cocaine song. We were actually going to call the album that but the record company wouldn't let us (laughs). We'd been through grass and hash and acid and cocaine was the big new drug at the time and we were recording in L.A. and coke was very big there so we wrote about it."

296 ROCK OF AGES
DEF LEPPARD

182 points *from Pyromania (Mercury '83)*

Probably the boldest move forward on **Pyromania**, *Rock of Ages* was a clever pastiche of pop, metal and dance styles, virtually "built" more than recorded, guitars converted, unlocatable, part of a seamless whole that was pure pulsing sound. *Rock of Ages* also ushered in Def Leppard's annoying habit of supplying lyrics that sounded like bits of mumbles of rock hoo-hah, Elliott's nasal delivery of these pearls not helping matters. But once again the rock rabbit is pulled from the hat with a heavily trudging chorus, the contrast between this and the anaemic verse making for valleys and platinum peaks which would rock our radios for years to come.

Rick Allen on *Rock of Ages* . . .

> "I think that was one of Mutt's ideas. We spent quite a bit of time getting the whole sort of cowbell intro going. It's funny, because Mutt had this whole counting game, where instead of saying 1-2-3-4, he would sort of make lighthearted fun of various groups around the world. And one of the counts was, 'Gutten-Gleben-Glatin-Globin' [sic], you know? And that was pretty interesting. Various people have written in saying, 'Oh, it means running through the forest softly,' all these different translations. Knowing Mutt, and his background, he speaks Dutch really fluently, so I think a lot of it came from his background. It was really just a bit of fun, as was *Rock of Ages* just being a play on the biblical Rock of Ages, as it were."

297 KILLING IN THE NAME
RAGE AGAINST THE MACHINE

181 points *from Rage against the Machine (Epic/Sony '92)*

I'd go with a couple or three from **Evil Empire** over *Killing in the Name*, but hey, this is where Rage honed their unique sound, so there you go. All the elements of this totally cool band are in (slightly under-produced) evidence here, Zack's venomous rapping, his mantra-like repetition, his politics, along with Morello's spare and Zeppelin-esque, slack stoner Alice riffing. As a bonus, Morello also massages in one of his noisemaker guitar solos, the gathered evidence over five albums resulting in the man being heralded as one of the few guitar heroes of the '90s. I called this record under-produced, but maybe it's more like under-arranged, the band daring in its power trio simplicity, by virtue of this ethic, ending up with a record that summarily explodes on the live stage.

298 CUM ON FEEL THE NOIZE QUIET RIOT

181 points *from Metal Health* (CBS '83)

Annoying to no ends of the earth, *Cum on Feel the Noize* pairs a sour-ish, duff, confused, quintessentially English glam 'n' glitter melody with dirty motorbike power chords, a distorted Spencer Proffer drum sound, and one of happy metal's great loudmouths. It's really the twisted sister track to *We're Not Gonna Take It*, both painted in primary colours so everyone gets it, both racked and pinioned with inane crowd participation bits which should have you disowning large swaths of your teenage life if you were there and cared. By the way, Slade's original version of the song came in 779th.

Frankie Banali on *Cum on Feel the Noize . . .*

> "*Cum on Feel the Noize* was not our idea. The producer we had at the time thought that it was a good song for us to cover for two reasons. One, he felt it was perfect for Kevin's range and vocal stylings. And number two, Slade, the band who wrote the song, had huge success with it everywhere in the world except the United States. So I guess he felt that the combination of Kevin's voice, and the fact that it was a known song outside of the United States, we would be the band to break it. We had no intention of doing the song. As a matter of fact, the band had pretty much agreed that we were not going to rehearse the song, which we didn't. The producer would call up and say how is the Slade song coming along? And we were like, 'Oh terrific! Sounds great!' And we weren't even playing it. And

Kevin said, 'Listen, when we go to play it, play it really, really poorly and probably what will happen is everyone will say hey, it doesn't sound as good as we thought it could and it will go by the wayside.' And when we went into the studio, there wasn't even an intro to the song. And the producer said, 'All right, let's roll tape,' and what you hear drum-wise is the first take. That intro is totally unplanned because I didn't have an intro and the drum track itself was unplanned. Unfortunately I get into this mode when I put headphones on that I get very focused and very direct (laughs) and I guess I did a better job than anybody expected because at that point Kevin just glared at me from across the room as the rest of the tracks were being laid down (laughs). We actually thought that if it was a prerequisite from the producer at that point to do a cover song, and especially a Slade song, we thought that *Mama Weer All Crazee Now* would be a better song to do, and that's why it ended up on the second record. But to be honest with you, I don't think that turned out as well as it could have."

299 RIDE THE SKY HELLOWEEN

181 points *from Walls of Jericho (Noise '85)*

You can hear the electricity in this song, especially within the churning roiling black seas of the chorus, and you can hear the majesty of manic metal. You can also hear about the power of flaming youth, Helloween being many things, most graphically the usurper to a petering-out Maiden, Helloween running faster, soaring higher, emphatically boxing the ears of those who would dare opine that the new wave of metal is over. We just got here! And we're Germans!

Kai Hansen on *Ride the Sky* . . .

"That was a song that was really pure metal and anger about being on top of things, not being depressed by parents and society's chains. A lot of anger in that, just the dream about getting away from all that."

300 I WANNA ROCK TWISTED SISTER

180 points

from Stay Hungry (Atlantic '84)

The ultimate Flintstones song on an album eons away from the Jetsons, *I Wanna Rock* outlined the band's new modus operandi: hit them hard, cold, dry and often. The early '80s was a time of many successful metal credo songs, and this was *Metal Health* Part II, *Denim and Leather* Part III, Dee finding a third, fourth and fifth way to say "stay hungry," his backing back of four rhythm players zigging down-strokes and zagging ups, producer Tom Werman fighting tooth, fang and claw with the boys, imposing his neutral tones on the pivotal career-or-towel record. The cards came up career as the multi-platinum **Stay Hungry** launched two big hits, a couple minors, and not much more than 18 months of Twisted mania.

Mark Mendoza on *I Wanna Rock* . . .

"That song came together really quick. It's not a tough song. Dee wrote the song basically and I helped him construct it and arrange it. It came together right away. The video went really quick as well unlike with most videos, where you end up standing around for a hundred hours doing nothing. I mean, it's a great rock song, one of our premier songs live. Live, we were an experience. In my opinion, our studio albums never did us justice. We were a live band and going to see us was like seeing a three-ring circus. It was a wall of sound; we had a huge sound. Even I forgot after awhile and in the last few months I was going through live tapes and I realize now how huge the band sounded . . . tremendous, massive sound. And we had the best weapon in the world. We had the best front man there ever was, live in concert. Had I not been in Twisted, I would have been a fan. The band knew how to handle crowds."

301 THE EVIL THAT MEN DO IRON MAIDEN

180 points *from Seventh Son of a Seventh Son* (EMI '88)

Riding on the sad saddle of a typical Maiden gallop, *The Evil That Men Do* grooves like crap, both Nicko and Harris demonstrating in tricycle tandem that when they're good they're metal incarnate, when they're bad, they're doddering. But the song is lifted by two stirring pre-chorus melodies, as well as a chorus that, if not any sort of creative apex, at least is impressionable in a drooling **Somewhere in Time/Fear of the Dark** manner.

Bruce Dickinson on *The Evil That Men Do* . . .

> "*The Evil That Men Do* was conceived . . . I got about halfway through writing a story to go with the album. And a couple of my songs that I did lyrics for fitted in with this general concept of the story. And *Evil That Men Do* was one of those, and the idea was the corruption of innocence. And in it, the seventh son of the seventh son is tempted to sleep with the Devil. And he comes down as this gorgeous woman who basically takes his virginity and disappears, basically leaving him lonely and pissed off and empty."

Chris Boltendahl from Grave Digger
Black Sabbath — *Paranoid*
Judas Priest — *Painkiller*
Rainbow — *Catch the Rainbow*
Led Zeppelin — *Stairway to Heaven*
Black Sabbath — *Sabbath Bloody Sabbath*

Led Zeppelin — *Whole Lotta Love*
Deep Purple — *Smoke on the Water*
Ozzy Osbourne — *Diary of a Madman*
Ozzy Osbourne — *Crazy Train*
Van Halen — *Runnin' with the Devil*

302 HOT FOR TEACHER VAN HALEN

179 points *from 1984 (Warner '84)*

I suspect we were all supposed to thank Van Halen for rocking out here, *Hot for Teacher* providing the speed metal mayhem on an album thin on metal. But thin applies here as well, *Hot for Teacher* being thin on premise, riff and arrangement, just like *Jump* and *Panama* and *I'll Wait*. In any event, we clapped, we stomped our feet, we hooted, we hollered, as Alex worked those tumbling double based drums (his fills are gorgeous), as Eddie played amphetamines blues, as Dave bounced his desk with his knees (I know, no one ever talks about the bass player). Close examination (grudgingly) reveals a sense of structure however, as mini-events blur by, methodically answering enough questions on the song test correctly to lift *Hot for Teacher* to a D+ pass. And if the good mood persists by record's end, it might be for the fact that Van Halen, in their do-no-wrong years, have managed to create a stop/start air guitar classic out of nothing more consequential than schoolroom chatter.

Michael Anthony on retaining inspiration . . .

> "I think it still comes from what it did 10, 15 years ago. I mean, I still feel like a teenager. If there's one occupation that keeps you young, it's playing music. We never try to put any undue pressure on ourselves to repeat or to sustain. If our material is hit material, it is, or it isn't. That non-pressure really helped us keep our sanity and inspiration together for all these years."

303 D.N.R. (DO NOT RESUSCITATE) TESTAMENT

179 points *from The Gathering (Spitfire '99)*

Very cool seeing such a new track vaulting this high, Testament's **The Gathering** impressing the discerning thrash throngs immediately with its all-star lineup and measured sampling of all the band's best characteristics. *D.N.R. (Do Not Resuscitate)* is the lead track and it's a hooky and majestic opener, well-recorded, well-executed and typically morbid, Chuck razor-honing his words with increasing intensity as the life experiences pile up.

Chuck Billy on *D.N.R. (Do Not Resuscitate)* . . .

> "All of them have to do with the same topic (laughs). It's about a guy having enough of this world and seeing how bad it is. Being in the choice of a life or death situation, he chooses death, because he doesn't want to see all the pain and misery in this world as it goes down the drain."

304 EPISODE 666 IN FLAMES

179 points *from Whoracle (Nuclear Blast '97)*

It was an exciting spectator sport, watching In Flames gleefully plunder the thunder of Maiden then flay the corpse in a particularly Swedish and deathly manner. Twin leads rifle gorgeously through this thick yet accessible song, while Anders succeeds in steadfastly standing his underground, burying a true death vocal amidst the seductive melody. Dirty guitars and dirty drums complete the bulking process, transforming a track that is embarrassingly hummable into something Scandinavian and sunsetting.

Anders Friden on *Episode 666* . . .

> "I like to play it live. It's a strange structure; it's like verse, verse, chorus, chorus, chorus, chorus, end, which is really weird (laughs). We've changed it a little bit now. Today it's not the same

song as when we wrote it. We've changed it for the live environment; we took some parts away that just went on, a big bunch of guitar riffing we didn't think was necessary. And we've done some parts a little more groovy. But I love to play it live because it's got good interaction between the band and audience because they always like to scream the famous numbers (laughs)."

305 THE BOYS ARE BACK IN TOWN THIN LIZZY

178 points *from Jailbreak (Vertigo '76)*

Sadly the band's only big hit, *The Boys Are Back in Town* successfully bridged Thin Lizzy's mellow melodies and their guitar firepower. Lyrically, Phil also bridges two worlds, his love of mythic heroes throughout literature and film with a modern, street-wise tale covering the same guy-gang terrain. Further establishing and securing the song's legendary status, *The Boys Are Back in Town* is rum-soaked in Phil's Springsteen and Van Morrison pub rock tones, the band as a whole creating a buoyant, optimistic bounce of a track, even the heavy, grounded, linear chorus chords evoking a celebration of the unique bond between the guys in any gang, be it a band, men of war, football hooligans, childhood friends or conspiring thugs, all of which have been proposed as the gist of the jingle. And as icing on the cake, you'll find one of the band's most spiritual twin leads of a vast catalogue full of them.

Scott Gorham on the band's writing chemistry . . .

"In those days, I don't think we knew how to credit the songs. I'm not saying that anybody was ripped off, but there weren't any sort of parameters or rules. The way the songs got written, somebody would bring something in and it would be a barebones kind of thing. Phil and I would sit around with the acoustic guitars and then bounce ideas off of each other. Everybody had a lot to do with the songs. It wasn't a one-man show, but Phil was the catalyst and would bring in most of the ideas. It was kind of a natural thing to give him the credit. There were certainly guitar parts in *The Boys Are Back in Town* that I came up with but you don't get credit for that. You get paid mechanically, but you can't claim a writing credit."

Mike Scott from The Waterboys
Blue Öyster Cult — *(This Ain't) The Summer of Love*
Deep Purple — *Child in Time*
Thin Lizzy — *Don't Believe a Word*
Jimi Hendrix Experience — *All Along the Watchtower*
Beatles — *Helter Skelter*
Iggy and the Stooges — *Search and Destroy*
Blue Öyster Cult — Harvester of Eyes
The Stooges — *Dirt*
Blue Öyster Cult — *Career of Evil*
Cream — *Strange Brew*

306 MEAN STREETS VAN HALEN

177 points *from Fair Warning (Warner '81)*

Opening with one of Eddie's most magical moments of many, *Mean Streets* then kicks into one of the band's least obscure, most precise metal tracks since the solidity of the fabled debut. It's a sinister minister of an anthem, full up with fireworks, Dave matching Eddie's malevolence lick for lick. As bonus, the band manages to raise their game come chorus time, coolest aspect being those unique backing vocals which Eddie marbles, brackets and punctuates with brief maneuvers that invoke the dark alley skullduggery of the lyrical concept.

307 JULY MORNING URIAH HEEP

177 points *from Look at Yourself (Bronze '71)*

Consider this Heep's answer to Purple's *Child in Time*, both tracks slowing down rip roarin' albums full of new metal fireworks. *July Morning* is a long, mellow, idealistic, proggy affair that placed Heep in yet another realm where they didn't quite belong, that of art rock, the band nevertheless touching on escapist realms that would become creatively and commercially advantageous places to visit come the next couple of records. Still, it's wholly out of place on **Look at Yourself**, even though over the years it's quietly gathered a sort of seriously reverential following.

Mick Box on *July Morning* . . .

> "I think that *July Morning* is one of the best examples of the way the band was developing at that point in time. It introduced a lot of light and shade into our sound. It was magic, a very powerful song that encompasses everything that Heep stands for then and now. Beautiful dynamics from the band. Manfred Mann playing over on the end section with his mini moog. No practice — he just played it and we recorded it in one or two takes from memory."

308 MODERN DAY COWBOY TESLA

177 points *from Mechanical Resonance (Geffen '86)*

Opening their greatest hits album and closing their 2-CD live album, *Modern Day Cowboy* is undoubtedly Tesla's most beloved moment. And of the band's two personas, Def Leppard done right and Mellenhead done heavy, this falls to the former. And done right it is, Tesla sliding (and *Foolin'*) into the dark and moody mellow verse before exploding into big riffs for the back end and the same chords for the chorus, which leans a little Bon Jovi jingoistic for my liking. Even if the production is a little sterile, you could hear that beneath the high stakes, there was soul, something which would breathe deeper as the band progressed through their underrated catalogue.

Troy Luccketta on *Modern Day Cowboy* . . .

> "It was our first single, so it means a lot to me. That was the track that actually broke us with radio and got us on the David Lee Roth tour, because he had seen the video and he thought the band and the song kind of stuck out a little bit over the other bands at the time, and he picked us for his tour. It was a song that opened all the doors for us. That was the tune that just kind of said, 'Hey! Here we are! Who are these guys? We're Tesla.' That first album is just a straight-ahead, honest record. We went in, minimal overdubs, recorded the record as live as we could. The second album, we probably got into more of the overdub processing at that time, a little more production on the record. The first record was probably a little less produced. But again, the first record, having *Modern Day Cowboy*, kind of jumpstarted things. Even back at the time of the debut, we were probably less produced than most of the albums coming out. But you can definitely hear it on the vocals, the saturation, the reverbs, things like that. Personally for me, that album's hard to listen to (laughs)."

309 REFUSE/RESIST SEPULTURA

176 points *from Roots (Roadrunner '96)*

Heartbeat, voodoo, metal heart, Igor, Max . . . the opening sequence of *Refuse/Resist* marks the apex of Sepultura's career, the moment of revelation before the actualization of **Roots**, the excitable cusp between old and new ideas. As the song progresses, what we get is an inspiring and violent protest anthem that is shaken and stirred, more volatile than any magic thrash moment from Metallica during their own divine molecular transformation, barely written but then so perfectly written. It is an arcing Molotov cocktail of a song, swirling, jagged, explosive, the riff flanged and flammed, banks and tanks of Marshalls destroying through sound alone. And stuffed in the middle, there's a modest hardcore breakdown that validates its existence once it drops back into the frenzied mob action of the opening riff and another resolute verse, followed by the rattle of dry bones.

Andreas Kisser on *Refuse/Resist* . . .

> "That was done in Phoenix, **Chaos A.D.**, we started working on the album in Brazil; we wrote *Propaganda* in Brazil, the first song from that album, and then we went to Phoenix. With *Refuse/Resist*, it's kind of funny, because we were trying to write songs and we were there for three hours and came up with nothing, absolutely nothing. It was just one of those days and we were almost giving up. And we tried one last time and we came up with that riff, and then we started working with the rest of the song and half of the song was pretty much done after we got that spark."

310 IGGY AND THE STOOGES SEARCH AND DESTROY

174 points *from Raw Power (Columbia '73)*

The try harder track on the last try record, *Search and Destroy* clearcuts a jagged path toward punk while making life uneasy for metal. In this latter laughing guise, *Search and Destroy* perhaps planted the self-extracting virus that would kill metal with the rise of Nirvana. Yet at the time, metal would pay no mind, Iggy and his autobiographical rant making more of an impression on the folks who would wobble and cobble together the New York punk movement. Guitars wrench, drums stomp and in a flashback to whatever rags from the past these walking trashcans have piled in the corners of their maniacal minds, there's even a bit of boogie woogie. But mostly it's squalid, accidental metal, arriving in that foreign place through chemicals, lack of sleep, malnutrition and anger.

311 I'M BROKEN PANTERA

174 points *from Far Beyond Driven (Atlantic '94)*

I'm Broken is perhaps the most accessible track on this difficult, experimental, extremely percussive record. Like *5 Minutes Alone*, it's got a tainted touch of blues swagger, or more pointedly, that part of doom that is tangled up in blue. Phil gets to call and answer with his bad self, using his increasingly raw scrape vocal, while Dime does simple math, adding, subtracting, resolving moving onto the next question. Blocky, angular and slow, with a pure and paramount break riff which also closes the show, creating a slow, grave-filling fade.

Phil Anselmo on *I'm Broken* . . .

> "I think there's just a killer fucking grove to that song. When it breaks into the chorus, that's pure Pantera; that's what we invented, that pure chug. Now of course, you hear so many bands do that today, it's ridiculous. But when it breaks into that chorus, it's pure unbridled Pantera. It's more about the groove and Pantera meeting up with it. It just turned out good."

312 PERFECT STRANGERS DEEP PURPLE

174 points *from Perfect Strangers (Polydor '84)*

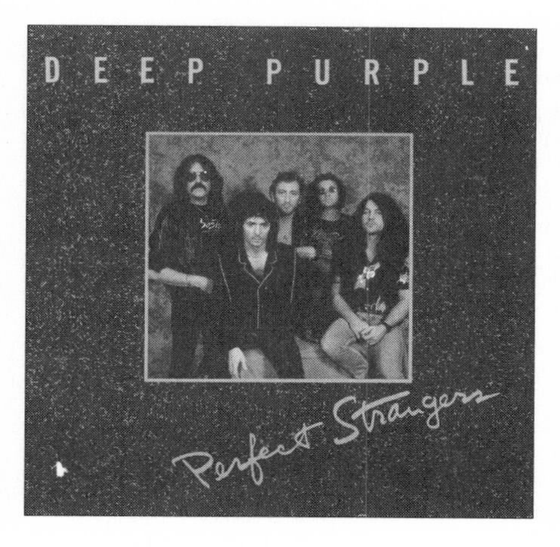

Rarely has a reunion (shotgun or otherwise) resulted in a record more beloved than **Perfect Strangers**, Purple's million-selling opus arriving on the tail end of one metal revolution, three years before the rise of another. The title track was the most dramatic bit of Ritchie rock enclosed, Gillan sent into a dreamy Robert Plant tizzy, Lord swelling swellegantly to a plodding pump from Paice and Glover, the band in total locking into a shameless bit of Rainbow rumination come break time. A case of giving the people what they want, connection definitely coupled, electric reverie flowing.

Ian Gillan on *Perfect Strangers* . . .

> "*Perfect Strangers* is one of those songs . . . if you go to my website, gillan.com, you can find, there's a wordography there, and that's one of the ones . . . I was going through all the lyrics that ever meant anything in my life, about 300 songs, and that's one of the ones up there. But I think the idea is that there's a certain amount of self-analysis in *Perfect Strangers*. It was difficult, the reunion at that time in '83. We had all carried on with our careers, our own music. And families get, you always have rows and disagreements, but there's some kind of spiritual bond or tie to hold you together, or at least make you want to give it another shot. And we were all doing OK individually, but having got together, there were two questions. Individually we were confident with our own abilities and contributions, but there was that nagging doubt, would it work a second time? And the answer to that was yes and no. And the other thing was, would anybody be interested? And the answer to that also was yes and no. And had we been able to rekindle the flame, with that thing you call, what-

ever you like, a love affair in torment, I think it might have been great. But there again, if you look at quantum theory, would we be where we are now had we been successful at that time or would it just have prolonged the agony? I don't know. It's just a different way of looking at it. So I think what happened with *Perfect Strangers* and the lyrics, it pretty much told the story of the album and the making of it and the reunion."

313 DIE YOUNG BLACK SABBATH

174 points *from Heaven and Hell (Warner '80)*

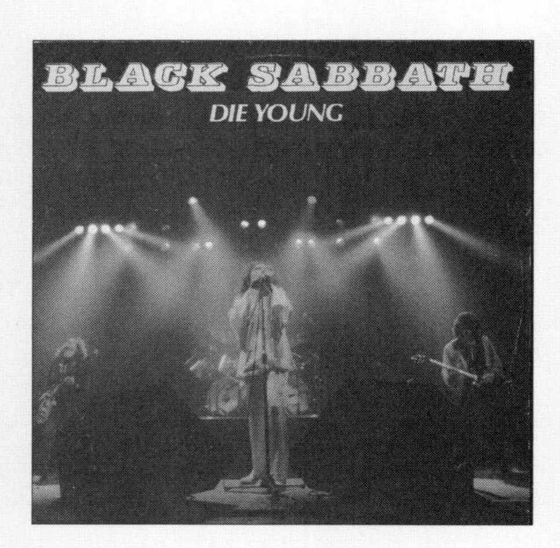

To my mind, *Die Young* is the emotional and creative apex of Sabbath's Dio years, and within the track, the moment is crystallized by the 'oomph!' just before the vocal kicks in. The beauty of this track is its hellish marriage between rhythm and melody, each and all instrumentalists virtually swept along by the song, each and all slaves to rhythm, only Ronnie spot-lit and starry. The lyric is universal yet also applicable to or synergistic with Ronnie's wizardly world. It is a high horse of a song, blessed with a forceful yet proggy yet hooky break, each fresh event building to regal metal starbursts. All combine for a worldly and world-weary quality that rises proudly above much of the rest of the album, which, classic as it is, works freely and willingly in juvenalia.

Ronnie James Dio on the **Heaven and Hell** experience . . .

"I think a lot of the success of that album has to do with the fact that I am so much different than Ozzy. Being so much different and being more of a writer than Ozzy is, I helped shape that band into a little bit more of me. It was still Black Sabbath. I think that Martin Birch, who produced that album, made an incredible difference. The sounds that he got were really wonderful. It was a real joint effort. It wasn't just one person. It was everybody really doing a great job on the album. I thought Bill Ward was great on it. I think Bill has always been under-appreciated. I think it shows the guys in that band can really play. We did shape the music a little differently. Ozzy used to call it Black Rainbow! I never tried to do that and I don't think that I did. I mean, the subject matter was very different and the riffs that Tony writes are very different from Ritchie's. We just made it Sabbath Mach II."

314 CHAINSAW CHARLIE
W.A.S.P.

173 points *from The Crimson Idol (Capitol '92)*

One of the emotional bits of turbulence on Blackie's somewhat well-regarded yet unsavoury concept album about a doped-up rocker, *Chainsaw Charlie* is quintessential W.A.S.P. recorded better 'n average. Blackie's bleak, vaguely Maiden-ish melodies are there, as well as the man's palpable sense of impatience, characterized by the vocals but more so W.A.S.P.'s trademark busy drumming, which goes plain nuts for the break preceding the obtuse, weak first guitar solo. Once it speeds up to a shoes-untied run just past the halfway point (this is really two songs), it sounds like Maiden again. **X-Factor** Maiden. Mixed with Jackyl.

Blackie Lawless on *Chainsaw Charlie* . . .

"Extremely angry at a record company president, someone who

lied right to my face. And when it hit me that I was a product and not a person, it actually got easier to deal with people in the music world because I realized then that hey, it's nothing personal. It's just a product. You're the new hula-hoop. When you don't sell any more, you get put in the bargain bin."

315 METAL GODS JUDAS PRIEST

173 points *from British Steel (CBS '80)*

The secret to this song is the double stroke shuffle hi-hat beat, that, and Ian Hill's pulsing bass, both driving a simple, almost optimistic and happy riff through to victory, Priest straddling the idea of uncompromising metal and clear compromise. In fact, *Metal Gods* is to **British Steel**, what *Sinner* is to **Sin After Sin**, the low background hum, the place for pause. But the band manage to make sure the chorus bulks up and gets dirty, much like the sister track on this album, *Grinder*.

Rob Halford on *Metal Gods* . . .

"Well if there was ever a great song in metal and if there was ever a metal anthem it would have to always be *Metal Gods,* talking about the robot scythes and the laser-beaming hearts and the molten breath. It's a great caricature for metal. It's almost like an animation idea put under cover of a piece of metal music. And when everyone sings along with that song I think they feel that they are a metal god too. It's just a great song that connects with people on an emotional metal level."

316 ANARCHY IN THE UK
SEX PISTOLS

172 points *from Never Mind the Bollocks, Here's the Sex Pistols (Virgin '77)*

One of the more lackadaisical musical structures on the one and only Pistols album proper, *Anarchy in the UK* is saved by Rotten's sloganeering lyric, one of his best both as poetry and social commentary. Plus the football hooligan, Cook 'n' Jones thuggery of the holler-along chorus is so damn dole and droll British, you can't help but see burning Union Jacks as those pints clink and chink. So to recap (or more like re-state): *Anarchy in the UK* sounds like Sid's silly, pretty vacant, tooth-protruded grin but there's 20 good bumper stickers here in Johnny's sneer, if plastering your Austin Mini with Pistols lyrics be your thing. Why's it in a metal book? 'Cos it's a metal album, a metal song, and on an expanded level, a phenomenon (badly translated rebellion) that dented the heads of many a metal mind making albums by the mid-'80s. Plus y'all voted for it.

317 SUPERNAUT
BLACK SABBATH

172 points *from Vol 4 (Warner '72)*

Supernaut sounds like Sabbath tackling itself, grappling with its insane ideas, falling about the place and not with laughter. Much of **Vol 4** does this, but *Supernaut* is particularly three-legged, Iommi wrapping up his hapless band mates in thick cables, driving the process into the yielding marshy ground of North England. Merely and impressively another volume on the man's bookshelf of doom, *Supernaut* is a tacit case-builder, a block on a record squared by them, another plow of sound deep into the nihilistic, answerless void.

Bill Ward on *Supernaut* . . .

"John Bonham really liked that song (laughs). It was one of his favourite songs. He came to Morgan Studios in London one time when we were recording, and they wanted to jam, there was Planty and Bonham, they came down and they were jamming, and we got together and Bonham wanted to play *Supernaut*, and he had it down. It sounded great (laughs). We know there's never been a recording of it with him, but it just sounded really cool. I love it because I think we originally did *Supernaut* in California. We recorded it right here where I am now, in L.A. It was a great time in our lives and I love the beginning. Tony's riff on that one totally rips. And I love the lyrics. Again, Ozzy and Geezer were totally on."

318 POUR SOME SUGAR ON ME DEF LEPPARD

117 points *from Hysteria (Mercury '87)*

Village Voice's Chuck Eddy has written the first and last intellectualized word on this band, and his prime area of study is this monster of a mainframe machine of a record. I choose not to participate in elevating its status past synthetic bubblegum rock into some sort of pioneering technology/art synthesis, but one can see the abstraction in a song like this, Joe Elliott mumbling and wheezing about this and that, guitars like armies of Prozac-bloated bees, drums that sound nothing like. Any anthem about pouring sugar on me is best left unexamined and unexhumed, but you bought it in droves, and you threw it more than a couple chicken bones in our pooch poll. While you indulge your sweet tooth, all I can dredge is the memory of one of those dreams where my teeth loosen and tinkle to the floor.

Rick Allen on *Pour Some Sugar on Me* . . .

"Actually, that was a line that Joe came up with and he just kept singing this thing in the studio. And Mutt got to hear it and really, they just based the whole song around the chorus. And the drum rhythm, we actually ripped straight from an LL Cool J song. It just seemed to fit. It's a bit of a silly song, but people seem to jump on it and love it. That was one of the songs responsible for **Hysteria** really going through the roof. Really, the philosophy is always, the best idea wins. If somebody comes along, or somebody in the band comes along and says, 'I don't like that; I just don't think that works there,' then it's always a good idea if you have another idea hanging out of your back pocket. That's always been the case. Mutt always instilled in us, try and not get too precious with whatever you record, because tomorrow we may change it. And it's purely to try and make the songs as good as they can be. I mean, many of the songs, they go through so many changes, by the time the thing is finished, Joe will have sung some of the songs 20, 25 times. It's just that constant process, polishing the thing, honing it down to where really, it's as good as it can be."

319 IMAGINATIONS FROM THE OTHER SIDE BLIND GUARDIAN

171 points

from Imaginations from the Other Side (Century Media '95)

Blind Guardian have endeared themselves to metal fans all over the world with their lush and plush power metal pageantry, taking the form beyond meticulous Helloween-derived speed metal into the truly operatic and multi-multi-tracked. Buttressed with classical passages and tales of Tolkien, Hansi Kursch and his assembled medieval Germans have succeeded by immersing themselves into gothic pomp well beyond levels other bands, save for Rhapsody, would find safe. Ambitious, daring and wholly committed like Manowar or Virgin Steele, Blind Guardian have become the unapologetic vanguard of all things castle-rocked.

Hansi Kursch on *Imaginations from the Other Side . . .*

"The most important thing there is that I did not like the chorus at all; I hated it. I was looking for any chance to get another chorus because I thought it was too mainstream, too easy. All the other guys in the band, they loved it and I basically did like the music but I did not like the lines I came up with. I did like the whole structure but it was simple-sounding. But that was probably the most important chorus on the whole album. That is what the album is considered to be unique for. Lyrically it's about something we experience a lot. People do not want to deal with fantasy themes but that's where a lot of individuality is. Music-wise, that was the strongest song on **Imaginations**, but because of my doubts about the chorus, we created at least two or three other choruses which were later on used in other songs. One chorus created for *Imaginations from the Other Side* is the chorus in *And the Story Ends*, for example."

Hansi Kursch from Blind Guardian
Iron Maiden — *Hallowed Be Thy Name*
Deep Purple — *Speed King*
Black Sabbath — *Black Sabbath*
Manowar — *The Crown and the Ring*
Led Zeppelin — *The Battle of Evermore*
The Who — *Smash the Mirror*
Thin Lizzy — *The Holy War*
Uriah Heep — *The Wizard*
Warlord — *Mrs. Victoria*
Omen — *Into the Arena*
Satan — *Key to Oblivion*

320 MANDATORY SUICIDE SLAYER

170 points *from South of Heaven (Def Jam '88)*

Dangerously into the catchy zone, Slayer simplify and get all cowboy hat rock 'n' rollsy. But it's a welcome directive as far as I'm concerned, the band really grooving, spurred on by the precious metal production of Rick Rubin and the automatic cool of Dave Lombardo, who applies his truck wreck, snare-and-tom-combo fills specifically and intelligently, never losing sight of the song's bloody and bloody entertaining backbone.

Dave Lombardo on *Mandatory Suicide* . . .

"Wow. We got a lot of stink for that, the suicide thing. We had a photo with some kid hanging himself, which was never used. It was staged, but that got a lot of flack from people. I think it eventually got used on a bootleg. But we were going to put it on a picture disk or on the back cover or something but we never did. I think Tom got a lot of ideas for that from **Full Metal Jacket**."

321 GOD OF THUNDER
KISS

170 points *from Destroyer (Casablanca '76)*

The darkest, most claustrophobic track on an album that is oddly uneasy even when partying, *God of Thunder* became the track most associated with Gene, as soundtrack to the man's superhero alter ego autobiography. Its smothered heft comes from its gangly difficult riff (*She* locked in a medieval dungeon) augmented by a percussive performance that evokes the lead drums of Bill Ward, topped by vocals that sounds like a grizzly late for hibernation. Wrapping a big black bow around the experience is the use of little kid noises, a creepy effect that is appropriate given the tenor of the times as the golden age of low budget high impact horror movies.

Gene Simmons on the reunion stage show . . .

> "Ace shoots mortars out of his guitar, blows up everything. I fly to the top of the light trust at eight feet per second, 50 feet plus the above the ground, throw up all over people's heads and sing the wonderful love ballad *God of Thunder*. There's tons of fireworks. Pete's drum kit levitates into the air. He'll wear a parachute just in case. There's hydraulic equipment that will lift the entire band, not just 50 feet, but out into the audience about 30 rows. We have enormous video banks that are over three stories high, so that no matter where you are, you'll be able to see the nose hairs sticking right out of my nose. It's finally the show of shows. The big rock show; now more than ever. There's the title of your article."

322 PICTURES OF HOME DEEP PURPLE

170 points *from Machine Head (Warner '72)*

The deep album track that bubbles with quiet sophistication, *Pictures of Home* is the unsung hero on **Machine Head**, every bit the keyboard/guitar ballet as are the segments from *Highway Star* and *Space Truckin'* that perform a similar thermal dance. And point in fact, this is the Purple place where Rainbow begins, *Pictures of Home* leaden with Nordic, Celtic, castle rock elitism, emitting quite the set of remarkable melodies this early in the building of metal's foundation. And later in the track, Jon Lord finds his finest moment, soloing as strongly as his piece on *Highway Star* but with even greater aristocratic authority.

Roger Glover on assembling Deep Purple albums . . .

> "I think we've always been a sort of self-contained band and for better or worse we've always given ourselves ridiculous handicaps under which to work, location being the main one. You know, setting ourselves up in the cellar of a ski house or a castle in France or a hotel corridor in Switzerland or a villa in Italy. For God's sake, why don't we just go into a proper studio with a proper producer and do a proper album? I've gotten to the point where I just want to get a great sounding album without all the headaches that go along with trying to make — how do they say that — a silk purse out of a pig's ear. Although I enjoy that, it's an unnecessary added stress. Just for once I would love us to do an album like the old-fashioned albums in a proper studio with a proper producer."

323 LOOK AT YOURSELF URIAH HEEP

169 points

from Look at Yourself (Bronze '71)

It is precisely what goes on in the engine room of this song that makes Uriah Heep arguably the greatest band that ever lived, although it is a earth-shattering chemistry that lasts for mere moments in a career spent reversing any (OK, ludicrous) claims such as the above. But man, when the stars (and this band was full of them) aligned, no one could touch them, Heep's cathedral-vaulted alloy of vocals, guitar, keyboards, bass and drums (yes, all of 'em!) standing Purple on their heads, winning the organ-grinding battle only occasionally but with more satisfying aesthetic wins. *Look at Yourself* is an intense drama, the band in command, driven by Lee Kerslake's powerhouse drumming, graced o'ertop with vocals that seemed to impart wisdoms from deep behind English history. Artfully controlled chaos, fidelity upon high, performances delivered from the frayed edges of rock possibility, *Look at Yourself* is all this plus a metal wallop up the backside.

Mick Box on *Look at Yourself* . . .

> "During the recording of the title song that the guys in Osibisa, who overdubbed some percussion, had some difficulty keeping up with the pace as the tempo increased. It's a good rock song. We were still experimenting after Salisbury in what direction we should go as a band and we decided that it should be melodic hard progressive rock. But yeah, my best memory is Osibisa's eyes popping out of their heads as the track got faster and faster at the end."

324 I DON'T BELIEVE IN LOVE QUEENSRYCHE

169 points *from Operation: Mindcrime (EMI '88)*

A rare patch of groove from a band who, let's face it, don't come equipped with much soul. So the bass and the drums wind up finding each other across the band's characteristic expanses. As with much of the larger album, the riffs are very much subjugated to the whole, as well as the loud percussion and the force of Tate's various vocal personas. One of very few anthemic choruses on an album not designed for such low-class concepts.

Michael Wilton on *I Don't Believe In Love . . .*

> "That's a special song for me because it reinvents the double leads, the trade-off harmonies. I've always enjoyed those. As we've grown older, we do less and less of those but I still like doing them. It was another good song that just came together really quickly."

325 METAL CHURCH METAL CHURCH

169 points *from Metal Church (Ground Zero '84)*

In a move almost worthy of Black Sabbath, Metal Church construct a song tall enough to bear the band name (and a cheeky band named it is, with the same last word connotations as their current competitor Metallica). Announced with a triumphant bass and drums groove joined by big slashing guitar chords, the track then gets down to business with one of metal's stellar riffs as of 1983 — really, no kidding — Kurdt Vanderhoof situating malevolent speed metal mayhem precisely over a drum rhythm reduced to half — and maybe even a quarter — the logical speed, a brilliant ploy, to this day arguably the high point of the catalogue. Also of note, the Peart-musical fills of drummer Kirk Arrington, who keeps the song grooving despite a few ugly bursts of metal busyness.

David Wayne on expanding his repertoire . . .

"I actually want to write a comedy routine. I know it's dicey, because comedy is not just telling funny stories, it's how you time the punches to each story to get them to laugh. I've written some routines and I keep telling myself I'm going to go down to Seattle and do an open mike (laughs). I haven't yet gotten the fortitude. It's easier for me to just grab my guitar and go down to a coffee shop and sing about topics of the day, and just play by myself, without Metal Church. There are quite a few places around here that do that as well. It's a gas, it's really fun. Still, one of these days I'd just like to skate out on that thin ice and try to make people laugh."

326 SPACE TRUCKIN' DEEP PURPLE

169 points *from Machine Head (Warner '72)*

As much of an enigma as *Smoke on the Water* was (once you got past that albatross track's drill-to-the-head riff — that point is crucial), *Space Truckin'* was as funky as it was heavy, as boogie woogied as it was sinister. Lord, Blackmore and Glover weave a tapestrophic history of hard-charging English music, putting on a clinic really, Gillan adding (as if more was necessary) a light-hearted psyche vibe, Paice spicing his halting one-and-three beat with smooth snare and turbulent toms, eventually squeezing in a bit of drum solo before the band meet once more at the pub for a phreak out set to the tune of the song's famous Devil music metal riff.

Ian Gillan on *Space Truckin'* . . .

"*Space Truckin'* was like a road song around the universe. Chuck Berry goes cosmic. At the time, it was amazing to think that there would be a time in the future when the space age would be a historical age rather than something very futuristic, and that's how quickly time has changed. But it was very exciting at the time. Sputnik was going around in the '60s and people were shooting rockets out in a haphazard fashion really."

Brian Vollmer from Helix
AC/DC — *Highway to Hell*
Black Sabbath — *Paranoid*
Steppenwolf — *Born to Be Wild*
Alice Cooper — *I'm Eighteen*
AC/DC — *Hells Bells*
Scorpions — *No One Like You*
W.A.S.P. — *I Wanna Be Somebody*
Deep Purple — *Woman from Tokyo*
Black Sabbath — *Iron Man*
Black Sabbath — *Sweet Leaf*

327 ROCKET QUEEN GUNS N' ROSES

168 points *from Appetite for Destruction (Geffen '87)*

Such is the commercial power of this record that a deep album cut like *Rocket Queen* (last song on the album to boot) can garner 168 points. Pretty much the least travelled track from **Appetite** (I don't believe I've ever heard it on the radio! Gasp!), *Rocket Queen* is really two songs in one, a typically punchy Perry-esqued funk-about (note Adler's signature two-fisted hi-hat work; Duff's swinging bass work) along with a more melodic and almost tender back end. Trivia note I: Axl sez it's about a girl he mooched off of, who was going to call her band *Rocket Queen*. Trivia note II: make-out noises at the halfway break were recorded authentically, live in the studio.

Slash on fame . . .

> "It makes people treat you differently. Even my dad! I got on my dad's case once. I said, 'The last thing I need is every time I come over to your house, you've got a bunch of people you introduce me to that I've never met before, and I've just come over to have dinner!' He treats me as a sort of celebrity, and that's the last

thing I want to deal with. I just want to go and see my family and some close friends I have. I can't go hang out in the same bars I used to go to. Heaven forbid I should go to Tower Records or something just to pick up some CD's, you know. That's awkward. I can't complain about it because at this point I've probably got as much of a vehicle to do whatever I want musically. A lot of kids would die for that. I know I would have before all this happened. So I don't like to bitch about it; that's not conducive to the whole creative element. You have to hole yourself up in some room somewhere, and lock the doors so can get anything done. It's like a little party that everyone wants to get in on."

328 TEARS OF THE DRAGON BRUCE DICKINSON

168 points

from Balls to Picasso (EMI '94)

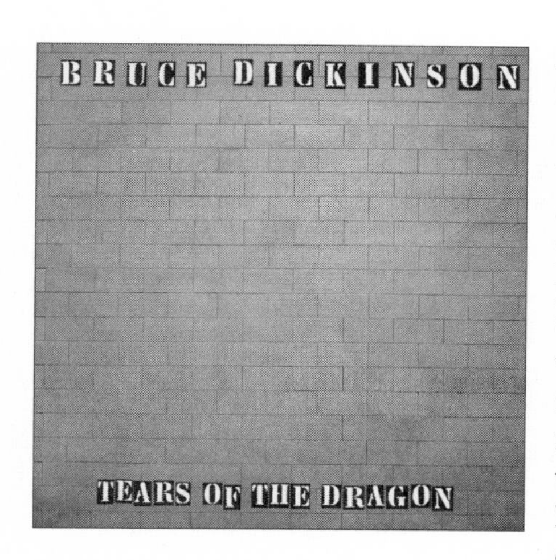

A **Chemical Wedding**/Maiden kind of track way out of context on the obscure, open architecture, lost in time **Balls to Picasso** album, *Tears of the Dragon* displays a proggy Bruce using his pipes passionately. Dickinson takes his vocals from a near whisper to his signature soar, nimbly navigating gothic English melodies along the way, best of which is the stormy verse line. Best to forget — or better yet, quickly scan past — the inexplicable reggae break within, after which we find Bruce duet-duelling with himself for the languished groove toward fade. Never too enamoured with the trashy live feel, I'd like to hear this recorded once again within the studio solidity of the man's gleaming **Chemical Wedding**-style production values.

Bruce Dickinson on *Tears of the Dragon* . . .

"*Tears of the Dragon* started off as being called *Pendragon's Day*, and was very much King Arthur, Knights of the Round Table, misty English hillsides, an atmospheric-type tune. And the producer I was working with at the time was like, 'Who is this Uther Pendragon!? Nobody knows who this guy is!' I said, 'Well, who cares?' And besides, they'll know after they listen to the song. And he said, 'That's not the point.' So I went away and scratched my head and said, 'Well, maybe there's a bit, there have been a lot of people singing about King Arthur and stuff like that. I can see how it can be seen as kind of a cliché. And out of that, I just started thinking, what do I feel and think of when I think about those kind of images? And I think it was something about water, you know, the Lady Of The Lake, Excalibur, and reincarnation. And that's how we got to all the water imagery in the song. And for me, it's still very much an Arthurian, romantic kind of song. It's the romance of throwing yourself into a raging torrent and just letting the water take you wherever. It's a very romantic sort of ideal. And of course *Pendragon's Day* to *Tears of the Dragon* isn't really that much of a leap of faith. It's manifestly a bloody good song. I mean I think it's one of those songs which you can keep coming back to time and time again. Every musician who's sort of ever been through my hands, as it were, has had to play that song and I've never gotten bored with listening to anybody play it yet. That pretty much works for me."

329 ARMED AND DANGEROUS ANTHRAX

168 points *from Spreading the Disease (Island '85)*

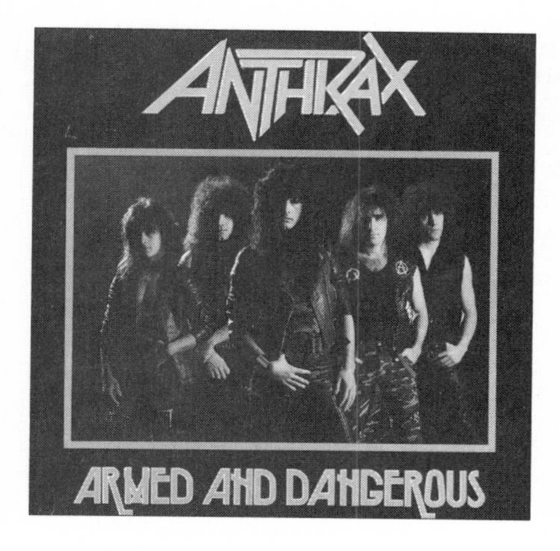

Not so much a power ballad as an epic in the somewhat discarded NWOBHM style (also practised, and according to this poll, perfected, by Metallica), *Armed and Dangerous* starts in gothic acoustic terrain unfamiliar to Anthrax and then leaps into battle, tossing off riffs that have Manowar's upstate NY Vikings in pitched, heated battle with marauding Cossacks. Throughout the song's cinematic journey, we also get to hear the band's effortless quick-picking, driven by Charlie Benante's hard-charging hardcore drum skills. All in all, a bit of an oddity for the band, a bit too musical, a bit pomp and circus pants.

Charlie Benante on the New Wave of British Heavy Metal's influence on Anthrax . . .

> "Oh yeah, I was totally into that more than anything. But I come from a punk rock background as well as a metal background. I was buying Motörhead and Discharge 45's, all that stuff. It was such an exciting time, Iron Maiden, buying Sounds and NME magazine all the time. . . ."

330 SPACE STATION #5
MONTROSE

167 points *from Montrose (Warner '73)*

One of American metal's most buoyant, hopeful and sledgehammer-heavy tracks as of '73, a mere three years into the life of metal as we know it, *Space Station #5* is frighteningly confident, well-paced, and rock starry for a band forcibly cobbled together to make their first album. The riff is pure amplified euphoria, Sammy singing like a rock god, the band dashing in little moody breaks and breakdowns before finally accelerating and blasting off for the climactic close, over which Ronnie turns in a foil of a solo, a soft meander, which itself is blown apart by synthesizer.

Ronnie Montrose on Sammy Hagar's late arrival . . .

> "Well, it wasn't a question of working together. The material was written and it was still a situation at that point we weren't cutting live vocals. We were cutting live rhythm tracks, and then we overdubbed the vocals and solos, because we were a trio obviously. We overdubbed guitar solos, any other extra little add-ons and Sam's voice. Sam was there for the recording, but literally, we would finish up the track, and I think we finished all of the tracks and then Sam came in and finished his vocals and we added the backgrounds as needed. We collaborated on a lot of different lyrics. For example *Bad Motor Scooter*, Sam wrote. *Space Station #5* we totally collaborated on."

331 THE SPIRIT OF RADIO
RUSH

166 points *from Permanent Waves (Anthem '80)*

One of the shining examples of loud electrics infusing with life the impossible conundrum that is progressive metal, *The Spirit of Radio* magically transforms from a fussy and difficult workout into a truly hummable and hooky er, radio song. Peart grooves gorgeously, splashing his myriad cymbals, while Lifeson turns in a gorgeous rain of melodic guitars. Sparking and spicing the event is a small bookcase of sonic chapters, including a smudge of reggae, but mostly variations on buoyant, inspiring electrocuted pop metal. All told, once the song flashes off, one has heard a track that could be a metaphor for a quick spin around the radio dial, Rush supplying quick samples of possible song ideas, strung together like a greatest hits pack, each piece a vignette, yet each interlocking logically under an umbrella of improbable power trio-ness.

Geddy Lee on Rush's changing sound . . .

> "If you were to analyze our history, I think you could say that the first period of our history was a band developing as players. And as time moved on, and we got more proficient as players, that came to surface in a very obvious way on albums like **Hemispheres** and so forth, where the records are very overtly complex. And then we got into this period with keyboards where we started thinking more in terms of making records and producing records. So really **Signals**, **Power Windows**, **Hold Your Fire** . . . that was a shift from being players to being producers. And we first got into the idea of adding things to our music that were not easy to reproduce live. And our albums became productions. There was a whole movement at that time. There was Midge Ure's band, Ultravox. I think we were influenced a lot by those kinds of bands at that time. They seemed to bring keyboards in in a very cool way. There were also records produced by Trevor Horne during that period, although that might have came a little bit later, that were very interesting. And I would say the last period focuses less on that and more on songwriting."

332 STILL LOVING YOU SCORPIONS

165 points *from Love at First Sting (Mercury '84)*

If one ignores the English lyrucks of our favourite six-string Teutons, words which clank loudest on the band's de-clawed kitties, one finds that a select few of their early power ballads actually progress with some sort of melodic, song-strong integrity. *Still Loving You* is like that, **Peter**

and the Wolf dark and dramatic, moving toward some purposeful conclusion, driven by big, stupid guitars, axes that would more or less draw the blueprint for the much maligned power ballad genre. Of course, having said that, count me on board only for that fleeting moment when those three deep metal chords smear into one big one, a power chord fill if you like. So yeah, great song for two seconds, grudgingly accepted sway 'n' stay gurl song for the (checking my watch) duration.

Rudolph Schenker on *Still Loving You* . . .

> "That was the same situation as *No One Like You.* It was composed seven years before it came out and I always tried to get the guys into it. And in 1983, I remember the day, we were in the rehearsal studio, and I again started to play the song. Sometimes people don't hear the special thing about it at any specific time, so I started playing it and Matthias started locking in and put his guitar in it, and Klaus always liked the song too. But as a band we couldn't play it and then we found the right link in it and the whole thing became very strong. I remember Klaus told me the story about how he put his lyrics together. Because you know how special the song is. He went out once in the winter time and he was walking in the park and there was a snowstorm, and he was walking into it, and he came up with it in his mind without writing the lyrics on the paper; he put the lyrics together, went home and wrote it down. This song was unbelievably big in France. We sold 1.8 million singles, just that song. Hey, and I'll tell you one thing, this is a good story. I remember we did four or five years ago a TV show in France that was the best live show in Europe. There was always a spot where the DJ or the guy who was running the show, did an interview part, and we were sitting there, Klaus and me and the guy, and he told us, 'You know you guys, that in 1985 there was a baby boom in France.' And we said, 'What, a baby boom in France?' And he said, 'You know why?' And we said, 'No.' And he said, 'Because of *Still Loving You.*' Everybody made love to this song (laughs). And the interesting thing is, two years later, we met this guy and this woman and they came up to us and said they were big fans and they said, 'We named our daughter Sly' and we said, 'Sly, why?' 'Because of *Still Loving You,* SLY.'"

333 LOST HORIZONS
MICHAEL SCHENKER GROUP

165 points *from The Michael Schenker Group (Chrysalis '80)*

Lost Horizons is a lumbering, doomy pre-power metal epic that laboriously crosses vast lands in search of *Kashmir*-level importance. And it pretty much achieves its aim, Michael, Gary Barden and inappropriate drummer Simon Phillips (see Priest's **Sin After Sin**: same fluttery, problematic lack of power, same happy eccentric moments), putting resolute step after step, past mirages, past feisty NWOBHM bands, past reinvigorated versions of Priest and Sabbath, past disconcertingly good UFO albums with Tonka Chapman. Surprisingly raw and uneventful for a major statement, but a welcome contemplation point on an album otherwise note-dense and pop metal rocking.

Michael Schenker on *Lost Horizons* . . .

> "It's one of my first solo songs with MSG. Working with Gary Barden was great. He and I got on very well. You know, I wrote all this stuff ahead of time and then I was looking for a suitable singer. I don't think my manager was too happy with him but I really liked his voice. And that was in the first bunch of songs I did for the first solo album, along with *Into the Arena*. On that album, we rehearsed like three days, and every time we played a particular song, Simon Phillips would play different drum parts. We would do the same song again, and he would play drums totally different. So basically there was no need for rehearsals because he was always experimenting. It was pretty incredible watching him, very entertaining. Some people don't like his drumming that much, especially for the time. Because he was very free and loose, and in the '80s, drums were very straightforward. But he was very open, adding fills, very unpredictable."

334 SIRENS
SAVATAGE

165 points *from Sirens (Par '83)*

There is not a more perfect couple of minutes of heavy metal guitar on the face of the planet than the first 1:32 (go witness those last four seconds) of this momentous album opener, *Sirens* cracking open the possibilities for traditional metal not heard so forcefully since perhaps **Sad Wings of Destiny**. Indeed, this was a potent form of doomy goth which killed Rainbow or Sabbath or whatever, and these guys were new nobodies on a corrupt and soon bankrupt Florida indie. Not for long, as the underground swarmed and catapulted them to, well . . . many say, their ruin, a commercialization that abated for a corrective and then returned for flowery concept rock. But pow! What an opener. Iommi could only wish to match the substrata struggle housed in this riff.

Jon Oliva on *Sirens* . . .

> "That was the beginning. I think that was the first song that me and my brother Criss wrote for the record and it ended up being the title track. And I remember going to the library . . . this is funny, we went to the library looking for song ideas. The dummies that we are, we go to the library. But I actually found this book on **The Odyssey** and that's where the whole thing for *Sirens* started. So that was very important to the band's career also. We did that album and *Dungeons Are Calling* in a day and a half. I mean, I thought the production was horrible (laughs), but for the time it was OK. I can't listen to it. I wish I could go in and remix those records. We were never in the studio before, and the producer, the so-called producer he had never done anything before either. So we were both in there, each never having done anything, and we recorded in Morrisound Studios who had never done a heavy metal band before (laughs). It was like three different groups. You had the studio guys, our so-called producer, record company guy, and us, all in the studio and we've never done this before. So it was kind of a hit and miss thing. We were kind of surprised that people made so many comments about the production. I mean, we spent maybe an hour on each song. It's like, I spend more time on the high hat now than we spent on the whole album."

335 ANGRY AGAIN MEGADETH

165 points

from Hidden Treasures (EMI '95)

Megadeth was undoubtedly in a zone with this non-LP soundtrack track and the songs surrounding it, deep underneath their hi-fi sound, gleaming guitars, equally shimmery ride cymbals, and ever-flowing bass driving one of the band's unique AC/DC-inspired groove rockers. Dave pulls out his mad old uncle mumble for this one, delivering a lyric that could be read as self-deprecatingly autobiographical (throw it on the pile). Good enough to have been high-class filler on **Countdown**, *Angry Again* was a microcosm of the more commercial,white pants, butt-shaking aspect of that buff 'n' stuffed album.

Dave Ellefson on *Angry Again* . . .

> "We were on a break toward the end of the **Countdown** tour, and we went out to Phoenix to record that song and it was the last session that was ever recorded in this old dilapidated recording studio on 64th Street and Lincoln, right in the heart of Paradise Valley, which is a beautiful old money part of town. There's like a fire department there or something because they mowed the studio down after we recorded there. And I remember going in and setting up and putting that song together within an afternoon. That night we were tracking drums. I remember Max Norman beating on the console to get the knobs to work. It was shorting out all the time. So again, that song came together very quick, it had a singleness of purpose, which was to be on the **Last Action Hero** soundtrack and I remember sitting there listening to the mix thinking, you know, this is probably the best bass tone we've ever had on a Megadeth record."

336 THE APPARITION FATES WARNING

165 points *from The Spectre Within (Metal Blade '85)*

It took a lot to make this kind of pioneering and difficult progressive doom metal connect, and *The Apparition* did so elegantly on the shoulders of John Arch's complex but tuneful vocal phrasings, culminating in the track's connecting, soaring, replenishing chorus. The parts don't exactly all add up synergistically, but all told, this is quintessential classic Fates Warning, dark, escapist, epic beyond any pre-power metal band plying their trade at the time.

337 KEEPER OF THE SEVEN KEYS HELLOWEEN

164 points *from Keeper of the Seven Keys Part II (Noise '88)*

A messy monster of a song, *Keeper*, like *Halloween*, is 13 minutes long, but while it's more sophisticated, it's also less purposeful. Oscillating between fresh mellow melodies for the band and a myriad of power metal postures, the song is a relentless stacking of hectic edits. Even the lyric is a confused tangle of good versus evil, the listener never quite sure who the enemy is. Despite the insane pastiche-ness of it all, there's a gritty live feel throughout, given the brash and boomy production values of the album as a whole, a "one sound" claustrophobia that only relents for a clean, bluesy and pretty much shoe-horned guitar solo.

Kai Hansen on *Keeper of the Seven Keys* . . .

> "That's a song that took a long time to finish. In the beginning, when the original version was even slower. Compared to the other epic, *Halloween*, it was a softer song and I always saw the song more in a harder way. And the first version was very soft in a way, and then we all pushed and tried to make it heavier in some parts and we kicked out some other parts. But finally, the outcome was very good."

338 HOLLOW PANTERA

163 points *from Vulgar Display of Power (Atlantic '92)*

'Ere's a wildly out of character power ballad that rings NWOBHM gothic like Maiden's *Remember Tomorrow* or the dank gloom tones of Angel Witch or Trespass. Phil does a fine and rare job crooning this tale of a friend in a coma, parallels with Metallica's *One* underscored further by the riff-delirious metal rave that inevitably bounds into the glare of the harsh hospital lights and doesn't leave until the song does, evoking images of Phil's durable anger at God and the shared deafening silence of addressor and addressee.

Vinnie Paul on *Hollow* . . .

> "Musically *Hollow*'s one of the most recognizable Pantera songs. It's something we really got in the mood for when we were in the studio. We dimmed all the lights down and really wanted to have that tranquil vibe on the front part of it and when it kicks in we really wanted it to move you. And it works so well. I remember it was the last song we wrote for **Vulgar Display of Power**. When you're writing, when you get past ten, or when you get to ten, anything on top of that is icing on the cake. And you know when to stop, when you've hit your final moment. And that's how we felt when we wrote that song. We said, 'That's it, we're done with this record.'"

339 SHOT IN THE DARK OZZY OSBOURNE

163 points *from The Ultimate Sin (Epic '86)*

Dipping as corruptedly into the waters of hair metal as he would dare go, Ozzy creates the uptempo power ballad, effortlessly scoring a hit single with it, getting a little work done on his unruly locks at the same time. I guess we're supposed to see the dark romantic side of Oz somewhere within this song's moody dynamics (wot a larf), but all I see is a lame song with an annoying chorus not too many notches below *Satisfaction* and *Rock 'n' Roll (Part 2)*, y'know, Gary Glitter's rink rocker. Jake doesn't do much of anything either here, other than squealing, a far cry from his perfect pyro all over **Bark at the Moon**. A bad year for metal, Oz doing nothing to cheer it up.

Phil Soussan on *Shot in the Dark* . . .

"I wrote *Shot in the Dark* originally in 1982. We performed it on a radio show called **Radio One In Session** at that time with my previous band Wildlife. When I joined Ozzy's band we went into the studio with the producer at that time and he didn't think that we had a good enough hit on **The Ultimate Sin**. We toyed with the idea of a cover song, *Born to be Wild*, I think, and then after that was dismissed, Randy Castillo and I were asked if we had any ideas. I presented *Shot in the Dark* and they loved it. Randy suggested to speed it up from the original version that was about 82 bpm to closer to 120 bpm. Ozzy did not like the lyrics that had to do with a mysterious girl and I set down to rewriting them. After a great deal of struggling with ideas, and after watching the movie **Prizzi's Honor**, I had an idea and rushed downstairs in my house - the song would be about a disgruntled assassin. I wrote the lyrics and presented them and the song was accepted. I was very glad that the song was such a success and put Ozzy back on the map; at that time I was being told by his office that this would be his last tour. That was in 1986! It was his biggest ever commercial hit. After we had some publishing disagreements I never wrote for him again."

340 JESUS CHRIST POSE SOUNDGARDEN

162 points *from Badmotorfinger (A&M '91)*

Wickedly, devilishly elevated songwriting here, with a disturbing video to boot, *Jesus Christ Pose* was an incendiary way to announce this album, unleashed as the first single, frankly freaking everybody out with its sin-draped metal vibe. Cornell is at his shriekfest best, stringing o'er top the song's rhythmic maelstrom a wide vocal melody that is pure sylvan Soundgarden. Guitars whiplash the track after the delivery of the verses, after which more guttural doom builds and builds the mood. One of those recurring grunge epiphanies, a smug six-minute justification for the hype raining down on Seattle during those golden years.

Ben Sheppard on making it . . .

> "I don't think we feel that way. We wouldn't know a good time if it bit us in the ass. We know we believe in ourselves and our career, and it's just been a slow process. We know that things come and go too, so were not living an illusion. One day you grab it and you go. I don't think we really feel like we've ever made it. Literally, probably like every other band that get signed or gets a chance to go for it, when you can quit your day job and go, 'Wow, now I can play a bar chord and play the same song a lot, and somehow not have to pay rent by going and doing this or that'. . . that's when you know you're onto something. Otherwise, regardless of the success we've reached, everyone is still as they were when I first met them years ago. No one has any strange drug habits or sexual deviance that they didn't have before (laughs). Kim, I've known for ages. He was friends with my little brother when he first moved from Chicago to Seattle, and I'd see him at punk rock shows that we'd be going out to, or that I would be playing at. We would talk and hang out. We'd go

see bands like Black Flag. After a while Seattle got more punk rock-oriented, then it kinda branched out. Basically you'd go and see Fear, and there would be weird bands opening up for them and they wouldn't be punk bands, they were college radio music. That's how Seattle was. It wasn't self-conscious. Most of it was bands playing for bands."

341 THE CALL OF KTULU METALLICA

162 points *from Ride the Lightning (Music for Nations '84)*

Proving their keen fans' ear for understanding how little tolerance the world has for instrumental music, Metallica write a truly interesting no-vocal track. And not only do they make it a long one, they make it logical and relatively simple, *The Call of Ktulu* advancing and retreating, always cognizant of hook, indeed offering a storehouse of riffs that shouldn't have vocals, riffs that are interesting without them, riffs that sparingly and tastefully use extra guitars in place of Hetfield's holler. The title comes from Lovecraft, and one can imagine the stories of the stony old school mythical creatures of this man out of time set to this substantial lost ruin of a track.

James Hetfield on widening horizons . . .

"Some bands get so trapped. They get so worried about what people think. We were never like that. When it comes down to it, it's the music. Looks or whatever just get in the way. People seem to hear the honesty and how pure it is to us and our 'not give a shit' attitude. That's kept true over all the years and that's the main goal for us."

Evan Seinfeld from Biohazard
Judas Priest — *Victim of Changes*
Motörhead — *Ace of Spades*
Black Sabbath — *After Forever*
Iron Maiden — *The Number of the Beast*
Iron Maiden — *Strange World*
Van Halen — *Mean Streets*
Jimi Hendrix Experience — *Axis Bold As Love*
Led Zeppelin — *Achilles Last Stand*
Accept — *Balls to the Wall*
Def Leppard — *Rock Brigade*

342 22 ACACIA AVENUE IRON MAIDEN

162 points *from The Number of the Beast* (EMI '82)

One in a long line of metal songs that curiously dramatizes the world's oldest profession (for some reason, metalheads usually find themselves relieved of their wallets after such visits), *22 Acacia Avenue* is quite an epic passion play given the subject matter. The opening riff, unadorned, mechanical, electric, strikes at the definition of metal's charms, after which the song flops into a set of pedestrian chords, releasing the tension but maintaining a grey and filmy melodic resonance, which is further reinforced by the transformation of the song into a proggy note-dense journey, seemingly a carryover from the debut album in its dressy gallop. Trust Maiden to wedge in a mellow bluesy part as well, although the ploy manages to provide a respite before saddling up the horses for a clip-clop to conclusion.

Bruce Dickinson on *22 Acacia Avenue* . . .

> "A fantastic song, isn't it? I love that one. Steve wrote the lyrics and I'm sure some Freudian psychoanalyst would have a field day with that one (laughs). I guess women are big, scary, spooky things, aren't they (laughs)? Much more complicated than beer cans."

343 ANTISOCIAL
ANTHRAX

162 points *from State of Euphoria (Island '88)*

The beginning of the end as far as I was concerned, *Antisocial* was just one cover too many, one cover too happy, one more bee in the bonnet, added to all the other novelties being added to the band's dumb smile repertoire. To say Trust was a French band that was sorta heavy is one thing, to call them a crucial and critical metal croissant, that's another. The song fits that middling appraisal, being an ordinary Green Day-style number, which Anthrax doesn't really mess with, even if their dry wit can't help but make a flak jacket racket of it.

Charlie Benante on *Antisocial* . . .

> "One of my favourite bands was Trust, from France. That band had so much attitude. I just loved them and I didn't care that they were singing in French; I just felt the attitude that was coming off of them. Of course they would do records in English too, but it just seems that when they would translate into English, it just wasn't the same. It lost something, I felt, but at least I could understand the lyrics. And with *Antisocial*, I kept saying to the guys, I definitely want to do this, do it as a B-side, and that's what we were doing. We were going to use it for a B-side, but everybody liked it so much, we put it on the record."

344 THE TOWER
ANGEL

161 points *from Angel (Casablanca '75)*

A swirling, regal way to kick off a record and career, *The Tower* is a formidable celebration of, well, progressive metal, before it even existed outside of uncooperative ill fits like Rush, Deep Purple and Zeppelin.

The production is airline pilot steady, an extraordinary conduit for Barry Brandt's percussive persuasion, the man driving the track with the dependable, virtuoso hand of a Lee Kerslake or an Ian Paice. Long track, but it doesn't feel long, with all this fortuitous chemistry and the song's seemingly bottomless melodic depth, provided by Frank Dimino's pipes nestling Greg Giuffria's grinding keyboard structurals.

Frank Dimino on the band's early influences . . .

> "Where our heads were at on the first album, is that we wanted to do a mixture of guitars and keyboards. Barry, myself and Punky were more guitar-oriented but we wanted creative fusion between guitar and keyboards and to keep it heavy. So that was the philosophy. Our influences were the usual ones, Led Zeppelin, Deep Purple, Queen. But we were trying to make it heavy but with synthesizer and guitar. We did that album in about ten days (laughs). We were so polished because that is the stuff we were doing and clubs. So that was the easiest record we did. We were playing every night, two shows a night, five or six nights a week. And then when we got to Los Angeles, we kept rehearsing."

345 LAY IT DOWN RATT

160 points

from Invasion of Your Privacy (Atlantic '85)

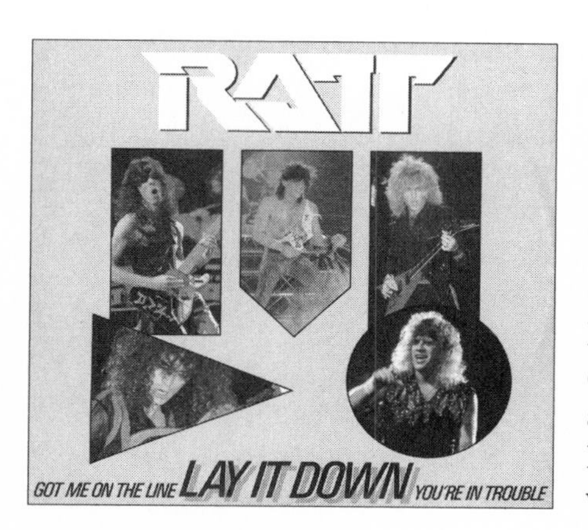

An arch and angled and somehow aristocratic song, *Lay It Down* bespoke of a certain rock starry sophistication that could only be found, amongst the new U.S. breed, in Northern brothers Queensryche. Those guitars sound like top secret aircraft, performing deliberate missions over a deep and delicious rhythm section even Beau Hill couldn't de-claw. Pearcy's voice is of course a key ingredient, his ragged roar distinguishing Ratt further as something special during what were still formative years for hair metal.

Juan Croucier on *Lay It Down . . .*

"*Lay It Down,* wow, man, that's a great song, thank you for asking. *Lay It Down* reminded me of when Ratt was in their prime. We had gone to Hawaii and we had just finished the **Out of the Cellar** tour and I mean, we went from one tour to another for about a year, ten months, and the final tour was with Billy Squier. So we ended up going to Maui, the entire band with girlfriends and wives and the whole thing. We all went to a place called The Maui Sands, which was right on the beach. And I had brought my recording studio, because I always carry a recording studio on the road. It was my version of what was then the state-of-the-art travelling studio which was nothing more than a four-track studio with a couple of accessories. We would all sit around and put our ideas together, ready to be recorded or presented to the group. In the day, we would usually pick a time and come to my hotel room, go into my little bedroom where the studio was set up and start recording. And for *Lay It Down,* Warren had the riff and then I kind of teamed up with him for the groove for it and then we all teamed up for the chorus. And to this day, it's really funny, I know I have this tape of us huddled around the studio, the four tracks, singing the chorus for *Lay It Down* for the first time, singing it together. And you could hear the beat, because it was a drum machine. I would program the drums and say, 'How about this, Bobby?' OK, that's cool. And then I added a bass line and Warren came down and did the guitars. So we had a little sketch of the guitars, and everybody is there singing, 'Lay it down' (laughs). It was just great, because creatively, it was the kind of thing every band wants to do writing-wise."

346 POST MORTEM SLAYER

159 points *from Reign in Blood (Def Jam '86)*

One of my favourite Slayer songs, *Post Mortem* is just this perfect piece of groovy metal power, Lombardo sort of waltzing in 4/4, creating a rhythmic bed that is more of a **South of Heaven** feel. The song is short, but like the brief album, gets the job done, creating a phalanx of mud-covered metal soldiers that, near the doomed conclusion, pick up the pace for the battle that is to come.

Dave Lombardo on *Post Mortem* . . .

> "It's hard to explain. It's the song before *Raining Blood* that sets up *Raining Blood*. It gives it that extra push."

347 IT'S A LONG WAY TO THE TOP (IF YOU WANNA ROCK 'N' ROLL) AC/DC

159 points *from High Voltage (Atlantic '76)*

. . . but it feels like we can all pile into the car, which is what makes this song so fun. Like all pre-**Let There Be Rock** Angus, this one's barely got flesh on those carbon datable bones, but there's no accounting for the attraction of simplicity, evidenced of course by the Grammys, radio and the Ramones. Another simple splash of power chords seductively stacked to get you all hot and bothered on a chilly Friday night, *It's a Long Way to the Top* is the inspiring, light-hearted tale of perseverance that is the band's life story, even if it wasn't that long for AC/DC compared to many harder luck stories. This track's distinguishing feature is its bag-pipe drone, something Korn's marching band-trained Jonathan Davis would recycle from his colourful past 20 years later.

Malcolm Young on the band's endurance . . .

> "Yeah, I'll be gettin' a gold watch soon, eh? I don't think there is any retirement in the music industry. I don't really know anyone that's retired. If they have, it means nobody wanted them anyway. With most musicians it's like the *Titanic*, they go down

with the ship. You feel a part of that responsibility, even with the kids. But you do feel that responsibility that if the kids keep wanting it, and I'm talking kids now that are 40, 45, we'll keep doing it for them. As long as we believe that we've got the right thing to put out, and that's what we always strive towards: the great song. We're still looking for it, like everyone else is. We would love to get something, somewhere near what the guys in the '50s were doing. Not sound-wise, but the quality of the rock 'n' roll. You know, back then they had it all, the swing and all that stuff that gets kids up for these days. AC/DC play basically what was going on with Chuck Berry, Little Richard, Jerry Lee Lewis, trying to create the excitement and get the mood. We want to keep the flag flying. I think we're the only guys except for the Rolling Stones. They're about ten years, 15 years older than us guys so we've still got a long way to go and we like to learn from their mistakes. Once you move, you're confusing the kids. They'd say, 'These guys have gone off rock 'n' roll. We want to keep that around for another millennium."

348 DISCIPLES OF THE WATCH TESTAMENT

158 points *from The New Order (Megaforce '88)*

Really digging into the grim scrape of the Testament identity, *Disciples of the Watch* demonstrates why this band always sounded heavier than Anthrax, despite somewhat the same underlying approach to songwriting. It was all in those back of the throat guitars, Alex Perialas capturing the band in desolate mechanical tones as they smashed their way through an old school thrash sound that was somehow both perfect for the time and two years too late.

Eric Peterson on *Disciples of the Watch* . . .

"*Disciples of the Watch* was the first song we wrote with Chuck. It was his first lyric offering and we were just blown away by the whole lyric and the title. The rhythms were very crushing and heavy and it was just a really powerful song and we really proved ourselves when we played that song at the Dynamo in '87. We were a big hit there."

349 AQUALUNG JETHRO TULL

157 points *from Aqualung (Chrysalis '71)*

Unwittingly creating progressive metal, Jethro Tull paddles in one of their many pools, *Aqualung* progressing obstinately, like a pregnancy's final hours, the band shoving the track around the schoolyard until Ian's relenting, yielding pure prog break deepens the enigma. Of course, Jethro Tull belong in a metal book about as clearly and cleanly as they do trumping Metallica for the metal Grammy. But as is proven by this song's demonic riff (and the number of Tull tracks that garnered votes), the band appeals to metalheads, much the way Floyd does. Plus Tony Iommi almost got the guitar gig when Mick Abrahams got sacked. How heavy metal history might have been different, indeed.

Ian Anderson on *Aqualung* . . .

"I think more than anything else, it's a song that has a grim reality. It's a bit like going onstage at the moment and singing a song, as I do on this concert tour, which is very tied up with the unfortunate aspects of the world's news stories at the moment, singing songs that do have to do with fundamentalist and radical religious applications. It's something that is pretty scary when you do it on stage every night. But to not do it would seem wrong. And to do it, it might seem like you're cashing in on it. But a song I've written some years ago, I feel that I should be able to still sing. And so it is with the song *Aqualung*. It's about something that's very real. And hardly a day goes by when I don't confront that sort of a person and feel the same mixtures of guilt and embarrassment and a degree of confusion. But at the same time you have to think well, hey, it's not going away. It's part of every day. Having to sing that song is a means of continuing to look at something. It's not exactly cathartic, but it's something you have to do. You have to keep confronting it and not pretend that it's something that doesn't exist. It's not at all alone amongst a bunch of songs that I sing. I don't necessarily find it very comfortable to sing, but they are things that I have to keep saying to remind myself of the degree to which they are important subjects. I guess I don't enjoy singing the song because I do focus very much on the words when I'm singing, visualizing what I'm singing. It's very important for me to do that and so it's not always an easy or comfortable song to do, not in the way that some other songs are fun. You sing them and they are upbeat or fun or humorous and are light-hearted. That's part of balancing up a show. You try and accept the songs a little bit so it does have its different resonances as it goes on, through a concert program."

Mikael Akerfeldt from Opeth
Black Sabbath — *Spiral Architect*
Judas Priest — *Dreamer Deceiver*
Ozzy Osbourne — *Diary of a Madman*
Iron Maiden — *Stranger in a Strange Land*
Morbid Angel — *Blessed Are the Sick*
Metallica — *To Live Is to Die*
Yngwie Malmsteen — *Far Beyond the Sun*
Scorpions — *The Sails of Charon*
King Diamond — *The Wedding Dream*
Mercyful Fate — *Satan's Fall*

350 COWBOY SONG THIN LIZZY
156 points

from Jailbreak (Vertigo '76)

Likely the warmest love-in between Thin Lizzy and Thin Lizzy listener, *Cowboy Song* finds the band with their guard down, meekly presenting a light boogie, laced with a twin lead that is among the most celebrated in rock. Phil had a penchant for the Wild West, along with a number of hero sagas and settings, so it's no surprise he handles the subject with passion. Built with a wise wink and a nod for the stage, *Cowboy Song* quickly and effortlessly became the magic moment of any Lizzy show, especially when followed by and fused to *The Boys Are Back in Town*, creating a one-two emotional punch that assured us all was well with the world.

Scott Gorham on Thin Lizzy's trademark sound . . .

> "I clicked big-time with Brian. He and I were the ones that actually came up with the Thin Lizzy sound, that twin guitar and harmony thing. There was no premeditation going on there at all. It was all by accident. That whole thing came about when we were sitting in rehearsals with an eight-track machine and one of us had a line, and someone suggested that we add a harmony line over it. We worked the notes out, put it down, recorded it, listened back and went, 'That's pretty cool.' We just started playing those things more and more. The only time that we realized that we actually had a sound was when we read it in a review — 'that amazing, harmony, twin lead guitar sound of Thin Lizzy.' I remember looking at Brian and saying, 'Shit man, we've got a sound!'"

351 MORE HUMAN THAN HUMAN WHITE ZOMBIE

154 points *from Astro-Creep: 2000 (Geffen '95)*

Perceptively combining industrial, hip-hop and metal, *More Human Than Human* also builds on the patter of the band's big *Thunder Kiss '65* hit, Rob raggedly, monotonously laying out his raps over a stiff backdrop of synthetic drum notions and occasional guitar explosions. Two very annoying things occur way too often throughout this song's urban pimp-roll caterwaul: that elastic band guitar riff and the awkward sentiments of the song title, stupid words spoke-sung like an itchy nursery rhyme. Still, it was a hit, because it kept whacking, despite the mere skin irritation inflicted by its quirky, annoying weapons.

Rob Zombie on the demise of White Zombie . . .

"For some reason, when I think about White Zombie, it seems long, like a lot of work and not a lot of fun for me. There was something about **Astro-Creep** . . . when I was making it, I thought that I'd never want to make another fucking record. White Zombie was very regimented. I had spent the better part of the past 13 years with White Zombie. In a certain way, I was bored with it. White Zombie had fallen into a pattern and something needed to inject new life into that band. A lot of times through the course of the years, that injection came when old member split and new members came in and that really kicked us in the ass. But I just wanted to do something different on my own, really just go for it."

352 DAVIDIAN MACHINE HEAD

154 points *from Burn My Eyes (Roadrunner '94)*

I'll never forget legendary metal scribe Mark Gromen's analysis of, and anger over, Machine Head's textbook sellout (in this case, a sellout to nu-metal), the man delivering his treatise at one of our mag's legendary Brave Bashes (a heavy-metal **High Fidelity** x 10). Gromen said the loss of Machine Head to the nu, dark side was a very real disappointment, a lost opportunity, this defection of a pulverizing, exciting band who on the surface weren't really doing anything new — turning in a cross between Pantera and maybe traditional metal and thrash — yet on an abstract level, becoming the fresh new hope for purists waiting for the wave. *Davidian* embodied this hope, as did the rest of the record. The next album coasted on the fumes of this hope, and it's been an unremarkable unimaginative cloning of average nu ever since, with crap sales numbers I might add.

Robb Flynn on *Davidian*'s impact on the cover art . . .

"That was by Dave McKean. We knew him from covers we liked and the **Enter Sandman** shit. We really liked his style. We really wanted an abstract feel, a surreal picture, and we thought he'd be perfect to do it. I talked to him once or twice. Before he did the picture I read him the lyrics to *Davidian* and then he sent us a couple of sketches, and we went with the one we liked the best and went and did that. We were extremely happy with it."

Ahrue Luster from Machine Head
Mötley Crüe — *Shout at the Devil*
Slayer — *Angel of Death*
Metallica — *Fight Fire with Fire*
Iron Maiden — *Run to the Hills*
Judas Priest — *Screaming for Vengeance*
Black Sabbath — *Black Sabbath*
Slayer — *South of Heaven*
Sepultura — *Chaos A.D.*
Ministry — *So What*
Accept — *Fast as a Shark*

353 SHOUT IT OUT LOUD KISS

153 points *from Destroyer (Casablanca '76)*

More of a **Love Gun** or **Rock and Roll Over** track, *Shout It out Loud* is a melted candy anthem that elevates, lifts, tucks, and then hums a happy tune until all teen problems evaporate. Four records in, this was the natural party rock successor to *Rock and Roll All Nite*, and within the context of **Destroyer**, the song provided a spot of reassuring comfort amongst tracks that could be disorienting and dark. The chorus is almost sweet and naïve, a gentle letdown after verse chords that are fairly heavy, chords topped by Paul in fine form, pep-talking the Kiss Army to go forth, multiply and above all, be proud.

Ace Frehley on his huge influence on other guitarists . . .

"It's probably because I'm still alive (laughs). I haven't died yet (laughs). You know, when you think about all the top guitar players in the world, they've either died or they kind of faded away. That's maybe one reason and another reason is probably because my style drew from all the greats. I took a little from Jimi Hendrix, a little from Jimmy Page, Jeff Beck, Eric Clapton, although a lot of those guys are still alive, God bless them. So you know, basically put it all together and mix it up in a stew and it comes out Ace Frehley. My hard-driving guitar sound is kind of what drives Kiss. From what I read. I didn't say that (laughs). Other people have said it. So don't quote me on that, you know?"

354 KNOCKING AT YOUR BACK DOOR DEEP PURPLE

153 points *from Perfect Strangers (Polydor '84)*

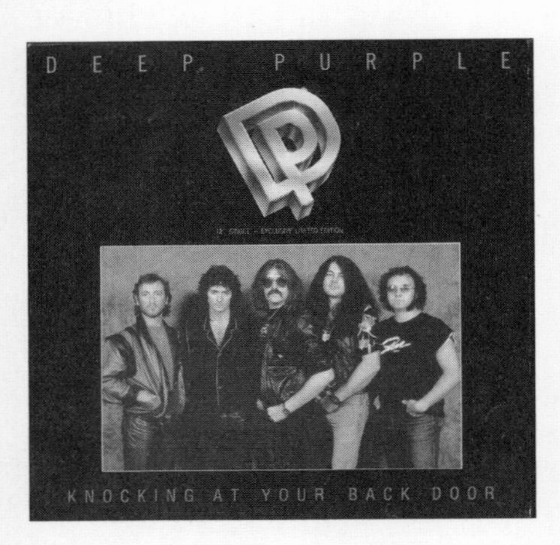

Accessible and royal Purple at once, *Knocking at Your Back Door* ascribes to the Free principle, which is basically letting the song breathe, letting the spaces tell the story. But if Ian's flip word games roll yer eyes, look deep and you will find two — not one but two — of Ritchie's most strident, well-composed, soulful guitar solos ever committed to tape, both chock full of signature Blackmore trademarks, both mini songs in themselves, the first carnal, the second pure blue blood rock aristocracy. And of course, that intro is emotion-rushed magic, Lord and Glover recreating the imminent attack of Jaws before the band collapse into a world-weary recline of a riff, one that oddly nourishes as it diminishes.

Ian Gillan on *Knocking at Your Back Door . . .*

> "Well, it's whimsical, it's humorous. There's this guy named Redbeard, from a radio station down in Texas. He phoned me up after it had been played on every radio station in America and said, 'Is this what I think it's about?' And I said, 'Yeah.' And he said, 'It's amazing, every radio station in America is playing a song written about anal sex and they don't even realize what's going on.' And I was like, well it's not in-your-face anal sex, it's just a joke. It just came about with the lyrics. It's no big deal. But it's a humorous thing and not meant to be offensive. And I think it was just an afterthought. It certainly wasn't what inspired the song."

355 THUNDERSTRUCK AC/DC

152 points *from The Razors Edge (Atlantic '90)*

A loveable but audacious track — and one similar in tone to *Who Made Who* — *Thunderstruck* is one of those modest showcases where the boys throw their couple o' tricks at the wall, and an audience starved for tricks reacts favourably. One is the recurring and memorable guitar widdle from Angus, another is the slow build, another is the (somewhat annoying and contrived) hockey barn chant, and yet another is the thawing of relations later in the track (see both break and chorus). All told, a semi-intelligent way to open the album, AC/DC holding their cards and then playing them when the timing is right.

Brian Johnson on flying the flag for rock . . .

> "I really hope that we can hold a torch out for this hard rock/heavy metal. Here in the States, they're dropping rock 'n' roll stations like hotcakes. I hope it's our job to get some of them back. Alternative is too serious. After awhile you've got to turn around and say, I just want a good time, where's that fucking AC/DC album? We're an enigma, especially with all the critics who say we've got nothing to say, that there's no message in our songs, that we're just a rock 'n' roll, have a good time band. But maybe that's the key to it because we haven't used our music for politics

or for personal crusades. All we've done it for is for the kids to come in and fucking rock for one night; to say, 'That was a great show, I had a great time; it was worth every penny I paid.'"

356 WILD SIDE MÖTLEY CRÜE

151 points *from Girls Girls Girls (Elektra '87)*

Dopey album, but man, this was a very infectious song, driven like a jackhammer by Tommy getting all rhythmic up and down the strip. It's also cool how the riffs criss-cross the depravity, and how the boys manage to perk up enough to chuck in a few abbreviated time change-ups. Once the desperate stripper blues kicks in you get the uneasy feeling that it ain't really about fun anymore, as Vince's seen-it-all lyric might attest. But despite the two atmospheres — both to be fair, quite menacing — the song gets across the idea that the time to drink and drug is now.

Tommy Lee on *Wild Side* . . .

"That's one that Nikki and I wrote. That's when I sort of brought in my new technology to Mötley Crüe. At that time, in 1984, is when I bought my first Macintosh and I was experimenting with recording direct to disc and using sequencers, so that (makes machine gun sounds) in that track, I sort of brought that in and I was trying to get Mötley Crüe to plunge forward, mine new territory with some sequencers and some electronics. I guess this is the part that sometimes throws people. I've been singing and playing guitar and writing music like, since '84. No one knew about it unless you read the credits on the Mötley Crüe records. It's weird, like I sort of taught myself to play guitar and sing, because the other guys in the band would never come over to work. It's kind of crazy. So I've got to thank those guys for not showing up (laughs)."

357 A FINE DAY TO DIE
BATHORY

151 points *from Blood Fire Death (Black Mark '88)*

Quorthon's a pretty interesting guy, and a virtual mythical universe is mapped out through his contemplative, strangely lonely records. *A Fine Day to Die* hails from the man's Viking era, Quorthon composing a dramatic and atmospherically successful look at men just doing what they have to do, going to war and getting offed. The soundtrack to this inward realization is a screeching mess of noise. Vestiges of early Bathory remain, as do necessarily meat scraps from Venom, but the new dimension is the cinematic, escapist quality, a fiercer northern chill. As well, either by accident or vision, Quorthon has created the blueprint for black metal, a style that would sound quite a bit like this, except faster, a style that would not get its act together for a good five years beyond this album's reclusive misanthropy.

Quorthon on the Bathory lifestyle . . .

> "I guess everything I've been doing with Bathory has been the dream of a lot of people my age. I've made all these records and I get to work at home alone. I mean sometimes I don't even get dressed. I sit in my robe and have my cup of tea and sit and read a good book or look at plane films. Life is very long. I've been around for 30 years, and a lot of things have been done since I was kicked out of school. And I'm supposed to be living for at least 60% more time. So there's a lot more to be done. But so far I owe it all to Bathory, so I'm going to have to stick with it."

358 CULT OF PERSONALITY LIVING COLOUR

150 points *from Vivid (Epic '88)*

Too smart and anti-social (same thing? Hell is other people?) for his own good, axe-razzer Vernon Reid at least managed to connect with this lone, anticlimactically early round punch. *Cult of Personality* begins with a memorable riff, pushes further the hit buttons with its open architecture percussive accents, and then cements a place in rock history with its socially responsible lyric, its Kennedy samples and its newsreel video. While still noisy and rudely Van Halen-esque (especially for the linear requirements of radio), *Cult of Personality* nevertheless tries to behave, edging out *Open Letter (To a Landlord)* as the first, second and last times Living Colour would extend the hand of conventionality, however accidentally, however begrudgingly. Fun fact: *Cult of Personality* won the first Grammy for hard rock.

Corey Glover on the "black rock band" tag . . .

> "For all intents and purposes, the shine is off the apple with that sort of thing. If you thought it was a gimmick, sorry, I can't rub this off! It's not, 'OK, I'm no longer black anymore, no longer an African-American, sorry!' I can't do that. Although the issues that I deal with come from my perspective, they're not exclusive to me because I am black. It's not because I'm black that I talk about homeless people or the ghetto. I talk about it because it exists. I talk about being alienated, not because I am black, but I have a unique perspective because I am black. But it is not, and has never been, exclusive to me. If you are a skinhead or a punk kid, a thrasher kid or skate kid, and you don't fit into the norm, you know what feeling alienated is about, just as much as you would know what alienation is like if you were a Rastafarian. It's about people who don't fit in, that's what all our records are actually about, the miscreant of the underworld that no one gives any credence to. I think the media has prompted the idea that we're talking about black issues in a rock format which is not the case — we're talking about people issues in a rock format."

359 FALLING OFF THE EDGE OF THE WORLD BLACK SABBATH

150 points — *from Mob Rules (Warner '81)*

Here's an example of Tony writing one of his sinister yet note-dense riffs, one that is perhaps a bit forced and machine-stamped. But then again, both the Dio albums (let's exclude **Dehumanizer**), as classic as they are, got that way by being forced, worked on, crafted, more perspiration than inspiration. So *Falling off the Edge of the World* is one of this version of the band's self-evident commercial numbers, one that takes care of business, rocks without much eccentricity, indeed, with a rote gothic gale that could have blown it onto a Rainbow album. Ronnie's vocal is leonine and carnivorous, evoking the hopelessness of damned infinity, and the lyric finds Ronnie well within his poetic element, Dio covering familiar territory, the downside of temptation.

Ronnie James Dio on *Falling off the Edge of the World . . .*

> "The writing process for that was weird, not just for that song but the whole album. We did it at this little studio that we had actually used before, Vinny and I, when we're doing some production for somebody else. We went there and did the rehearsals and it was weird, just a strange room and a strange place. *Falling off the Edge of the World* was one of the latter songs we wrote for that album and it was not as smooth as *Sign of the Southern Cross*; but again, the locale was different."

360 ALL WE ARE WARLOCK

149 points — *from Triumph and Agony (Vertigo '87)*

Doro's old band were a well-regarded patch of hard-riding hair metal, and *All We Are* is the band's biggest anthem, a true Germanic festival-format singalong. Its hook is that "look at our fine English" wordplay chorus, driven by a few extra bass drum beats, infused with Euro tones that are all headbanged and hammered onto a steady Accept backbone, even if the main thrust of the song is one that grapples with '87's irrepressible commercial temptations. One of these temptations lies within big, fussy, fought over production values, which fortunately on this album, utilize the best qualities of this golden era, and none of its dated gizmo-driven elements. Not too heavy, not to light, *All We Are* is both accessible and metal, something which made it a live favourite against the more oppressive, note-dense speed of the band's power-ish tracks.

Doro Pesch on touring with W.A.S.P . . . .

> "There was this one W.A.S.P. tour where Blackie decided that he wasn't going to do a show with all the blood and guts anymore because I guess he got in trouble with some people. So he wanted to make a great show but without all the blood. So we played in England and the fans heard about it, that there wasn't going to be any bloody scenes, and they went into the butcher store before the concert. And we were the back-up act, and before the show, being a girl, I always want to put on the makeup and do my hair nice, and I looked great, and I go on stage and within one minute, I was covered in all this bloody stuff they threw. And after the first concert I said to myself, 'Oh man, I can't do this. How will I survive this tour?' And then by the second show I thought, okay, I just have to go through it. When you are the support act you just have to do your best and take it. It was fun, but it wasn't so funny sometimes. And I thought, okay, I have to adjust my look. Also in England, they have a strange way of showing appreciation which came from the punk days. They would spit on you so I was covered in blood and spit all the time."

361 T.N.T.
AC/DC

149 points *from High Voltage (Atlantic '76)*

The original Oi! anthem, *T.N.T.* is one of those barely visible tracks that are all over AC/DC's first two albums. It features a key AC/DC ace, the absence of a full drum beat until the chorus which frankly doesn't add much. Barely there, the song is practically a vocal showcase as Bon warns us laundry list-style against getting involved with the likes of his bad, mean drunk self. Two/thirds through however, we get a truncated ripster of a guitar solo from Angus presaging the tone we'll hear all over the next album, **Let There Be Rock**.

Malcolm Young on staying grounded . . .

> "We just try hard to please ourselves really. You gotta do what you do best. You get lots of people saying, 'Oh, when are they going to change?' and plenty say, 'Don't change.' We couldn't change cause we only know the stuff we like — straight ahead rock 'n' roll, no frills and good performances. The music really is the important thing, that's the bottom line, personally that's all I'm interested in. I'm not even much up for the rest of the thrills of it. Even the press, I'm not a big mover and shaker in those areas and never wanted to be. If I were out of a job, I'd be back at the factory I think. We were all fitters and turners. That's what they called 'em back then in the metal trade, steel work. It was like apprenticeships, four of the guys were fitters and turners and Angus worked with lead. You don't forget the meaning of a dollar. I get amazed at it sometimes when you see a lot of young bands have come up from tough parts of town, especially the rap guys. You see them just buying everything straight away and then six months later they've no more hits, no more money. Scots are thrifty, you know. We're not tight, but we do know what the value of a dollar is."

362 LONG LIVE ROCK 'N' ROLL RAINBOW

148 points *from Long Live Rock 'n' Roll (Polydor '78)*

I've always found this trash-faced boogie song low-rent compared to the rest of this album's moody, mystical, misty material. But its verses, both lyrically and musically, are better than its chorus, and even though it rollicks (badly, stiffly), the song faintly glows with Ritchie's wizardly melodies. Ronnie sells the lyric with a sense of tragedy that almost seems to say that rock 'n' roll is a fatal and final curse, turning the song into anything but a party anthem. But the general structure harkens back beyond **Rising** to the first album, to Elf, making it an odd choice for side one, track one, not to mention title track.

Bob Daisley on the **Long Live Rock 'n' Roll** line-up . . .

> "Ronnie and Ritchie were starting to not see eye to eye, and on the American tour in 1978, Ronnie was beginning to sort of hint to me that he was about to form a band at the end of the tour himself. And David Stone the keyboard player was really only brought in as an emergency to do the world tour. Ritchie always had this funny thing with keyboard players; I think he kind of picked on all keyboard players, and David Stone was no exception. David Stone had the right name; he was a little bit of a 'stoner' (laughs), but he was a good player, and I got on OK with him. A lot of people refer to that line-up as the 'classic' line-up. And we only did one album, and then after the world tour Ritchie went on to put together another version of Rainbow. And they had a lot of success as a slightly more commercial version of Rainbow. But I tend to agree that that was more or less the classic Rainbow line-up."

363 RUNNING FREE IRON MAIDEN

148 points *from Iron Maiden (EMI '80)*

Running Free was perhaps the most participatory of NWOBHM anthems, written and launched in the punted thick of the movement and then serving as a template for a couple dozen songs by other lesser new metal sprouts on stout. Its gallop is positively tribal, nodding to Di'Anno's beloved punk roots, but it is also Sabbatherian and something entirely new. The track easily hooked in Britain's jean jacket army and the rails were lubricated by the fact that the chorus and the verse were pretty much the same chords stacked the same way, Di'Anno bellowing out a credo that any pint-lifting lugan could appreciate, the urge to break those chains. It is a rare example in the Maiden catalogue where there is symbiosis between guitar and bass, or at least an endearing but begrudging kinship, something between oil and water or fire and gasoline. The same elusive relationship exists between the band's twin leads which would work themselves out of the shell forthrightly once Bruce joined and tingled the band's creative cockles.

Paul Di'Anno on *Running Free* . . .

> "Aah, now this is my baby. You see, Steve got a writing credit on that because he sort of put the bass line down. But I had the whole rough idea of how I wanted it to be. And I actually got the idea from one of me mum's records, Gary Glitter (laughs), would you believe, just the idea of that drumbeat, *Rock and Roll Part 1* or whatever that hit was called. My mum was playing it, because she was a big Gary Glitter fan, although she's not too fond of him at the moment (laughs). So I listened to this and thought, 'Ooh, might get an idea out of that.' And the lyrics obviously represent me and my youth, sort of thing, and that was it. Once you actually have the idea, it normally sort of fits around pretty easy, and that came together in less than a couple of hours I reckon. But then Steve put the bass line down on it, so he got a credit on it."

364 HARVESTER OF SORROW METALLICA

147 points *from . . . And Justice for All (Elektra '88)*

Released in the year nobody talks about, **. . . And Justice for All** was a woodshed/turning point/anomaly for the bubbling under Metallicats. *Harvester of Sorrow*, as the album's second shortest track, was one of the record's simpler precepts, somewhat forecasting the sluggish greys of the Black Album, galumphing along like a dry, gated version of *Sad but True*. But its dressy subplots tag it as **Justice** wankery, *Harvester* sampling from a belt-buckling buffet lunch of darting and fading directives, Kirk and James trying out riff, lick and lead ideas that in later years, would alone or in pairs, form entire songs.

Jason Newsted on alternative music . . .

> "People are too worried about being cool, the alternative elitist.

The ironic thing about some of these alternative bands that are making their move, they've got bigger egos and rock star shit then we've ever come across. They are the weird race, trying to outdo each other, trying to bring more attention to themselves. What the fuck about the music? They brush aside all that shit. We're going against the grain again. The people who have always been with Metallica and know what we mean, they're still going to be there for us. We're still going to crush them live like we always have. They expect a lot out of us and we expect a lot out of ourselves."

365 LEFT HAND PATH ENTOMBED

147 points *from Left Hand Path (Earache '90)*

Freshly firebranding to our foreheads a new thing called Swedish death, Entombed opened the gates to chaos like no band had since, well, Nirvana and Mudhoney. The parallels are apt, for what you've got within this album and song, is a sense of deafening scatter, unpredictability, rock 'n' roll danger . . . the very qualities that were opined as those that killed the meticulously executed and expensive hair band albums of '91, '92 and '93. Florida death wasn't really impressing anybody at the time, but this was something different, something alcoholic. And Skogsberg's production, although not yet to his trademark gut-guitar standards, already contains the germination of better things to come. The result: death that seems fed up with death.

Uffe Cederlund on the **Left Hand Path** material . . .

"**Left Hand Path** is mostly Nihilist songs. Basically we broke Nihilist up and then we did one demo with Entombed and then Earache signed us and we were back on track. So we just wrote two songs from when Earache signed us. So all the songs on **Left Hand Path** were from '87 to '89. All the stuff from **Clandestine** was written from '90 to '91. But that was a time when everyone in the scene had to do everything complex."

366 HIGH 'N' DRY (SATURDAY NIGHT) DEF LEPPARD

146 points *from High 'n' Dry (Mercury '81)*

Virtually indistinguishable philosophically from *Let It Go, High 'n' Dry* proved that Def Leppard were to AC/DC what Tank was to Motörhead, a note-dense version of a potential dragon slayer, although that isn't exactly how things worked out in either case, Tank tanking and AC/DC eventually winning the long ball battle for hearts and minds if not wallets (call it a gold-certified tie in '00). But I envision Johnson and his johnson covering this tune in some sort of heavenly parallel universe, 'cos fact is, this would be the last truly fist-pumping anthem from these youthful upcountry stallions, at least as far as their aging and long-suffering original fanbase are concerned.

Joe Elliott on the second album's AC/DC vibe . . .

> "Well, I mean, sonically, there's a big comparison between **Highway to Hell** and **High 'n' Dry**, because of the studio, the producer, the equipment available. That's like, you can listen to Gerry And The Pacemakers and it doesn't sound that different to the early Beatles stuff either; it's a time thing as well. But of course, the way Mutt got the two guitars to play against each other, or with each other, depending on what suited each part, was very much a Mutt Lange thing. If you listen to those Mutt albums, and compare them to the Vanda and Young AC/DC, you'll hear — maybe only a tiny bit — but you'll hear a difference."

367 ANGEL OF DEATH ANGEL WITCH

146 points *from Angel Witch (Bronze '80)*

Arguably the most Sabbatherian song from the Angel Witch catalogue, *Angel of Death* turns on a carbonic and sinister verse riff which gets even blacker come chorus time. Drummer Dave Hogg goes for a variation of the signature NWOBHM gallop, crossed with a full metal stomp, but there are all sorts of twists, pre-choruses and breaks causing this eventful track to steamroll with purpose. The echoey close is sheer brilliance, Heybourne strafing out a conclusion with high guitar shrieks and a warning that Satan is within our midst and actually down at the pub.

Kevin Heybourne on the reviews for **Angel Witch** . . .

> "I'd say about 50/50. We had some bad ones and some good ones. Some people raved about it and some people absolutely hated it. This is where the . . . you're talking about one person's opinion of your album. And that sort of annoys me. It goes out to the public and you say, 'They believe this?!' You've got a mind of your own. It's dangerous. I really like that whole album. I'm very proud of it because it's the first one and because of the fact that I wouldn't be where I am now without it. I feel I have a bit of respect because of that album. You can't be 100% original, you know what I mean? Everybody's got to get their influence from somewhere. I don't see it as a bad thing. I've never hidden the fact that Black Sabbath is my favourite band."

368 THUNDER KISS '65 WHITE ZOMBIE

145 points *from La Sexorcisto: Devil Music Vol. 1 (Geffen '92)*

Finally, the band's kaleido-colours find the mainstream, thank Beavis. *Thunder Kiss '65* stood out from the dreck of the catalogue like a severed thumb, the road signs aligning for a groovy, hip-hopped, Rob-rapped tour of craptatious America. The riff contains the same ghoulish charms as *Enter Sandman*'s, or for that matter, much of the Misfits canon. As well, White Zombie were one of the first bands to really become known for soundtracky samples, *Thunder Kiss '65* introducing us to dangerous women in short skirts while it cruises the desert on bad, bouncy shocks in search of folks to kill and bury.

Rob Zombie on the White Zombie sound . . .

> "White Zombie was always a sort of a weird mixture of . . . I don't know how this actually mixes into our sound, but Black Sabbath and Van Halen with Black Flag and the Bad Brains. And it wasn't consciously mixing sounds, it's just that those were the bands I liked. It's just kinda what came out of it. It's everything. I kinda think of the band as just one big magnet for all kinds of weird American culture. It's everything from movies to TV to books to comic books to news reports, just any kind of crazy shit."

369 THE YEARS OF DECAY OVERKILL

145 points *from The Years of Decay (Megaforce '89)*

Heirs to East Coast homeboys Anthrax but more akin in spirit to the Bay Area bands, Overkill, like Exodus and like Testament, were always considered great but late. **The Years of Decay** hit at a turning point year for thrash, everybody doing quite well, frankly riding Metallica's coat-tails, the bubble bursting before anybody really got to cash in. This eight-minute monster of a title track is a pretty depressing road tale, sorta like *Turn the Page*, Blitz lamenting over an **. . . And Justice for All**-journey how the years slip away with the miles, how life wanes with each identical club clubbed. Last record for Bobby Gustafson, and the last before major advancements would be made on coming transitional records.

Bobby "Blitz" Ellsworth on attitude . . .

> "I hate to say it, but it's something that we believe has carried us over the top and that is that we can beat anybody. Like a prizefighter, you don't go into the ring thinking you're going to lose. I feel that we've never written a perfect record, but we've come damn close to doing the perfect show. The mistakes, the

spontaneity, the immediacy of it, the 'what the hell's gonna happen next?' aspect of the live performance makes the perfect show. It's like taking your life into your own hands. I think the feeling people get from this band is, 'Oh my God, it's out of control. We're gonna crash!' And this is a good feeling. It's not necessarily planned. When you come off the roller coaster at the amusement park you're going, 'Holy fuck!' And if we do our job right, you should be saying the same thing after one of our shows."

370 THE EAGLE HAS LANDED
SAXON

144 points *from Power & the Glory (Carrere '83)*

Inclined to rock out unsafely or stick with an AC/DC plod line, Saxon mix it up with this slow, doomful, mourning dirge, respectfully drama-charged in tribute to the first manned mission to the moon. The pensive, measured build of the track evokes the majesty of the feat, but it also seems to urge the army of technicians involved to remain calm, collected and focused, to remember that this is planned as a round trip. A regal, mature way to end an album of frenetic screeching exultant metal magic, the NWOBHM's ultimate travel agents arranging the ultimate trip, which unfortunately would cap off the band's last great record until the solid modern parodies of this very album, commencing with '95's **Dogs of War**.

Biff Byford on *The Eagle Has Landed* . . .

"*Eagle Has Landed*, again, it's from my youth really, the first landing on the moon. These things that happened during this period stuck in my head obviously. I just thought the riff lent itself to a great song. And *The Eagle Has Landed* fitted with our eagle (laughs). And just the whole concept of landing on the moon was such a fabulous thing. I like to write what I call picture lyrics. I like each line to paint a picture in your head. It's very important that the songs, when you hear the lyric, that you see a picture in your head. It's quite hard actually. It's quite hard to write a song about landing on the moon in four verses and get the spirit. But I think I did do that. And the music, don't forget that myself and Paul Quinn were very heavily into progressive rock, and maybe there's a lot of that coming out on that song."

371 WHEELS OF STEEL SAXON

144 points *from Wheels of Steel (Carrere '80)*

Saxon's gritty determined version of the *Bad Boy Boogie* takes a tough rednecked riff into the world of bikers, visually reinforcing the pro-Quo rattle and hum with a winged logo ready-made to be slapped on the back of a well-worn leather jacket. The track swigs and quaffs like a hot summer run as well, facilitating, lubricating ploy being Steve Dawson's bobbing one-note bass line. *Wheels of Steel* is built on a time-honoured rock 'n' roll structure, and two records in for Saxon, it is probably the most convincing headbang of the bunch thus far, elevating then sustaining for its middle metal mission.

Biff Byford on *Wheels of Steel* . . .

"We had an American car at the time, an Oldsmobile Towne Car and I just fancied writing a song about it, that's all. I mean, originally my ideas for *Wheels of Steel*, was the *Princess of the Night* song but I switched mid-stream and went with a song about a car. It was basically about people's competition between each other with their cars, the hot rod thing. That's the type of song it is. If you listen to it, it's basically a song about street rods and beating each other. The riff is very AC/DC-ish. I was heavily into early AC/DC when I was getting the band together. **Dirty Deeds Done Dirt Cheap** etc. I suppose that riff is influenced by them although it's not really their style because it's just continuous. But it's in sort of the same register. I mean, they're more likely to go (he sings a riff), where we just played it continuous, more like an English riff."

372 LICK IT UP KISS

144 points *from Lick It Up (Mercury '83)*

Bravely under-written in the fine tradition of Twisted Sister, *Lick It Up* is all rarified air, abstract space spinning gold, the ambition and will of Paul Stanley causing giddy epiphany for the first time since, oh, let's say the chorus of *Detroit Rock City*. The rest of the three album cluster around this song is much fussier and critically valid, but *Lick It Up* gets the last laugh, keeping it simple stupid, as a result, getting the girl, the fast car, and most of the hoots and hollers.

Paul Stanley on keeping the spirit alive . . .

> "The drive comes from your own demons and desires; the things that challenge us, or everyone. It's the things that started you off when you were young, the self-challenge, and hurdles you wanted to jump. Eventually you have to find your own record to break. That's what it's all about."

373 DESPERATE CRY SEPULTURA

143 points *from Arise (Roadrunner '91)*

Part of the appeal of a song like this is its datedness, most pertinently its love of, and dependence on, riff, the band trying out a couple before randomly stripping the gears and collapsing into an unrelated verse one. Touchpoints are Metallica '85 or Slayer from any era, although the production might go beneath and behind both of those ideas. Combine the sound and the hurried construction, and you've got a metaphor for the uneasy chaos that is underground metal, the same fragile coalition of sounds one felt with punk and grunge, *Desperate Cry* falling about the place, running into concrete guitar walls, picking itself back up and then hitting another one, over and over again, for about three forehead-bloody minutes too long.

Andreas Kisser on *Desperate Cry . . .*

> "That's pretty much a demonstration of the **Arise** feeling. That one and *Under Siege* had clean introductions and stuff. We were trying to be a little more diverse, and Igor had that double bass in there."

374 JESUS BUILT MY HOTROD MINISTRY

143 points

from Psalm 69 (Warner '92)

A frantic spot of pioneering industrial, *Jesus Built My Hotrod* lodged nicely between Butthole Surfers, White Zombie and Ministry's own bad vibes, scurrying along through video's second golden age, converting droves to this new shotgun marriage between tough metal rock and computers. It was all ripe for picking within the optimistic alternative tenor of the times, grunge exploding to the north, all things weird being considered for major label push. Ministry got that push, but they still scared the bejesus out of people with their scary graphics, trick album titles and all-too-real heroin chic. Linear, dark, considerably uncommunicative, but somehow the soundtrack to the great flaming road movie escape, *Jesus Built My Hotrod* would turn out to be the first and last big hit for Jourgensen and Barker, who, in coming years, — if it was even possible — would make records that were even uglier, more caustic and less commercial than this landmark breakthrough.

Richard Kruspe from Rammstein
Led Zeppelin — *Kashmir*
AC/DC — *Whole Lotta Rosie*
Judas Priest — *Breaking the Law*
Kiss — *I Was Made for Loving You*
Ministry — *Jesus Built My Hotrod*
Metallica — *Sad but True*
Marilyn Manson — *The Beautiful People*
Faith No More — *We Care a Lot*
Black Sabbath — *Heaven and Hell*
AC/DC — *Dirty Deeds Done Dirt Cheap*

375 TEN TON HAMMER MACHINE HEAD

143 points *from The More Things Change . . . (Roadrunner '97)*

Looking back, it all kind of makes sense, this band's transformation into an unsuccessful, petering-out nu-metal act. Because there it was, *Ten Ton Hammer* creating the blueprint with its spookycore (where did that tag go so fast?) chords, its disconnected Fear Factory croons, its large and loathsome guitar scrape. But it's a bridge song really, still rocking out pretty heavy compared to the trend-fit that would come, producer Colin Richardson impactfully pounding the percussiveness of the band home with imposing force.

Robb Flynn on Machine Head's influences . . .

> "It's hard to pinpoint because we all listen to lots of different music, from Fear Factory and Sepultura to old hardcore bands, Discharge, GBH, KFDK to Wu Tang Clan, House of Pain, to just regular rock like Soundgarden and Stone Temple Pilots. It all has some type of the effect on us and just comes out. We listen to anything. In terms of any one person into strange stuff, Logan's into really hardcore industrial, some of the more obscure shit that just kind of annoys me, like Coil and Pailhead."

376 WELCOME HOME
KING DIAMOND

143 points *from "Them" (Roadrunner '88)*

Tricky, intricate and simply another chunk of proof supporting the King as one of the grandfathers of power metal, *Welcome Home* is practically a Mikkey Dee showcase, the expert skinsman offering a wild assortment of snap, crackle and pop rhythms and fills, utilizing double bass, single bass, and for the note-dense verse, a cool ride cymbal pattern. *Welcome Home* is also the erstwhile opener (after long intro), on a wildly successful album for King, selling strongly, second only to **Abigail**, its predecessor, and that is enough reason as any for it to stick in the creeped-out minds of King's dark ride disciples. Ripping solos all over the place.

King Diamond on *Welcome Home* . . .

> "As least as much if not more of a King Diamond milestone than *Abigail*. There isn't the same difficulty singing it; I love singing that song live. There's a lot of stuff going on in there; it's very progressive. That's one of those I really enjoy live. The fans have pretty much given it its own new name. People are like, 'Grandma! Hey, are you playing Grandma!?' 'OK, you mean *Welcome Home*?' 'Yeah, yeah!'"

377 KILLED BY DEATH
MOTÖRHEAD

142 points *from No Remorse (Bronze '84)*

A raffish charmer, *Killed by Death* is Lemmy's cockroach credo set to a stirring metal swagger that doesn't forget to sup a few pints with the likes of Quo or perhaps old crime-mates Girlschool. Expertly constructed for maximum electric charge, *Killed by Death* casts more than a few hooks, while retaining the dirt of the band's celebrated trinity of records (you know the ones). Its crouching all-attitude break is legendary, Philthy and his shotgun trash cans being a big part of this portion's magic as well as the general hoary hardware delivery of the song as a whole. But Lemmy makes you believe in his indestructibility against all alcoholic odds, and for this we must slip the man a bottle and whatever else he needs to get him through soundcheck.

Lemmy on *Killed by Death . . .*

> "Well, we had a great time doing the video down in Arizona, great fun. We got to party with all those girls who were in it which was also great fun. Apart from that, it was a great song. It comes from the Goon Show, you know, 'Killed by death! Killed by death?' (laughs). Death by killing. It was just tongue-in-cheek. Killed by death; you know, everybody is (laughs)."

378 BLOOD OF THE KINGS MANOWAR

142 points *from Kings of Metal (Atlantic '88)*

Comes as a surprise for me, seeing this track hailed as one of the Manowar classics. I mean, I always found *Blood of the Kings* a thick paste that was the average of all the band's stomping mid-paced workhorses, another faceless "of"-er, but granted, blessed with a steely-eyed persistence that threatens to break out of its blocky, bass drum on all beats plod. Plus that chorus contains catchy vocal phrasings that ring moderately poetic, even if the lyrics are your basic Manowar spoo.

Eric Adams on *Blood of the Kings . . .*

> "Yeah, I remember screaming (laughs). I learned a trick there in the studio. When I went to scream the really, really high scream, I actually stood on a chair in the studio, because I bend down when I scream, to push the air out. And in the studio, the microphone was already set up at a certain level, so I ended up standing up on a chair, just for that one scream and bending down so my mouth was right with the microphone. And I belted that scream out and hit it. It was really funny."

379 I AM A VIKING
YNGWIE MALMSTEEN

142 points *from Marching Out (Polydor '85)*

Impacting for the fact that Yngwie gets down and dirty on this one, *I Am a Viking* proves that ornate medieval metal does not always have to sound like muso music for the privileged aristocracy, but that it can also reflect the doom of the guillotine and the fatal sores of the plague. The track finds Yngwie in a hot, infested Sabbatherian trench, stomping out dark chords, searching with little bridges, but moving with grand, belaboured paces. As usual, melodies are of extreme and intense goth, but given its low guttural movements, the song both fits and adds contrast within what was a shockingly classy metal album for 1985.

Yngwie Malmsteen on *I Am a Viking* . . .

> "Yes, I remember that song and I remember it very, very well. You see, it's so funny that those first couple of albums had such a huge impact. Because I never realized it. I was just a fucking crazy kid! I was 20 years old, I was running around, fucking being crazy! And I didn't really concentrate that much on music. I was just being a nutcase. On the last album, I wrote a song about it, it's called *The Wild One*, and that's about myself. To be honest with you, I think the music and the songs from that era, they're OK. But compared to what I write now, they're very banal. And they're kind of childish in a way, musically and lyrically. I'm not knocking it. But the thing that is so amazing, what never ceases to amaze me, just because it was that time, that it came out THEN, it had a very, very big impact. I didn't realize it at the time. Now I do, but at the time I didn't realize it. But I wrote the lyrics five minutes before they were put on the record. Well actually, not all of them; some of them I wrote on the airplane, leaving the band Alcatrazz. (sings them) 'As the shores of my home disappear' or 'you're such a loser and it's such a shame that you don't know I am Viking and by my sword you shall die'; it was dedicated to Graham Bonnet. And then there was some verse that I just finished writing in the studio. And musically it's very simple, it's just an E minor. Kind of a cool riff, but . . ."

Yngwie Malmsteen
Deep Purple — *Fools*
Deep Purple — *Demon's Eye*
Deep Purple — *Pictures of Home*
Rainbow — *Gates of Babylon*
Queen — *Bohemian Rhapsody*
Kansas — *Carry on Wayward Son*
Queen — *Was It All Worth It*
Scorpions — *The Sails of Charon*
Rush — *Anthem*
Jimi Hendrix Experience — *Manic Depression*

380 TRASHED BLACK SABBATH

142 points *from Born Again (Warner '83)*

Trashed provides a winning combination as Sabbath's thickest thicket of rhythm collides quasar-like with **Born Again**'s most purposeful patch of melody. It's really *Neon Knights* and *The Mob Rules* refried, pan-fried, reprised, Sabbath giving it the ol' college binge try, throwing a few accessible sweet and sour bones at a demon-driven freight train metaphysically puncturing the night. Trivia note: lyric wilts a bit miniature when you find out it's actually about racing and crashing go-karts!

Ian Gillan on his stint in Sabbath . . .

> "That was the craziest year I ever had in my life. It was just unbelievable. I went out for a drink with Tony and Geezer in a place called The Bear Hotel in Woodstock, which is in Oxfordshire in England. And it's halfway between Birmingham and where I used to live. And I had a car wreck on the way there. Someone drove into my car. So I parked what was left of my car outside the hotel, went in and had a stiff whiskey. And Tony turned up a few minutes later, and we went into the restaurant and we

started drinking. I can't remember much, but apparently they dragged us out from under the table at about 7:00 so they could open the restaurant for the evening. So they got us home, and the next day I got a call from my manager who was pretty pissed off and said, 'You know Ian, if you're going to start making serious career moves I think we should talk about it first.' I said, 'I don't know what you're talking about.' He said, 'Apparently yesterday afternoon you agreed to join Black Sabbath and record an album and do a tour.' So I said, 'No I didn't.' And he said, 'Well, you signed papers.' So anyway, whatever. I never regretted it. It was a fantastic, great experience. We spent God knows how long at the Manor Studios, Richard Branson's studio in Oxfordshire, near Oxford. I lived in a tent for the duration. We had . . . I mean it was just wild, fantastic. And then we did a tour which lasted a year and then I went straight into **Perfect Strangers** after that, the reunion of Purple. And Tony and I are still good buddies."

381 RIFF RAFF
AC/DC

141 points *from Powerage (Atlantic '78)*

On of the band's early master blasters, *Riff Raff* abstractly gets a whiff of some of those southern rock qualities found more clearly elsewhere on **Powerage**, qualities which wouldn't really rear up again until **Ballbreaker** and **Stiff Upper Lip**. The groove is unstoppable, a no-brakes locomotive, hot-railed by a riff that steps aside for the big mouth of Bon and the resolute rumble of the Evans/Rudd rhythm section until the chorus reprises what is Angus' most note-dense widdle thus far.

Angus Young on meeting Bon Scott . . .

"When Bon first came along and saw me and Malcolm, he sat behind the drums and started bashing away. We said, 'We know a good rock 'n' roll drummer, what we want is a great rock 'n' roll singer.' Hence the song. This is what we wanted. For us it was great. He was a striking person. He did have the stuff legends are based on. I was in awe too, being the youngest. I laughed my head off and he laughed when he saw me! He said to Malcolm, 'Do you want me to sing like someone?' Malcolm said, 'No, we're asking for you, not anybody else. We don't want a clone, we want you and what you are.' He loved that. He loved the fact that he could get on and be himself. He said to himself, 'I never got to be what I wanted to be.' Being in a pop band, the front guy would always have the image for the little girls. Bon used to call himself the background singer, the rhythm singer. He had the talent and nice-guy looks. Some people wanted him to cover up his tattoos and all sorts of stupid things."

382 FUTURE BREED MACHINE MESHUGGAH

140 points *from Destroy Erase Improve (Nuclear Blast '95)*

Staggering, really, to think Meshuggah were forging their distinct stutter gun sound as early as '95. Now it's seeped into the thoughtspace of Tool, as well as the burgeoning mathcore scene, not to mention the works of Meshuggah's agitated Swedish cohorts. But the catalogue is chaotic and occasional, this album and sound, perhaps marking the heart of the experience, *Future Breed Machine* containing all of the band's stunning mad muso manoeuvres, most notably the upset apple cart time signatures, dry monotone deliveries, and an exotic oasis where guitars swim like Holdsworth, all the while drummer Tomas Haake providing the bone-breaking percussive efficiency that is actually the lead character trait of the band.

Marten Hagstrom on *Future Breed Machine* . . .

"Right now it means it's a hassle. You gotta play it. People expect us to play it; that's the closest we'll ever come to a hit song (laughs). The song was written somewhere around 1994 and I would say that that song stands very much for what Meshuggah was about at the time. So for me, *Future Breed Machine*, when I think about that song, and how we wrote it and how it came together, it was very much an imprint of what we were all about, and what our state of mind was way back in '94, '95. It's a pivotal song for us, because it's the first song off the album and it caught the attention of many people. In terms of that song and the album as a whole, it's very rhythmic. Our drummer's really good. He has lots of heroes; I know he likes the drummer from Cynic, but his favourites are probably guys like Vinny Colauita, Dennis Chambers, Chad Weckl, fusion drummers. But to be honest, a lot of the drumming basics, we do — me, Fredrik and Jens — on drum machines each of us have at home. And then Tomas adds those little touches. I'm the only one in the band that hasn't been a drummer in the past. Fredrik and Jens both played drums for a couple years, and even I can do simple beats. Sometimes Tomas is really devastated, especially when Fredrik's done something, because he's the best drummer in the band that's not the drummer (laughs). So sometimes, he comes up the stuff that Tomas is like, 'Aw shit, now I gotta practise' (laughs)."

383 I SEE THE LIGHT TONIGHT YNGWIE MALMSTEEN

140 points *from Marching Out (Polydor '85)*

Frighteningly talented for 1985, Yngwie and his band of meticulous alchemists absolutely stormed all sense of gothic rock normalcy and took it over the talented top for this pristine and triumphant metal riff. The verse feels obtuse like Hendrix, a bit filmy and arcane, which just adds to its effect when the chorus chops into the potential of what metal can be. Live, this song takes on a new light with these interesting full stops, the band making way for soaring vocal harmonies and those alone. A gorgeous assemblage of plush castle rock well ahead of its time.

Yngwie Malmsteen on *I See the Light Tonight . . .*

"That was also once again very simply put together, just basically thrown together. To me, if I was to compare that song to something like *Crucify* or *Wild One* or *Miracle of Life*; to me it's rubbish. It's not rubbish! But there's no depth. I wasn't mature enough to write music that had the kind of depth that I write now. The timing was perfect and I think that, you know, Alcatrazz was a good band. I think they had some good songs. Steeler was a joke. I never liked that. But when I came out to do my own thing, that's when I really started getting it right. But at the same time, comparing to what I do now, the new stuff is light years ahead. But it's just like what you said, which has to be said, at the time it came out it was very outstanding. Alcatrazz was pretty good I thought, but I thought Rising Force was better (laughs)."

384 SUNSHINE OF YOUR LOVE CREAM

140 points *from Disraeli Gears (Reaction '67)*

Heavy metal or not, *Sunshine of Your Love* is at minimum, diabolus in musica, spooking along like the worst song on Black Sabbath's witchy debut, Ginger Baker sounding like a zombified metronome, turning in a stupid metalhead performance before such a notion existed. Clapton's verse riff finds electricity though, and come chorus time, he reaches into the darkness for a few half-hearted power chords like some sort of incremental upratchet on The Kinks. Jack Bruce as usual steals the show with his disaffected, unattached vocal, a rare spot of intrigue on a track that just kind of flops around like a fish.

Jack Bruce on *Sunshine of Your Love* . . .

"Oh yes, I remember exactly about writing it. Let me tell you about it. Pete Brown, who is my lyricist, and myself, we always had to write the songs for the albums very quickly, because we never had much time. So we were trying to write some stuff, and we had been up all night and weren't really coming up with anything and we were in my flat in London and I just picked up my double bass and played the riff, the line of *Sunshine of Your Love* (sings it), and Pete looked out the window, and he wrote, 'It's getting near dawn.' Just like that. It's true."

385 BECOMING PANTERA

139 points *from Far Beyond Driven (Atlantic '94)*

Nothing says **Williard** like the gnawing rats of this track's opening chaos feast fest, *Becoming* featuring the band impatiently gathering toward a doomy, cloying verse, Phil unemotionally outlining the transformation from insignificant kicking post to skilled Satanist with a long to-do list. Vinnie's ballet-bouncy bass drum patter is an interesting subplot to the sturm and drang of Dime's irrepressible critical mass. Those rats we talked about earlier return just past two minutes, Dime getting tangled up in one of the funniest guitar solos ever to escape the cutting room floor. Essentially more grist for Pantera as closet absurdists.

Phil Anselmo on *Becoming* . . .

> "*Becoming* to me is all about the drumbeat. The drumbeat is fucking insane, especially what Vinnie Paul does with his feet. It's just not a common thing you hear heavy metal drummers playing, not that what he's playing is not heavy metal. It's heavy metal times fucking 50. It's very unique what he does and the drive to that song is infectious. And in a live situation, I have to say that the crowd goes fucking ballistic."

386 THE PRISONER IRON MAIDEN

139 points *from The Number of the Beast (EMI '82)*

Before launching into the track's triumphant and rhythmic castle siege intro riff, *The Prisoner* begins with an appropriately chilling spoken sample, which, from the far-flung reaches of Western Canada, I always associated with the album's Devil theme, vaguely along the lines of conspiracy theories which would have us all, post-apocalypse, stamped with numbers and UPC codes. But it's about a TV show, mate, set to a brisk verse riff that further builds the case for Maiden as business-like weavers of platinum guitar lines. Come chorus time, Bruce sing-songs a silly melodic line over a similarly saccharine guitar tinkle from the boys in back, the only odd bit out, unless of course, one counts the quick gear change (first to fifth) after the song's aforementioned heavy hallo intro stomp (OK, you didn't like castle siege; then picture Mussolini, crossed arms, basking in applause).

Bruce Dickinson on *The Prisoner* . . .

> "*The Prisoner* was a favourite of mine, obviously being a huge fan of the TV series. I always remember the moment when we got Patrick McGoohan, who was star of **The Prisoner** and who also wrote the series, and we got his permission to use the opening lines of the series. We phoned him up. He's in Malibu; he's a recluse and you can't normally get in touch with him at all. And we got through to him on the phone at home! And we said, 'Hello, we're a rock band from England and we'd like to use your bit.' And he said, 'What did you say you were called?' And we went, 'Um, Iron Maiden,' and he said, 'Do it,' and just put the phone down."

387 FATES WARNING THE IVORY GATE OF DREAMS

139 points *from No Exit (Metal Blade '88)*

Vocalist Ray Alder replaces John Arch and the band gleam with the production acumen of Max Norman. But Fates Warning is as progressive as ever, writing this sprawling — yet almost power metallic — epic, *The Ivory Gates of Dreams* switching between dark acoustic passages and crushing underground doom riffs which recall a Queensryche-intellectualized cross between Trouble and Warlord. Its sheer ambition would help push **No Exit** to status as a fan favourite (arguably second behind **Awaken the Guardian**), the band taking one last gasp and grasp toward making it as obscure art wizards before crafting a couple half-hearted attempts at something a little more simpler.

Ray Alder on some fans and their obsession with the band . . .

> "Most of the letters are directed to Jim. Obviously the lyrics are pretty obscure, and they can be taken different ways.

Sometimes they hit the nail on the head and sometimes they are way off base. They try to explain the lyrics to us. The Satan thing comes up quite a lot. Mostly when John Arch was in the band. But I remember, it's funny, it went back and forth. People thought we were either a Christian band or that we were Devil worshippers, because of the lyrics that John wrote; very strange, very obscure. The Christian thing I can understand, but the Satan thing, no. Maybe it's because we put a witch on the cover of the first record or something. I think in later years people realized that we were just a band, not these strange floating phantoms who write music. It's just a couple of guys writing music."

388 TRIAL BY FIRE TESTAMENT

138 points *from The New Order (Megaforce '88)*

Trial by Fire was indicative of a Testament glowing with European reviews for the first album, the band mixing up the tempos, trying a little Megadeth, even opening things with a tinkly mellow intro. As well, there were some memorable vocal melodies come chorus time, although for the most part, Chuck sticks to his scary old school mode. But the engine room of the song, as always, was stoked with those dry-lung guitars, Peterson and Skolnick creating a dark, cave-dwelling version of the Metallica guitar team, defiantly metalizing well off the map of commercial concerns.

Chuck Billy on the golden era of thrash . . .

"**The Legacy** and **The New Order** came out at the right time, an era when thrash metal was on its rise when Metallica, Anthrax and stuff like that were getting very popular. **The Legacy** did well in Europe. Then we got into **The New Order**, which we went into right after **The Legacy**. It's pretty much in the same vein as the first one, but a lot more thrash and speed-type metal."

389 YOU'RE IN LOVE RATT

138 points *from Invasion of Your Privacy (Atlantic '85)*

Hard to separate these airtight flying cigars from the current bloated, unravelled state of affairs that is the drunken Ratt camps, Pearcy over in his corner crowing how he is they, Warren shredding while rodent burns behind this week's Pearcy replacement. But once upon a time, the band was hot property, shining rock star vibes all around, songs like this swaggering smartly, heavy as a mallet without relenting on the radio charms.

Juan Croucier on *You're in Love* . . .

"*You're in Love* was a song I was putting together sort of as a follow-up to *Lack of Communication*. Basically what ended up happening was, I had a different concept for the lyric, and Stephen and Beau Hill went in a different direction. They loved the track and at that point I said, 'Look, hey, use whatever you want,' because I wasn't really particularly tied to it as a song. It was more of a track. I remember the title I had for the song was *Victory* and it was a very different melodic phrase approach than what ended up being *You're in Love*. So I give credit where credit is due, and that credit would have to go to Beau Hill and Stephen Pearcy as writers of the melody, although I helped out with the melody a little bit. But they're the ones that really came up with it and I just gave them the track."

390 OUTSHINED SOUNDGARDEN

137 points *from Badmotorfinger (A&M '91)*

The perfect synthesis of Soundgarden's Sabbath, Zeppelin and prog influences, *Outshined* rumbles like a gone dead train, hiccupped by Matt's 7/4 beat. The song's a relaxed grungster akin to Alice in Chains and serves as an essential building block of a multi-dimensional record. As well, the chorus injects a little of the band's interesting "Geronimo" metal sound, before collapsing back into the slinky vibe of the verse riff, and the pre-chorus is a rare spot of sweet Beatle-esque melody.

Ben Sheppard on **Badmotorfinger** versus **Superunknown** . . .

> "It all comes with the song. And the song comes about any number ways with four people contributing. How we recorded it is another thing. For **Badmotorfinger**, we recorded the rhythms first for the whole record, one song at a time, got the drum tracks down, then the bass tracks, and then when Matt and I were done, Kim and Chris did their parts. With **Superunknown**, we actually took it in four song blocks, and did the four songs' drum tracks, then we go to the first song and I put my bass on it, and Kim would put his guitars on it, and Chris his vocals. Then we would go to the second and work on that and so on. So we just concentrated on one song at a time. That freed us up to get a method going where each song was treated as its own song. That's why you'll hear different guitar tones. You know, some of those tones took a few days to get! Amazingly enough, communications or technical difficulties, or the exact opposite of that, would add or detract at the time to the song. That's why I don't really see **Superunknown** being that much different from **Badmotorfinger**, because even on that recording, even though we did the formulaic drums, rhythm tracks first, we still always treated the song like 'that' song. For **Superunknown**, however, we were more condensed in treating the individual song."

391 CITIES ON FLAME WITH ROCK AND ROLL BLUE ÖYSTER CULT

137 points *from Blue Öyster Cult (Columbia '72)*

Quite the stack of power chord pancakes so early in the game, *Cities on Flame* nevertheless delivers the bulky bulkhead of metal only halfway home, Krugman too inexperienced to capture the frequencies, Al Bouchard too complex to lose his jazz, the band in total, too crafty to drool happily like Sabbath. Many new and old rock emotions swirl through this astonishingly mature track, the band briefly boogieing barrelhouse, briefly progging like *21st Century Schizoid Man*, before collapsing back into the track's boldly drawn angles. The end result: an apocalyptic rock battle, electrified, electrocuted and finally reduced to powdery ash, taking with it, the world's last lonely headliner.

Al Bouchard on *Cities on Flame with Rock and Roll* . . .

> "Patti Smith was loft-sitting for Johnny Winter. I don't know if she had anything going on with him or just taking care of his loft. Anyways, she was there, and that was the first time I met her. I think that was the first time for all of us, and we rehearsed there in Johnny Winter's loft. And that first day, we wrote *Cities on Flame with Rock and Roll.* That was our first attempt at imitating Black Sabbath. And of course we stole the lick from *The Wizard*; it's well-documented. We stole the first part from *The Wizard* and the second part from *21st Century Schizoid Man*. So, two of our favourite licks."

392 MEAN STREAK Y&T

136 points *from Mean Streak (A&M '83)*

Fully the fourth, by last count, of seven stylistic shifts for the band, **Mean Streak** also marked the apex of the band's chemistry, distinction and sense of purpose. Meniketti's voice is the little Hagar that could(n't), and his guitar work is like a comfortably sorted out fireplace fire, blending with the glow of Leonard Haze's highly dependable percussive grooves (looks like, sounds like, and is shaped like, Vinny Appice. Lyrically, well, throw it on the pile of evil woman songs, Meniketti keeping the tale somewhat self-deprecating and light (like his silly song about incredulously realizing how prostitution works).

Dave Meniketti on *Mean Streak* . . .

> "Yeah, that was obviously *the* song on the **Mean Streak** record. It's just one of those songs that comes to you when you're a hard rock band that just says, 'This is what a hard rock band is all about.' It just says exactly what we were into and in a way that just flowed perfectly out of us. A lot of times, we have all these different melodic ideas and they tend to change the way hard rock sounds, from a standpoint of how we play. But this was just straight-ahead, blistering hard rock, and it's been one of our favourite songs we ever played and ever wrote."

393 LOVE YOU TO DEATH
TYPE O NEGATIVE

136 points *from October Rust (Roadrunner '96)*

This protruding forehead rocker probably vaulted onto the nether regions of our list because for once, the band have created something that doesn't nag like ear damage. Now it's a more manageable wax blockage, the band limiting the buzz to the behaved guitars, everything else sounding plush and lush, Pete more or less presenting the Goth cliché affixed to the band's breastplates by fans who need to see things a certain way. As well, the hype for this album was palpable, given the slow, surprise success of **Bloody Kisses**. And this is the album's first track, after the quite humorous grounding joke and an oddly refreshing hallo from the band, included as the untitled track #2. Basically, sexy necro autumnal doom metal with none of the band's undisciplined collateral injury.

Pete Steele on **October Rust**'s laid-back vibe . . .

> "It's slower I think because our testosterone levels have fallen, I think significantly, and we're just not able to perform like we

used to. And we're getting old now, so the arthritis has set in, so it's a matter of need, not because we want to play at this speed."

394 MY LAST WORDS MEGADETH

136 points *from Peace Sells . . . But Who's Buying? (Capitol '86)*

One of the anonymous fast thrashers from the band's early unconscious blur of songs, *My Last Words,* despite being impenetrable and the last song on the record, evidently caught favourable fan attention, vaulting into the working musician region of our Top 500. An inordinate amount of bass guitar fills the cracks of this one, as Dave Sr. turns in a mature and colourful lyric obliquely ridiculing his stupid decisions thus far in life. Thrashing, swimming and drowning in a sea of nasty tones, *My Last Words* at least keeps a loose grip on Megadeth's reputation as fearless speed progenitors.

Dave Ellefson on *My Last Words . . .*

"That song was written even before **Killing Is My Business**, I believe. Because there were a bunch of songs on **Peace Sells** that weren't developed enough yet to put on the first record, which is probably good, so those songs had their best shot at coming to the light of day when they got to a major label, Capitol at that point. And there again, from a bass player's point of view, the bass line during the verse is just smokin'. There's no sitting still when you're in Megadeth."

395 MISTY MOUNTAIN HOP
LED ZEPPELIN

136 points

from IV *(Atlantic '71)*

Hippie music that actually makes you pine for those times, *Misty Mountain Hop* is a celebration of life, a track that swaggers due to the unexpected sparks between Jonesy's throbbing organ work and Bonham's fat shuffle. And Robert is at his most thespian, massaging in all sorts of blues technique, sounding cynical with reason beyond his years through use of a monotone that seems to say that Led Zeppelin has become a machine. Jimmy is curiously absent from this one although when he does visit, he makes an impression with meticulous placements of lines you will remember forever.

396 BE QUICK OR BE DEAD
IRON MAIDEN

136 points

from Fear of the Dark (EMI *'92)*

These wastrel years for the once mighty Maiden had their place, a certain age demographic getting their own Maiden records to spin as soundtrack to their cat-sacrificing teenage years. *Be Quick or Be Dead* was designed as the focal point or a violent hello to **Fear of the Dark**, getting advance single and video treatment as well as the most sweat and toil from the band, the musicians note-dense and quick to arrive there, Bruce breathing fire like a diminutive dragon (or maybe just blowing smoke). It's lively, a real (yawn) live showstopper, and I guess given **No Prayer** and the rest of **Fear of the Dark**, this is what passes for aggression in the Maiden camp circa '91.

Bruce Dickinson on *Be Quick or Be Dead* . . .

> "That's as close as you can get to Maiden doing a thrash song. We haven't played that one at all for quite a few years. **Fear of the Dark** as an album sounds considerably better that **No Prayer**, much more like a Maiden album. But at that point, I guess I was starting to get a little disenchanted with the complacency — I suppose complacency would be the right word, at least that's the way I saw

it. We weren't doing anything on **Fear of the Dark** that we didn't do on every other damn Maiden album. And I was like, 'Ah, shouldn't we be trying to a bit harder? Like shouldn't we be worried?'"

David Defeis from Virgin Steele
Led Zeppelin — *Immigrant Song*
Black Sabbath — *Black Sabbath*
Black Sabbath — *War Pigs*
Deep Purple — *Burn*
Angel — *The Fortune*
Queen — *Great King Rat*
UFO — *Love to Love*
Queen — *Ogre Battle*
Rainbow — *Stargazer*
Nazareth — *Please Don't Judas Me*

397 STRANGER IN A STRANGE LAND IRON MAIDEN

136 points — *from Somewhere in Time* (EMI *'86*)

Easily my favourite Maiden track from any of the albums after **Powerslave**, *Stranger in a Strange Land* is a thick, urgent, black and blue rocker with great hooks, vocal melodies and lots of guitars, which are used more multi-dimensionally than usual, adding colour as well as prominent riffs. The rhythm bed is a little *Heaven and Hell*, which is fine by me — and odd for Maiden — Nicko turning in some of his best short, small, micro, grace note fills of his career while Harris behaves, playing bass-like bass, recorded like bass. In rapt possession of passionate, lifting melodies, a darkness maintained throughout, unflashy yet poetic lyric from Bruce, and only one mellow watch-watching part (that should have found the cutting room floor), *Stranger in a Strange Land* is a bright spot of creative angst on a downward coast to drifted ennui.

Bruce Dickinson on *Stranger in a Strange Land* . . .

> "They had just brought out the first Roland guitar synthesizers, and you could play kind of Hammond organ and guitar at the same time. Well, all the new toys came out so all of a sudden we sounded like Deep Purple on that one. It's strange that some of my favourite songs on the records sometimes don't seem to make it live. *Strange World* is another one of my favourite Maiden songs that just didn't really happen live. But *Stranger in a Strange Land*, again, everybody in the band thought it should be a great live song but it just never seemed to work."

398 DEATH OR GLORY HOLOCAUST

136 points *from The Nightcomers (Phoenix '81)*

Rife with trashy integrity and the teenage blues, *Death or Glory* is a sinister little bottle rocket of a track, Mortimer delivering lines like a bedheaded punk idler, while guitars announce and define the unselfconscious evil of the NWOBHM. I'm surprised it's this track that rose to the top, but in truth, it could have been any of them, all of them readily identifying with the magic of the times, any one of them the soundtrack to some punter's shiftless experience of Britain's magic metal explosion.

John Mortimer on recording **The Nightcomers** . . .

> "Well it was actually a very top-notch studio, so we were extremely excited by all the flashing lights and dials. It wasn't really bashed down live; it was very much track by track. I thought it was great, really exciting and really fascinating. I remember one journalist at the time saying that it sounded like

we had been overawed by the occasion, going into a big studio to record. But I don't remember us as being overawed by it."

399 BILLION DOLLAR BABIES ALICE COOPER

136 points *from Billion Dollar Babies (Warner '73)*

Probably both the smartest and hardest Alice Cooper track, *Billion Dollar Babies* floats on a riff that is pure melodic euphoria, despite its stilted, stunted parade pains toward resolution. And it's a bit spooky as well, what with all those psychotic characters poking in succession their heads out of Alice's vocal deck. With an exotic lyric, an exotic martial rhythm and a break that makes fun of old folks and their music, *Billion Dollar Babies* is a remarkable song, more so when sight, touch and sound conspire through a frightening album cover and the attendant decadent goodies therein enclosed.

Alice Cooper on *Billion Dollar Babies* . . .

> "*Billion Dollar Babies* was actually a song that was written off the drums. It was a drum riff. And we used to do that a lot. Dennis Dunaway would write a bass riff, let's say on a song like *Blue Turk*, and we would write the song around a bass line, and this time it just happened to be off the drum riff. And *Billion Dollar Babies* was basically just making fun of ourselves. Here we were, the most hated band in Los Angeles, couldn't get a job. Went to Detroit, met this guy Ezrin and all of a sudden we're the biggest thing in the world. We were voted number one band in the world and we were just making fun of ourselves. Here we are, *Billion Dollar Babies* and it was also a bit of a play on words from the old Busby Berkeley movies."

400 MOTORBREATH METALLICA

135 points *from Kill 'Em All (Music for Nations '83)*

Proto-speed metal that is almost comical, *Motorbreath* revolves around a carousel of melodies that eventually causes a sort of happy motion sickness for the new breed of punter growing and learning in tandem with these brash upstarts. But Metallica marbles the track's gleeful switchbacks with some wicked breaks, James playing his quick hand, the band working their need for speed effortlessly and charmingly, enforcing through this song's punk rock mayhem, a believable identification with their growing legion of Brit metal-weaned fans.

Lars Ulrich on who runs things . . .

> "Me and James have a tendency to kind of point the direction of the band every time we make a record; what music evolves into songs, that's mostly something me and James do."

401 BADLANDS METAL CHURCH

135 points *from Blessing in Disguise (Elektra '89)*

Capable of creating massive concrete grooves at will, Metal Church turn in one of their progressive showstoppers, *Badlands* opening side two (vinyl) of what was an intellectual metal album ponderously, taking 7:21 to lather it up and then fade it out. The riffs are impermeable, timeless, gothic, and Mike Howe (ex-Heretic) shows us the modern low-key Geddy Lee part of his thespian repertoire, set to an eventually pounding force, once again driven hard by Kirk Arrington's drum cannons.

Kurdt Vanderhoof on his old-time tastes . . .

> "I'm a '70s freak. As far as I'm concerned, it's 1974. Unfortunately, I have a hell of a time buying new records, because when I hear a new song I go out and buy the record and I usually get burned. There's usually one or two good songs and the rest of it is crap. But I love the new Stone Temple Pilots, I love the new Spock's Beard, The Flower Kings, lots of old Kansas, Thin Lizzy."

402 NIGHTFALL BLIND GUARDIAN

135 points *from Nightfall in Middle-Earth (Century Media '99)*

With a sound honed through seven previous albums, Blind Guardian create what is arguably, their masterpiece. *Nightfall* is the erstwhile title track and the sound is triumphant Blind Guardian, the band creating a mead-hall power ballad layered with a myriad of vocal tracks and guitars which are Queen-befitting renaissance-rich. Production-wise, this track is a technological marvel, swirled with old and new world tones which never seem out of place or too plentiful, in total, creating a living, breathing anthem that places delicately forth, the unmistakable, signature sound of this singular power metal brigade.

Hansi Kursch on *Nightfall* . . .

> "That's my favourite song on the **Nightfall in Middle Earth** album. It was either the first or second song we composed for that album and I was considering having a lyrical topic at that point connected to an old German mythological thing which Wagner has done a lot of stuff with. It was a very good experience because we started with that one and it was as far away from the intense **Imaginations** songwriting than any Blind Guardian song at that point possibly could have been. And that was a good starter. Considering the situation we had with **A Night at the Opera**, that was like a dream, because

from that point on, we could continue working in any direction we wanted."

Marcus Siepen from Blind Guardian
Iron Maiden — *Purgatory*
Black Sabbath — *Die Young*
Fates Warning — *The Apparition*
Thin Lizzy — *The Holy War*
Queensryche — *Suite Sister Mary*
Ozzy Osbourne — *Diary of a Madman*
Queen — *Bohemian Rhapsody*
Savatage — *Sirens*
Rainbow — *Stargazer*
Rush — *Tom Sawyer*

403 HIT THE LIGHTS METALLICA

134 points *from Kill 'Em All (Music for Nations '83)*

Maybe the usual suspects invented speed metal through the '70s, and maybe thrash was wobbling out of the pubs all around the NWOBHM, but it took *Hit the Lights* to really bring the two together with any sort of attack-ready acumen, Metallica applying American know-how to extreme metal and sealing the band's star-vaulting fate through the process. *Hit the Lights*, however, was the rickety, unsure track on **Kill 'Em All**, the one closest to punk's youthful exuberance. But its chorus was lethal, the band dropping to a stomp while James shrieks his way into your itchy ear until an impression is left you will never forget. Ultimately, *Hit the Lights* and *Metal Militia* form iron-clad bookends to this crucial, seminal album, but it's kind of amusing how much more technically advanced *Metal Militia* is, almost as if the band was that fast, learning by leaps and bounds, in the space of a little over half an hour, how to kick metal black and blue and leave footprints.

Lars Ulrich on his NWOBHM roots . . .

"I don't really follow it at that level anymore. I really don't listen to what these bands are doing these days and I haven't for quite a while. Somewhere along the line, I lost interest probably because most of these things weren't innovative enough. They weren't doing things that interested me anymore. I could talk to you about **Wheels of Steel** from now until midnight, but if you asked me about a Saxon album from 1989, I have no idea what you're talking about. I really haven't listen to it and that's the God's honest truth."

404 BLOOD OF MY ENEMIES MANOWAR

133 points *from Hail to England (Megaforce '84)*

Dirty tinkle tones open this coagulated bass-faced power surge, *Blood of My Enemies* announcing **Hail to England** with a measured methodical statement of intent. All the band's Viking-proud ingredients are there, including hailing backing vocals which sound like those same strong winds of which Eric foretells. Production was courtesy of legend Jack Richardson who seems to stand aside as Joey converts Thor's distorted paranormal messages into the eccentric clank of the Manowar sound.

Eric Adams on *Blood of my Enemies* . . .

"That's one of those songs that is just undeniable. The beat on it I think is 120. I'm not sure what it is, but when you hear it, you just can't stop tapping your toe. It's one of those things that comes directly from the heart. The lyrics come directly from the fucking heart. It came from a time when the band was having hard times, people stabbing us in the fucking back and the only thing that kept us going were the fans. They are the true brothers, the true fans, our true friends. These other people, they can go fuck themselves, and I was going to let them know it. That's where that song really got its emotion from."

405 LOVE BITES JUDAS PRIEST

132 points *from Defenders of the Faith* (CBS '84)

Sounds like a Sabbath song with those turgid intro tones, and it still sounds like one as it lumbers into Lifer's tale of velvety vampire love. But *Love Bites* is also a sly pop construct, K.K. and Glenn, slaves to the rhythm, keeping things minimal, really showing their craftiness come solo time, after which Holland gongs us back into the song proper. Lots of little echo effects throughout make it a bit of a production piece, even if its basic premise is thin, deliberate and workmanlike.

Ian Hill on **Defenders of the Faith** . . .

> "Obviously, putting the new one side, because the new one is always your favourite because you just poured your heart and soul into it for the last couple of years, but of the back catalogue I would have to say **Defenders** is my favourite, only because it was the last of the traditional Priest albums, know what I mean? Because after that came **Turbo**, which was quite different, not content-wise but sound-wise, with the synth guitars. And from then the band took on a much harder edge with **Ram It Down** and **Painkiller**. It was a harder, more aggressive direction than we had been known for, culminating with **Jugulator**, which was the end of that sort of line. And **Demolition** is the start of the new one with the inclusion of the more subtle passages and some more subtle songs. **Defenders of the Faith** was a step forward. **Screaming for Vengeance** was the combination of what we were doing on **British Steel** with **Point of Entry**, which is arguably the most commercial album we've done. Other than that, it's been a natural progression from the early days, really, culminating with **Defenders**, which is why it's one of my favourite albums because it's the end of an era."

406 I AM THE BLACK WIZARDS EMPEROR

132 points *from In the Nightside Eclipse (Century Media '95)*

Vastly more primitive than the retiring Emperor of **Prometheus**, *I Am the Black Wizards* creates a frozen place, speeds beyond a blur, vocals thrashing madly deep within the alien, eerie melodies, Ihsahn weaving a fantastic tale of realities mixed with impossibilities, the concrete morphing into dreamscapes. The production makes sure all one pulls from the flames is sharp, wary emotion, a vibe that is as anti-commercial and singularly isolationist as music can get, save for pure sound effects. A primitive black metal classic, forged during the period's golden age.

Samoth on his writing style versus Ihsahn's . . .

> "I have my periods, you know. I can be very non-creative for a long time and then all of a sudden I get a rush of creativity and I write a lot of material for a couple of months and then work on it in the rehearsal room and make the tracks that way. I also work in a very spontaneous way and in the end things fall into place. Whereas Ihsahn is more of the composer attitude. He has his own studio and he basically works with music every day from music to evening, that's what he's doing all the time. So he's more the accompanist, working with orchestration and huge melodies and I'm more straightforward. I've been working together with Ihsahn for ten years now and in the later years now, we've been going in kind of different directions and we have different ideas of what we really want to do. And I want to work maybe a little more with Morbid Angel aspects of metal and he wants to work more with progressive aspects of metal. We still work together in Emperor and we have the balance between those two points but we also both have the creativity to do something on the outside."

407 ZERO THE HERO BLACK SABBATH

132 points *from Born Again (Warner '83)*

Arguably the last smelly swamp monster from the Sabbath catalogue, *Zero the Hero* is also the largest and the loudest, surprising everybody with its frightening rhythmic plow and its bass-faced burrow through solid rock. Gillan plays one of his only appropriate characters, the overwhelmed eccentric asthmatic curmudgeon, as the album's accidentally legendary production values turn the song into a glorious last wheeze for this sleeping giant. The subsequent Tony Martin years would prove that after *Zero the Hero*, there was in fact nothing more to say.

Ian Gillan on recording **Born Again** . . .

> "Geezer Butler was totally responsible for destroying the production on that thing. I've got the rough mixes. It sounds sensational. Geezer took it away to London to another studio. Next thing I hear was on plastic, on vinyl. I couldn't believe it. He just obviously cranked the bass up, not only the bass guitar but the bass. I can't even listen to it. It's just a disgusting production. We were told it was unplayable on the radio."

408 I DON'T NEED NO DOCTOR HUMBLE PIE

131 points *from Performance Rockin' The Fillmore (A&M '71)*

A thick loogie of an early concerted, serious riff rocker, *I Don't Need No Doctor* bruised the folks at the Fillmore with a rumble of a chug as strong as Free. But it wasn't exactly metal, more like a predecessor to American roots metal, something which wouldn't exist until Aerosmith. In this spirit and in that of Zeppelin, Humble Pie adapt a number of classics on the **Fillmore** album, converting them through ham-fisted decibel-crazy deliveries, into songs that sound like new power chord-wrapped originals. Somewhat of a supergroup, Humble Pie featured Steve Marriott and Peter Frampton, with Jerry Shirley later ending up in Fastway.

409 THE WIZARD URIAH HEEP

130 points *from Demons and Wizards (Bronze '72)*

The Wizard places lovingly in a velvet jewel box, all of the exotic, escapist, positive traits from both psych rock and prog rock, Heep swirling together a tale of magick using to their advantage, an exalted chemistry most prevalent between vocals, keyboards and drums. The melodies on *The Wizard* are unapologetically lush, almost fey, certainly twee, possibly precious. Mix it all up and what you have is a sound that presages American pomp rock, *The Wizard* being one of the few bits of art rock that is actually radio-friendly versus random prog hits that seem shoved or cajoled onto the charts (see *Roundabout*). It's an escape you want to take; it's a world you begin to believe exists.

Mick Box on *The Wizard* . . .

> "You can hear a high-pitched string sound which goes over the verse. It was actually the kettle! When we were playing back the track, it boiled. We all thought it sounded good, so we recorded it a few times, multi-tracked it, and added it onto the track. So yeah, we were playing the song back through the speakers in the studio with the door open. In the next room was the kitchen and somebody had put a kettle on for a cup of tea. This was a kettle with a whistle to tell you it had boiled. So the whistle went off and that gave us an idea to recreate a string line on the song. We recorded the kettle boiling and whistling away and tracked it many times to give it some body. Then we tuned it to pitch, recorded it and that is how we got the string note on *The Wizard*!"

410 ASSAULT ATTACK MICHAEL SCHENKER GROUP

130 points *from Assault Attack (Chrysalis '82)*

Writing in some sort of stellar hallowed zone, the frightfully talented MSG came up with this complex, melodically sublime rocker. Set to a geometric shuffle, the song contains fitful stops and starts over which Graham Bonnet turns in an impassioned, embittered vocal performance. The break is vintage Schenker-ized Germanic goth, keyboards swirling, Michael's solo melancholically building to a guitars and drum barrage before one final heroic verse, another lush go at the chorus and then a final instrumental flare-up. Highly innovative track all 'round, and incredibly well-appointed and pin-striped for 1982, a year or so before the advent of the time-consuming studio trickery practised by the first wave of L.A. hair bands and their meticulous song doctors.

Michael Schenker on the **Assault Attack** years . . .

> "What I remember about that time, that's how I lost my manager, Peter Mensch. He wanted me to make a record with David Coverdale and I said, 'No, I want Graham Bonnet,' so we had a fight and that was it; that was the end of that. And I guess he knew better, because Graham Bonnet never lasted. He only . . . I mean, excellent singer, the whole album, great producer, Martin Birch. We were in France in a kind of castle. Musically, it was very inspiring because it was a really good band. We had Graham Bonnet, Ted McKenna and Chris Glen from the Alex Harvey Band, so it was a very healthy kind of thing. That album is actually a musician's favourite. The whole **Assault Attack** album in general was very strange because I wrote all the music, and when it was time for Graham Bonnet to sing, he didn't know what to do. And I was very, very confused about it because I mean . . . he had been with Rainbow; how did he manage there? So it was a very strange process to watch. What's the word for it? He acted very immature. But once it clicked, he was there all the way. But it was kind of a strange start."

411 KICKSTART MY HEART MÖTLEY CRÜE

130 points *from Dr. Feelgood (Elektra '89)*

One of Mötley's more upbeat and supercharged smash hits, *Kickstart My Heart* also houses one of the band's magic live moments, its pointed climax being the part where everybody blisses out with the blues for a second and Vince reminisces about the ride thus far, band and fan huddling and celebrating why they are here together right now. Blessed with a great shout-along chorus, its backbone is the hard-tail, post-*Radar Love* military snare of Tommy, which rumbles like a freight train (or the long determined history of great train songs), o'er which Vince turns in an aggressive boogie woogie vocal, more snarly than his usual twangy delivery.

Nikki Sixx on songwriting . . .

> "The listener has to go on the journey. What it all comes down to is the music. The listener who's out there waxing his car on a Sunday afternoon or throwing a football around in the park or drinking a beer with a buddy in the bar and it comes across the sound system, it's a song, man. Either you like it or you don't. All that other stuff is unimportant if the song's not good. So our first mission is to write great songs."

412 ALL ALONG THE WATCHTOWER JIMI HENDRIX EXPERIENCE

130 points *from Electric Ladyland (Reprise '68)*

The definitive version of the Bob Dylan song, *All Along the Watchtower* is first and foremost a triumph of production — self-production, incredibly — Jimi adding an impatient, psychedelic sheen to the song even before he frills and thrills us with ornate self-accompaniment that tacitly, with a wink of an eye, steals the show. As well, Jimi's vocal, with its oscillation between meander and unease, is a fine example of the man's unaffected but exhaustive blues vocabulary. Above all, the convergence of all these sonic cues creates a psychedelic classic with a compressed urgent feel, overloaded with sensuality and spontaneity, a straight-forward (though literary) ballad dressed to the fine nines.

413 UNDER THE BLADE TWISTED SISTER

129 points *from Under the Blade (Secret '82)*

If you are a true blue Manowar-hailing metalhead, *Under the Blade* is probably your favourite Twisted track. Sinister, flashy, rifled through with rock 'n' roll drama, *Under the Blade* kicks ass when it kicks in, and drops you on yours when it screeches to a stop, Dee left to roar his thespian tale over a crazy cuckoo clock of a riff. It is also a prime example of the band's simplified version of the twin guitar attack, how it can be used in a speed metal context versus less critically embraced, primary-coloured pursuits. It is also a demonstration of the band's street-tested precision, its tight attack built from slaving away in New York bars for most of the '70s before catching a break.

Dee Snider on *Under the Blade* . . .

> "The one key thing I would like to say is that for a number of years I've been saying that *Under the Blade* is the first song I ever wrote. That was a lie (laughs). I've been lying about that every night. And it's not a blatant lie. It's one of the first Twisted Sister songs that really starts to focus the band as a metal band. But I remember writing *Under the Blade,* and playing that one and the audience just immediately reacted. It was our first really big song where a unified core of our fans really liked a song. It became a sort of battle cry, and it became the title of our first album as well as the flip side of our first single. It was also one of the songs that Tipper Gore sunk her teeth into. And it was so funny, because she accused me of writing a song about sado-masochism and bondage, when in fact it was inspired by Eddie Ojeda's throat operation. He had polyps. He was going in for an operation and he was very nervous. And I told him, 'Dude, I'm going to write you a song called *Under the Blade.*' And I did. My vision for the song is that there were three different kinds of

blade. One of them is that you were being jumped in an alleyway. The second verse was about being strapped to a table and being operated on and that was Eddie getting his throat operated on. The third verse was sort about the band being the blade. It was sort of this cerebral, audience's view of a concert. But none of the verses were about sadomasochism or bondage. I then said to Senator Gore, 'I can't help it if Ms. Gore has a dirty mind.' And he was fit to be tied! He'll probably have me shot if he becomes president. He'll hunt me down because he was angry. And then Rockefeller accused me of insulting his wife, and I said, 'I didn't insult anybody. She accused me of writing a song about sadomasochism and bondage. She heard what she wanted to hear. I didn't put those thoughts in her mind.' So that song has always had a special place for me. It's the one song I have played at every single performance I've ever done in any of my bands in any incarnation. *Under the Blade* has been played every night without exception. It's a special one."

414 OGRE BATTLE QUEEN

129 points

from II (EMI '74)

If an elevation of hyperactivity was possible over the action-packed epics on Queen's debut, then this track was it. Compressed, claustrophobic and smothering, *Ogre Battle* piled on the engineering, assaulting the listener with impatient, in-patient sonics. Surprise to see it rank so high really, but there you go, a happenstance I figure comes from the song's prog metal madness and its placement squarely within the band's golden critical years, spanning roughly the first three albums. And don't forget the title. Titles are important and this one is both colourful and demonstrative of the beefy collisions within the song. And metalheads just love ogres.

Brian May on then and now . . .

"It's very heartening to come into the States and hear your songs. A couple of weeks ago my first stop was in Boston, and while I was collapsed in front of the TV, I began watching a basketball game and the first thing I hear is the boom boom crash of *We Will Rock You*. It just says to me that we're still on the consciousness of people, and that's great to know. The thing is that once people accept something, they tend to keep it in their hearts as it was, so the history is well-accepted and documented. But that doesn't mean that they're in touch with what we are now. What made me think today was I saw William Shatner on the cover of a mag, and everybody must walk up to him saying Captain Kirk. And that for him is now 20 years ago, and I'm sure he's tired of hearing it. But to people it's something that's warm to them, something they love, but I'm sure he has great problems getting across what he does now. It's the same for us. Thanks be to God for our past being so loved, but it's history, and you can't live on history. You have to live on what's happening now, and in the future."

415 SACRIFICIAL SUICIDE DEICIDE

129 points *from Deicide (Roadracer '90)*

Once state of the art death metallers, Deicide could blister paint off of all comers, as this debut-era classic attests. A combination of fast, grind, groove and distressingly note-dense axe acrobatics, *Sacrificial Suicide* is a bit large like *Raining Blood*, Deicide blasting a triumphant epic that is paced just right. In their day, they were the uncompromising world-beaters, but a decade later, critics were carving their albums as boring, rushed rehash, opening the gates for new lethal forces, most notably (and visibly it seems), Nile.

Glen Benton on his lyrics . . .

"The storylines are right out of my head, clear and simple. I'm just in my own little world here, hating God."

416 WITCHFINDER GENERAL
WITCHFINDER GENERAL

128 points *from Death Penalty (Heavy Metal '82)*

Lovably hapless, irresistibly unravelling, Witchfinder General were the first '80s band aside from Trouble to dig into the crux of Sabbatherian doom, indeed unwittingly creating doom and/or stone rock with their turgid bass-quaked pre-Entombed guitar reverberations. Their lusty namesake track was a power-packed one-and-three romp that takes an uneasy pride in the burning of witches. In many ways, it is a time-honoured parallel to the masters before them, Witchfinder General and Black Sabbath both putting out plainspeak public service admonishments to those who would dare become crafters.

John Gallagher from Raven
Judas Priest — *Victim of Changes*
Black Sabbath — *Symptom of the Universe*
The Who — *Young Man Blues*
Montrose — *Space Station #5*
Budgie — *Breadfan*
Deep Purple — *Hard Loving Man*
Uriah Heep — *Gypsy*
Aerosmith — *Toys in the Attic*
King Crimson — *Lark's Tongues in Aspic Part 2*
Black Sabbath — *Supernaut*

417 RUSTY CAGE
SOUNDGARDEN

128 points *from Badmotorfinger (A&M '91)*

Yet another quixotic proposition from this fecund collection of musicologizing disparates, *Rusty Cage* exhibited a band smartly tidy, the track opening **Badmotorfinger** with a wake-up call similar to the effect the title track had on Aerosmith's *Toys in the Attic.* It's a fast rocker and it's got purpose and critical mass and for the first time in Soundgarden's career, uplifting production, pointing Cornell and crew in the direction of mainstream success, despite their steadfast refusal to write by the rules, cramming this song and others on the album with odd time signatures and tangled metal heft.

Ben Sheppard on the grunge explosion . . .

> "There's really no one sound out of Seattle, or any other town for that matter. Why Seattle has done so well has to do with Soundgarden somewhat, because before I joined them, they were one of the first bands to be pursued here. And it came at a time when there was a lull in the music world. The industry knew something was up, yet they couldn't figure out how to cap the underground flow that was going on. And suddenly there was this big blanket in sales from bands, say like Warrant, and there was a drop in rock. They probably started watching indie labels and saw how well they were doing. After Soundgarden started getting pursued, other people started coming to Seattle; the bands that were out here were just like all the other bands around the country. It's easy to cap and guide: the epitome of the 'sensitive angry young man of the world' was going on around here. All the bands hitting each different sense, I guess. Hitting different nerves."

418 TALK DIRTY TO ME
POISON

128 points *from Look What the Cat Dragged In (Capitol '86)*

Wind 'em up and watch 'em go. You may want to shoot yourself, or them, but you can't deny that Poison have succeeded in executing a specific vision. Or they've stumbled on something that works and really has little to do with this bull about being the real punk rock. But stop the presses, *Talk Dirty to Me* is in effect, Sid's version of *Something Else,* sent gravely and soul-incineratingly neon, so maybe there's some truth to this slightly intelligent philosophical device both C.C. and Rikki

"Richard Ream" Rockett tend to stroke. Not sure where Brett stands, but he's always struck me as closer to the glam rock surface. Gawd, always hated these guys but I must confess, I've seen them live twice lately — way out of context, in another world, with much too big of a crowd — and I had nothin' but a good time.

Bobby Dall on *Talk Dirty to Me* . . .

> "That was actually the song that got C.C. DeVille the job in the band. We had just lost our guitar player after moving to Los Angeles. We had been out there for about a year, and our guitar player had left, and we were auditioning guitar players in L.A. Amongst them was Slash, C.C. and the third guy was the guy who filled in for Joe Perry in Aerosmith; I forget his name right now. Those were the three guys we had narrowed it down to. And obviously the Aerosmith guy and Slash I had the utmost respect for, but C.C. Deville came through the door and he's this obnoxious, rude, Brooklyn, loudmouth, in-your-face kind of guy (laughs). And he played a little ditty for us and that song turned into *Talk Dirty to Me*. So that song originated with C.C. DeVille and I think it's one of the quintessential rock 'n' roll songs of our genre. You know, Poison gets slagged for having the makeup or whatever but if that song had been done by . . . what was the band out of England? If that song had been done by the Sex Pistols, it would've been a punk anthem. And the fact it was done by Poison maybe took a bit of respect away from it."

419 POISON
ALICE COOPER

419 points *from Trash (Epic '89)*

Hard to fathom this peddle-by-numbers corporate power ballad vaulting so far up the list but such is the environmental, contextual, temporal effect of music, our dear voters obviously muddling through some important life experiences with this fat song as soundtrack to the shenanigans. Who knows who wrote it or played on it. I mean, it's basically the blueprint for the Kiss way of doing business, the first 10% of the work meticulously thrown at it being the only part that matters, the rest, all ego, all fidelity fiddling that no room of ten metalheads would agree upon as better or worse or necessary or detrimental. Fact is, sounds like crap now, whereas any record with four guys in a room playing more or less live has stood the test of time, sonically speaking.

Alice Cooper on *Poison* . . .

> "We took three days writing that song. Now usually I say, a hit is written in five minutes. So maybe the basics of *Poison* was written in a half-hour. But when you're working with Desmond Child, he is a song doctor, he is a surgeon. He spent two days just on the background vocals. I mean he really, really made that song work. The basics were written, yeah, in maybe an hour. But he really sat down at the piano and worked out every one of those background vocals, which is something I never would be able to do."

420 IN LEAGUE WITH SATAN VENOM

127 points *from Welcome to Hell (Neat '81)*

If we're going to get to the crooked crux of Venom, why not dive into their worst disaster of an album, and then to the song that barely gets given a beat? That would be *In League with Satan*, a nasty, sneering direct credo crapster that finds Abaddon pounding on pot lids to a tribal nursery rhyme buried deep within his noggin. If criticism be kind, you might call this a rudimentary gallop, but really, it's barely constructed. To my mind, a surprise choice, saddled with **Welcome to Hell**'s horrid, shuddering recording values, buried deep into the album (second to last track), and not one of the band's better known er, singles.

Cronos on going out of tune . . .

> "Yeah, we didn't give a shit. All the first Venom records are all in a different tuning. We used to just say, 'Who sounds in tune?', and then we'd just change to match that guy. And we changed speeds a lot too. That was all part of it. A song should change; it

should never be the same time after time after time. One other thing about the tuning as well, which is quite interesting. Like Mantas would go home and put on a Kiss album and sit and play his guitar to it, but he would have to tune his guitar to the album. And when he came to rehearsals the next time we would just tune to him. So it was whatever we had been playing in the house, we would tune to whatever we were playing last."

421 MONKEY BUSINESS SKID ROW

127 points *from Slave to the Grind (Atlantic '91)*

More than a bit of Aerosmith in this one, from the creaky rocking chair blues intro to the funky Joe Perry riffs to Baz's Tyler-rapped vocal. And ain't it nice to hear the return of the cowbell? Lyrically, once again it's all Aerosmith, Baz spitting out an apocalyptic observance of sleaze types walking the strut in front of his equally sleaze-sagging eyes. A powerful and grindingly hypnotic way to open what was a surprisingly hefty bag record.

Dave "Snake" Sabo on *Monkey Business* . . .

"When we were out on the Aerosmith tour, I had some riffs and whatnot that I was working on. Rachel and I would sit down on our days off and fool around, throw ideas back at each other and that was the first song we worked on. It was something we would work on a weekend here, a weekend there, but Rachel is such a prolific lyricist that he's got all this great imagery, using metaphors and whatnot; he's just got this stream of consciousness sometimes where words just flow out onto the paper. And I sit there and I'm awe-struck by it. So I start playing this riff and he's like cool, and all of a sudden he starts reeling off these lyrics on paper. And he said 'I don't know where this is going, but here's the start.' And we basically just kept building it on that tour, and by the time we got started working on the next record, which was literally a couple months after we had gotten done touring, we had the basic skeletons down for a number of songs, with that being the one that was closest to being done. We knew we had something pretty special our hands, lyrically and musically, and it was a really great first track for **Slave to the Grind** because it set the tone for the rest of that album and the rest of the touring year."

422 GOD OF WRATH METAL CHURCH

127 points *from Metal Church (Ground Zero '84)*

Proving their versatile skills right out of the lead boot blocks, Metal Church construct a left-field power ballad, framed on Kirk Arrington's groovy backbeat. *God of Wrath* moves majestically through many dark modes, changing speeds, spreading, compressing, and then of course metalizing late in the game. Terry Date's production is as good as it gets, proving to all these people fussing over the 20 years since that once you have all the bass and treble anybody would ever request, the rest is just abstract, subjective opinion. An arrangement destined for the thrash metal wake song Metallica would ride to great success on at least four occasions.

David Wayne on his lyrical modus operandi . . .

"I think it's part poetry, and part writing stories, and I think a song is just this story that is crafted onto paper. One thing I've always enjoyed is storytellers. If you can tell a good story, be that in song, poetry, or books . . . I admire those who can craft a good story and keep your attention. Maybe you are not asking me this question, but I'm going to throw it in anyway, for any aspiring writers or rock 'n' rollers out there. I have one simple rule of thumb that works for me, and it is no matter what you are writing about. I know this is so simple and yet sometimes even for myself, very hard. You need to do, no matter where you start your story, when you get done with it, remember to have a beginning, a middle and an end (laughs)."

423 CAN YOU DELIVER ARMORED SAINT

127 points *from March of the Saint (Chrysalis '84)*

No surprise seeing this modest anthem break through the morass of Saint coulda's for one simple subjective reason: its chorus is the stickiest, hookiest part of the whole catalogue. Otherwise, the song is a tame mid-mosh chugger with a nice Priest-style break which is riddled with tasty guitar runs. The story's old now, but the sentiment is unanimous: Saint were one of the archetypes of a band that was better live and raw versus the watery performances captured on their shackled recordings.

Joey Vera on staying true to metal . . .

> "We're just a rock band that's trying to write good music. We just want to write good songs. One thing I'm very glad about was that we never tried to follow something else. That's not to say it made any easier. It was very confusing for us to look around and see trends happening, and people liking the trends. We suddenly would find ourselves out. It wasn't enough for us to change, or follow anybody else, but it was a little bit confusing and it made us second-guess ourselves a little bit. Well, what are we doing? Why doesn't anybody like us? It's a fine line, doing something that you create for yourself, and then having somebody else like it. To some degree, we don't give a shit, but to another degree we do. After all, this is what we want to do for our livelihood. This is our life. When you think of it in that light, it made us wonder, are we doing something wrong?"

424 SEX TYPE THING STONE TEMPLE PILOTS

126 points *from Core (Atlantic '92)*

Does anybody remember irony? That's what Scott was asking on this smart commentary on rape or date rape or one step back, just getting your way. His menacing vocal is set to a big linear grunge bulldozer of a track, even if this is the number one band to which you never say grunge. They get mad, trust me. In any event, STP were the L.A. parallel to the new fat, mean sawed-off metal from up north, and this was their first of three or four pretty big songs from **Core**, *Sex Type Thing* 4-by-4ing a smeary churn deep into radio, adding fuel to the alternative fire scattershot sparked by Faith No More, Red Hot Chili Peppers, Jane's Addiction and the big three from Minneapolis.

Dean DeLeo on writing perfect pop songs . . .

> "We are pop whores! I'm 38, and I got to say man, I could not wait to get home from school and sit in front of the AM radio and hear songs like *Cisco Kid* from War. I would sit there until they played that and *Stuck in the Middle with You* by Stealer's Wheel and *Close to You* by The Carpenters. My mom actually took us to see The Carpenters when we were kids, and the music that was filtering down from what my mom was playing, all those killer Andy Williams records, those Carpenters records, Dusty Springfield records. And then from my older brother's bedroom you would hear Hendrix. And then from our sister's room you would hear Spanky And Our Gang, Rascals, Motown. There are just some killer pop songs out there. And then our dad had this incredible collection out of Edith Piaf stuff. I mean we could go on and on. . . . Our outlet wasn't video games back then, it was music, including prog rock. I realized that prog rock was a definite outlet, but it wasn't the foundation of a good song. So the challenge for us is taking musicianship and combining it with well-written songs. That's the link right there, you know?"

425 ATTITUDE SEPULTURA

126 points *from Roots (Roadrunner '96)*

Groovy to the dub point of almost sounding submerged, *Attitude* is the ultimate expression of the band's extreme creativity on this pivotal album for the band. *Attitude* digs deep into the mud for a twangy, tangy vibe that placed Sepultura at the forefront of "world" metal while simultaneously providing blueprints for the Ross Robinson-inspired nu-metal revolution to come. The song's beating heart is Igor's negating cymbal work, playing against a down-tuned throb that is hypnotic like jungle heat. Out front, it's all Max, sounding very angry indeed, his accent adding to the exotic nature of the little emerging nation the band had created.

Max Cavalera on *Attitude* . . .

> "*Attitude* was a song I wrote with the help of Dana, Gloria's son, my stepson, who was murdered. I was working on the song and he started reading the lyrics and he was like, 'Wow, those are awesome lyrics' and he said, 'I wrote some lyrics as well.' And I said, 'You write lyrics?!' And he said, 'Yeah, let me show you' and he showed me some stuff and I was so impressed by what he wrote, because he was just a kid; he wasn't a musician or anything. And he had the words, 'Live your life not the way they taught you. Do what you feel,' and that's actually what's written on his grave, on his tombstone. So I have those memories of working and writing with Dana. Even though the Sepultura guys were against that, I didn't care; I gave Dana the credit. It was a song that was really between me and Dana, lyrically and the idea of the song, and I'm proud that I didn't back down and I'm really proud I gave him the credit on the album."

426 MERCYFUL FATE
THE OATH

126 points *from Don't Break the Oath (Roadrunner '84)*

It takes a couple minutes to get past the cheesy vampire stuff, but once it does, what an onslaught of glorious metal *The Oath* bestows upon yer dented head. Musical, fast, artfully complex, rhythmic and simply grand, this is a seven minuter that unfolds entertainingly, even if in the final analysis, there may be a handful too many riffs without tasks assigned to them, riffs which could be served lay-off notices with little effect on the corporation. And that little bass showcase . . . don't think I forgot that little bit of fromage. But all is forgiven as the rousing twin leads of Shermann and Denner return for a recapitulation of the opening moments, in essence, a quickly vanishing spot of Maiden mania that is the album's most passionate passage.

King Diamond on mixing **Don't Break the Oath** . . .

> "When you'd do a mix in the old days, it was a nightmare, complete nightmare! It was maybe more like school, you know? You're waiting outside, and then the producer comes and gets you and takes you inside, 'OK, listen to this,' and we're saying, 'Oh God, that's not loud enough; we need more reverb on this.' 'OK, go outside again and I'll change those things,' and it's like, 'What!?' So we would go outside, and then he'd call us back in, 'OK, listen to this one.' Ugh. We did that through all of **Melissa** but halfway through **Don't Break the Oath** we finally put our foot down and told the producer at the time that we want to be in the room. We're not going to say anything, but we want to be in there. Finally it was like, I don't care what anyone says, I'm staying in here. We're not going to waste all this fucking time. I can sit here and tell you, 'No, that's not enough, that guitar is not loud enough, as you're doing it and then you can do it again.' 'Well . . . OK.' But God, what a nightmare! These days it's so automated, whereas once you've done it, you listen to it, you readjust it, and the mixing desk moves those things itself."

427 SURPRISE! YOU'RE DEAD!
FAITH NO MORE

126 points *from The Real Thing (Slash/Warner '89)*

Probably the most supreme audio reproduction of thrash metal outside of Megadeth, and probably the only extreme metal waltz in existence, *Surprise! You're Dead!* was merely another elevated creative moment on an action-packed, gorgeously recorded and meticulously mixed album. The riff is a steamroller, picking its holes through 3/4 time, as Patton does his best to sound metal. But hey, really in the spirit of no less than Zeppelin or Soundgarden, this is a band who thinks metal is lame, trying, and succeeding, in kicking some intellect into it every chance they get.

Mike Bordin on the band's big metal fan, Jim Martin . . .

"Definitely, he was metal, is metal. I grew up in the East Bay of San Francisco, where there was a lot of metal. I was a huge metalhead as a kid. I was in school and I was friendly with this guy called Cliff Burton, who every metalhead knows. And we used to smoke funny cigarettes and listen to Sabbath records and Trower and Blue Öyster Cult, Mahogany Rush, Tommy Bolin, Deep Purple, Led Zeppelin, Scorpions, everything, anything metal. That's all we listened to. And we both decided to start playing instruments; he obviously played bass, and I played drums. And about two or so years into having started playing, at about the age of 15 or 16, we met Jim. Jim was in a band that needed a bassist and a drummer. So yes, Jim is hugely a metal guy. The point is that after I was playing with those guys for awhile and I stopped playing with them, I started listening to punk rock and lots of other music, and he never really did. So we sort of come from the same place but I went to some different places as well. So in that band, yes, he was definitely the most metal guy."

428 MAN IN THE BOX ALICE IN CHAINS

126 points *from Facelift* (CBS '90)

The boyz with toyz in Alice in Chains quickly shed their old glam ways before becoming one of the big four grunge conglomerates, lead big-shot song being this simple, beautiful Sabbath-bound bouncer, a song that combines a certain rock starry axe hero swagger with pacing pouncing to pay-off. What made the band's sound irresistible was this new kind of droning, melodic, depressed vocal, plus a crux-bound understanding of what kind of heavy can crack a smile on the most seasoned metalhead; ergo, the open architecture riff and the subcycle chorus riff, both parts cloaked in plush druggie purple corduroy curtains.

Layne Staley on *Man in the Box* . . .

"It's a song about living for yourself. Don't live your life for another person. It's not anti-religious at all. It's the highest god-figure I can think of. Some people will base their whole life around another person, or this person's teachings and forget about what it's all about. They tend to excuse everything they do in the name of that person or that idea. I think you should live for yourself and not for someone else's ideas."

429 ANTHEM TO THE ESTRANGED
METAL CHURCH

125 points *from Blessing in Disguise (Elektra '89)*

With Mike Howe banshee-wailing like a blond-tressed Blackie Lawless, Metal Church turn in a sorrowful, hopelessly metal, astonishingly lengthy classic somewhere between power ballad in tone and doom metal in execution. The production values are pulverizing, as Howe delivers an empathetic paean to those who have fallen through the cracks and become homeless, the track becoming merely one of the band's many classy, intelligent, responsible social commentaries. Note: contains one of the most thrilling, melodic and resolving guitar solos of the Metal Church canon.

Kurdt Vanderhoof on the band's two vocalists . . .

"I think the David Wayne voice and Mike Howe voice are two completely different things. Some of the songs from the Mike Howe era I like better, but overall I think the vibe of the first two is more correct, because we were in our mid-20s, full of energy, ready to take over the world type thing. Of the three from the Mike Howe era, I would have to say definitely my favourite is **Human Factor**. I think **Blessing in Disguise** was great, but the mix was a little funny for me. It didn't sound right, and that was really a transition period for the band. A lot of people really dig that record, but for me it would be **Human Factor**."

430 CAN I PLAY WITH MADNESS
IRON MAIDEN

128 points *from Seventh Son of a Seventh Son* (EMI '88)

A happy dumpling of a song that says we, as a band have faults too, *Can I Play with Madness* is a friendly mess of things tried, things botched, things that bravely go bump in the night and finally, by crooked hook, things that win you over. The title reminds me of something Klaus Meine would say, only he'd call it *Can I Play with Your Madness Baby* or *Can Madness Rock the House Now!* Anyway, the riff possesses that specific twee charm that rides the little static electricity carpet spark between *I Don't Know* and *Crazy Train*, humming a hopping tune as record reviews burn. Wildly inappropriate to the verse as it is, the chorus is however a winner, a rare bit of groove on this stilted album.

Bruce Dickinson on *Can I Play with Madness* . . .

> "Again, we had a big row in the writing of that one. There's that whole bit in the middle where it goes into a sort of guitar solo bit and then just stops abruptly and goes 'Can I play with madness?' And you get the a cappella bit and then it goes back into the chorus. That whole bit in the middle was just completely inserted, like plunk, stuck in the middle. And it was Steve's bit. And he said, 'Oh, this will work,' and he put it in there, and Adrian absolutely hated it. I was unfortunately the one who sat in the corner thinking, 'Well, Adrian hates it, and Steve thinks it really works,' and then I was thinking actually, 'It does kind of work,' so I chimed in and said, 'Actually, it does seem to work guys,' and it was like, 'Oh dear' . . ."

431 DETHRONED EMPEROR
CELTIC FROST

125 points *from Morbid Tales (Noise '84)*

One of the band's more immediate rock 'n' rollsy metal sledges, *Dethroned Emperor* further benefits from a fat sacrificial goat of a guitar sound, backed with a rhythm section that is all heads-down, see you in the front. But as is Celtic Frost's wont, the track contains simple but simply escapist sections that are proggy in nature or at least spirit, the slow bit sounding sublime and ethereal despite the track's direct but effective power trio toolings.

Tom G. Warrior on his early influences . . .

> "I grew up with Black Sabbath and The Who as far as hard music goes. That was really aggressive music in the '70s. I mean, they would thrash their interest instruments and they were dark and everything. And those bands rose from the early metal that was basically a form of revolution in the late '60s, the revolution against your parents, against your boss, the establishment. And this kind of spirit was always part of it. And when I started to listen to music and play music myself, I always had that picture in my mind, that the music has to be aggressive and adrenalizing and revolutionary and that it has to scratch and kick at things."

432 BRING THE NOISE ANTHRAX

125 points *from Attack of the Killer B's (Island '91)*

Kicking off with an intense Benante double bass, *Bring the Noise* quickly explodes into an innovative, pioneering rap metal number, driven by the band's no-nonsense hardcore metal riffs, set to spare but full-contact production values. A surprise blow-up hit for the band, *Bring the Noise* never came out on an album proper, beginning life appropriately as a 12" then lurching onto both this B-side compilation and, also appropriately, **Attack of the Killer A's**. Touched off an explosion of healthy cross-polinations, one large flag-waver being Biohazard.

Charlie Benante on *Bring the Noise* . . .

> "*Bring the Noise* has a big story to it because that was one of the first rap/rock partnerships, of course the first being Aerosmith and Run DMC, and then of course we did the *I'm the Man* thing. But living in New York, you can't help being influenced by things coming off the street. Rap music was of course something that

was originated in New York and me being from the Bronx, the first rapper came from the Bronx. So to me heavy metal or thrash was totally a street thing, and same with rap and I always just loved it. One of the bands we totally loved was Public Enemy. They came out and just man, fuckin' ripped it up. And I kind of knew people who knew them, and I met Chuck before the first album came out and got some T-shirts and we would wear the T-shirts and he saw Scott wearing a T-shirt in this paper; I think it was Sounds from Britain. He was doing the song *Bring the Noise* and he gave Anthrax a namecheck in that song. So we were doing the **Persistence of Time** record and we were going to do a bunch of B-sides again, and we decided to do *Bring the Noise*, but we didn't put it out. We waited and then put it out on the **Attack of the Killer B's**. It was just great; we did a video for it and then we did a tour with Public Enemy. And this was like pre-Lollapalooza; it was us, Public Enemy, Primus, and it was great."

433 IN MY WORLD ANTHRAX

125 points *from Persistence of Time (Island '90)*

Quite surprising to think that Anthrax was making dry-angled, fish-hook, tackle box thrash like this in 1990, but there you go, **Persistence of Time** (too) full of the stuff, *In My World* indicative of the kitchen sink ethic of a band at the height of a game that was now getting hard on the ears. Ergo, *In My World* is a bit mathematical, chop-blocked and forced, but still, one of the serious meaty bits on this frantic album.

Charlie Benante on *In My World* . . .

"The funny thing about *In My World* is that we played that song on that episode of **Married with Children** and everyone thought Scott was the singer in the band."

434 CHILDREN OF THE DAMNED
IRON MAIDEN

124 points *from The Number of the Beast* (EMI '82)

Children of the Damned manages to fan the flames for those who saw evil in this record, providing a dark and moody mellow moment, y'know, a quiet space where the five punks in Maiden could contemplate their impending damnation. Of course, it's not all mellow, the chorus revealing an epic and triumphant stand of oaks, Bruce soaring above the treetops with his endearing bit of overacting. The break's the real spot of fun though, Smith and Murray unravelling a nice harmony solo o'er one of Clive Burr's odd but appealing double-fisted hi-hat patterns. Big, big close on this one too, again, supplying a fairly creepy and mournful cloak of seriousness to album that is pretty uptempo much of the time.

Bruce Dickinson on *Children of the Damned* . . .

> "I love that song. I have to say that we were heavily influenced by *Children of the Sea*, the Black Sabbath song. Take a listen (laughs). There's a little bit of that about that song, in terms of structure. But other than that, it's a beautiful song, almost plaintive at times, until it gets going (laughs)."

435 MR. BROWNSTONE
GUNS N' ROSES

124 points *from Appetite For Destruction (Geffen '87)*

With pretty much the funkiest, most circular and note-dense Slash riff on the album, *Mr. Brownstone* gets even punchier with Axl's rapid-fire vocal callisthenics, Axl also affecting a strange crocodile voice that recalls Tyler and Osbourne and their odd low frequency deliveries on their respective debut albums. Again, the record is cranked full of chemistry and chemicals, and a subtle part of selling these songs is the rhythmic gangbang of Duff and Adler, who are a little bit punk rock, a little bit bar brawl, all black and blue.

Duff McKagan on *Mr. Brownstone* . . .

"Yeah, Izzy came up with the main riff and it's a song about, I mean . . . heroin. And it was really prevalent within the collective band's life at that time. One we got our record advance, before we made the record, we all of a sudden found ourselves with money. It wasn't a lot of money, but to us then it was. It allowed you to exercise your drug habits and stuff (laughs). But it came time for us to do the record and get serious. And Slash and Izzy were both strung out at that point. So they got off it. They took this stuff, I forget the name of it, but it puts you through a three-day withdrawal in one day. And you get incredibly sick and stuff. So I think the words, or the idea for the words came after this withdrawal."

436 TOO HOT TO HANDLE
UFO

122 points *from Lights Out (Chrysalis '77)*

Containing one of golden era metal's best cowbell parts (king cow being *Hair of the Dog*), *Too Hot to Handle* is one of UFO's laddish pub rock songs, a personable pint-lifting way to open an album fraught with a lot of serious music of one sort or another. Its English glam rock verse chords (same as the chorus chords) greet you at the door with a smile, and then its sinister break taketh away the warmth with a bit of power metal posturing. But it's all in the context of a solid traditional oak table boogie, dependable *Louie Louie* hummables rocking your buzzed self into Phil's world of rogues, rascals and unredeemed rockers.

Pete Way on *Too Hot to Handle* . . .

"It's just a simple riff I had, which is almost like Grand Funk's *American Band*, or something like that; it has that feel to it. My part within UFO is that I tend to write more of the rock things, things that Michael doesn't normally touch. It's one of those things; my whole attitude toward music tends to go to the live side of things, so there is always an energy in it. In those days, and this might seem strange, we used to go to the pub and come back from the pub and play things, if I had an idea or Michael had an idea. It wasn't like nowadays where we'd come in and say, 'This is my idea for the song; it starts like this, goes like that.' In those days, there was a good chemistry there. I'm not saying there isn't in the new stuff, because you always find a way back to the chemistry; you just adapt it. But in those days it was very much a touring band and I think that came into the way that song came across. Ron Nevison came in for **Lights Out** and he added production into it. I think the hard rock songs . . . he let things like *Too Hot to Handle* be raw, but it gave it and overall bigger sound. Actually, we always wanted the Led Zeppelin drum sound, because he was the engineer on **Physical Graffiti**. That record was kind of smoothed out for American radio but at that point in time, we kind of resented smoothing stuff out too much. But unfortunately, to a certain extent then, we went after Top 30 singles. America and Canada, they liked to hear that kind of thing, didn't they?"

437 YOU CAN'T STOP ROCK 'N' ROLL TWISTED SISTER

122 points *from You Can't Stop Rock 'n' Roll (Atlantic '83)*

Heavy and tensely melodic, compared to future fare, *You Can't Stop Rock 'n' Roll* nevertheless sounds grounded compared to the precisions strikes on **Under the Blade**. And indeed, it's indicative of its namesake album as a whole, a bit of a street-level bash, an anthem for the lunchbox set, an actualization of the band's evolution from a chaotic, unfocused '70s catch-all to something Priest- and NWOBMH-affected, to something simpler, Dee's near obsession with AC/DC seeping into the backbeats.

Dee Snider on *You Can't Stop Rock 'n' Roll . . .*

"That was written while **Under the Blade** was being recorded. I was writing that album then because there was a lot of downtime. And by the way, **Under the Blade** was supposed to be called **You Can't Stop Rock 'n' Roll**. We were recording that song and it was decided by the record company at the last minute that album titles with rock 'n' roll in the title weren't happening. So we didn't put the track on **Under the Blade** because we had been playing that song for a long time. But we did wind up using it on the next album."

438 S.A.T.O. OZZY OSBOURNE

122 points *from Diary of a Madman (Jet/CBS '81)*

One of the silent unsung sentinels deep within the Ozzy catalogue, *S.A.T.O.* features, to my mind, Randy's greatest riff, even if that riff is more of an abstract melody with a flurry of mini-riffed angels and devils flitting and flirting around that axis. In this respect, Rhoads performs the track more like Eddie Van Halen would, an idea that is reinforced with the song's solo, which is three part conventional guitar solo, one part meaty and substantial enough to be called a riff, or at least serve as riff, given no backing rhythm guitar track. Melodically, Ozzy is also at his sorrowful best, demonstrating his ability to be doomy, ornately gothic and commercially accessible all at once. A great "album" track, *S.A.T.O.* cracked our Top 500 as the 12th and last Ozzy solo track to do so.

Bob Daisley on *S.A.T.O.* . . .

> ""I'll tell you exactly what that meant. Funnily enough, I had been reading some Buddhist doctrines at that stage and I wrote that song really about what was said in the Buddhist doctrine. But after I left the band . . . originally that song was called *Strange Voyage*, and after I left the band, they changed the name to *S.A.T.O.* and all that meant was a Sharon Adrian Thelma Ozzy. Because Sharon at the time had a boyfriend called Adrian, and Ozzy's current wife at the time was Thelma, and that was it. People were trying to figure out, 'Oh, it stands for Sail Across the Ocean' and all sorts of things, but it just meant that."

439 PULL THE PLUG
DEATH

122 points *from Leprosy (Relativity '88)*

One, Hollow, Pull the Plug from Starz, *Pull the Plug* from Death . . . the coma/invalid/active mind without the physical ability to die . . . this is healthy metal terrain. Seminal death metal underlords Death of course give us the scorched earth version, Chuck chillingly and agonizingly requesting eternal peace through a mournful grinding melody that marked a new sophistication for this band, on album #2, already making baby steps towards the high falutin' progressive death of their late '90s fare. Chuck: R.I.P. Thursday, December 13th, 2001 at 4 PM EST.

Chuck Schuldiner on staying true to metal . . .

> "What makes me stubborn is basically my love for music, just like any fan. I'm a fan first and then I'm a guy in a band. For me remaining a fan has helped me not turn my back on what I believe in. That's crucial. You just can't be someone in a band that doesn't care about what's going on around you. But I don't see any barriers. If you start out as a heavy metal artist then what's the problem? Keep growing and pushing things. That's where Death is, pushing things to the maximum limit, if there is one. If you put on the new Death album, you're going to hear the most rebellious metal going."

440 TO LIVE IS TO DIE
METALLICA

121 points *from . . . And Justice For All (Elektra '88)*

An insufferable bore of a track, *To Live Is to Die* is more or less the last stop on this train of thought for Metallica. Thankfully arriving late in the record, *To Live Is to Die* plods bloatedly while bloating ploddingly, stuffed full of parts, mellow, heavy, entirely grooveless, Lars making a failing contraption of the thing. It is a demonstration how not to write instrumental music, the antithesis of the good taste Metallica exhibited with *The Call of Ktulu.* Still folks sent in the votes, perhaps due to the involved, escapist and sorrowful quality to the thing. Indeed, one could imagine this as some sort of a thrash version of a Pink Floyd experience for a new breed of metal listener. I imagine not.

Jason Newsted on *To Live Is to Die . . .*

"*To Live Is to Die . . .* God, was a really heavy thing; just the whole vibe around the recording because it was for Cliff, you know? Nobody has really said those words, but it really was, and everybody knew it, without saying it. There was that kind of feeling that was around. It was just very present; you could feel it. I don't know how to explain it. The lyrics were something that Cliff had written down in a notebook somewhere. I think James found them in his belongings or something, or it was something that he had given James earlier, some kind of exchange. I think Cliff might have gotten them from . . . he might have twisted the words around from some other famous writer, but James really liked the way he put it."

441 DEMANUFACTURE FEAR FACTORY

121 points *from Demanufacture (Roadrunner '95)*

Arguably at the height of their game, less arguably at the height of their original purpose, Fear Factory crafted this harsh, cold, unfeeling album of classic cyber metal. The opening title track defined the band's distinct sound, percussive production past Pantera, riffs impossibly rigid, keyboards adding techno ambience, Burton barking angstified man versus machine philosophies through a dry hardcore attack. The impressive result of a collision between extreme production detail and extreme metal.

Burton C. Bell on *Demanufacture . . .*

"That's a classic riff. **Demanufacture** was a very tough record to make, very difficult, a very rough time, a disgruntled time and it ended up being one of the most classic albums. It didn't have any bass on it. *Demanufacture* is a song that is so memorable; musically, lyrically, it just hits people so hard they're sent reeling. We can't even play a show without playing that song or we'll get our ass kicked (laughs)."

Burton C. Bell from Fear Factory
AC/DC — *Back in Black*
Black Sabbath — *Black Sabbath*
Iron Maiden — *The Number of the Beast*
Judas Priest — *You've Got Another Thing Comin'*
Kiss — *I Was Made for Loving You*
Metallica — *Trapped under Ice*
Slayer — *South of Heaven*
Pantera — *Walk*
Ministry — *Burning Inside*
Dio — *The Last in Line*

442 SAY WHAT YOU WILL FASTWAY

121 points *from Fastway* (CBS '83)

The big party rocker on an album that overflows with celebratory ebullience, *Say What You Will* had two things built for strip joints: a pumping burlesque bassline and a widdly riff that took a while to climax. O'ertop, wonder bread wunderkind Dave King screeches like Plant reborn, enunciating viciously, really selling the track's naff sentiments, set to a sparkly musical soundtrack that was destined for the hit single status it briefly enjoyed.

Dave King on *Say What You Will* . . .

"A lot of stuff back then was more about phrasing, if it sounded good, you know what I mean? Which took a lot of heat off the lyrics, in a sense. Don't get me wrong, I enjoyed them and I had a great time doing it. The first two Fastway albums for me were some of the greatest memories of my life. The only reason I cringe sometimes is that I remember some of the lyrics not quite being probably smart enough, I don't know. Maybe I'm being hard on myself, I don't know. I come from a completely different angle in my life right now."

Dave King from Fastway
Yardbirds — *Shapes of Things*
Led Zeppelin — *Good Times Bad Times*
Free — *The Mover*
AC/DC — *High Voltage*
Black Sabbath — *War Pigs*
The Who — *Baba O'Reilly*
Queen — *Father to Son*
Cream — *Spoonful*
Rush — *Bastille Day*
UFO — *Lights Out*

443 POWER OF THE NIGHT SAVATAGE

120 points *from Power of the Night (Atlantic '85)*

Major label, new logo, but the shocking skills of this modest Florida collective could not be stopped. Authoritative album, but its calling card is this brusque, brisk, sinfully perfect smart bomb, *Power of the Night* demonstrating Criss Oliva's knack for castle rock with crunch. And Dr. Killdrums, Steve Wacholz is a big part of the game, Savatage's stringsmen answering his cannons pound for pound while Jon Oliva puts his frightwig on the line, the man quickly becoming one of metal's rich in personality vocal masters.

Jon Oliva on *Power of the Night* . . .

"That was one of the first tuned-down songs. We dropped the low E string to C, and kept the rest of the guitar in scale, which was also the tuning for *Hall of the Mountain King*. So *Power of the Night* was definitely a very experimental track. That was my brother's idea. He was trying to come up with a weird tuning idea. Actually the funny thing about *Power of the Night* is that the synthesizer introduction was something that was played by accident. I was just messing around with this synthesizer and I didn't even know they were recording it. I was just screwing around hitting all kinds of different buttons. And I went back into the room and I hear the thing coming back and I said, 'What's happening?' And they say, 'Oh, that's the thing you just played.' And I was like, 'Well, that's cool. Let's use that for the intro.' And I remember the note C, and my brother just tuned his low string down to C and he started playing that riff and I just went 'Hmm . . . Mondo like candy!'"

444 BLACK NIGHT DEEP PURPLE

120 points *from 24 Carat Purple (Warner '75)*

Rushed together as a single without a homeful album, *Black Night* sounds like old tired pre-psych rock 'n' roll from somewhere between '64 and '67 coal mine-transformed into heaving heavy metal. On paper, it's more about keyboards than power chords, but the delivery is so thick with backwash that you become convinced it's Black Sabbath knocking over a liquor store. Never too beloved and no smash hit, *Black Night* pales in production and vision compared to the material on **In Rock** or **Machine Head**. But you gotta admire the gumption of the extended band family proposing such a burnin' up belly-churner as an innocent little 45 RPM household item.

Roger Glover on improvisation . . .

"I've worked with so many bands that don't know what improvisation is. It really comes from knowing your instrument. I've worked with a — I won't say who — but a lead guitarist who was doing his solo, many years ago now, and I said, 'OK, now we've got the sound,' and he did the solo and I said, 'Yeah, well that's pretty good, now let's try another one.' And he played it exactly the same. And I'm like, 'What's the point of doing another one,' and he said, 'Well, you asked me to do another one,' but I'm like, 'Well, do a different one.' And he looked at me like I was mad, and said, 'But that's the solo!' The whole idea of just having fun with music was gone. He had learned it by rote and that was that. And that kind of thinking is something that Deep Purple has helped to change. I mean, lots of people were doing it though. We were a jamming band. I suppose back in the in the late '60s there were quite a few jamming bands, long solos. I listened to some old Cream stuff where they would go on for 25 minutes, and it actually wasn't that good either. But I love Cream; don't get me wrong. But that sort of self-indulgence is what we were born into."

445 GYPSY ROAD CINDERELLA

120 points *from Long Cold Winter (Mercury '88)*

Always the bluesier, nastier face of hair metal, Cinderella turn in a rough 'n' tumble twangy nu-country punk rock song here, Keifer doing his best Blackie McCafferty over a barroom brawl of a riff that is both warmly beer-goggled and glam at once. No question, Cinderella and Poison overlapped on the roots thing, but Cinderella took to it more resolutely, Keifer wanting (and never really getting) that street cred so elusive to every hair band teasing the scene. But this is a nice handshake of a track, written somewhere between the sophistication of Aerosmith and the paint-by-numbers patter patterns of Sammy Hagar.

446 LOW
TESTAMENT

119 points *from Low (Atlantic '94)*

To my mind this is when Testament really found their own headspace, rocking with hardened arteries through a bad time for metal, returning renewed, with fresh flesh and blood for an imposing stack of riff monsters that finally shed the vestiges of the old school. There's almost a sense of positive self-parody in this song, a mining of all the great qualities of the band, Chuck newly carnivorous, drums like cannons, the guitars, catchy, punky, but thick as a black brick. Bonus boner: new boy James Murphy (Death, Obituary) rips off a solo that is the nasty high register emotional equivalent of the wide-load riffs punching their way through the album as a low whole.

Eric Peterson on *Low* . . .

> "*Low* is a song that we wrote when we were kind of lost after **The Ritual**. We were really going towards commercialism with the old members. After Lou and Alex had left we really wanted to get back to the heaviness and *Low* was the first riff that I wrote at that point. And Chuck had the pattern; we were jamming it in his office. He had an acoustic guitar and it worked out really cool. It was a welcome home for us."

447 NO LOVE LOST
CARCASS

119 points *from Heartwork (Earache/Sony '94)*

Another catchy mosh happy meal from the band's first pop album, *No Love Lost* mines new lyrical terrain, Bill Steer hilariously quill-penning a lament to faded love half-heartedly wrapped in a handful of gore images, arriving at a power ballad with 10% medical content. But of course power ballad is a relative term, this sounding more like electrocuted Cathedral or Trouble, deeply convincing doom metal power-punched by Colin Richardson's production body blows, hacked to pieces by odd time signatures and Jeff Walkers witchly crowings, which sound truly misplaced for that purely sentimental chorus, one conspicuously lacking in words like regnant, osculatory, magniloquent or smelting.

Michael Amott on *No Love Lost* . . .

> "Those were Bill Steer's riffs, if I remember correctly. But I really liked it because it had more of a rock groove to it, rocky for Carcass anyway (laughs). I mean, you've got to remember in those days, people didn't mix stuff up like they do nowadays. But that one reminded me of Trouble or something. I remember we called it the Trouble riff. I did some pretty off the wall lead guitar in it as well, if I remember correctly."

448 SUFFER THE CHILDREN NAPALM DEATH

118 points *from Harmony Corruption (Earache '90)*

An old punk rock moshnut from a band of legendary English nutters, *Suffer the Children* showed that true speed was often more beloved than blasting, able to cause more fervent moshing than mere double time, able to evoke chaos through the particular angry charms of old school hardcore. And in terms of the early output, it was one of the band's more logically written tracks, even though it skirts the edges of good tastes with its many velocities. Seminal grim grindcore from the grey nation that invented it.

Shane Embury on change . . .

> "It got to the point where blastbeats didn't seem extreme to me. It was getting boring to a point. You get buried and you learn to play better as musicians. We could sit down and come up with **Utopia** II in about two hours. What's the point in doing that really, just to satisfy a few kids who just don't want the band to change? We've always tried to do an album different than the last one in some ways. For a band it's difficult to create something fresh. There's something different about Napalm. We're lumped in with a lot of bands and we don't listen to that type of

stuff nowadays. We're into a totally different trip. If we did just concentrate on listening to the bands in our genre of music, we'd find ourselves doing the same stuff because there'd be no new ideas coming from anywhere. I think it got to a point where we looked at what we were into and realized it had nothing to do with the scene which we were supposedly involved with. Obviously we're still into aggressive and heavy music, but when we had spare time on the road, we didn't put on the new Cannibal Corpse album. Nothing against them, but the whole scene just started to thrive off each other's records. That's why it became samey. Some people get scared of change."

449 WAR MACHINE KISS

118 points *from Creatures of the Night (Mercury '82)*

War Machine is a partial throwback to the band's Gene genes, although given the new realities of heavy music so apparent in the low '80s, there's purpose and critical mass here, no stumble, just a thick black felt pen line from point A to point B. *War Machine* therefore dents an impression in the metalhead, due partially to the clear movement of its ideas, due also to this song's vaguely predictable, charmingly stupid, old-time rock patterns. An additional clear positive (not that any of the preceding is meant to sound negative) is the fact that this track, with its oppressive lumber, does its duty to widen admirably and unexpectedly the range of metal styles on **Creatures of the Night**.

Gene Simmons on achieving goals . . .

"I've always had it all. I'm not a big fan of material goods. For me, it's always been about keeping my mind busy and having a good time. Imagine being in Fort Knox with all that gold and money, by yourself. You might as well be in a jail. The sound of one cricket is not very exciting."

450 SILENT SCREAMS HALFORD

118 points *from Resurrection (Sanctuary '00)*

Silent Screams is pretty much the integrity anchor to the sometimes safe and obvious **Resurrection** album. It's cool how it broods low and builds, Rob's lyric evoking pain, his vocal melody one of the best on the record. Then of course, it rocks out, and here it seems a little forced. But all is forgiven as it collapses back into the ennui and angst of the final slow metal moment. Rob's duets with his high self are particularly effective, and by track's end, you feel this was one of a handful of songs on the record that asked to be written, an epic wrapped in a lot of words, many that might have been floating in the lonely ether above Rob's recent career excursions for quite some time.

Rob Halford on the motivation behind the Halford band . . .

> "It came out of the live shows with Two in Switzerland. I was coming off stage and I was thinking this just isn't right. I don't feel like I know how I want to feel. I want to come off stage mentally and physically depleted. I want to feel that certain way. And I wasn't getting that from the Two stuff. And I'm not dissing the Two record. It just wasn't happening for me live. So I went back to the States and then spoke to Bob and I said, 'Look, this is what's been going on and this is what I want to do.' And he said, 'Let's start writing.' So we did, and the germ of the album therefore is the *Silent Screams* track. And I stuck that on the internet and everybody went ballistic. 'This is great, Rob; is this what you're going to do, are you coming on to metal?' Yeah, this is it. This is where all the best things happen for me. So I worked with Bob for a few more weeks and at the same time I was building my friendship with Roy Z and then the cut off point came and I went from Bob's place to Roy's place and that's when we proceeded."

451 THE FINAL COUNTDOWN EUROPE

118 points *from The Final Countdown (Sony '86)*

Drilled into your head like a hockey puck at the barns in which the song so infinitely careens and echoes, *The Final Countdown* (and more often just its wimpy synth line — then play resumes), was a huge and quite unexpected hit for this band of shiftless foreigners. Gaggle and gag with *We Are the Champions* and *Eye of the Tiger*, and you've got the recipe for a victory of which you, sadly, are only a spectator. But bear no mind, for a moment soundtracked by that one spray of old school synthesized electronics, you feel light (and vacant) as air. Thenceforth the band break into a vaguely Swedish and frosty metal chug, buried way back behind the frills and nonsense and sweetly naïve vocals of Joey Tempest (in a teapot), all a faint reminder of the stormy, snowy force this band once was way back on their godless, peerless self-titled debut.

452 A SORCERER'S PLEDGE CANDLEMASS

118 points *from Epicus Doomicus Metallicus (Black Dragon '86)*

Candlemass were somewhat akin to Celtic Frost in temperament, most pointedly in their immobility, this sense that once a riff started bulldozing its way through the rhythm section, watch out, step aside and let nature take its course. But of course, Candlemass were a doom band, kind of like Mercyful Fate without the window dressing, just this massive surge of simple power elements, performances drowning in light of the imposing idea of the thing. *A Sorcerer's Pledge* does all this and more, including mellow bits, a post-NWOBHM gallop, lots of slow doom and some additional epic touches, including an early, innovative dip into female operatics.

Leif Edling on the band's early influences . . .

> "We listened to all the current metal. I mean, we were young when we started, 17, 18 years old. Of course we were huge Black Sabbath fans; we also loved Venom, the NWOBHM, Angel Witch. And with Trouble, we were pretty crushed when that record came out because they were the only band doing what we were doing in Nemesis, our band before Candlemass. When the first Trouble record came out, we had played with Nemesis for two years or something, and we thought we were the only heavy band on the planet (laughs). So we thought, wow, here we've got some guys in Chicago that are doing exactly the same thing that we're doing, but they did it before us. So we were just thrilled that somebody was doing it, because nobody was doing it at that point."

453 BACK IN THE SADDLE AEROSMITH

118 points *from Rocks (Columbia '76)*

Reprising Tom Hamilton's role as four-string riff-driver last subcycled on *Sweet Emotion*, *Back in the Saddle* slow-trots through dust and tumbleweed with all sorts of textures served up as trail mix along the way. The song features Steve Tyler's most painful screech, as well as riffs that help brush-stroke a picture rather than hog the road. The song's creative heat-treated soundtrack of a close simply underscores the wealth of talent poured into what is widely considered the best album by America's best rock 'n' roll band.

Joe Perry on sobriety . . .

> "I can remember a time in the late '70s, early '80s, when I thought I had written all the best songs I was ever gonna write and that was it. When in fact, I was finally closing down because

of drugs and alcohol. My imagination had shut down. Now it feels like it's slowly being revved up, and I feel as energetic about rock 'n' roll as I ever have."

454 GIRLS, GIRLS, GIRLS MÖTLEY CRÜE

117 points *from Girls Girls Girls (Elektra '87)*

Here's an example of Crüe clinging to the thin part of a premise, the verse hardly there at all, Tommy all ham-fisted and of singular brain-dead purpose. But that riff behind Vince's lame chorus vocal is something special, thick, dirty and searching, and as a big cockroach-infested package, the song at least mumbles chemistry, as well as effectiveness through big red truck simplicity. Became one of the era's miserable, trampled dead-end double-vision stripper numbers for obvious drooling reasons. Man, the '80s, what a larf.

Nikki Sixx on **Girls Girls Girls** . . .

"It was a direct rebellion against **Theater of Pain**. If you take those records out and look at them, what we went from, Vince wearing a pink on the back of that. And in a sense, **Theater of Pain** was a rebellion against **Shout at the Devil**. It's what **Dope Show** is for Marilyn Manson, against **Antichrist Superstar**. You can see the parallel: **Antichrist Superstar — Shout at the Devil**, **Theater of Pain**, with what Marilyn Manson is doing now. They're doing the same thing. They are rebelling against themselves. I think we were getting so much heat for focusing more on the way we looked. So it was like for **Girls Girls Girls**, we decided, you know what? Let's just go leather and motorcycles, because we were all into that. We were like a gang, and don't forget, there was high drug addiction at that time."

Brian Milner from Skrape
Dio — *Rainbow in the Dark*
Ratt — *Back for More*
Metallica — *Ride the Lightning*
Judas Priest — *Electric Eye*
Iron Maiden — *Where Eagles Dare*
Ozzy Osbourne — *Bark at the Moon*
Deftones — *My Own Summer (Shove It)*
Mötley Crüe — *Looks That Kill*
Pantera — *5 Minutes Alone*
Slayer — *Angel of Death*

455 I WAS MADE FOR LOVING YOU KISS

117 points *from Dynasty (Casablanca '79)*

Hey, everybody at a certain level was trying it, or maybe it was everybody period, but the press only noticed the big franchises. Anyway, blah blah blah, this was Kiss trying disco and dammit if it wasn't a big hit, somehow, somewhere (Italy? Israel? Japan?), meaning something to someone. Who? You? I doubt it. It's crap of course, as good or bad as anybody at it, a little rock, a little hooky, stiff like disco's expected backbone, oddly appropriate for a fop like Stanley, also unsurprisingly bass-percolated given the presence of a Gene, Gene, dancing machine in the band.

Ace Frehley on *I Was Made for Lovin' You* . . .

> "Yaddah yaddah yaddah (laughs). I didn't particularly like that one (laughs). A disco rock song. Actually, when I first heard it I was like, 'I don't even want to get involved with this song,' even though it was one of our biggest hits, more outside the United States than inside the United States, from what I understand. I think we gained new fans when that song became a hit but I think we also lost some of the hardcore heavy metal fans who were turned off by it. But you know, music is a double-edged sword. But the hardcore Kiss fans, they've always hung around, or else I wouldn't be here today."

456 RAPID FIRE JUDAS PRIEST

117 points

from British Steel (CBS '80)

I never liked the way this song just sort of ambles into the room. But after **British Steel** winds down eight hummable hardballs later — surprise — we find that *Rapid Fire* was the record's heaviest song, only *Steeler* matching it for speed, *Grinder* for malevolence. For my liking, Halford plays too fully the part of metal rube, forcing the lyric whereon past Priestly pre-thrashers, a subtle intelligence once hovered, no actorly hamming necessary. Still, there are subtleties in the guitar performance (behind Rob's vocal, and of course in the break), and the track does serve the purpose of purifying what is elsewhere a primary and poppy rock ride.

Rob Halford on **British Steel** drummer Dave Holland . . .

> "Well, after we had been through the experience of those two writing modes, **Stained Class** and **Killing Machine**, we hooked up with Tom Allom. The band was suddenly writing in this **British Steel** format. There was just this feeling that we wanted to get back, if you will, to that very simple, steady, solid, almost Bonham-esque style of drumming. And we found all of those things we needed in Dave Holland."

457 ROISIN DUBH (BLACK ROSE) A ROCK LEGEND THIN LIZZY

116 points

from Black Rose (Vertigo '79)

To my mind, this is only as euphoric as Celtic music, not Thin Lizzy's subtle inclusion of Celtic music clues, *Black Rose* perhaps clutching at straws, laying things out too clearly, foretelling a creative well gone dry in **Chinatown**. Still, it's newly proggy and committedly epic, Phil playing his hand, visiting his roots evidently and methodically, Moore and Gorham doing the same with their medley of Celtic riffs, Downey shuffling an expansive 7/4 sweep with his usual grace and style. The hero returns home, perhaps for the last time.

Scott Gorham on his chemistry with Phil . . .

> "Phil and I were on this mission and we were on it together. We understood each other. I knew what he was all about; he knew what I was all about. We were extremely close with each other. It seemed that other people who joined weren't completely led into the private mini-circle that we had created. Maybe that was a fault of ours. We had done too many things together and had spent so much time together to maybe let the new face in completely."

458 BENEATH THE REMAINS SEPULTURA

116 points *from Beneath the Remains (Roadrunner '89)*

Part of the mystique and sheer metal draw of a track like this is its unapologetic, almost naïve retro feel, 1989, in some respects, being half a decade late for this sort of raw, punked-out Bay Area thrash. But one does ascribe naïvety to Sepultura, the band having honed its chaos far from the metal centres, as a result bringing abstract alterings of metal's chromosomal make-up to the vicious game. *Beneath the Remains* is a prime example of one of the band's charming traits, their grabbing, holding onto, and shaking of a riff until it is lifeless or at least amusingly dizzy, an operation that is performed a bunch of times on this progressive but not too progressive Slayerized feast from the band's third album and first Roadrunner issue.

Max Cavalera on *Beneath the Remains* . . .

> "*Beneath the Remains*, believe it or not, is influenced by U2. Nobody really knows that, but I was listening a lot to the album **War** at that time. Even the words 'Under a pale grey sky,' coming from *Arise*, the title track to the follow-up album to **Beneath the Remains**, was a U2 influence; it was a time when I was listening

to a lot of old U2 and I was picking up a lot of Bono's inspiration. There is something like, 'Who has won, who has died, beneath the remains.' Throughout U2's **War** album, there are some words that are totally connected, his antiwar-type lyrics. Of course the music has nothing to do with U2 (laughs), but the message, I was very influenced by Bono's antiwar statements at that time."

459 KISS OF DEATH DOKKEN

116 points *from Back for the Attack (Elektra '87)*

Kiss of Death's cracking of the Top 500 goes to prove that the fans who are still there lived for the heavy stuff, George Lynch firing up this guitar hero rocker to Viv Campbell/Zakk Wylde proportions, galloping grandly to the bloody backbeat of "Wild" Mick Brown. Don's vocal melodies are also central to the track's charms, his silken delivery providing striking contrast to Lynch's combative attack. Highlights elsewhere: cool modulation and a memorable and forceful pre-chorus punch-out.

Don Dokken on *Kiss of Death* . . .

"I don't know if people understand this or not, but it's a song about AIDS. Mick made a comment one night, kind of a naïve comment, if you sleep with a good-looking girl, a model, you get AIDS, if you sleep with a ho backstage, you get AIDS. We were talking about that and I said AIDS doesn't discern between good-looking girls and fat, ugly chicks. And this is all around '85, '86, so that partly inspired the lyrics for *Kiss of Death*. It's about the kiss of death. It's, oh, she looks bitchin', she looks beautiful, gorgeous; she says, 'I've never been backstage before.' You take her back to the hotel room, and you get it."

460 AT DAWN THEY SLEEP
SLAYER

115 points *from Hell Awaits (Metal Blade '85)*

One of the slower songs on **Hell Awaits**, *At Dawn They Sleep* is an example of Slayer getting down to business and honing their sound, pounding through a one-and-three mid-mosher that has King and Hanneman working out their angular equations. The band at this point had established all their basic premises, but the delivery was still blocky, with Araya sounding like a horror movie hawker rather than the real life frightwig of later years. And writing in the long song style at the time, Slayer could have used some judicious editing here, and elsewhere on the album.

Tom Araya on *At Dawn They Sleep . . .*

> "Wow, I was a co-author to that. There were three authors to that song, Kerry, Jeff and me. The song was basically about vampires. I had some stuff written and I asked them if they cared if I put my two cents into the song, because I hadn't really written anything for anything. And when I showed them what I had, they really liked it. That was from a book I had read a long time ago, Stephen King's **Salem Lot**, and that gave me the idea about the philosophy behind vampires, which I've also learned a lot about from **Interview With The Vampire.**"

461 SLAVE TO THE GRIND
SKID ROW

115 points *from Slave to the Grind (Atlantic '91)*

Gotta give the boys credit for this one, bulking up the guitars into a force of nature, *Slave to the Grind* rumbling and roiling like some sort of pumped-up punk annihilator. It's an escape hatch, a release valve, but a dark one, you (the victim) getting the impression that Baz might not be left behind, but you will. Why? Because he's hit the ground running all spindly and unpredictably and has knocked you over before you've located that first cuppa java. All you can do is shuffle sheepishly to the record store and buy his new album, you, along with millions of others, who upon returning home, found a collection of songs much thornier than those preening on the milky white debut.

Sebastian Bach on *Slave to the Grind* . . .

> "I definitely think our best song is *Slave to the Grind*, especially those opening chords and all of *Monkey Business*. And *Darkened Room* is a beautiful piece of music. And critically it was the favourite, although they all like **Subhuman Race** too. But **Slave to the Grind** was the album we did most collectively. You can hear all of us come together as a real rock band. We rehearsed it in my basement, and we cut it in Rob's basement. I came up with *Slave to the Grind* musically, and Rachel said, 'Wow that sounds like a grind and then he came up with the title."

462 GENOCIDE JUDAS PRIEST

115 points *from Sad Wings of Destiny (Gull '76)*

One of **Sad Wings Of Destiny**'s deep album tracks, *Genocide* is an expert example of the band's postmodern metal riff-writing abilities, Tipton and Downing shoving their way past Schenker, Blackmore and Iommi in terms of sheer artful intelligence. The way the guitars segue into breaks, choruses and the song's thrilling battle royale . . . you just gotta crack a smile, or a beer, preferably in a can, to the way Priest were dumping the apple dumplings out of the hard rock cart. Of course their little experiment in thinking man's metal would only last for another three albums before the band, ribs showing through their smart leather togs, would start showing up in shifts on the steps of CBS (beginning well before office hours), flashing placards saying "Will play for food," "Will play what you want, for food," and "Will exchange drummer for food."

Rob Halford on *Genocide* . . .

> "Once again, *Genocide* carries for me the same types of feeling that *Tyrant* does in that the language is quite strong and graphic, and I'd like to feel that some of the things that I've at

least done with my lyrics is to be provocative and somewhat controversial and to stimulate people. When they're listening to these things, I want them to see what I'm trying to express. I leave the listener up to their own choice of what they wish to do with them. That's one of the great things I love about the power of music, that you can either take it in and enjoy it or take it to a deeper level. But again, *Genocide* has a very strong story to tell. Some of the great unfortunate moments in history have come from genocidal situations. But again, it's great too because of the complexity of the song and the journey that it takes you on."

463 LA VILLA STRANGIATO RUSH

114 points *from Hemispheres (Anthem '78)*

La Villa Strangiato marks the summit of Rush's slow rise to, and then gradual withdrawal from, progressive metal density, this instrumental featuring the band full-on showcased, working in concert with their warmest, most glowing and electric set of production tones thus far, a happenstance that makes this track and album soar with youthful ambition. What this means is that Geddy sounds precise yet fat enough to blend, while Alex's meteor storm of guitar ideas sounds metal even though fusion might better describe the man's mindspace. Driving from below, Peart grooves in his gangly manner, simultaneously showing us his collection of bells and whistles, most celebrated being his army of calibrated tom toms, the scintillating sonics of which caused many a young percussive pup to order up the monster set, please. Yes, all 11 pieces. No, the glockenspiel will have to wait 'til next payday, but can I try that gong over there?

Alex Lifeson on long songs . . .

"Will we do those long songs again? I would probably say never. You're talking about an era that's almost 20 years old. There was certainly a segment of our fans that were disappointed after **Hemispheres**. For everybody, music from a certain era in their lives has a very special place in their hearts. I think for a lot of

Rush fans, that whole epic era was like that. We enjoyed doing it and I don't think we want to go back to that. We decided late in the '70s and the early '80s that we wanted to write more concise songs and we've kind of stuck with that format. To do those long full-side concept things, we have no interest in that. Neil's writing from a whole different headspace now. We don't miss it."

464 ROCK THE NATION MONTROSE

114 points *from Montrose (Warner '73)*

If anything threw open the oak and wrought iron doors to American rock 'n' metal, it was this anthemic call to arms, Ronnie unwittingly galvanizing a nation, creating a voracious public that would one day fill sun-dappled stadiums groping and toking to the sounds of **Montrose**'s wicked stepchild, Van Halen — **Van Halen**. *Rock the Nation* started the ball rolling, no-nonsense metal riff clutched tightly, cowbell ringin' out, monster vocalist Sammy Hagar sounding like the kingdom-conquering American Robert Plant. But people forget the Quo-table boogie woogie in the song, as well as that glammy lick stuck right in the middle of this blue jean break. And the verse riff: pure modulation elation.

Ronnie Montrose on the heaviness of the debut album . . .

"Well, I wouldn't say that it was much of a surprise because we were already playing that kind of a heavy rock with the Edgar Winter Group; basically an extension of that, if not exactly an extension of that group, an extension of the way my playing was evolving. For me there wasn't any intention to make a specific kind of music, it just happened to be where I was at the time, a.k.a. the words to *Rock the Nation*, 'I've got it in me, ain't gonna quit until it all comes out.'"

465 COUNTDOWN TO EXTINCTION MEGADETH

114 points *from Countdown To Extinction (Capitol '92)*

One of the mellower (yet philosophically tragic) songs on the album, *Countdown to Extinction* was a predictor of things to come, its melody and its laid back pocket of a groove soon to be the norm for the rest of Megadeth's '90s. Dave is almost singing, even if he keeps the effort low, resentful and bitter, an approach that matches well to the artful chorus riff. I dunno, this is surprisingly under-written for a title track, and the subject matter pretty specific and unmatched to the cover concept or the concept of the album as a whole. But as with everything on the record, it is painstakingly assembled and sonically gleaming, a winner through sweat and toil.

Dave Mustaine on *Countdown to Extinction* . . .

> "I remember Nick Menza coming to me with the lyrics for that song and then about a week later seeing the same exact story in, I think it was *Time* magazine, and I thought, 'You little fucker!' (laughs), so he plagiarized *Time* magazine, I think. So I reworked the lyrics so they would be flowing and semantically correct and have some kind of continuity to it. And I get all these letters from people all the time (in crying voice), 'God, I'm so glad you love the animals!' And I feel like writing back and saying, 'Yeah, with the proper spices, those fuckers taste good, don't they?' But what the song is about is really a dreadful topic. In Texas they have a lot of ranches, as well as in other mid and southern states, where they take these exotic animals, and they just let them out of the cages and these pussy hunters just shoot them a few feet away from the cage. And you know, in reality they've bagged the animal, but they didn't go to the Serengeti jungle to do it."

466 CREATURES OF THE NIGHT KISS

114 points *from Creatures of the Night (Mercury '82)*

Perhaps egged and prodded by the new metal explosion, Kiss respond with their heaviest song ever, *Creatures of the Night*, firing and recoiling with an artillery barrage of performances this band never knew. Riffs are note-dense and complex, drums fall all over themselves, and Paul sings with a conviction that brings back all those distinct and worthy qualities in his voice that had lain dormant since **Love Gun**'s two showcase tracks. Still, there's something non-metal about this track's overweight production values, the quality that keeps it from lift-off. But that is also part of the charm, this notion that beneath the blurry, semi-contrived bluster, Kiss is a babysitting glam band at heart.

Paul Stanley on the music . . .

> "I don't ever want to lose sight of the other stuff, because that's who we are too. In an arena, that counts for half of what's going on. But let's not kid ourselves: nobody's ever put a smoke bomb into an album. I think it's important to stake your turf and claim it. If anyone's crazy enough to think that a hairy chest or a nice ass is what's kept this band going, they're sadly mistaken (laughs). Music is what it's all about for me. I'm as happy in a club playing as in an arena; there's nothing like having a guitar in your hand and destroying the airwaves!"

Jason and Mike from Godhead
Iron Maiden — *Run to the Hills*
Ozzy Osbourne — *I Don't Know*
Ozzy Osbourne — *Mr. Crowley*
Metallica — *One*
AC/DC — *Highway to Hell*
AC/DC — *Back in Black*
Mötley Crüe — *Shout at the Devil*
Black Sabbath — *War Pigs*
Yngwie Malmsteen — *Riot in the Dungeons*
Slayer — *Raining Blood*

467 RATS IN THE CELLAR AEROSMITH

114 points *from Rocks (Columbia '76)*

The wicked redheaded stepchild of *Toys in the Attic, Rats in the Cellar* is what happens when speed metal strikes back, Aerosmith rocking nasty and reckless in a New York minute. Perry slashes and burns on what is arguably Aerosmith's heaviest track, *Nobody's Fault* at the other end of the speed spectrum, being another caustic candidate. How far the mighty have fallen. And you know (and they don't), if the band just got in a room and punched out a few of these — analogue, chemical relapse, no song doctors — it would sell precisely as many copies as **Just Push Play**. And they'd have their integrity back, the only thing (besides love, eternal youth and one of those **Star Trek** transporter things) a guy could want when money is no longer concern.

Steven Tyler on the band's dark past . . .

> "Joe and I used to get inebriated all the time, to say the least. Along with that, you get some super feelings, like tripping. You can't go to the moon, but you can certainly get close enough by taking LSD and, if you remain that way, you really aren't on earth. You're not experiencing stuff, as your emotions are tainted because of all the drugs. Coming back into reality is hard; shit's hard to deal with. It's really hard being sober all the time. Trust me. I've gotten plastered a lot of times over a lot of angry things, plain, 'Goddamn, I work so hard so I need to get loaded.' Drugs are like a bungee cord: you can try it once and say you did it, or you can live it until the rope snaps. You can do it every day and eventually the rope may snap. Drugs are even better; they make you feel so good you feel inhuman. That's when they snap your life right out from underneath you. For a musician, it's the kiss of death, because it really loops you in. It gets you away from your fears, your doubts, and your insecurities, and it steals your inspiration. At the beginning it helped me, but in the end, it will steal from you."

468 WALK ALL OVER YOU
AC/DC

114 points *from Highway to Hell (Atlantic '79)*

Well, it's my favourite AC/DC song, if that counts for anything, followed closely (just like on the album) by *Touch Too Much*. But yeah, this thing just ripsaws with old timey rock 'n' roll values, a little boogie, a little southern rock, a desert head-on collision of blood, sweat and white line fever. And it's really so simple (granted, medium to high complexity in the AC/DC canon), chords everyone can understand and not a lot of them, a nice slowdown for the fairly mean chorus before firing up again, the band bubbling ever more intensely toward my favourite Angus solo and then Bon's crowning vocal performance of the catalogue, one where you can just hear him pulling out his shaggy, tangled locks.

Angus Young on brotherhood and the basics . . .

> "When Malcolm asked me to join when I was young, it was always the case that the music is what we were there for. We have the brothers thing but between the two of us it's always the music that you look at and that's your end-game. As kids we would scrap a lot I suppose, but as we joined together in playing and making music it was more professional. When we were working out all our ideas, the thing that we wanted the most was to make a good rock 'n' roll record and something that was toe-tapping all the way through and that's what we aim for. We weren't thinking of anything like Top 40 hits or anything; we were just aiming to make a good rock 'n' roll record. That's why we also brought in our other brother George because he made a lot of the early rock 'n' roll with AC/DC, and it just seems so natural — the three of us. And if Malcolm's sitting between the two of us he makes a good referee too! We all get on together. We are a family that grew up very bonded, very tight and we're all in agreement — we all love what's good in rock 'n' roll, especially George. He's a big fan of rock 'n' roll, especially the past; he knows a lot of the history of it. When he's got his two brothers there really belting it out, he loves it."

469 THE IDOL
W.A.S.P.

113 points *from The Crimson Idol (Capitol '92)*

Gratuitous shades of Pink Floyd's **The Wall** all over this one, as the Jonathan character deals with all that fame (gag), Blackie going into a wheezy croon over a dark acoustic track that builds nicely to some plush multi-tracked vocals. The guitar solo is all steel-on-steel electric with a feel like Slash. But again, it's the plain jane song around it that counts, Blackie keeping *The Idol* well within the rulebooks for a reflective downtime moment on a concept record.

Blackie Lawless on *The Idol* . . .

> "Well, *The Idol* was pretty much the pinnacle of the record, where he wakes up, he looks around, and then he says, 'Is this all there is? This is everything I've worked for. I'm still not happy. Is this all it's ever going to be?' It's kind of like when a person is on the road, or traveling down the road where they meet themselves, and they're not sure what to say when they finally become acquainted with themselves."

470 AND THE CRADLE WILL ROCK . . .
VAN HALEN

113 points *from Women and Children First (Warner '80)*

Featuring one of Van Halen's most sophisticated arrangements, *And the Cradle Will Rock* . . . builds a complicated yet sweet melody through a series of abstracts, one of the most ambitious being Dave's vocal circuitry, applied to a tale of youth that cannot be stopped. Of course, Eddie's swirling, scraping guitar magic is a big part of the mix, as is the welcome addition of multiple layers of guitars, one of which is reserved for what amounts to commentary. Come solo time, Ed is accompanied by a shower of cymbals from a rock steady Alex, Ed responding with a very metallic attack and a somewhat conventional storm of notes. All told, a fairly bizarre song, and one of many examples of the band expanding their palette.

471 THE THING THAT SHOULD NOT BE METALLICA

113 points *from Master of Puppets (Elektra '86)*

A woolly mammoth of a track, *The Thing That Should Not Be* is a Lovecrafted tale of an "old one" lurking beneath the sea. And the soundtrack to the spare and sparse lyric is about as appropriately awkward, blocky and voluminous as could be. It's one of those tracks that is unique and uniquely put to service as a foil to much of the rest of the record, squatting low to the ground as the song sentinel with spaces and stone and friction. A mature exercise in restraint, building on the legacy of *Escape* and *For Whom the Bell Tolls.*

Lars Ulrich on getting away from work . . .

> "I spend most of my free time completely ignoring music and dealing with other things. Dealing with movies, dealing with hanging out. I'm not as absorbed by music 24 hours a day like I was five, 10 or 15 years ago. I find that by playing it, I choose to spend my free time differently than chasing it. Certainly a lot of things in my life have changed over the last few years. I can sit down and be philosophical about whether it was due to the fact that we sold a gazillion records or not, but certainly, my musical tastes have changed a lot. I don't think my musical taste change has anything to do with how many records we've sold though. I think it has more to do with the fact that I've always been one to explore and check different things out."

472 SHE
KISS

113 points *from Dressed to Kill (Casablanca '75)*

Toughened from its roots as a fey and Tull-ian Wicked Lester track, *She* is one of the early Kiss tracks both sung by Gene, with music that sounds like Gene's personality. Its riff is a buffalo burger of a BTO beefsteak, never quite resolving, always in search of that final burp that spells relief. It is an essential component of Kiss' quite unique early repertoire, this bassy throbbing thing that is integral to a third of the original trio of albums. But it is, for this reason, also the odd (wo)man out on the album of the original three that is the brightest and most buoyant.

Peter Criss on the ritual of the makeup . . .

> "Of course it's a pain in the ass, because there's a lot of it. It's not like putting on a little bit of makeup and looking like Steven Tyler. This is a lot of work. It's a two-hour procedure to get into it, to do the makeup, to get your hair all teased up and go through all of that. But when you find the get up there and look out into the audience and you see people dressed like you, it just hits my heart. How cool is it that somebody else took the time to go through this to pay homage to us? It's as high a form of compliment as you can get far as I'm concerned. So it's worth it."

473 MADHOUSE
ANTHRAX

113 points *from Spreading the Disease (Island '86)*

After an amusingly diabolical laugh, *Madhouse* opens with one of the band's purest wood grain alcohol metal moments (first they throw the brick, then comes the sirens). *Madhouse* captures the gravity of Anthrax's early sound, the gelling with the new singer, a sense of settling down and finding the songs within the metal. The riff is monster, as is the cut and dried production. The song's all about groove, combining Accept (the solo is all Wolf) and Metallica (the chorus?), with little of the hysterical hardcore soon to become the band's itchy trademark.

Charlie Benante on *Madhouse* . . .

"That was our first video, and it was one of those things I have fond memories of. I had all my friends involved in the video. We did it at this old mental ward and we all had to be there at seven in the morning. So all my friends were there at the crack of dawn getting in makeup and stuff and the shoot lasted all day and I remember it being really cold in there. It was one of the first things of a band coming together and being a band, you know, shooting a video. That was the first one and the most exciting one and I've hated doing videos ever since."

474 MEAN MAN W.A.S.P.

112 points *from The Headless Children (Capitol '89)*

Great beer-drinking gunrack chorus, pretty good verse performance, but for once we've got drums that ain't busy enough or, for that matter, able to make this snarling beast groove, part of the problem being the thinning, disappearing mix. Still, Blackie unleashes a great vocal swinging through a lyric that convinces you that the subject of this tribute is, in fact, trouble with a capital "T." Would like to hear Crüe wastecase a few braincells through this one, with Tommy drumming, maybe **Girls Girls Girls** production. Yeah, wicked.

Blackie Lawless on *Mean Man* . . .

"Chris had come to me for years telling me, 'You gotta write a song about me, you gotta write a song about me.' He originally had an idea for a song called *Born to Raise Hell*. And I thought it was OK but I didn't really think it encapsulated him. So I waited until the right title again came along. Because titles to me are very important. They are at least half the song. They set up the entire framework for what the song's going to be."

475 REVOLUTION IS MY NAME PANTERA

112 points *from Reinventing the Steel (Atlantic '00)*

Glory-bound, foot-stomping, guitar-chomping riffs open up this **Munsters**-rocking track, but then things get a bit confused, Dime lurching from grey-brown idea to non-starter back to discoloration. The verse riff is definitely still prime time Dime, chopping along a bit self-deprecating (if it's possible for a guitar to do that), Phil augmenting with a lyric that works on two levels, as autobiography and as a biography of revolution. I dunno, after wading through this one, it seems like one of the band's junkyards, riffs, rebar, rusted cables and rock chunks jutting out at all angles, not my choice for bad-ass **Reinventing** ambassador, but evidently yours.

Phil Anselmo on *Revolution Is my Name* . . .

> "Now, *Revolution Is my Name*, when we did that record, **Reinventing the Steel**, I was really hell-bent on the fact that yeah, we had out-heavied heavy, we had done heavy metal 20 times over. But what I wanted out of that song especially was a catchy chorus. I really wanted a hook that would stick, and I think we achieved that pretty well. I like that song."

476 RIDE THE SKY LUCIFER'S FRIEND

112 points *from Lucifer's Friend (Philips '71)*

This one track is the overwhelming reason people call Lucifer's Friend heavy, although their unfortunate moniker also takes some of the credit. Far and away the airtight metal machine on the band's seminal (but not all that power-packed) debut, *Ride the Sky* seems more so one of those fortunate accidents of healthy musical adventure, than the product of metal know-how meeting metal purpose. But some of the best few heavy minutes come from foggy foghorns who don't know the rules, and this heavy-handed Heep Purple people-eater fits that bill quite splendidly and expandedly.

John Lawton on joining Lucifer's Friend . . .

> "I hooked up with Lucifer's Friend through Peter Hesslein, the guitarist, who happened to play guitar with Les Humphries as well. He said to me that they had a German band called Lucifer's Friend and they were looking for an English singer, and if I fancied doing it, and I said yes! In regards to the Asterix album, the pre-Lucifer's Friend album, I wrote a few things on there, but the majority of the backing tracks were done. What we needed were some English lyrics, which I did, together with the other guy who sang on it, Tony Cavanna. And that was it. It seems to be a collector's item, a bit of a cult album. I think a lot of the influences came from Sabbath, Purple . . . I'm not so sure about Heep?! I hadn't heard so much about Uriah Heep, only a couple of tracks from various albums. I was never a Heep fanatic in that respect. So I'd say more of the influences came from Sabbath, Purple, and lots of Gothic stuff that was around the time. We always played how we felt. The tracks were written between myself and the rest of the guys in the band. It was just how the songs were written and how we felt about recording them."

477 STILL LIFE IRON MAIDEN

112 points *from Piece of Mind (EMI '83)*

Still Life is one of those deep album tracks on a record full of showy showstoppers. But it's an example of the band's heavy, heaving passionate melodies applied to metal music (I sound like Rob Halford there, don't I?). It's a cool little tale about staring into a pool, seeing spirits and being psychically dragged to a watery death. Set to a light Nicko touch, *Still Life* features one of the band's smartest, most logically integrated breaks, beginning with a behaved yet emotional harmony solo, then into the break proper, which modulates before collapsing back to a military marching version of a verse, followed by one more kick at the song's climactic chorus. An underrated gem on an action-packed album.

Steve Harris on the writing process . . .

"Well, to be honest with you, I have different lyrics and melodies over a period of time. Mainly music I guess. But lyrics is usually the last thing. It's kind of restricting sometimes, if you get a strong melody line. If the melody line is that strong you have to stick to it, and find the syllable, and certain words you might want to use don't fit there, and you have to find something else. And that can be a bit frustrating. I think it's most important that the melody is strong. I mean, that's the way we've always written anyways, since the first album."

478 SHOOT TO THRILL
AC/DC

112 points *from Back in Black (Atlantic '80)*

Lame puns aside, *Shoot to Thrill* fits comfortably in that happy, hummable zone, Johnson cawing out a tribute to his johnson, a pocket pistol with a mind of its own. Heady AC/DC manoeuvres are all over this hook-heavy hit for Friday, most effective being the build to a chorus, an explosive high-flying break and then a crouch-down break followed by another round for the boys. Put it on that bloke's tab, o'er there. Gotta go.

Brian Johnson on the tour grind . . .

"You really do need a break, just to get away from everything, if not just to find out where the fucking light switch is in the house we live in! When I went home I said, 'Who are you?' And she went, 'I'm your wife!' I had to learn all that stuff again. The trouble is after two months off, your feet start getting itchy; this addiction called rock 'n' roll is calling. We've always had this great camaraderie, this great feeling of fellowship that not many bands have. That's never died during all the years we've been together. But we never got bored with it; never got to the point were we thought that we'd burn ourselves out because we like each other so much, and we laugh together so much. I know we're pretty serious up there onstage, but to be on the bus or playing with this band, or in the hotel, they're the funniest bunch of fuckers I've ever been with in my life. I'm always laughing. That sounds dumb, but I don't care. It's fun. It keeps you sane."

479 TAROT WOMAN RAINBOW

111 points *from Rising (Polydor '76)*

After Tony "Dream Weaver" Carey does his thing, *Tarot Woman* kicks in with a flash bit of Cozy and we're off to the races, Ritchie and Ronnie (the gloomer twins?) flipping a few cards and coming up with a productive, if brief future together. *Tarot Woman* is a classic bit of stomping castle rock, Ronnie's vocal melodies really making the track, given Ritchie's fairly behaved monotone riff. Even Carey gets to flex his fingers, adding nice washes throughout and then closing the book with a classy, understated synth solo. And Cozy? He's just Cozy, hammering down a stiff 4/4, vaguely Bonham-esque in style, underscored in that respect by Martin Birch's dry production tones.

Ronnie James Dio on his and Ritchie's shared interests . . .

"I think maybe classical music. He liked Bach and I liked Bach. I liked Beethoven. He didn't like him as much as Bach but we really liked most of the same classical themes. I think that was reflected in the writing as well. That is one of the reasons that we were able to come together. We thought the same way musically. We thought in big melodic orchestral terms. That was our point of contact. And in terms of stories about our interest in the occult, well, they are all true. They are very, very true. I don't bother to dabble in that anymore because we had some rather scary experiences. I've given it up. Once you invite the Devil into your house he doesn't go away! We did all those things and they were sometimes scary and sometimes they were really interesting. But we weren't demonic. We weren't trying to converse with the Devil or anything. As soon as the Devil popped up we all got away pretty fast!"

480 SPIRAL ARCHITECT BLACK SABBATH

111 points *from Sabbath Bloody Sabbath (Warner '73)*

Perhaps a harbinger of things to come, *Spiral Architect* presented a miasma of deflated, rainy Sunday afternoon emotions. It is a flustered track with draining batteries and waning ambitions, a mellow, complex bucket full of ideas, but ideas that sound like the last brainers the band might ever propose. There is a finality to the strings, a finality to the lyric, a finality to Ozzy's detached vocal, and a sly play on the idea of finality, with the song's false ending, followed by a false start, followed by a fade, followed by the silence that marks the end of this uneasy, unearthly album.

Geezer Butler on his Sabbath favourites . . .

> "Lyrically I really like *Spiral Architect* and *National Acrobat* — my two favourite lyrics — and *After Forever* as well. I loved the **Sabbath Bloody Sabbath** album. I mean, I love the first three as well, but they were done almost unconsciously (laughs) in every sense of the word."

481 AT THE GATES SUICIDE NATION

111 points *from Slaughter of the Soul (Earache '95)*

Shocking really, how tightly wound and yet melodic these pioneering death riffs were, *At The Gates* reverently cited in hushed tones along the likes of Soundgarden, as a seminal, important band that broke up at the height of their powers. The band's distinct skill was in creating these fast, accessible whipsaws of songs and then capture them in skull-frying hi-fidelity, every bass drum beat clearly heard halfways to Pantera, each riff precisely slashing, twin leads in disciplined tandem, metal possibilities endless. The result: probably the least dated, most prescient metal record you will find from the mid-'90s, even if Meshuggah might have something to say about that.

Tomas Lindberg on *Suicide Nation* . . .

> "Well that entire album has a bit of a theme, lyrics-wise. The songs fit together so nice; all the songs have the same ingredients. The lyric to that one relates somewhat to the idea of Sweden being such a safe country and people don't like to think that there are any problems there. But we have one of the highest suicide rates in the world. So that triggered the title and some the lyrics. But then again, there's a little bit of that **Slaughter of the Soul** idea, suicide of the soul. So it's kind of a mishmash of those two concepts, kind of like how society kills off your feelings. I like that track a lot, how it kicks off with the loading of the gun, the shell sound."

482 LACK OF COMMUNICATION RATT

110 points *from Out of the Cellar (Atlantic '84)*

Not as elegant as *Round and Round, Lack of Communication* was more of a cut and dried and directly catchy metal number, a little darker and low-slung than the album as a whole, a little more Crüe, and with that hanging chord verse, a little Hagar. A nice set of melodies though, the break not really a break, but more of a chorus, the chorus . . . well there really isn't one. In total, a little dirtier than one remembers of Ratt.

Juan Croucier on *Lack of Communication* . . .

> "I remember that song very well. I wrote that song myself. It's basically a statement I made a long while back, 20 years ago and it's a song about not being able to get along, not communicating in many circumstances, lovers at close range to nations around the world, simply not being able to see eye to eye and therefore causing all these silly problems we have in the world that seemingly should be easy to fix. I can get into examples but it's best

to leave it as a picture. Actually I brought that one to Dokken and we were going to do it and I remember George Lynch looking at me and going, 'Juan, we can't do this song, it's too simple, we need a hot guitar riff.' And I said, 'George, it's really not about just the guitar riff alone, it's the song. You need to listen to the lead vocals, the backups, the beat, the whole thing together and see if you like it.' And that's right about the time I started going, you know, I get the feeling I won't be able to get a song in here edgewise."

483 NOTHING ELSE MATTERS METALLICA

110 points *from Metallica (Elektra '91)*

Closer to *One* than the three year gulf might attest, *Nothing Else Matters* is another one of those half-baked ballads that is arranged such that (other than the orchestration) it could be more or less faithfully rendered at a soundcheck. Everybody is electric, loud, but playing softly, most pointedly Lars, who sounds no different in the metal bits than the kill myself bits. True, it's a power ballad, but Metallica find dark, modestly intellectual gothic tones through which to sell themselves out just a little bit less, some of these guitar lines sounding like minstrel music from the days of the Plague.

Lars Ulrich on *Nothing Else Matters . . .*

"Well, James wanted to sing I guess. I've always known he had that shit buried in him. I think it was just a matter of timing and it felt like the right time to get some of that out. That song itself came up after a few shows we did last year after an eight-month holiday. After these European gigs, James gave me this tape of all his new ideas. I went back to Copenhagen and I just sat and listened to what he came up with and that was one thing that really stuck out. When I met up with him the next week at home, I said, 'We gotta fuckin' write this song!' It hit me right away, and it seems to hit everybody else too. Bob really felt that James was a great singer. And James has always been underrated, being more of a frontman than a singer. Bob really wanted to bring some of that shit out of James, try to get him to prove himself as a first-rate singer, instead of the guy that can just stand there and growl and look like he wants to kill your family. In terms of the orchestration, we were just looking at each other saying there was only 90% there. It needed something else. Bob suggested that we use string arrangements and we tried to keep an open mind so we kind of went for it. But renting a keyboardist and having a guy play string arrangements on a fuckin' synthesizer didn't seem right. If you're going to go for it, you've got to go for it all the way. Bob suggested this guy Michael Kamen who's done orchestral arrangements for Pink Floyd and a lot of movie soundtracks. We sent a tape over to him and two weeks later he came back and he put a fucking 30-piece orchestra on there playing our song. It was a little over the top, so we had to tone it down. We just had to maintain a balance to what was originally written. I just wish I could've seen it. Thirty fuckin' guys in a symphony orchestra playing a Metallica song."

484 ALL RIGHT NOW FREE

110 points *from Fire and Water (Island '70)*

It was nothing new to stack power chords methodically next to each other, but Free managed the task with such basic beauty, especially on this wildly successful hit. With all that clear air, the track becomes a vocal showcase for one of rock's most enduring voices, Paul Rodgers dancing his phrasings amidst time-honoured chord patterns and big dumb drums from Simon Kirke. The chorus positively placates, both through melody and lyric, and all seems well with the communal gathering that is Free on stage, bass, guitar, drums and vocals weaving politely through values that were not rocket science to dream up, espouse or execute.

Paul Rodgers on an early Free influence . . .

"Well, for us we had a mentor in a guy called Alexis Korner, who was a jazz musician. And it was great for us because he was like from an older generation, but at the same time he was hip, you know? He could talk music with us and it was so great because he had so much experience and he had seen bands come and go and he had seen trends and fads and this and that. I mean, he had seen a blues boom that came and went ten years prior to that, which was just awesome to us. Of course, it was all new to us, the blues. But then we had to stop and think, of course this music is 40 years old, what are we talking about here? And he opened us up to the wisdom that says sometimes it's important what you don't play. And we would go away scratching our heads thinking what the heck does that mean? Like the gaps in between. And we finally figured it out and that helped us, you know? You have to have some reserve and hold back so that the listener is urging you to play more. You're holding back and holding back and then you release."

Josh and Keith from Buckcherry
AC/DC — *Problem Child*
The Cult — *Love Removal Machine*
AC/DC — *You Shook Me All Night Long*
Aerosmith — *Sweet Emotion*
Guns N' Roses — *It's So Easy*
Sex Pistols — *God Save the Queen*
Ramones — *I Wanna Be Sedated*
Love/Hate — *Blackout in the Red Room*
Cheap Trick — *Surrender*
Free — *All Right Now*

485 THE MIRROR DREAM THEATER

110 points

from Awake (Eastwest '94)

A perfect metaphor for what people think of this album as a whole, *The Mirror* is a surprisingly dark, low-cycled metal weight bench from a band usually more positive and into spiritual well being. The chords are thick as Metallica, maybe even Pantera, and LaBrie gamely plays along with a twist of the black moustache. But as usual, the song is sweetened with keyboards, as well as complicated breaks in the scraping action. Reminds me of the bleak psychic landscapes of Queensryche's *Suite Sister Mary*.

John Myung on **Awake** . . .

> "**Awake** was the very fast-paced album for us. We basically wrote and recorded the album as soon as we got straight off the road in January, had 75 or 80 minutes of music, nothing left over, and went straight in and recorded it, a very opposite situation from **Images and Words**. There was no time at all to refine anything. We went in, recorded it, and went straight back out on the road. It was kind of a reactive album."

486 BREADFAN BUDGIE

110 points

from Never Turn Your Back on a Friend (MCA '73)

OK, few people heard it, but sign *Breadfan* up for *Space Station #5*, the two comprising the hottest high octane metal riffs of 1973. *Breadfan* was of course made famous through Metallica's respectful cover thereof, but as a musical entity it needed no improvement, its production values curious, idiosyncratic but full range, its guitar specifically projecting and proud. Really, combining songwriting, arrangement and production, *Breadfan* marks Budgie's clearest sense of purpose until perhaps the NWOBHM-exploitative **Power Supply** album seven years hence; and this from a band, album and song, all oddly, maybe even deceptively or at minimum elusively, monikered.

487 BLACK WINTER DAY
AMORPHIS

110 points *from Tales from the Thousand Lakes (Relapse '94)*

Making their left turn from death into a quixotic, exotic style of folk-tainted doom, Amorphis almost overnight attracted a larger fanbase. The key here was the frosty Finnish melodies, topped with a traditional Finnish lyric translated into English, actually a rather brief and humorous description of the winter blues. As well, keyboardist Kasper Martenson drizzles o'er top a dated prog rock synthesizer tone which again perked and itch-scratched the ears of death/black purists, fierce weather fans who would shortly find themselves running, clanky chain-mail, battle axe and all, in the other direction, come the next three lush and wonderfully art-rocked studio spreads.

Esa Holopainen on understanding Amorphis . . .

> "People who usually are not familiar with metal, but know of Amorphis are mainly older people who dig some psychedelic stuff; these guys are very open-minded to our music. Still, I guess it's quite an impossible idea to get any 'Britney teenagers' to get into our stuff. This music is still too complicated for them. Perhaps when they grow up and smoke a few joints they'll realize the point of music."

488 CARRY ON WAYWARD SON
KANSAS

110 points *from Leftoverture (Columbia '76)*

More Than a Feeling, Black Betty, all of Saga's hits, Hell, even *21st Century Schizoid Man* . . . these are all songs with hooks that are ultimately married to, and buried in, rhythms, rhythms that are necessarily and distinctly complex, else they wouldn't be hooks, they'd just be rhythms. *Carry on Wayward Son* is stuffed full of the same scattershot spice, while also managing to be a pomp and circumstance form of hard rock, as well as the rare beast that is the succinct, well-edited, well-reasoned epic, *Bohemian Rhapsody* defining the state of this art. 'Course *Carry On* also possesses the quilt work Kansas chemistry, which rears all too rarely despite many awkward introductions, and it also contains the band's best three guitar riffs. Add the spiritually searching vocals of Steve Walsh and man, that's a lot of substance, grist, food for thought, cause for alarm, cause for ridicule and cause for punk.

Kerry Livgren on the Kansas sound . . .

> "I don't think we fit anywhere, and I'm very proud of that (laughs), meaning that the band to me defies easy categorization. And that's something I personally hold very highly. I like that fact. Now of course you have to come up with some sort of descriptive term, so I would say what we are is an American — and I would underline that word — progressive rock band. We're very different from the British progressive rock bands, which we always get lumped together with, because we have elements in our music that I don't think they have. There's a blues influenced and we also rock a lot harder than Yes or Genesis or those other bands that we get compared to. In addition to that, Kansas' original style was pretty well developed before we even heard any of those bands. Not to say that we weren't influenced by them at some point in time, but I would consider them parallel to us rather than progenitors."

489 BAD COMPANY
BAD COMPANY

110 points *from Bad Co. (Swan Song '74)*

A big thick burger of a band, Bad Co. took all that was left of the British blues explosion and brought it ever so slowly and patiently into the '70s. Free was already that conduit, as were label and management mates Zeppelin, but Bad Company, and to a lesser extent, Humble Pie, seemed to carry on the tradition best, updating slightly with a wider palette, a more direct and obvious stack of power chords, an ego-less dumbling down for the pure joy of rock 'n' roll radio. Elements of southern rock seep into this song, as do strange signals from Canada's BTO, as do literary references to tales of the wild west, a recurring theme throughout the Bad Company catalogue.

Paul Rodgers on the Bad Company sound . . .

> "The essence of Bad Company in what we do is a simplistic thing. And I actually think that for me, that's harder to do. It's very easy to play a million notes a minute, which a lot of guys do. And very often, even the Buddhists says, life is lived between the notes. That's where the real atmosphere is. It's what you don't play. It's what you imply that is the real mastery of music. So I mean, I like the simplicity. The space that is left is where you can put yourself as a listener."

490 STORMBRINGER DEEP PURPLE

110 points *from Stormbringer (Warner '75)*

Flooding into being through an elegant merger between metal and cosmic funk, *Stormbringer* then gets down to the business of appeasing Ritchie's castle rock muse with what is one of the album's two lone metal numbers. The song is all-Purple all the time, Ritchie icing the proceedings late in the game with a snake charmer of a slide solo, Paice, Lord and Hughes pumping and percolating along, creating a rhythmic backbone that is much more assured and resolute than the exploding headspace of the band as a whole at the time. Considered by fans, critics and the band itself as something thrust onto the tired back of the Purple legacy, *Stormbringer* and the brash flash it emitted, have combined to become the only glowing ember on an album that drops to the bottom of any Purple poll presumed. A sort of wiener by default. Trivia note: compare with rare Joe Lynn Turner-era track *Slow Down Sister*.

David Coverdale on *Stormbringer* . . .

> "Oh my God! I wrote two songs which could be termed heavy

metal or whatever. I've never embraced the expression 'heavy metal' because all my themes are emotional. But I wrote two songs to keep Ritchie Blackmore happy, which was *Burn*, which is, I still think, a classic and *Stormbringer*, which basically if you look at the lyrics, they are more or less sci-fi poems. But it never felt comfortable for me to have those. In fact, I think that's where Ritchie got the name Rainbow from, the hook in *Stormbringer*. *Burn* I can enjoy any time of the day but I don't really go for *Stormbringer*."

491 THUNDER AND LIGHTNING THIN LIZZY

109 points *from Thunder and Lightning (Vertigo '83)*

I always found this swansong of a title track the weak link on an otherwise gritty, determined, impassioned album. To me, the riff is aggro for aggro's sake (see also *Angel of Death*), the lyric bluntly macho versus the many, many times Phil could and did discuss a man's world poetically, without losing the power, laying waste without throwing a punch. But the track definitely blasted holes in a new direction for the band, John Sykes as arsonist at the fireworks factory, this album's harsh and assaultive production providing a tension-filed boxing ring, Phil's failing voice weakly drowned out by the crowd of crowers.

Scott Gorham on Thin Lizzy's final days . . .

"The year before he died, I had told Phil I had had enough. I couldn't take it any longer. We were just too nuts with the drinking, the drugs and the craziness of it all. It was he that actually talked me into another album and another tour. He said, 'Let's end on a high.' When I look back, I realize how completely stupid that scene was. Thinking that you're actually playing better and you need that shit in your system. The drugs destroy your guitar playing and your writing. It completely fucks you around to the point where you don't even want to play the guitar, you even can't. You definitely lose control and you lose control quickly. I would say it doesn't enhance writing or playing at all."

492 METAL ON METAL ANVIL

109 points *from Metal on Metal (Attic '82)*

Canada's early thrash pride and joy Anvil had a leg up on competition around the world with the force of Lips' riffs and the drum tornado madness of power groover Robb Reiner. *Metal on Metal* was a wily, left field calling card, slow, but ironically busy, seething with electricity, yet doomful. Already, at this early stage, Anvil had soaked up all of the new metal force from the NWOBHM and created a sound that Metallica wouldn't catch up to until **Ride the Lightning**. A metal necessity, as is the rest of the album, as is the speed science follow-up.

Robb Reiner on *Metal on Metal* . . .

> "I'm going to have to lie to you about it (laughs). Because *Metal on Metal* is my least favourite song that Anvil ever wrote. I've learned to accept it after all these years, because it's an anthem and fans just go ballistic over it. But on an artistic level about where Robb Reiner's at, I just don't like the track. That's the truth. But for the record, yeah great, I love it! I guess the **Metal on Metal** days would be the prime of Anvil media hype-wise, but not the prime of Anvil musically. You have to be very careful about that. Because it was the furthest thing from our prime musically that can possibly be. But you know, even **Forged in Fire** was quite slagged at the time. I could dig you up press stuff from Sounds and Kerrang! and I think they shit all over that record in its day. Sounds barfed on it I believe. I didn't give a fuck. I just said, 'Hey, these guys just missed the boat on it.' And only now, when people speak about that record, they are like, 'Man, that had legendary riffs on it!' The stuff I've heard from people, you have no idea. It just blows me away. And I never thought about that at the time. We just made music and hoped people liked it."

493 GANGLAND
TYGERS OF PAN TANG

109 points *from Spellbound* (MCA '81)

Record two for these eager NWOBHM beavers featured a new lead singer in the rock starry Jon Deverill, who would become the presentable focus of this second-tier band over the next couple of successful records. The sound was polished but still modest and punky, as is evidenced by this compact little speed nugget. Many British metal characteristics rifle their way through this combative bit of fireworks but the overall effect was always spoken of as thin, a bad surprise given that bigshot producer Chris Tsangarides was the man at the board. Me fears that this beat out everything else on the album simply because it's the lead track on the album.

Robb Weir on the personalities within the Tyger camp . . .

> "Brian was always very happy and liked to have a drink. Rocky was the 'thinker,' lots of fun but would always be strategizing our next career move. John Sykes was mad, full of fun, ready for anything! And Jon Deverill, he kept to himself mostly, went to bed early and rarely partied."

494 GREEN MACHINE
KYUSS

108 points *from Blues for the Red Sun (Dali/Elektra '92)*

Green Machine is an example of Kyuss locking onto a rare, less than sloth-like groove, but still loading up on quaking Sabbatherian frequencies that trick the blood into coagulating into a glutinous mess. The riff is simple, but you pretty much don't care, because all you can hear (or comprehend) is bass guitar, open high-hats and crashing, swinging Bill Ward cymbals for miles. Stoner rock is born, and the desert is its birthplace.

Nick Oliveri on *Green Machine* . . .

> "*Green Machine* is actually . . . you know when you were a kid, and they had the Big Wheel, but they also had the Green Machine? And you had the little handles on the side that actu-

ally turned you? That's what a Green Machine is (laughs). The sound on that album, that was something we went in to do on purpose. We wanted to make an album that had more bass, basically make it heavier than anything that was out there at the time just by having such a rumble that like, 'Holy shit, what the fuck was that?!' Know what I mean? It's really one of those records that if you put it on, and you had been listening to something else you're definitely going to have to fuck with your EQ. If you just put it on and had it turned up full blast, never hearing it before, there's a good possibility that you'll blow your woofers. That was one of our things, let's blow people's speakers! You know, when you're kids, you want to do fun, silly shit like that. It was like, what if we had something that was so heavy if people just left their shit turned up and they'd never heard it before it could possibly blow their speakers."

495 THUS SPAKE THE NIGHTSPIRIT EMPEROR

108 points

from Anthems to the Welkin at Dusk (Century Media '97)

Pure black metal from a vanguard band operating arguably at their peak, blazing forth at the crossroads of their raw distorted past and their elegant progressive future, *Thus Spake the Nightspirit* is a whirling, swirling, howling firestorm of melancholic speed. None of the very busy, mathematical performances rise above, each subsumed to the frenzy, indeed Ihsahn's vocals buried within the agony as well. One of many Emperor songs which impossibly involves the listener in a wall of sound that is as enigmatic as it is brutal.

Ihsahn on his belief system . . .

"It's a personal thing when you say, I'm a Satanist. People get all these thoughts of what you mean by that, so sometimes it doesn't feel right to call yourself a Satanist because it gives people the wrong impression. Whereas on the other hand, who cares? People tend to think what they want about you anyways. I'm a very relaxed and personal Satanist. It's for me. It's not important for me to say that I am right about this and that. But it would be better if everybody was like me and it would be better if I could be king. I'm just satisfied to have my beliefs. There's much more to it than Satanism."

496 OVER MY HEAD KING'S X

from Gretchen Goes to Nebraska (Megaforce/Atlantic '89)
108 points

Swimming, concentric and blessed alternative metal from slightly before such a thing existed, King's X are one of the unsung procreators of grunge and all the fecund creative intensity for which the genre is known, the band especially touching the lives of Soundgarden, who seem to be the band that took Ty Tabor's metalized jazz chords to big wallets. Ergo, *Over My Head* is an example of the left field hard rock obtusely angling its way through **Superunknown**, for example. And *Over My Head* is also King's X's most recognizable number, built and lubricated for crowd participation, its hypnotizing chorus celebrating the avalanche of great innovative music one might hear at any emotionally charged King's X gig.

Doug Pinnick on *Over My Head* . . .

"*Over My Head* was a big hit, huh? (laughs). Wow. I wrote that song a long time ago and I thought it sucked, so I just kept it in an old cassette with all my other crappy demos. And one day Sam Taylor, who was our manager back then, said, 'I want to hear all your demos.' Because we were getting ready to do **Gretchen**, and after the first record, we were on tour the whole time, so we really didn't have a lot of new songs. We had a bunch of older ones and he wanted to pull out some of them, so he played that one and he liked it. And he played it for Ty and Jerry and they loved it. And I went, OK, because I didn't think they would like it. And oh God, you should hear it, because it's like a

Mattel drum machine, it's so awful. And I thought the chorus was weak because it didn't go up, it didn't lift, it went down. And then I thought about Lenny Kravitz's *Let Love Rule*; I thought it was cool that when you got to that point, it dropped. So I took that approach and got the music thing going. It's sort of a gospel kind of thing. The pastor at the church I grew up in, there's a lot of mimicking of him on that song. And it's not really about my grandma, but it is at the same time. I remember I used to hear her praying late at night and I kind of elaborated on it. It's not all true but it comes from hearing sounds coming from her bedroom in the middle of the night. I always thought she was praying because she was a really religious woman, but she could have been having nightmares for all I know. And musically, it's just this bizarre kind of funk song that I like to write. I put that weird chord in there and I thought it was stupid (laughs), and Ty goes, 'Wow, I like that chord!' Go figure. You can't judge your own music. But that was it, and we put it out and people liked it and it became the showstopper, which was a surprise to me."

Ty Tabor from King's X
Beatles — *I Wanna Hold Your Hand*
Badfinger — *No Matter What*
Black Sabbath — *Iron Man*
Led Zeppelin — *Black Dog*
Led Zeppelin — *Rock and Roll*
Aerosmith — *Train Kept a Rollin'*
Deep Purple — *Woman from Tokyo*
Accept — *Balls to the Wall*
AC/DC — *Shot down in Flames*
Gamma — *Fight to the Finish*

497 WAIT AND BLEED SLIPKNOT

107 points

from Slipknot (Roadrunner '99)

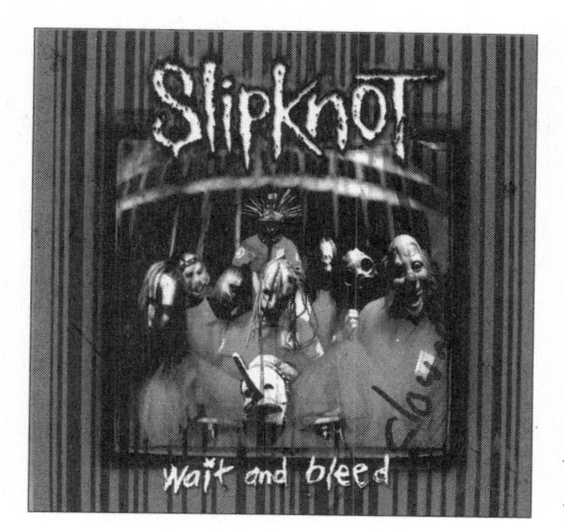

Slipknot is one of those cyclical forces of nature that causes ageing hard rock fans to throw in the towel and admit the gulf between their definition of heavy and what is plainly heavier, and most pertinently, to admit that this new ass-itch of a sound is designed for a generation that they, from this epiphany forward, are not allowed to comprehend. Whipped across bare backs with too many too rough vocals, too many drums, too many unlocate-able sound textures, and more rancour than any metal and/or hardcore before it could muster in five generations of broken families, the recorded works of Slipknot have dented young heads with a sonic and visual firestorm that is as destructive on their bald domes as the inferno heat of the band's hellish outdoors Ozzfest performances. Expect more of the band's aggro-acrobatic anthems, like a cancer, to invade and climb the list in future years. God help us.

Corey Taylor on *Wait and Bleed . . .*

"When I joined Slipknot, basically what I had done is I went back and rewrote the lyrics to a lot of their older songs, and that's what we performed. The first one we ever wrote together as a band, when I joined the band, was *Spit It Out,* which is a very in-your-face volley of hip-hop madness. But I had a melody in my head that I couldn't get out, and I came to practice one day, and they had this music written, for what was going to be *Wait and Bleed.* And for some reason, it just fit with the melody that was going on in my head and I just started belting it out, and that is actually the second song we wrote as a band. And it was the first song that kind of pushed Slipknot in that direction, that kind of melodic direction. Because before, their old singer, amazing as he was, he didn't have that melodic background. I mean, he attempted it but it didn't sound right. With me, I've always been very entrenched in that; it was second nature. And we got together and I wrote the lyrics right there and it just came out that way. I remember just playing it over and over and over and we couldn't believe we had written something like this. It was really cool. I could really see in their faces that there weren't a lot of boundaries be couldn't break through with this. Slipknot was really kind of known for what they had done, and this was a departure for them."

Joey Jordison from Slipknot
Kiss — *Deuce*
Terrorizer — *After World Obliteration*
Alice Cooper — *Cold Ethyl*
Slayer — *Post Mortem*
Black Sabbath — *Black Sabbath*
Hanoi Rocks — *Malibu Beach Nightmare*
Faster Pussycat — *Bathroom Wall*
Ramones — *Commando*
Mayhem — *Pure Fucking Armageddon*
Melvins — *Honey Bucket*

498 BOMBER MOTÖRHEAD

107 points *from Bomber (Bronze '79)*

I always found this song a little happy-go-glam amongst the bleak slog of Lemmy's otherwise cynical dirt rock. The melody is almost yobbo punk from jolly ol' circa '77 at The Roxy, but then again, it's contrast like this that is immensely welcome on a Motörhead album, given the band's unrelenting wall of gargly argle bargle. Philthy Phil turns in one of his snappy, energetic percussion performances, one that recalls the "traps" sound of Albert Bouchard, jazzy skin-basher for another umlaut band, Blue Öyster Cult.

Fast Eddie Clarke on *Bomber* . . .

"Lemmy would be playing the rhythm on the bass so you got this 'grr' sound and Phil and I would work around that and try to see what we could do within it. When you're talking about *Bomber*, I remember it was a similar thing — Lemmy doing his 'grr' — so we did sort of a riff power noise thing and then I thought afterwards, what can I put on this to make it a bit more interesting? So it wasn't just me playing the same as the bass. So that's what I came up with, which was essentially a *Johnny B. Goode* riff (sings it). So I managed to stick that over it. It was really fast so it was quite tricky and I think that's one of the things that gives it its flavor, that little lick that you get. But with Lemmy, it's like any song that we would do, we'd have to work around Lemmy's bass sound. All those years I was fucking struggling all the time to get a really nice guitar sound. It was really hard, onstage especially. And I just sort of fought with it the whole time."

499 POWERTRIP MONSTER MAGNET

107 points *from Powertrip (A&M '98)*

The pinnacle of Monster Magnet fame thus far (given the follow-up album's miserable demise), **Powertrip** marked a euphoric power rock high for Dave Wyndorf and his long-suffering anti-commercial sludge rock combo. The song manages to be giddy in its anthemic upper register reach, while dredging the Bo Diddley beat memory of many arcane garage acts, a particularly fond area of study for Dave. The pay-off of the song is an emphatic and permanent vacation from work, a hollered vow from the horned hirsute one that quickly drove this demon driver deep left toward feel good hit of the summer. I can imagine Dave's wisecracking chuckle getting voted 499th greatest metal song of all time. I think he'd frame that one.

Dave Wyndorf on the **Powertrip** concept . . .

"Sex, money, power, you know? Anger. Elation. All the stuff that goes on when you don't have the amount of money you want and you don't have the amount of power you want. Or you do, and you mishandle it. Lyrically, it's completely different because I was coming from a different spot on the last album. I was coming from a really hardcore dose of reality, running up lots of bills, doing psychedelic light shows, tripping out for three years, spending lots of money. So on this particular album I make comments on American lifestyles, advertising, my own pathetic experiences with those things, relationships with women I've had. It's all there. I don't really expect everyone to understand it."

Dave Wyndorf from Monster Magnet
Sir Lord Baltimore — *Master of Heartache*
Highway Robbery — *Promotion Man*
Grand Funk Railroad — *People Let's Stop the War*
The Troggs — *Wild Thing*
Hawkwind — *Born to Go*
The Stooges — *1970*
Atomic Rooster — *Sleeping for Years*
Frijid Pink — *Black Lace*
Roachpowder — *Galactic Blues*
Blur — *Tracy Jacks*

500 ASTRONOMY BLUE ÖYSTER CULT

107 points *from Secret Treaties (Columbia '74)*

A gorgeous, ethereal, predecessor to *(Don't Fear) The Reaper*, *Astronomy* is both a lush, inviting piece of melodic soft rock and a dark, progressive semi-metallic epic. The weapons in this band, both musical and literary, are too numerous to mention, and many of their stars are aligned here, creating an uneasy easement into a cosmic infinity that thankfully seems like an interesting place in which to dissolve. The track builds through elegant soft rock into hooky, well-blended AOR-ist artiste rock and back again, steered by an army of talent that is already well-tested through years in a tough market, already bolstered and reinforced by outside advisers like Krugman, Pearlman and Meltzer. In the end, it just went over everyone's heads.

Albert Bouchard on *Astronomy* . . .

"I don't think I wrote very many lyrics at all; the most lyrics I wrote on was *Flaming Telepaths*. But I must say, I'm prouder of *Astronomy*, although I probably did less lyrically on that. And of course, I'd only written half the music because my brother Joe had already started it and he got stumped and left it. I grabbed a hold of it and used what he had done and expanded it. Basically he did the slow part and I did the fast part plus the transition between the two. That's one of my favourite songs. It's very simple. There's not much to it, but I really dig it. I think it has a quality that's really enduring. And the Cult fans really like it too."

APPENDIX I: TOP 500 AT A GLANCE

The handy, dandy reference checklist Part I: the songs ranked by points.

Artist	Song Title	Points	Album	Year
Black Sabbath	Paranoid	3588	Paranoid	70
Metallica	Master of Puppets	3578	Master of Puppets	86
Motörhead	Ace of Spades	3165	Ace of Spades	80
Osbourne, Ozzy	Crazy Train	2940	Blizzard of Ozz	80
Slayer	Angel of Death	2936	Reign in Blood	86
Iron Maiden	The Number of the Beast	2896	The Number of the Beast	82
Iron Maiden	Hallowed Be Thy Name	2591	The Number of the Beast	82
Black Sabbath	War Pigs	2355	Paranoid	70
AC/DC	Back in Black	1995	Back in Black	80
Black Sabbath	Iron Man	1915	Paranoid	70
Black Sabbath	Heaven and Hell	1835	Heaven and Hell	80
Judas Priest	Painkiller	1784	Painkiller	90
Metallica	One	1758	. . . And Justice for All	88
Deep Purple	Highway Star	1729	Machine Head	72
Black Sabbath	Black Sabbath	1700	Black Sabbath	70
Megadeth	Holy Wars . . . The Punishment Due	1692	Rust in Peace	90
Judas Priest	Victim of Changes	1665	Sad Wings of Destiny	76
Judas Priest	Electric Eye	1643	Screaming for Vengeance	82
Guns N' Roses	Welcome to the Jungle	1611	Appetite for Destruction	87
Slayer	Raining Blood	1564	Reign in Blood	86
Metallica	Creeping Death	1539	Ride the Lightning	84
Metallica	Fade to Black	1489	Ride the Lightning	84
AC/DC	Highway to Hell	1469	Highway to Hell	79
Iron Maiden	The Trooper	1463	Piece of Mind	83
Deep Purple	Smoke on the Water	1460	Machine Head	72
Accept	Balls to the Wall	1389	Balls to the Wall	84
Megadeth	Peace Sells	1332	Peace Sells . . . but Who's Buying?	86
Iron Maiden	Run to the Hills	1321	The Number of the Beast	82

Artist	Song Title	Points	Album	Year
Judas Priest	You've Got Another Thing Comin'	1317	Screaming for Vengeance	82
Dio	Holy Diver	1251	Holy Diver	83
Metallica	For Whom the Bell Tolls	1244	Ride the Lightning	84
Mötley Crüe	Shout at the Devil	1243	Shout at the Devil	83
Accept	Fast as a Shark	1225	Restless and Wild	83
Black Sabbath	Sabbath Bloody Sabbath	1118	Sabbath Bloody Sabbath	73
Led Zeppelin	Stairway to Heaven	1065	IV	71
Metallica	Enter Sandman	1058	Metallica	91
Rainbow	Stargazer	1041	Rising	76
AC/DC	Hells Bells	1003	Back in Black	80
Dio	The Last in Line	972	The Last in Line	84
Slayer	Seasons in the Abyss	971	Seasons in the Abyss	90
Deep Purple	Burn	960	Burn	74
Pantera	Cowboys from Hell	947	Cowboys from Hell	90
Judas Priest	Beyond the Realms of Death	924	Stained Class	78
Black Sabbath	Symptom of the Universe	922	Sabotage	75
Slayer	South of Heaven	911	South of Heaven	88
Dio	Rainbow in the Dark	906	Holy Diver	83
Kiss	Detroit Rock City	881	Destroyer	76
Pantera	Walk	877	Vulgar Display of Power	92
Deep Purple	Child in Time	797	In Rock	70
Metallica	Seek and Destroy	768	Kill 'Em All	83
Van Halen	Runnin' with the Devil	758	Van Halen	78
Osbourne, Ozzy	Over the Mountain	750	Diary of a Madman	81
Black Sabbath	Children of the Grave	748	Master of Reality	71
Osbourne, Ozzy	Diary of a Madman	736	Diary of a Madman	81
Iron Maiden	Aces High	736	Powerslave	84
Led Zeppelin	Whole Lotta Love	727	Ii 69	
Judas Priest	Breaking the Law	719	British Steel	80
Whitesnake	Still of the Night	709	1987	87
Van Halen	Ain't Talkin' 'Bout Love	690	Van Halen	78
Kiss	Rock and Roll All Nite	675	Dressed to Kill	75
Iron Maiden	2 Minutes to Midnight	668	Powerslave	84
Slayer	Hell Awaits	664	Hell Awaits	85

Artist	Song Title	Points	Album	Year
UFO	Lights Out	658	Lights Out	77
Metallica	Four Horsemen	647	Kill 'Em All	83
Dream Theater	Pull Me Under	633	Images and Words	92
Megadeth	Hangar 18	630	Rust in Peace	90
Metallica	Battery	615	Master of Puppets	86
Rainbow	Kill the King	605	Long Live Rock 'n' Roll	78
Black Sabbath	Into the Void	600	Master of Reality	71
Led Zeppelin	Black Dog	598	IV	71
Metallica	Fight Fire with Fire	592	Ride the Lightning	84
AC/DC	For Those About to Rock (We Salute You)	592	For Those About to Rock We Salute You	81
AC/DC	You Shook Me All Night Long	589	Back in Black	80
Iron Maiden	Rime of the Ancient Mariner	573	Powerslave	84
Venom	Black Metal	567	Black Metal	82
Osbourne, Ozzy	Bark at the Moon	556	Bark at the Moon	83
Led Zeppelin	Immigrant Song	552	III	70
Led Zeppelin	Kashmir	550	Physical Graffiti	75
Iron Maiden	Killers	532	Killers	81
Osbourne, Ozzy	Mr. Crowley	531	Blizzard of Ozz	80
Slayer	War Ensemble	527	Seasons in the Abyss	90
Iron Maiden	Powerslave	512	Powerslave	84
Savatage	Hall of the Mountain King	510	Hall of the Mountain King	87
Queensryche	Take Hold of the Flame	509	The Warning	84
Sepultura	Roots Bloody Roots	506	Roots	96
Judas Priest	Screaming for Vengeance	505	Screaming for Vengeance	82
Def Leppard	Photograph	504	Pyromania	83
Black Sabbath	Neon Knights	504	Heaven and Hell	80
Pantera	Cemetary Gates	495	Cowboys from Hell	90
Led Zeppelin	Rock and Roll	492	IV	71
Black Sabbath	Nib	477	Black Sabbath	70
W.A.S.P.	I Wanna Be Somebody	475	W.A.S.P.	84
Scorpions	Rock You Like a Hurricane	474	Love at First Sting	84
Mötley Crüe	Live Wire	473	Too Fast for Love	81
Iron Maiden	Revelations	463	Piece of Mind	83

Artist	Song Title	Points	Album	Year
UFO	Rock Bottom	461	Phenomenon	73
Rush	2112	457	2112	76
Quiet Riot	Metal Health (Bang Your Head)	454	Metal Health	83
Judas Priest	Living After Midnight	453	British Steel	80
Ratt	Round and Round	451	Out of the Cellar	84
Iron Maiden	Fear of the Dark	447	Fear of the Dark	92
Scorpions	Blackout	446	Blackout	82
Metallica	Whiplash	444	Kill 'Em All	83
Van Halen	Unchained	435	Fair Warning	81
Iron Maiden	Wasted Years	434	Somewhere in Time	86
UFO	Doctor Doctor	434	Phenomenon	73
Motörhead	Overkill	433	Overkill	79
Judas Priest	The Ripper	431	Sad Wings of Destiny	76
Queensryche	Queen of the Reich	430	Queensryche	83
Judas Priest	Hell Bent for Leather	429	Killing Machine78	
Pantera	Mouth for War	428	Vulgar Display of Power	92
Megadeth	Symphony of Destruction	428	Countdown to Extinction	92
Osbourne, Ozzy	Flying High Again	428	Diary of a Madman	81
Rush	Tom Sawyer	423	Moving Pictures	81
Mercyful Fate	A Dangerous Meeting	422	Don't Break the Oath	84
Iron Maiden	Wrathchild	415	Killers	81
Saxon	Power and the Glory	414	Power & the Glory	83
Judas Priest	Tyrant	414	Sad Wings of Destiny	76
Celtic Frost	Circle of the Tyrants	413	To Mega Therion	85
Helloween	I Want Out	413	Keeper of the Seven Keys Part II	88
AC/DC	Whole Lotta Rosie	409	Let There Be Rock	77
Metallica	Ride the Lightning	401	Ride the Lightning	84
Mötley Crüe	Looks That Kill	399	Shout at the Devil	83
Iron Maiden	Phantom of the Opera	399	Iron Maiden	80
Iced Earth	Dante's Inferno	398	Burnt Offerings	95
Megadeth	Tornado of Souls	397	Rust in Peace	90
Black Sabbath	Mob Rules	397	Mob Rules	81
Judas Priest	The Sentinel	391	Defenders of the Faith	84
Steppenwolf	Born to Be Wild	388	Steppenwolf	68
Queensryche	Revolution Calling	384	Operation: Mindcrime	88

Artist	Song Title	Points	Album	Year
Metallica	Disposable Heroes	379	Master of Puppets	86
Metallica	Orion	376	Master of Puppets	86
Pantera	Fucking Hostile	375	Vulgar Display of Power	92
Skid Row	Youth Gone Wild	374	Skid Row	89
Rainbow	Gates of Babylon	374	Long Live Rock 'n' Roll	78
Helloween	Halloween	373	Keeper of the Seven Keys Part I	87
Cannibal Corpse	Hammer Smashed Face	369	Tomb of the Mutilated	92
Danzig	Mother	367	Thralldemonsweatlive	93
Queensryche	Eyes of a Stranger	366	Operation: Mindcrime	88
Black Sabbath	Sweet Leaf	362	Master of Reality	71
Diamond Head	Am I Evil?	359	Borrowed Time	82
Megadeth	Wake Up Dead	358	Peace Sells . . . but Who's Buying?	86
Guns N' Roses	Paradise City	355	Appetite for Destruction	87
Osbourne, Ozzy	No More Tears	353	No More Tears	91
Scorpions	Sails of Charon	351	Taken by Force	78
Van Halen	Jump	350	1984	84
Iron Maiden	Flight of Icarus	349	Piece of Mind	83
Judas Priest	Freewheel Burning	346	Defenders of the Faith	84
Iron Maiden	Where Eagles Dare	346	Piece of Mind	83
Judas Priest	Sinner	346	Sin After Sin	77
Dream Theater	Metropolis — Part I	345	Images and Words	92
Scorpions	No One Like You	345	Blackout	82
Aerosmith	Toys in the Attic	344	Toys in the Attic	75
Osbourne, Ozzy	Suicide Solution	343	Blizzard of Ozz	80
Judas Priest	Exciter	336	Stained Class	78
Led Zeppelin	Achilles' Last Stand	335	Presence	76
Tool	Sober	332	Undertow	93
Kiss	Deuce	332	Kiss	74
Kiss	I Love It Loud	330	Creatures of the Night	82
Anthrax	Among the Living	327	Among the Living	87
Black Sabbath	Children of the Sea	327	Heaven and Hell	80
Beatles	Helter Skelter	326	White Album	68
Anthrax	Indians	320	Among the Living	87
Guns N' Roses	Sweet Child O' Mine	319	Appetite for Destruction	87
Riot	Swords & Tequila	317	Fire Down Under	81
Blue Öyster Cult	(Don't Fear) the Reaper	317	Agents of Fortune	76

Artist	Song Title	Points	Album	Year
Aerosmith	Dream On	314	Aerosmith	73
Cooper, Alice	I'm Eighteen	314	Love It to Death	71
Uriah Heep	Easy Livin'	313	Demons and Wizards	72
AC/DC	Let There Be Rock	312	Let There Be Rock	77
Saxon	Denim and Leather	311	Denim and Leather	81
Thin Lizzy	Emerald	310	Jailbreak	76
Riot	Outlaw	306	Fire Down Under	81
Carcass	Heartwork	306	Heartwork	93
Van Halen	Eruption	305	Van Halen	78
Motörhead	Orgasmatron	305	Orgasmatron	86
Nugent, Ted	Cat Scratch Fever	304	Cat Scratch Fever	77
Iron Maiden	Murders in the Rue Morgue	301	Killers	81
Queen	Bohemian Rhapsody	300	A Night at the Opera	75
Manowar	Hail and Kill	299	Kings of Metal	88
Sepultura	Arise	299	Arise	91
Metallica	Damage Inc	298	Master of Puppets	86
Savatage	Gutter Ballet	295	Gutter Ballet	90
Guns N' Roses	November Rain	294	Use Your Illusion I	91
Cooper, Alice	School's Out	293	School's Out	72
Aerosmith	Sweet Emotion	290	Toys in the Attic	75
Nirvana	Smells Like Teen Spirit	289	Nevermind	91
Cooper, Alice	Welcome to My Nightmare	288	Welcome to My Nightmare	75
Osbourne, Ozzy	You Can't Kill Rock and Roll	287	Diary of a Madman	81
Kiss	Black Diamond	287	Kiss	74
Deep Purple	Speed King	286	In Rock	70
Anthrax	Caught in a Mosh	285	Among the Living	87
Helloween	Eagle Fly Free	285	Keeper of the Seven Keys Part II	88
Dio	Don't Talk to Strangers	284	Holy Diver	83
Iced Earth	Something Wicked (Trilogy)	282	Something Wicked This Way Comes	98
Skid Row	18 and Life	282	Skid Row	89
Jimi Hendrix Experience	Voodoo Child (Slight Return)	282	Electric Ladyland	68
Metallica	Blackened	280	. . . And Justice for All	88
Mercyful Fate	Come to the Sabbath	280	Don't Break the Oath	84

Artist	Song Title	Points	Album	Year
Testament	Practice What You Preach	278	Practice What You Preach	89
Type O Negative	Black No. 1	276	Bloody Kisses	93
Van Halen	Panama	275	1984	84
Jimi Hendrix Experience	Purple Haze	275	Are You Experienced?	67
Accept	Restless & Wild	275	Restless and Wild	83
Sepultura	Dead Embryonic Cells	273	Arise	91
Manson, Marilyn	The Beautiful People	272	Antichrist Superstar	96
Metallica	Welcome Home (Sanitarium)	266	Master of Puppets	86
Sepultura	Territory	266	Chaos A.D.	91
Scorpions	The Zoo	263	Animal Magnetism	80
Metallica	Sad but True	262	Metallica	91
W.A.S.P.	Wild Child	257	The Last Command	85
Pantera	5 Minutes Alone	252	Far Beyond Driven	94
Exodus	The Toxic Waltz	252	Fabulous Disaster	89
Black Sabbath	Fairies Wear Boots	252	Paranoid	70
Manowar	Metal Daze	249	Battle Hymns	82
Osbourne, Ozzy	I Don't Know	247	Blizzard of Ozz	80
Mercyful Fate	Evil	246	Melissa	83
Iced Earth	A Question of Heaven	245	The Dark Saga	96
Motörhead	(We Are) the Road Crew	245	Ace of Spades	80
Anthrax	I Am the Law	244	Among the Living	87
Alice in Chains	Would?	243	Dirt	92
Accept	Princess of the Dawn	241	Restless and Wild	83
Thin Lizzy	Cold Sweat	239	Thunder and Lightning	83
AC/DC	Dirty Deeds Done Dirt Cheap	239	Dirty Deeds Done Dirt Cheap	76
Saxon	Princess of the Night	237	Denim and Leather	81
Iron Maiden	Iron Maiden	235	Iron Maiden	80
Led Zeppelin	Communication Breakdown	235	Led Zeppelin	69
Uriah Heep	Gypsy	234	Very 'Eavy Very 'Umble	70
Suicidal Tendencies	You Can't Bring Me Down	229	Lights . . . Camera . . . Revolution	90
Mountain	Mississippi Queen	229	Climbing!	70
Dio	Stand up and Shout	227	Holy Diver	83
Cream	White Room	226	Wheels of Fire	68

Artist	Song Title	Points	Album	Year
UFO	Love to Love	225	Lights Out	77
Metal Church	Beyond the Black	224	Metal Church	84
Rainbow	Man on the Silver Mountain	224	Ritchie Blackmore's Rainbow	75
AC/DC	Sin City	224	Powerage	78
Angel Witch	Angel Witch	223	Angel Witch	80
Dream Theater	A Change of Seasons	221	A Change of Seasons	95
Thin Lizzy	Jailbreak	221	Jailbreak	76
Nevermore	Dreaming Neon Black	220	Dreaming Neon Black	99
Def Leppard	Foolin'	220	Pyromania	83
Annihilator	Alison Hell	219	Alice in Hell	89
Van Halen	Atomic Punk	218	Van Halen	78
Nugent, Ted	Stranglehold	218	Ted Nugent	75
Black Sabbath	The Sign of the Southern Cross	217	Mob Rules	81
Nazareth	Hair of the Dog	217	Hair of the Dog	75
Rush	Working Man	217	Rush	73
Judas Priest	Dissident Aggressor	215	Sin After Sin	77
Metallica	Trapped under Ice	214	Ride the Lightning	84
Mercyful Fate	Satan's Fall	214	Melissa	83
Queen	Stone Cold Crazy	212	Sheer Heart Attack	74
Led Zeppelin	Dazed and Confused	212	Led Zeppelin	69
Megadeth	Rust in Peace . . . Polaris	211	Rust in Peace	90
King Diamond	Abigail	211	Abigail	87
Black Sabbath	Hole in the Sky	211	Sabotage	75
Judas Priest	Desert Plains	210	Point of Entry	81
Slayer	Chemical Warfare	209	Haunting the Chapel	84
Manowar	Battle Hymn	207	Battle Hymns	82
Judas Priest	Heading out to the Highway	207	Point of Entry	81
Led Zeppelin	When the Levee Breaks	205	IV	71
Anthrax	Only	204	Sound of White Noise	93
Mötley Crüe	Dr. Feelgood	204	Dr. Feelgood	89
Iron Maiden	Seventh Son of a Seventh Son	204	Seventh Son of a Seventh Son	88
MC5	Kick Out the Jams	203	Kick Out the Jams	69
Def Leppard	Let It Go	202	High 'n' Dry	81
Sex Pistols	God Save the Queen	202	Never Mind the Bollocks	77

Artist	Song Title	Points	Album	Year
Loudness	Crazy Nights	202	Thunder in the East	85
W.A.S.P.	Animal	201	Animal	84
Blue Öyster Cult	Godzilla	201	Spectres	77
Black Sabbath	After Forever	201	Master of Reality	71
Motörhead	Iron Fist	200	Iron Fist	82
Pantera	This Love	199	Vulgar Display of Power	92
Black Sabbath	The Writ	199	Sabotage	75
Whitesnake	Here I Go Again	198	1987	87
Mercyful Fate	Melissa	196	Melissa	83
Twisted Sister	We're Not Gonna Take It	195	Stay Hungry	84
Sepultura	Inner Self	195	Beneath the Remains	89
Black Sabbath	The Wizard	194	Black Sabbath	70
Slayer	Dead Skin Mask	193	Seasons in the Abyss	90
Pantera	Domination	193	Cowboys from Hell	90
Judas Priest	The Green Manalishi (With the Two-Pronged Crown)	193	Hell Bent for Leather	79
Halford	Resurrection	191	Resurrection	2000
Faith No More	Epic	191	The Real Thing	89
Rush	Limelight	191	Moving Pictures	81
Black Sabbath	Megalomania	188	Sabotage	75
Led Zeppelin	Heartbreaker	188	II	69
Thin Lizzy	Don't Believe a Word	187	Johnny the Fox	76
Judas Priest	Grinder	186	British Steel	80
At the Gates	Blinded by Fear	186	Slaughter of the Soul	95
Queensryche	Suite Sister Mary	185	Operation: Mindcrime	88
Saxon	747 (Strangers in the Night)	185	Wheels of Steel	80
Krokus	Screaming in the Night	185	Headhunter	83
Accept	Metal Heart	185	Metal Heart	85
Exodus	Bonded by Blood	184	Bonded by Blood	85
Black Sabbath	Snowblind	183	Vol 4	72
Def Leppard	Rock of Ages	182	Pyromania	83
Rage Against the Machine	Killing in the Name	181	Epic	92
Quiet Riot	Cum on Feel the Noize	181	Metal Health	83
Helloween	Ride the Sky	181	Walls of Jericho	85
Twisted Sister	I Wanna Rock	180	Stay Hungry	84

Artist	Song Title	Points	Album	Year
Iron Maiden	The Evil That Men Do	180	Seventh Son of a Seventh Son	88
Testament	D. N. R. (Do Not Resuscitate)	179	The Gathering	99
Van Halen	Hot for Teacher	179	1984	84
In Flames	Episode 666	179	Whoracle	97
Thin Lizzy	The Boys Are Back in Town	178	Jailbreak	76
Tesla	Modern Day Cowboy	177	Mechanical Resonance	87
Van Halen	Mean Streets	177	Fair Warning	81
Uriah Heep	July Morning	177	Look at Yourself	71
Sepultura	Refuse/Resist	176	Chaos A.D.	91
Pantera	I'm Broken	174	Far Beyond Driven	94
Stooges	Search and Destroy	174	Raw Power	73
Deep Purple	Perfect Strangers	174	Perfect Strangers	84
Black Sabbath	Die Young	174	Heaven and Hell	80
W.A.S.P.	Chainsaw Charlie	173	The Crimson Idol	92
Judas Priest	Metal Gods	173	British Steel	80
Sex Pistols	Anarchy in the U. K.	172	Never Mind the Bollocks	77
Black Sabbath	Supernaut	172	Vol 4	72
Def Leppard	Pour Some Sugar on Me	171	Hysteria	87
Blind Guardian	Imaginations from the Other Side	171	Imaginations from the Other Side	95
Slayer	Mandatory Suicide	170	South of Heaven	88
Kiss	God of Thunder	170	Destroyer	76
Deep Purple	Pictures of Home	170	Machine Head	72
Queensryche	I Don't Believe in Love	169	Operation: Mindcrime	88
Metal Church	Metal Church	169	Metal Church	84
Deep Purple	Space Truckin'	169	Machine Head	72
Uriah Heep	Look at Yourself	169	Look at Yourself	71
Guns N' Roses	Rocket Queen	168	Appetite for Destruction	87
Anthrax	Armed and Dangerous	168	Spreading the Disease	86
Dickinson, Bruce	Tears of the Dragon	168	Balls to Picasso	94
Montrose	Space Station #5	167	Montrose	73
Rush	The Spirit of Radio	166	Permanent Waves	80
Megadeth	Angry Again	165	Hidden Treasures	95
Fates Warning	The Apparition	165	The Spectre Within	85
Savatage	Sirens	165	Sirens	83

Artist	Song Title	Points	Album	Year
Schenker Group, Michael	Lost Horizons	165	Michael Schenker Group	80
Scorpions	Still Loving You	165	Love at First Sting	84
Helloween	Keeper of the Seven Keys	164	Keeper of the Seven Keys Part II	88
Pantera	Hollow	163	Vulgar Display of Power	92
Osbourne, Ozzy	Shot in the Dark	163	The Ultimate Sin	86
Soundgarden	Jesus Christ Pose	162	Badmotorfinger	91
Anthrax	Anti-Social	162	State of Euphoria	88
Metallica	Call of Ktulu	162	Ride the Lightning	84
Iron Maiden	22 Acacia Avenue	162	The Number of the Beast	82
Angel	Tower	161	Angel	76
Ratt	Lay It Down	160	Invasion of Your Privacy	85
Slayer	Postmortem	159	Reign in Blood	86
AC/DC	It's a Long Way to the Top	159	High Voltage	76
Testament	Disciples of the Watch	158	The New Order	88
Jethro Tull	Aqualung	157	Aqualung	71
Thin Lizzy	Cowboy Song	156	Jailbreak	76
White Zombie	More Human Than Human	154	Astrocreep 2000	95
Machine Head	Davidian	154	Burn My Eyes	94
Kiss	Shout It Out Loud	153	Destroyer	76
Deep Purple	Knockin' at Your Back Door	153	Perfect Strangers	84
AC/DC	Thunderstruck	152	The Razors Edge	90
Mötley Crüe	Wild Side	151	Girls Girls Girls	87
Bathory	A Fine Day to Die	151	Blood Fire Death	88
Living Colour	Cult of Personality	150	Vivid	88
Black Sabbath	Falling Off the Edge of the World	150	Mob Rules	81
Warlock	All We Are	149	Triumph and Agony	87
AC/DC	TNT	149	High Voltage	76
Iron Maiden	Running Free	148	Iron Maiden	80
Rainbow	Long Live Rock 'n' Roll	148	Long Live Rock 'n' Roll	78
Metallica	Harvester of Sorrow	147	. . . And Justice for All	88
Entombed	Left Hand Path	147	Left Hand Path	90
Def Leppard	High 'n' Dry (Saturday Night)	146	High 'n' Dry	81
Angel Witch	Angel of Death	146	Angel Witch	80

Artist	Song Title	Points	Album	Year
White Zombie	Thunderkiss '65	145	La Sexorcisto: Devil Music Vol.1	92
Overkill	The Years of Decay	145	The Years of Decay	89
Kiss	Lick It Up	144	Lick It Up	83
Saxon	The Eagle Has Landed	144	Power & the Glory	83
Saxon	Wheels of Steel	144	Wheels of Steel	80
Machine Head	Ten Ton Hammer	143	The More Things Change	97
Ministry	Jesus Built My Hotrod	143	Psalm 69	92
King Diamond	Welcome Home	143	"Them"	88
Sepultura	Desperate Cry	143	Arise	91
Manowar	Blood of the Kings	142	Kings of Metal	88
Motörhead	Killed by Death	142	No Remorse	84
Black Sabbath	Trashed	142	Born Again	83
Malmsteen, Yngwie	I Am a Viking	142	Marching Out	85
AC/DC	Riff Raff	141	Powerage	78
Cream	Sunshine of Your Love	140	Disraeli Gears	67
Meshuggah	Future Breed Machine	140	Destroy Erase Improve	95
Malmsteen, Yngwie	I See the Light Tonight	140	Marching Out	85
Pantera	Becoming	139	Far Beyond Driven	94
Fates Warning	Ivory Gate of Dreams	139	No Exit	88
Iron Maiden	The Prisoner	139	The Number of the Beast	82
Testament	Trial by Fire	138	The New Order	88
Ratt	You're in Love	138	Invasion of Your Privacy	85
Soundgarden	Outshined	137	Badmotorfinger	91
Blue Öyster Cult	Cities on Flame with Rock and Roll	137	Blue Öyster Cult	72
Type O Negative	Love You to Death	136	October Rust	96
Megadeth	My Last Words	136	Peace Sells . . . but Who's Buying?	86
Y & T	Mean Streak	136	Mean Streak	83
Cooper, Alice	Billion Dollars Babies	136	Billion Dollars Babies	73
Iron Maiden	Be Quick or Be Dead	136	Fear of the Dark	92
Iron Maiden	Strange in a Strange Land	136	Somewhere in Time	86
Holocaust	Death or Glory	136	The Nightcomers	81
Led Zeppelin	Misty Mountain Hop	136	IV71	
Metal Church	Badlands	135	Blessing in Disguise	89
Metallica	Motorbreath	135	Kill 'Em All	83
Blind Guardian	Nightfall	135	Nightfall in Middle Earth	98

Artist	Song Title	Points	Album	Year
Metallica	Hit the Lights	134	Kill 'Em All	83
Manowar	Blood of My Enemies	133	Hail to England	84
Judas Priest	Love Bites	132	Defenders of the Faith	84
Black Sabbath	Zero the Hero	132	Born Again	83
Emperor	I Am the Black Wizard's	132	In the Nightside Eclipse	95
Humble Pie	I Don't Need No Doctor	131	Performance: Rockin' the Fillmore	71
Mötley Crüe	Kickstart My Heart	130	Dr. Feelgood	89
Schenker Group, Michael	Assault Attack	130	Assault Attack	82
Jimi Hendrix Experience	All Along the Watchtower	130	Electric Ladyland	68
Uriah Heep	The Wizard	130	Demons and Wizards	72
Deicide	Sacrificial Suicide	129	Deicide	90
Twisted Sister	Under the Blade	129	Under the Blade	82
Queen	Ogre Battle	129	II	74
Soundgarden	Rusty Cage	128	Badmotorfinger	91
Cooper, Alice	Poison	128	Trash	89
Poison	Talk Dirty to Me	128	Look What the Cat Dragged In	86
Witchfinder General	Witchfinder General	128	Death Penalty	82
Skid Row	Monkey Business	127	Slave to the Grind	91
Metal Church	God of Wrath	127	Metal Church	84
Armored Saint	Can U Deliver	127	March of the Saint	84
Venom	In League with Satan	127	Welcome to Hell	81
Stone Temple Pilots	Sex Type Thing	126	Core	92
Alice in Chains	Man in the Box	126	Facelift	91
Faith No More	Surprise You're Dead	126	The Real Thing	89
Mercyful Fate	The Oath	126	Don't Break the Oath	84
Sepultura	Attitude	126	Roots	96
Anthrax	Bring the Noise	125	Attack of the Killer B's	91
Anthrax	In My World	125	Persistence of Time	90
Metal Church	Anthem to the Estranged	125	Blessing in Disguise	89
Iron Maiden	Can I Play with Madness	125	Seventh Son of a Seventh Son	88
Celtic Frost	Dethroned Emperor	125	Morbid Tales	84
Guns N' Roses	Mr. Brownstone	124	Appetite for Destruction	87
Iron Maiden	Children of the Damned	124	The Number of the Beast	82
Death	Pull the Plug	122	Leprosy	88

Artist	Song Title	Points	Album	Year
Twisted Sister	You Can't Stop Rock 'n' Roll	122	You Can't Stop Rock 'n' Roll	83
Osbourne, Ozzy	S. A. T. O.	122	Diary of a Madman	81
UFO	Too Hot to Handle	122	Lights Out	77
Fear Factory	Demanufacture	121	Demanufacture	95
Metallica	To Live Is to Die	121	. . . And Justice for All	88
Fastway	Say What You Will	121	Fastway	83
Cinderella	Gypsy Road	120	Long Cold Winter	88
Savatage	Power of the Night	120	Power of the Night	85
Deep Purple	Black Night	120	24 Karat Purple	75
Testament	Low	119	Low	94
Carcass	No Love Lost	119	Heartwork	93
Halford	Silent Screams	118	Resurrection	2000
Kiss	War Machine	118	Creatures of the Night	82
Aerosmith	Back in the Saddle	118	Rocks	76
Napalm Death	Suffer the Children	118	Harmony Corruption	90
Europe	The Final Countdown	118	The Final Countdown	86
Candlemass	A Sorcerer's Pledge	118	Epicus Doomicus Metallicus	86
Mötley Crüe	Girls, Girls, Girls	117	Girls Girls Girls	87
Kiss	I Was Made for Lovin' You	117	Dynasty	79
Judas Priest	Rapid Fire	117	British Steel	80
Dokken	Kiss of Death	116	Back for the Attack	87
Thin Lizzy	Roisin Dubh (Black Rose) a Rock Legend	116	Black Rose	79
Sepultura	Beneath the Remains	116	Beneath the Remains	89
Skid Row	Slave to the Grind	115	Slave to the Grind	91
Slayer	At Dawn They Sleep	115	Hell Awaits	85
Judas Priest	Genocide	115	Sad Wings of Destiny	76
Megadeth	Countdown to Extinction	114	Countdown to Extinction	92
Kiss	Creatures of the Night	114	Creatures of the Night	82
Aerosmith	Rats in the Cellar	114	Rocks	76
Montrose	Rock the Nation	114	Montrose	73
Rush	La Villa Strangiato	114	Hemispheres	78
AC/DC	Walk All Over You	114	Highway to Hell	79
W.A.S.P.	The Idol	113	The Crimson Idol	92
Anthrax	Madhouse	113	Spreading the Disease	86
Metallica	The Thing That Should Not Be	113	Master of Puppets	86

Artist	Song Title	Points	Album	Year
Van Halen	And the Cradle Will Rock . . .	113	Women and Children First	80
Kiss	She	113	Dressed to Kill	75
Pantera	Revolution Is My Name	112	Reinventing the Steel	2000
W.A.S.P.	Mean Man	112	The Headless Children	89
Iron Maiden	Still Life	112	Piece of Mind	83
Lucifer's Friend	Ride the Sky	112	Lucifer's Friend	71
AC/DC	Shoot to Thrill	112	Back in Black	80
Rainbow	Tarot Woman	111	Rising	76
Black Sabbath	Spiral Architect	111	Sabbath Bloody Sabbath	73
At the Gates	Suicide Nation	111	Slaughter of the Soul	85
Dream Theater	The Mirror	110	Awake	94
Metallica	Nothing Else Matters	110	Metallica	91
Ratt	Lack of Communication	110	Out of the Cellar	84
Kansas	Carry on Wayward Son	110	Leftoverture	76
Deep Purple	Stormbringer	110	Stormbringer	75
Bad Company	Bad Company	110	Bad Company	74
Budgie	Breadfan	110	Never Turn Your Back on a Friend	73
Free	All Right Now	110	Fire and Water	70
Amorphis	Black Winter Day	110	Tales from the Thousand Lakes	94
Tygers of Pan Tang	Gangland	109	Spellbound	81
Thin Lizzy	Thunder and Lightning	109	Thunder and Lightning	83
Anvil	Metal on Metal	109	Metal on Metal	82
Kyuss	Green Machine	108	Blues for the Red Sun	93
King's X	Over My Head	108	Gretchen Goes to Nebraska	89
Emperor	Thus Spake the Nightspirit	108	Anthems to the Welkin at Dusk	97
Slipknot	Wait and Bleed	107	Slipknot	99
Monster Magnet	Powertrip	107	Powertrip	98
Blue Öyster Cult	Astronomy	107	Secret Treaties	74
Motörhead	Bomber	107	Bomber	79

APPENDIX 2:
TOP 500 SORTED BY BAND

The handy, dandy reference checklist . . . Part II. You will find this interesting, believe me. I did. It allows for all sorts of cool analysis, mainly around how a specific band did, what their winning tracks were and by what margins. Make your own greatest hits packs! Put together a set list! Get a life!

Artist	Song Title	Points	Album	Year
AC/DC	Back in Black	1995	Back in Black	80
AC/DC	Highway to Hell	1469	Highway to Hell	79
AC/DC	Hells Bells	1003	Back in Black	80
AC/DC	For Those About to Rock (We Salute You)	592	For Those About to Rock We Salute You	81
AC/DC	You Shook Me All Night Long	589	Back in Black	80
AC/DC	Whole Lotta Rosie	409	Let There Be Rock	77
AC/DC	Let There Be Rock	312	Let There Be Rock	77
AC/DC	Dirty Deeds Done Dirt Cheap	239	Dirty Deeds Done Dirt Cheap	76
AC/DC	Sin City	224	Powerage	78
AC/DC	It's a Long Way to the Top (If You Wanna Rock 'n' Roll)	159	High Voltage	76
AC/DC	Thunderstruck	152	The Razors Edge	90
AC/DC	TNT	149	High Voltage	76
AC/DC	Riff Raff	141	Powerage	78
AC/DC	Walk All Over You	114	Highway to Hell	79
AC/DC	Shoot to Thrill	112	Back in Black	80
Accept	Balls to the Wall	1389	Balls to the Wall	84
Accept	Fast as a Shark	1225	Restless and Wild	83
Accept	Restless & Wild	275	Restless and Wild	83
Accept	Princess of the Dawn	241	Restless and Wild	83
Accept	Metal Heart	185	Metal Heart	85
Aerosmith	Toys in the Attic	344	Toys in the Attic	75
Aerosmith	Dream On	314	Aerosmith	73
Aerosmith	Sweet Emotion	290	Toys in the Attic	75
Aerosmith	Back in the Saddle	118	Rocks	76
Aerosmith	Rats in the Cellar	114	Rocks	76

Artist	Song Title	Points	Album	Year
Alice in Chains	Would?	243	Dirt	92
Alice in Chains	Man in the Box	126	Facelift	91
Amorphis	Black Winter Day	110	Tales from the Thousand Lakes	94
Angel	Tower	161	Angel	76
Angel Witch	Angel Witch	223	Angel Witch	80
Angel Witch	Angel of Death	146	Angel Witch	80
Annihilator	Alison Hell	219	Alice in Hell	89
Anthrax	Among the Living	327	Among the Living	87
Anthrax	Indians	320	Among the Living	87
Anthrax	Caught in a Mosh	285	Among the Living	87
Anthrax	I Am the Law	244	Among the Living	87
Anthrax	Only	204	Sound of White Noise	93
Anthrax	Armed and Dangerous	168	Spreading the Disease	86
Anthrax	Anti-Social	162	State of Euphoria	88
Anthrax	Bring the Noise	125	Attack of the Killer B's	91
Anthrax	In my World	125	Persistence of Time	90
Anthrax	Madhouse	113	Spreading the Disease	86
Anvil	Metal on Metal	109	Metal on Metal	82
Armored Saint	Can U Deliver	127	March of the Saint	84
At the Gates	Blinded by Fear	186	Slaughter of the Soul	95
At the Gates	Suicide Nation	111	Slaughter of the Soul	85
Bad Company	Bad Company	110	Bad Company	74
Bathory	A Fine Day to Die	151	Blood Fire Death	88
Beatles	Helter Skelter	326	White Album	68
Black Sabbath	Paranoid	3588	Paranoid	70
Black Sabbath	War Pigs	2355	Paranoid	70
Black Sabbath	Iron Man	1915	Paranoid	70
Black Sabbath	Heaven and Hell	1835	Heaven and Hell	80
Black Sabbath	Black Sabbath	1700	Black Sabbath	70
Black Sabbath	Sabbath Bloody Sabbath	1118	Sabbath Bloody Sabbath	73
Black Sabbath	Symptom of the Universe	922	Sabotage	75
Black Sabbath	Children of the Grave	748	Master of Reality	71
Black Sabbath	Into the Void	600	Master of Reality	71
Black Sabbath	Neon Knights	504	Heaven and Hell	80
Black Sabbath	NIB	477	Black Sabbath	70
Black Sabbath	The Mob Rules	397	Mob Rules	81

Artist	Song Title	Points	Album	Year
Black Sabbath	Sweet Leaf	362	Master of Reality	71
Black Sabbath	Children of the Sea	327	Heaven and Hell	80
Black Sabbath	Fairies Wear Boots	252	Paranoid	70
Black Sabbath	The Sign of the Southern Cross	217	Mob Rules	81
Black Sabbath	Hole in the Sky	211	Sabotage	75
Black Sabbath	After Forever	201	Master of Reality	71
Black Sabbath	The Writ	199	Sabotage	75
Black Sabbath	The Wizard	194	Black Sabbath	70
Black Sabbath	Megalomania	188	Sabotage	75
Black Sabbath	Snowblind	183	Vol 4	72
Black Sabbath	Die Young	174	Heaven and Hell	80
Black Sabbath	Supernaut	172	Vol 4	72
Black Sabbath	Falling off the Edge of the World	150	Mob Rules	81
Black Sabbath	Trashed	142	Born Again	83
Black Sabbath	Zero the Hero	132	Born Again	83
Black Sabbath	Spiral Architect	111	Sabbath Bloody Sabbath	73
Blind Guardian	Imaginations from the Other Side	171	Imaginations from the Other Side	95
Blind Guardian	Nightfall	135	Nightfall in Middle Earth	98
Blue Öyster Cult	(Don't Fear) the Reaper	317	Agents of Fortune	76
Blue Öyster Cult	Godzilla	201	Spectres	77
Blue Öyster Cult	Cities on Flame with Rock and Roll	137	Blue Öyster Cult	72
Blue Öyster Cult	Astronomy	107	Secret Treaties	74
Budgie	Breadfan	110	Never Turn Your Back on a Friend	73
Candlemass	A Sorcerer's Pledge	118	Epicus Doomicus Metallicus	86
Cannibal Corpse	Hammer Smashed Face	369	Tomb of the Mutilated	92
Carcass	Heartwork	306	Heartwork	93
Carcass	No Love Lost	119	Heartwork	93
Celtic Frost	Circle of the Tyrants	413	To Mega Therion	85
Celtic Frost	Dethroned Emperor	125	Morbid Tales	84
Cinderella	Gypsy Road	120	Long Cold Winter	88
Cooper, Alice	I'm Eighteen	314	Love It to Death	71
Cooper, Alice	School's Out	293	School's Out	72
Cooper, Alice	Welcome to My	288	Welcome to My	75

Artist	Song Title	Points	Album	Year
	Nightmare		Nightmare	
Cooper, Alice	Billion Dollars Babies	136	Billion Dollars Babies	73
Cooper, Alice	Poison	128	Trash	89
Cream	White Room	226	Wheels of Fire	68
Cream	Sunshine of Your Love	140	Disraeli Gears	67
Danzig	Mother	367	Thralldemonsweatlive	93
Death	Pull the Plug	122	Leprosy	88
Deep Purple	Highway Star	1729	Machine Head	72
Deep Purple	Smoke on the Water	1460	Machine Head	72
Deep Purple	Burn	960	Burn	74
Deep Purple	Child in Time	797	In Rock	70
Deep Purple	Speed King	286	In Rock	70
Deep Purple	Perfect Strangers	174	Perfect Strangers	84
Deep Purple	Pictures of Home	170	Machine Head	72
Deep Purple	Space Truckin'	169	Machine Head	72
Deep Purple	Knockin' at Your Back Door	153	Perfect Strangers	84
Deep Purple	Black Night	120	24 Carat Purple	75
Deep Purple	Stormbringer	110	Stormbringer	75
Def Leppard	Photograph	504	Pyromania	83
Def Leppard	Foolin'	220	Pyromania	83
Def Leppard	Let It Go	202	High 'n' Dry	81
Def Leppard	Rock of Ages	182	Pyromania	83
Def Leppard	Pour Some Sugar on Me	171	Hysteria	87
Def Leppard	High 'n' Dry (Saturday Night)	146	High 'n' Dry	81
Deicide	Sacrificial Suicide	129	Deicide	90
Diamond Head	Am I Evil?	359	Lightning to the Nations	80
Dickinson, Bruce	Tears of the Dragon	168	Balls to Picasso	94
Dio	Holy Diver	1251	Holy Diver	83
Dio	The Last in Line	972	The Last in Line	84
Dio	Rainbow in the Dark	906	Holy Diver	83
Dio	Don't Talk to Strangers	284	Holy Diver	83
Dio	Stand Up and Shout	227	Holy Diver	83
Dokken	Kiss of Death	116	Back for the Attack	87
Dream Theater	Pull Me Under	633	Images and Words	92
Dream Theater	Metropolis — Part 1	345	Images and Words	92
Dream Theater	A Change of Seasons	221	A Change of Seasons	95

Artist	Song Title	Points	Album	Year
Dream Theater	The Mirror	110	Awake	94
Emperor	I Am the Black Wizard's	132	In the Nightside Eclipse	95
Emperor	Thus Spake the Nightspirit	108	Anthems to the Welkin at Dusk	97
Entombed	Left Hand Path	147	Left Hand Path	90
Europe	The Final Countdown	118	The Final Countdown	86
Exodus	The Toxic Waltz	252	Fabulous Disaster	89
Exodus	Bonded by Blood	184	Bonded by Blood	85
Faith No More	Epic	191	The Real Thing	89
Faith No More	Surprise You're Dead	126	The Real Thing	89
Fastway	Say What You Will	121	Fastway	83
Fates Warning	The Apparition	165	The Spectre Within	85
Fates Warning	Ivory Gate of Dreams	139	No Exit	88
Fear Factory	Demanufacture	121	Demanufacture	95
Free	All Right Now	110	Fire and Water	70
Guns N' Roses	Welcome to the Jungle	1611	Appetite for Destruction	87
Guns N' Roses	Paradise City	355	Appetite for Destruction	87
Guns N' Roses	Sweet Child O' Mine	319	Appetite for Destruction	87
Guns N' Roses	November Rain	294	Use Your Illusion I	91
Guns N' Roses	Rocket Queen	168	Appetite for Destruction	87
Guns N' Roses	Mr. Brownstone	124	Appetite for Destruction	87
Halford	Resurrection	191	Resurrection	2000
Halford	Silent Screams	118	Resurrection	2000
Helloween	I Want Out	413	Keeper of the Seven Keys Part II	88
Helloween	Halloween	373	Keeper of the Seven Keys Part I	87
Helloween	Eagle Fly Free	285	Keeper of the Seven Keys Part II	88
Helloween	Ride the Sky	181	Walls of Jericho	85
Helloween	Keeper of the Seven Keys	164	Keeper of the Seven Keys Part Ii	88
Holocaust	Death or Glory	136	The Nightcomers	81
Humble Pie	I Don't Need No Doctor	131	Performance: Rockin' the Fillmore	71
Iced Earth	Dante's Inferno	398	Burnt Offerings	95
Iced Earth	Something Wicked (Trilogy)	282	Something Wicked This Way Comes	98
Iced Earth	A Question of Heaven	245	The Dark Saga	96

Artist	Song Title	Points	Album	Year
In Flames	Episode 666	179	Whoracle	97
Iron Maiden	Number of the Beast	2896	The Number of the Beast	82
Iron Maiden	Hallowed Be Thy Name	2591	The Number of the Beast	82
Iron Maiden	The Trooper	1463	Piece of Mind	83
Iron Maiden	Run to the Hills	1321	The Number of the Beast	82
Iron Maiden	Aces High	736	Powerslave	84
Iron Maiden	2 Minutes to Midnight	668	Powerslave	84
Iron Maiden	Rime of the Ancient Mariner	573	Powerslave	84
Iron Maiden	Killers	532	Killers	81
Iron Maiden	Powerslave	512	Powerslave	84
Iron Maiden	Revelations	463	Piece of Mind	83
Iron Maiden	Fear of the Dark	447	Fear of the Dark	92
Iron Maiden	Wasted Years	434	Somewhere in Time	86
Iron Maiden	Wrathchild	415	Killers	81
Iron Maiden	Phantom of the Opera	399	Iron Maiden	80
Iron Maiden	Flight of Icarus	349	Piece of Mind	83
Iron Maiden	Where Eagles Dare	346	Piece of Mind	83
Iron Maiden	Murders in the Rue Morgue	301	Killers	81
Iron Maiden	Iron Maiden	235	Iron Maiden	80
Iron Maiden	Seventh Son of a Seventh Son	204	Seventh Son of a Seventh Son	88
Iron Maiden	The Evil That Men Do	180	Seventh Son of a Seventh Son	88
Iron Maiden	22 Acacia Avenue	162	The Number of the Beast	82
Iron Maiden	Running Free	148	Iron Maiden	80
Iron Maiden	The Prisoner	139	The Number of the Beast	82
Iron Maiden	Be Quick or Be Dead	136	Fear of the Dark	92
Iron Maiden	Strange in a Strange Land	136	Somewhere in Time	86
Iron Maiden Son	Can I Play with Madness 88	125	Seventh Son of a Seventh	
Iron Maiden	Children of the Damned	124	The Number of the Beast	82
Iron Maiden	Still Life	112	Piece of Mind	83
Jethro Tull	Aqualung	157	Aqualung	71
Jimi Hendrix Experience	Voodoo Child (Slight Return)	282	Electric Ladyland	68
Jimi Hendrix Experience	Purple Haze	275	Are You Experienced?	67

Artist	Song Title	Points	Album	Year
Jimi Hendrix Experience	All Along the Watchtower	130	Electric Ladyland	68
Judas Priest	Painkiller	1784	Painkiller	90
Judas Priest	Victim of Changes	1665	Sad Wings of Destiny	76
Judas Priest	Electric Eye	1643	Screaming for Vengeance	82
Judas Priest	You've Got Another Thing Comin'	1317	Screaming for Vengeance	82
Judas Priest	Beyond the Realms of Death	924	Stained Class	78
Judas Priest	Breaking the Law	719	British Steel	80
Judas Priest	Screaming for Vengeance	505	Screaming for Vengeance	82
Judas Priest	Living After Midnight	453	British Steel	80
Judas Priest	The Ripper	431	Sad Wings of Destiny	76
Judas Priest	Hell Bent for Leather	429	Killing Machine	78
Judas Priest	Tyrant	414	Sad Wings of Destiny	76
Judas Priest	The Sentinel	391	Defenders of the Faith	84
Judas Priest	Freewheel Burning	346	Defenders of the Faith	84
Judas Priest	Sinner	346	Sin After Sin	77
Judas Priest	Exciter	336	Stained Class	78
Judas Priest	Dissident Aggressor	215	Sin After Sin	77
Judas Priest	Desert Plains	210	Point of Entry	81
Judas Priest	Heading Out to the Highway	207	Point of Entry	81
Judas Priest	The Green Manalishi (With the Two-Pronged Crown)	193	Hell Bent for Leather	79
Judas Priest	Grinder	186	British Steel	80
Judas Priest	Metal Gods	173	British Steel	80
Judas Priest	Love Bites	132	Defenders of the Faith	84
Judas Priest	Rapid Fire	117	British Steel	80
Judas Priest	Genocide	115	Sad Wings of Destiny	76
Kansas	Carry on Wayward Son	110	Leftoverture	76
King Diamond	Abigail	211	Abigail	87
King Diamond	Welcome Home	143	"Them"	88
King's X	Over My Head	108	Gretchen Goes to Nebraska	89
Kiss	Detroit Rock City	881	Destroyer	76
Kiss	Rock and Roll All Nite	675	Dressed to Kill	75
Kiss	Deuce	332	Kiss	74

Artist	Song Title	Points	Album	Year
Kiss	I Love It Loud	330	Creatures of the Night	82
Kiss	Black Diamond	287	Kiss	74
Kiss	God of Thunder	170	Destroyer	76
Kiss	Shout It out Loud	153	Destroyer	76
Kiss	Lick It Up	144	Lick It Up	83
Kiss	War Machine	118	Creatures of the Night	82
Kiss	I Was Made for Lovin' You	117	Dynasty	79
Kiss	Creatures of the Night	114	Creatures of the Night	82
Kiss	She	113	Dressed to Kill	75
Krokus	Screaming in the Night	185	Headhunter	83
Kyuss	Green Machine	108	Blues for the Red Sun	93
Led Zeppelin	Stairway to Heaven	1065	IV	71
Led Zeppelin	Whole Lotta Love	727	II	69
Led Zeppelin	Black Dog	598	IV	71
Led Zeppelin	Immigrant Song	552	III	70
Led Zeppelin	Kashmir	550	Physical Graffiti	75
Led Zeppelin	Rock and Roll	492	IV	71
Led Zeppelin	Achilles' Last Stand	335	Presence	76
Led Zeppelin	Communication Breakdown	235	Led Zeppelin	69
Led Zeppelin	Dazed and Confused	212	Led Zeppelin	69
Led Zeppelin	When the Levee Breaks	205	IV	71
Led Zeppelin	Heartbreaker	188	II	69
Led Zeppelin	Misty Mountain Hop	136	IV	71
Living Colour	Cult of Personality	150	Vivid	88
Loudness	Crazy Nights	202	Thunder in the East	85
Lucifer's Friend	Ride the Sky	112	Lucifer's Friend	71
Machine Head	Davidian	154	Burn My Eyes	94
Machine Head	Ten Ton Hammer	143	The More Things Change	97
Malmsteen, Yngwie	I Am a Viking	142	Marching Out	85
Malmsteen, Yngwie	I See the Light Tonight	140	Marching Out	85
Manowar	Hail and Kill	299	Kings of Metal	88
Manowar	Metal Daze	249	Battle Hymns	82
Manowar	Battle Hymn	207	Battle Hymns	82
Manowar	Blood of the Kings	142	Kings of Metal	88
Manowar	Blood of My Enemies	133	Hail to England	84
Manson, Marilyn	The Beautiful People	272	Antichrist Superstar	96

Artist	Song Title	Points	Album	Year
MC5	Kick Out the Jams	203	Kick Out the Jams	69
Megadeth	Holy Wars . . . The Punishment Due	1692	Rust in Peace	90
Megadeth	Peace Sells	1332	Peace Sells . . . but Who's Buying?	86
Megadeth	Hangar 18	630	Rust in Peace	90
Megadeth	Symphony of Destruction	428	Countdown to Extinction	92
Megadeth	Tornado of Souls	397	Rust in Peace	90
Megadeth	Wake Up Dead	358	Peace Sells . . . but Who's Buying?	86
Megadeth	Rust in Peace . . . Polaris	211	Rust in Peace	90
Megadeth	Angry Again	165	Hidden Treasures	95
Megadeth	My Last Words	136	Peace Sells . . . but Who's Buying?	86
Megadeth	Countdown to Extinction	114	Countdown to Extinction	92
Mercyful Fate	A Dangerous Meeting	422	Don't Break the Oath	84
Mercyful Fate	Come to the Sabbath	280	Don't Break the Oath	84
Mercyful Fate	Evil	246	Melissa	83
Mercyful Fate	Satan's Fall	214	Melissa	83
Mercyful Fate	Melissa	196	Melissa	83
Mercyful Fate	The Oath	126	Don't Break the Oath	84
Meshuggah	Future Breed Machine	140	Destroy Erase Improve	95
Metal Church	Beyond the Black	224	Metal Church	84
Metal Church	Metal Church	169	Metal Church	84
Metal Church	Badlands	135	Blessing in Disguise	89
Metal Church	God of Wrath	127	Metal Church	84
Metal Church	Anthem to the Estranged	125	Blessing in Disguise	89
Metallica	Master of Puppets	3578	Master of Puppets	86
Metallica	One	1758	. . . And Justice for All	88
Metallica	Creeping Death	1539	Ride the Lightning	84
Metallica	Fade to Black	1489	Ride the Lightning	84
Metallica	For Whom the Bell Tolls	1244	Ride the Lightning	84
Metallica	Enter Sandman	1058	Metallica	91
Metallica	Seek and Destroy	768	Kill 'Em All	83
Metallica	Four Horsemen	647	Kill 'Em All	83
Metallica	Battery	615	Master of Puppets	86
Metallica	Fight Fire with Fire	592	Ride the Lightning	84
Metallica	Whiplash	444	Kill 'Em All	83

Artist	Song Title	Points	Album	Year
Metallica	Ride the Lightning	401	Ride the Lightning	84
Metallica	Disposable Heroes	379	Master of Puppets	86
Metallica	Orion	376	Master of Puppets	86
Metallica	Damage Inc	298	Master of Puppets	86
Metallica	Blackened	280	. . . And Justice for All	88
Metallica	Welcome Home (Sanitarium)	266	Master of Puppets	86
Metallica	Sad but True	262	Metallica	91
Metallica	Trapped Under Ice	214	Ride the Lightning	84
Metallica	The Call of Ktulu	162	Ride the Lightning	84
Metallica	Harvester of Sorrow	147	. . .And Justice for All	88
Metallica	Motorbreath	135	Kill 'Em All	83
Metallica	Hit the Lights	134	Kill 'Em All	83
Metallica	To Live Is to Die	121	. . . And Justice for All	88
Metallica	The Thing That Should Not Be	113	Master of Puppets	86
Metallica	Nothing Else Matters	110	Metallica	91
Ministry	Jesus Built My Hotrod	143	Psalm 69	92
Monster Magnet	Powertrip	107	Powertrip	98
Montrose	Space Station #5	167	Montrose	73
Montrose	Rock the Nation	114	Montrose	73
Mötley Crüe	Shout at the Devil	1243	Shout at the Devil	83
Mötley Crüe	Live Wire	473	Too Fast for Love	81
Mötley Crüe	Looks That Kill	399	Shout at the Devil	83
Mötley Crüe	Dr. Feelgood	204	Dr. Feelgood	89
Mötley Crüe	Wild Side	151	Girls Girls Girls	87
Mötley Crüe	Kickstart My Heart	130	Dr. Feelgood	89
Mötley Crüe	Girls, Girls, Girls	117	Girls Girls Girls	87
Motörhead	Ace of Spades	3165	Ace of Spades	80
Motörhead	Overkill	433	Overkill	79
Motörhead	Orgasmatron	305	Orgasmatron	86
Motörhead	(We Are) the Road Crew	245	Ace of Spades	80
Motörhead	Iron Fist	200	Iron Fist	82
Motörhead	Killed by Death	142	No Remorse	84
Motörhead	Bomber	107	Bomber	79
Mountain	Mississippi Queen	229	Climbing!	70
Napalm Death	Suffer the Children	118	Harmony Corruption	90
Nazareth	Hair of the Dog	217	Hair of the Dog	75

Artist	Song Title	Points	Album	Year
Nevermore	Dreaming Neon Black	220	Dreaming Neon Black	99
Nirvana	Smells Like Teen Spirit	289	Nevermind	91
Nugent, Ted	Cat Scratch Fever	304	Cat Scratch Fever	77
Nugent, Ted	Stranglehold	218	Ted Nugent	75
Osbourne, Ozzy	Crazy Train	2940	Blizzard of Ozz	80
Osbourne, Ozzy	Over the Mountain	750	Diary of a Madman	81
Osbourne, Ozzy	Diary of a Madman	736	Diary of a Madman	81
Osbourne, Ozzy	Bark at the Moon	556	Bark at the Moon	83
Osbourne, Ozzy	Mr. Crowley	531	Blizzard of Ozz	80
Osbourne, Ozzy	Flying High Again	428	Diary of a Madman	81
Osbourne, Ozzy	No More Tears	353	No More Tears	91
Osbourne, Ozzy	Suicide Solution	343	Blizzard of Ozz	80
Osbourne, Ozzy	You Can't Kill Rock and Roll	287	Diary of a Madman	81
Osbourne, Ozzy	I Don't Know	247	Blizzard of Ozz	80
Osbourne, Ozzy	Shot in the Dark	163	The Ultimate Sin	86
Osbourne, Ozzy	S. A. T. O.	122	Diary of a Madman	81
Overkill	The Years of Decay	145	The Years of Decay	89
Pantera	Cowboys from Hell	947	Cowboys from Hell	90
Pantera	Walk	877	Vulgar Display of Power	92
Pantera	Cemetary Gates	495	Cowboys from Hell	90
Pantera	Mouth for War	428	Vulgar Display of Power	92
Pantera	Fucking Hostile	375	Vulgar Display of Power	92
Pantera	5 Minutes Alone	252	Far Beyond Driven	94
Pantera	This Love	199	Vulgar Display of Power	92
Pantera	Domination	193	Cowboys from Hell	90
Pantera	I'm Broken	174	Far Beyond Driven	94
Pantera	Hollow	163	Vulgar Display of Power	92
Pantera	Becoming	139	Far Beyond Driven	94
Pantera	Revolution Is My Name	112	Reinventing the Steel	2000
Poison	Talk Dirty to Me	128	Look What the Cat Dragged In	86
Queen	Bohemian Rhapsody	300	A Night at the Opera	75
Queen	Stone Cold Crazy	212	Sheer Heart Attack	74
Queen	Ogre Battle	129	II	74
Queensryche	Take Hold of the Flame	509	The Warning	84
Queensryche	Queen of the Reich	430	Queensryche	83
Queensryche	Revolution Calling	384	Operation: Mindcrime	88

Artist	Song Title	Points	Album	Year
Queensryche	Eyes of a Stranger	366	Operation: Mindcrime	88
Queensryche	Suite Sister Mary	185	Operation: Mindcrime	88
Queensryche	I Don't Believe in Love	169	Operation: Mindcrime	88
Quiet Riot	Metal Health (Bang Your Head)	454	Metal Health	83
Quiet Riot	Cum on Feel the Noize	181	Metal Health	83
Rage Against the Machine	Killing in the Name	181	Epic	92
Rainbow	Stargazer	1041	Rising	76
Rainbow	Kill the King	605	Long Live Rock 'n' Roll	78
Rainbow	Gates of Babylon	374	Long Live Rock 'n' Roll	78
Rainbow	Man on the Silver Mountain	224	Ritchie Blackmore's Rainbow	75
Rainbow	Long Live Rock 'n' Roll	148	Long Live Rock 'n' Roll	78
Rainbow	Tarot Woman	111	Rising	76
Ratt	Round and Round	451	Out of the Cellar	84
Ratt	Lay It Down	160	Invasion of Your Privacy	85
Ratt	You're in Love	138	Invasion of Your Privacy	85
Ratt	Lack of Communication	110	Out of the Cellar	84
Riot	Swords & Tequila	317	Fire Down Under	81
Riot	Outlaw	306	Fire Down Under	81
Rush	2112	457	2112	76
Rush	Tom Sawyer	423	Moving Pictures	81
Rush	Working Man	217	Rush	73
Rush	Limelight	191	Moving Pictures	81
Rush	The Spirit of Radio	166	Permanent Waves	80
Rush	La Villa Strangiato	114	Hemispheres	78
Savatage	Hall of the Mountain King	510	Hall of the Mountain King	87
Savatage	Gutter Ballet	295	Gutter Ballet	90
Savatage	Sirens	165	Sirens	83
Savatage	Power of the Night	120	Power of the Night	85
Saxon	Power and the Glory	414	Power & the Glory	83
Saxon	Denim and Leather	311	Denim and Leather	81
Saxon	Princess of the Night	237	Denim and Leather	81
Saxon	747 (Strangers in the Night)	185	Wheels of Steel	80
Saxon	The Eagle Has Landed	144	Power & the Glory	83
Saxon	Wheels of Steel	144	Wheels of Steel	80

Artist	Song Title	Points	Album	Year
Schenker Group, Michael	Lost Horizons	165	Michael Schenker Group	80
Schenker Group, Michael	Assault Attack	130	Assault Attack	82
Scorpions	Rock You Like a Hurricane	474	Love at First Sting	84
Scorpions	Blackout	446	Blackout	82
Scorpions	Sails of Charon	351	Taken by Force	78
Scorpions	No One Like You	345	Blackout	82
Scorpions	The Zoo	263	Animal Magnetism	80
Scorpions	Still Loving You	165	Love at First Sting	84
Sepultura	Roots Bloody Roots	506	Roots	96
Sepultura	Arise	299	Arise	91
Sepultura	Dead Embryonic Cells	273	Arise	91
Sepultura	Territory	266	Chaos A.D.	91
Sepultura	Inner Self	195	Beneath the Remains	89
Sepultura	Refuse/Resist	176	Chaos A.D.	91
Sepultura	Desperate Cry	143	Arise	91
Sepultura	Attitude	126	Roots	96
Sepultura	Beneath the Remains	116	Beneath the Remains	89
Sex Pistols	God Save the Queen	202	Never Mind the Bollocks	77
Sex Pistols	Anarchy in the U. K.	172	Never Mind the Bollocks	77
Skid Row	Youth Gone Wild	374	Skid Row	89
Skid Row	18 and Life	282	Skid Row	89
Skid Row	Monkey Business	127	Slave to the Grind	91
Skid Row	Slave to the Grind	115	Slave to the Grind	91
Slayer	Angel of Death	2936	Reign in Blood	86
Slayer	Raining Blood	1564	Reign in Blood	86
Slayer	Seasons in the Abyss	971	Seasons in the Abyss	90
Slayer	South of Heaven	911	South of Heaven	88
Slayer	Hell Awaits	664	Hell Awaits	85
Slayer	War Ensemble	527	Seasons in the Abyss	90
Slayer	Chemical Warfare	209	Haunting the Chapel	84
Slayer	Dead Skin Mask	193	Seasons in the Abyss	90
Slayer	Mandatory Suicide	170	South of Heaven	88
Slayer	Postmortem	159	Reign in Blood	86
Slayer	At Dawn They Sleep	115	Hell Awaits	85
Slipknot	Wait and Bleed	107	Slipknot	99

Artist	Song Title	Points	Album	Year
Soundgarden	Jesus Christ Pose	162	Badmotorfinger	91
Soundgarden	Outshined	137	Badmotorfinger	91
Soundgarden	Rusty Cage	128	Badmotorfinger	91
Steppenwolf	Born to Be Wild	388	Steppenwolf	68
Stone Temple Pilots	Sex Type Thing	126	Core	92
Stooges	Search and Destroy	174	Raw Power	73
Suicidal Tendencies	You Can't Bring Me Down	229	Lights . . . Camera . . . Revolution	90
Tesla	Modern Day Cowboy	177	Mechanical Resonance	87
Testament	Practice What You Preach	278	Practice What You Preach	89
Testament	D. N. R. (Do Not Resuscitate)	179	The Gathering	99
Testament	Disciples of the Watch	158	The New Order	88
Testament	Trial by Fire	138	The New Order	88
Testament	Low	119	Low	94
Thin Lizzy	Emerald	310	Jailbreak	76
Thin Lizzy	Cold Sweat	239	Thunder and Lightning	83
Thin Lizzy	Jailbreak	221	Jailbreak	76
Thin Lizzy	Don't Believe a Word	187	Johnny the Fox	76
Thin Lizzy	The Boys Are Back in Town	178	Jailbreak	76
Thin Lizzy	Cowboy Song	156	Jailbreak	76
Thin Lizzy	Roisin Dubh (Black Rose) a Rock Legend	116	Black Rose	79
Thin Lizzy	Thunder and Lightning	109	Thunder and Lightning	83
Tool	Sober	332	Undertow	93
Twisted Sister	We're Not Gonna Take It	195	Stay Hungry	84
Twisted Sister	I Wanna Rock	180	Stay Hungry	84
Twisted Sister	Under the Blade	129	Under the Blade	82
Twisted Sister	You Can't Stop Rock 'n' Roll	122	You Can't Stop Rock 'n' Roll	83
Tygers of Pan Tang	Gangland	109	Spellbound	81
Type O Negative	Black No. 1	276	Bloody Kisses	93
Type O Negative	Love You to Death	136	October Rust	96
UFO	Lights Out	658	Lights Out	77
UFO	Rock Bottom	461	Phenomenon	73
UFO	Doctor Doctor	434	Phenomenon	73
UFO	Love to Love	225	Lights Out	77
UFO	Too Hot to Handle	122	Lights Out	77

Artist	Song Title	Points	Album	Year
Uriah Heep	Easy Livin'	313	Demons and Wizards	72
Uriah Heep	Gypsy	234	Very 'Eavy Very 'Umble	70
Uriah Heep	July Morning	177	Look at Yourself	71
Uriah Heep	Look at Yourself	169	Look at Yourself	71
Uriah Heep	The Wizard	130	Demons and Wizards	72
Van Halen	Runnin' with the Devil	758	Van Halen	78
Van Halen	Ain't Talkin' 'Bout Love	690	Van Halen	78
Van Halen	Unchained	435	Fair Warning	81
Van Halen	Jump	350	1984	84
Van Halen	Eruption	305	Van Halen	78
Van Halen	Panama	275	1984	84
Van Halen	Atomic Punk	218	Van Halen	78
Van Halen	Hot for Teacher	179	1984	84
Van Halen	Mean Streets	177	Fair Warning	81
Van Halen	And the Cradle Will Rock . . .	113	Women and Children First	80
Venom	Black Metal	567	Black Metal	82
Venom	In League with Satan	127	Welcome to Hell	81
W.A.S.P.	I Wanna Be Somebody	475	W.A.S.P.	84
W.A.S.P.	Wild Child	257	The Last Command	85
W.A.S.P.	Animal	201	Animal	84
W.A.S.P.	Chainsaw Charlie	173	The Crimson Idol	92
W.A.S.P.	The Idol	113	The Crimson Idol	92
W.A.S.P.	Mean Man	112	The Headless Children	89
Warlock	All We Are	149	Triumph and Agony	87
White Zombie	More Human Than Human	154	Astrocreep 2000	95
White Zombie	Thunderkiss '65	145	La Sexorcisto: Devil Music Vol.1	92
Whitesnake	Still of the Night	709	1987	87
Whitesnake	Here I Go Again	198	1987	87
Witchfinder General	Witchfinder General	128	Death Penalty	82
Y & T	Mean Streak	136	Mean Streak	83

APPENDIX 3: POINTS BY COUNTRY: TOP 10

Fairly obvious results here, the US and the UK running away with it, the US entries spread amongst many bands, the UK vaulting big time due to Maiden, Sabbath and Deep Purple. Australia is 100% entirely due to AC/DC. Brazil is all Sepultura: nine songs. For Canada, it's six Rush songs, plus one from Anvil and one from Annihilator. Ireland, you guessed it . . . eight Thin Lizzy songs and that's it. Rounding out the bottom end, Sweden's got a good mix, Switzerland gets on through two Celtic Frost and a Krokus, and Denmark, through six Mercyful Fate songs, which isn't too fair given the band's metropolitan status, although fairer given that we're talking old stuff here.

Country	Points
United States	88,182
United Kingdom	79,154
Australia	7659
Germany	7342
Brazil	2100
Canada	1896
Ireland	1516
Sweden	1432
Denmark	1484
Switzerland	723

APPENDIX 4:
SOME FREEWHEELING OBSERVATIONS

This is just some stuff that surprised me. Take that for what it's worth. But hey, part of the fun of this is pointing out such surprises. Admit it, that's what you're gonna do.

Vote Splitting

There were approximately 4500 different songs voted for in this poll. Obviously, for this project, we've focused on only 500. One thing that I wanted to do as a bit of a heavy hail to those who didn't make the grade was to mention a few bands that seemed to have stalled out of the Top 500 due to "vote-splitting," i.e., they had a number of songs that all did OK, at the expense of having clear focal tracks that kicked at least something past our Top 500 radar screen. Here are some observations, like the heading sez, freewheeling, because it's not scientific. It's just me telling you some stuff that I've noticed in the master list. And really, take this with a grain of salt for this reason. Even though I am pointing these out, many big winners also had a proportional amount of songs below the 500 mark. For example, AC/DC had an additional 35 songs that didn't make the radar. And even mid-ringers like Accept had 21 songs below the five that made it. So, what this is is a list of select bands that had *no* songs creep into the Top 500, followed by the number of songs that made the master list. In the parlance of sport, these bands are better than their records.

> Angra — 7, Bon Jovi — 10, Cradle Of Filth — 12, Dark Tranquillity — 7, Destruction — 8, Gamma Ray — 7, Hammerfall — 9, Immortal — 9, Kreator — 21 (!), Mayhem — 7, Morbid Angel — 16, My Dying Bride — 8, Opeth — 14, Paradise Lost — 11, Pearl Jam — 7, Rage — 7, Raven — 11, Running Wild — 8, S.O.D. — 8, Sentenced — 7, Sodom — 7, Soulfly — 7, Stratovarius — 11, Trouble — 18, Voivod — 12 and The Who — 11.

So . . . the above list hails a bunch of bands that had a lot of different songs for which votes were respectfully cast, but did not make the list with a single track. Here's a handful of bands that I'm just plain surprised didn't make the list AND did quite bad on the master list of 4500 songs. You would be correct in assuming they had less than seven songs on the master list, as the above exercise includes all the bands with seven or more. So, yeah, here are some bands who were forgotten, for whatever reason, main one likely being that the general demographic didn't think they were heavy. But then again, they just might be dropping out of consciousness, or for newer bands, not jumping into it in parallel with the hype. Look, I'm not saying these bands should have done way better, I'm just saying they definitely stunk up the joint. And I'm saying that while looking at the master list, something which you, dear reader do not get with this book. You might be saying, "Wha . . . he thinks they shoulda been higher? Slaughter?!" And I'm telling you, I'm looking at some really, really, pathetic, paltry marks here . . . 4500 songs includes a lot of weird votes, and these bands just were not getting any respect. See further down the dustpipe for something similar: actual songs I thought would have done better. OK, so, bands:

> Biohazard, Blackfoot, Cheap Trick, Corrosion Of Conformity, The Cult, Deftones, Exciter, Foghat, Gillan, Sammy Hagar, Hanoi Rocks, Hawkwind, Helmet, Helstar, Hypocrisy, Jag Panzer, Korn, Kittie, L.A. Guns, Limp Bizkit, Moonspell, Nightwish, Nile, Nine Inch Nails, Papa Roach, Pretty Maids, Primal Fear, Rammstein, Razor, David Lee Roth, Royal Hunt, Samson, Satyricon, Savage, Sevendust, Slaughter, Staind, Status Quo, Strapping Young Lad, Stryper, Styx, Sweet, Tank, Pat Travers, Triumph, Robin Trower, U.D.O., Virgin Steele, Warrant, Warrior Soul, White Lion, Witchery, Rob Zombie and ZZ Top.

More trite observations . . .

All four Savatage tracks are the title tracks of albums.

Three Soundgarden tracks made it, all from **Badmotorfinger**.

Testament, Anthrax, Megadeth and Metal Church all did better than I expected, pointing perhaps to the supposition that traditional Big Four-style thrash is near and dear to the heavy hearts of our poll respondents. Megadeth had an astounding 34 extra songs voted for that didn't make the Top 500. Anthrax notched an additional 25.

Van Halen with David Lee Roth: 10 songs. Van Halen with Sammy Hagar: 0. Dave solo: 0. Sammy solo: 0. Do the math. Past the Top 500, Van Halen notched an additional 18 songs, 15 of which feature Diamond Dave.

Rainbow with Ronnie James Dio: 6. Rainbow with Joe Lynn Turner: 0.

Nevermore had one song crack the Top 500, and 22 additional tracks voted on that didn't. Overkill? One made the list, 31 additional songs voted for did not.

And speaking of Ronnie James Dio . . . well, you love him: Black Sabbath songs with Ronnie: 6. Rainbow songs with Ronnie: 6. Dio songs: 5.

Metallica songs: 26. Metallica songs from either Load or Re-Load: 0.

Deep Purple's **Perfect Strangers** album came on strong with two tracks picked, but there was nothing from the five studio albums since.

Black Sabbath songs in the Top 500: 28. Black Sabbath songs with Tony Martin singing, in the Top 500: 0.

Every Aerosmith song on the list is 25 years old or older.

Songs I'm surprised didn't make the list (granted, a lot of these are old and not that heavy, but I just thought they'd get more votes):

> AC/DC — *High Voltage,* AC/DC — *Shot Down in Flames,* Aerosmith — *Walk This Way,* Aerosmith — *Draw the Line,* Anvil — *Forged in Fire,* Black Sabbath — *Hand of Doom,* Black Sabbath — *Electric Funeral,* Alice Cooper — *Elected,* Alice Cooper — *Under My Wheels,* The Cult — *Love Removal Machine,* The Cult — *She Sells Sanctuary,* Deep Purple — *Hush,* Deep Purple — *Fireball,* Def Leppard — *Bringin' on the Heartache,* Dio — *We Rock,* Dio — *Straight through the Heart,* Exodus — *Piranha,* Foghat — *Slow Ride,* Golden Earring — *Radar Love,* Guess Who — *American Woman,* Sammy Hagar — *Heavy Metal,* Jimi Hendrix — *Manic Depression,* Iron Butterfly — *In-A-Gadda-Da-Vida,* Iron Maiden — *Sanctuary,* Judas Priest — *Running Wild,* Judas Priest — *Jawbreaker,* Judas Priest — *Delivering the Goods,* Kiss — *Cold Gin,* Kiss — *Parasite,* Kiss — *Strutter,* Led Zeppelin — *The Song Remains the Same,* Led Zeppelin — *The Ocean,* Metallica — *No Remorse,* Metallica — *Metal Militia,* Metallica — *Phantom Lord,*

Motörhead — *Motorhead,* Nazareth — *Razamanaz,* Ozzy Osbourne — *Miracle Man,* Queen — *Tie Your Mother Down,* Riot — *Fire Down Under,* Rush — *Fly by Night,* Scorpions — *Virgin Killer,* Scorpions — *Dark Lady,* Stooges — *I Wanna Be Your Dog,* Sweet — *Ballroom Blitz,* Thin Lizzy — *Bad Reputation,* Twisted Sister — *Stay Hungry,* UFO — *Let It Roll,* Van Halen — *Jamie's Cryin',* Van Halen — *Beautiful Girls,* Van Halen — *Poundcake,* Venom — *Countess Bathory,* Whitesnake — *Slide It In,* Whitesnake — *Fool for Your Loving,* ZZ Top — *Tush.* and ZZ Top — *La Grange.*

One hit wonders: these are bands who sent one song (I was going to allow up to two, but then you're not a one hit wonder, are ya?) way up the charts, but nothing else very high at all, as well as having few other songs getting any votes in the extended master list. OK big shot, without looking, try naming the band's "big hit."

Angel, Annihilator, Beatles (something seems wrong with calling the Beatles a one hit wonder, don't it?), Cannibal Corpse (and something also seems wrong with listing Cannibal Corpse right next to The Beatles), Danzig, Diamond Head, Bruce Dickinson, Entombed, Europe, Humble Pie, In Flames, Jethro Tull, Kansas, Krokus, Living Colour, Loudness, Marilyn Manson, MC5, Ministry, Mountain, Nazareth, Nevermore, Nirvana, Rage Against The Machine, Stone Temple Pilots, Stooges, Suicidal Tendencies, Tesla, Tool, Warlock, Y&T.

APPENDIX 5: POINTS BY BAND

The number of different bands represented in the Top 500 Songs is 129. Here are all of them, and the number of points each garnered, in total. You may (but I'm not forcing you) consider this a list of the greatest metal bands of all time, on (the very unscientific) basis of how beloved their key songs were. Oh, forget it, do with it what you will!

Band	Points
Black Sabbath	19,374
Metallica	17,130
Iron Maiden	16,147
Judas Priest	13,251
Slayer	8419
AC/DC	7659
Ozzy Osbourne	7456
Deep Purple	6128
Megadeth	5463
Led Zeppelin	5295
Motörhead	4597
Pantera	4354
Dio	3640
Van Halen	3500
Kiss	3434
Accept	3315
Guns N' Roses	2871
Mötley Crüe	2717
Rainbow	2503
Sepultura	2100
Anthrax	2073
Scorpions	2044
Queensryche	2043
UFO	1900
Rush	1568
Thin Lizzy	1516
Mercyful Fate	1484
Saxon	1435
Def Leppard	1425
Helloween	1416
W.A.S.P.	1331
Dream Theater	1309
Aerosmith	1180
Alice Cooper	1159
Savatage	1090
Manowar	1030
Uriah Heep	1023
Iced Earth	925
Whitesnake	907
Skid Row	898
Testament	872
Ratt	859
Metal Church	780
Blue Öyster Cult	762
Venom	694
Jimi Hendrix Experience	687
Queen	641
Quiet Riot	635
Twisted Sister	626
Riot	623
Celtic Frost	538
Ted Nugent	522
Exodus	436
Soundgarden	427
Carcass	425
Type O Negative	412
Steppenwolf	388
Sex Pistols	374

Band	Points
Alice In Chains	369
Angel Witch	369
Cannibal Corpse	369
Danzig	367
Cream	366
Diamond Head	359
King Diamond	354
Tool	332
Emperor	331
Beatles	326
Faith No More	317
Halford	309
Blind Guardian	306
Fates Warning	304
White Zombie	299
At the Gates	297
Machine Head	297
Michael Schenker Group	295
Nirvana	289
Yngwie Malmsteen	282
Montrose	281
Marilyn Manson	272
Mountain	229
Suicidal Tendencies	229
Nevermore	220
Annihilator	219
Nazareth	217
MC5	203
Loudness	202
Krokus	185
Rage Against the Machine	181
In Flames	179
Tesla	177
Stooges	174
Bruce Dickinson	168
Angel	161
Jethro Tull	157

Band	Points
Bathory	151
Living Colour	150
Warlock	149
Entombed	147
Overkill	145
Ministry	143
Meshuggah	140
Fear Factory	139
Holocaust	136
Y&T	136
Humble Pie	131
Deicide	129
Poison	128
Witchfinder General	128
Armored Saint	127
Stone Temple Pilots	126
Death	122
Fastway	121
Cinderella	120
Candlemass	118
Europe	118
Napalm Death	118
Lucifer's Friend	112
Amorphis	110
Bad Company	110
Budgie	110
Free	110
Kansas	110
Anvil	109
Tygers Of Pan Tang	109
King's X	108
Kyuss	108
Monster Magnet	107
Slipknot	107

APPENDIX 6: POINTS BY ALBUM

The total number of different albums represented in the Top 500 Songs poll is 286. Here are all of them. Surprise! AC/DC's life and death affirming **Highway to Hell** sneaks past more obvious choices, to perch at the top. Partly in the interest of saving space, I'm going to ascribe to you a shred of intelligence and assume you know the respective names of the pop combos who created the below travesties (although there might be a few roman numerals and such you'll have to guess at) . . .

Album	Points
Highway to Hell	11,583
Paranoid	8110
The Number of the Beast	7233
Ride the Lightning	5641
Master of Puppets	5625
Reign in Blood	4659
Blizzard of Ozz	4061
Back in Black	3699
Machine Head	3528
Screaming for Vengeance	3465
Ace of Spades	3410
Rust in Peace	2930
Heaven and Hell	2840
Piece of Mind	2733
Holy Diver	2668
Sad Wings of Destiny	2625
Appetite for Destruction	2577
IV	2496
Powerslave	2489
Black Sabbath	2371
Diary of a Madman	2323
. . . And Justice for All	2306
Kill 'Em All	2128
Vulgar Display of Power	2042
Van Halen	1971
Master of Reality	1911
Peace Sells . . . But Who's Buying?	1826
Painkiller	1784
Restless and Wild	1741
Seasons in the Abyss	1691
British Steel	1648
Shout at the Devil	1642
Cowboys from Hell	1635
Sabotage	1520
Metallica	1430
Balls to the Wall	1389
Stained Class	1260
Killers	1248
Sabbath Bloody Sabbath	1229
Destroyer	1204
Among the Living	1176
Rising	1152
Long Live Rock 'n' Roll	1127
Operation: Mindcrime	1104
In Rock	1083
South of Heaven	1081
II	1044
Lights Out	1005
Images and Words	978
The Last in Line	972
Burn	960
1987	907
Pyromania	906
Phenomenon	895

Album	Points
Defenders of the Faith	869
Jailbreak	865
Don't Break the Oath	828
Keeper of the Seven Keys Part II	826
1984	804
Blackout	791
Dressed to Kill	788
Iron Maiden	782
Hell Awaits	779
Mob Rules	764
Let There Be Rock	721
Arise	715
Melissa	656
Skid Row	656
Love at First Sting	639
Metal Health	635
Roots	635
Toys in the Attic	634
Fire Down Under	623
Killing Machine/Hell Bent for Leather	622
Kiss	619
Moving Pictures	614
Fair Warning	612
For Those About to Rock	592
Fear of the Dark	583
Somewhere in Time	570
Black Metal	567
Far Beyond Driven	565
Creatures of the Night	562
Out of the Cellar	561
Sin After Sin	561
Power & the Glory	558
Bark at the Moon	556
III	552
Physical Graffiti	550
Denim and Leather	548

Album	Points
Countdown to Extinction	542
Metal Church	520
Hall of the Mountain King	510
Seventh Son of a Seventh Son	509
The Warning	509
W.A.S.P.	475
Too Fast for Love	473
2112	457
Battle Hymns	456
Led Zeppelin	447
Demons and Wizards	443
Chaos A.D.	442
Kings of Metal	441
Overkill	433
Queensryche	430
Badmotorfinger	427
Heartwork	425
Point of Entry	417
To Mega Therion	413
Electric Ladyland	412
Burnt Offerings	398
Steppenwolf	388
Stay Hungry	375
Never Mind the Bollocks	374
Keeper of the Seven Keys Part I	373
Angel Witch	369
Tomb of the Mutilated	369
Thralldemonsweatlive	367
Powerage	365
Borrowed Time	359
Vol 4	355
No More Tears	353
Taken by Force	351
High 'n' Dry	348
Thunder and Lightning	348
Look at Yourself	346
Presence	335

Album	Points
Dr. Feelgood	334
Undertow	332
Wheels of Steel	329
Perfect Strangers	327
White Album	326
Agents of Fortune	317
The Real Thing	317
Aerosmith	314
Love It to Death	314
Beneath the Remains	311
Resurrection	309
High Voltage	308
Orgasmatron	305
Cat Scratch Fever	304
A Night at the Opera	300
Invasion of Your Privacy	298
Slaughter of the Soul	297
The New Order	296
Gutter Ballet	295
Use Your Illusion I	294
School's Out	293
Nevermind	289
Welcome to My Nightmare	288
The Crimson Idol	286
Marching Out	282
Something Wicked This Way Comes	282
Montrose	281
Spreading the Disease	281
Practice What You Preach	278
Bloody Kisses	276
Are You Experienced?	275
Born Again	274
Antichrist Superstar	272
Girls Girls Girls	268
Animal Magnetism	263
Blessing in Disguise	260

Album	Points
The Last Command	257
Fabulous Disaster	252
The Dark Saga	245
Dirt	243
Slave to the Grind	242
Dirty Deeds Done Dirt Cheap	239
Very 'Eavy Very 'Umble	234
Rocks	232
Climbing!	229
Lights . . . Camera . . . Revolution	229
Wheels of Fire	226
Ritchie Blackmore's Rainbow	224
A Change of Seasons	221
Dreaming Neon Black	220
Alice in Hell	219
Ted Nugent	218
Hair of the Dog	217
Rush	217
Sheer Heart Attack	212
Abigail	211
Haunting the Chapel	209
Sound of White Noise	204
Kick out the Jams	203
Thunder in the East	202
Animal	201
Spectres	201
Iron Fist	200
Johnny the Fox	187
Headhunter	185
Metal Heart	185
Bonded by Blood	184
Epic	181
Walls of Jericho	181
The Gathering	179
Whoracle	179
Mechanical Resonance	177
Raw Power	174

Album	Points
Hysteria	171
Imaginations from the Other Side	171
Balls to Picasso	168
Permanent Waves	166
Hidden Treasures	165
Michael Schenker Group	165
Sirens	165
The Spectre Within	165
The Ultimate Sin	163
State of Euphoria	162
Angel	161
Aqualung	157
Astrocreep 2000	154
Burn My Eyes	154
The Razor's Edge	152
Blood Fire Death	151
Vivid	150
Triumph and Agony	149
Left Hand Path	147
La Sexorcisto: Devil Music Vol. 1	145
The Years of Decay	145
Lick It Up	144
Psalm 69	143
The More Things Change	143
Them	143
No Remorse	142
Destroy Erase Improve	140
Disraeli Gears	140
No Exit	139
Blue Öyster Cult	137
Billion Dollars Babies	136
Mean Streak	136
October Rust	136
The Nightcomers	136
Nightfall in Middle Earth	135
Hail to England	133
In the Nightside Eclipse	132
Performance: Rockin' the Fillmore	131
Assault Attack	130
Deicide	129
Under the Blade	129
Death Penalty	128
Look What the Cat Dragged In	128
Trash	128
March of the Saint	127
Welcome to Hell	127
Core	126
Facelift	126
Attack of the Killer B's	125
Morbid Tales	125
Persistence of Time	125
Leprosy	122
You Can't Stop Rock and Roll	122
Demanufacture	121
Fastway	121
Carat Purple	120
Long Cold Winter	120
Power of the Night	120
Low	119
Epicus Doomicus Metallicus	118
Harmony Corruption	118
The Final Countdown	118
Dynasty	117
Back for the Attack	116
Black Rose	116
Hemispheres	114
Women and Children First	113
Lucifer's Friend	112
Reinventing the Steel	112
The Headless Children	112
Awake	110
Bad Company	110
Fire and Water	110
Leftoverture	110

Album	Points
Never Turn Your Back on a Friend	110
Stormbringer	110
Tales from the Thousand Lakes	110
Metal On Metal	109
Spellbound	109
Anthems to the Welkin at Dusk	108

Album	Points
Blues for the Red Sun	108
Gretchen Goes to Nebraska	108
Bomber	107
Powertrip	107
Secret Treaties	107
Slipknot	107

APPENDIX 7:
POINTS BY YEAR: TOP 10

The number of different years being represented in this poll is 34, every year from 1967 until 2000, with nothing from 2001 making the list, even though it was pretty much over when we closed the gate. The '80s ran away with the top decade prize, pointing to something we critic types have been discussing a lot lately: the farther we get away from the '70s, the less people even think bands and rekkids from that ancient era qualify as heavy metal, the term hard rock being imbued with new meaning as of late, to refer to a lot of what might have made the grade say, even five years ago. Here are the Top 10 best years for metal songs, derived from the Top 500. Note that 1980 through 1984 pretty much seem to comprise, by a long though arguably imprecise shot, the hallowed golden deadly dynasty years of metal.

Year	Points
1980	18,204
1984	17,335
1983	16,148
1986	13,793
1982	13,770
1970	12,689
1990	9235
1981	8934
1976	8192
1988	7586

APPENDIX 8: MARTIN POPOFF'S TOP 25

Hey, I did a list too! Glancing o'er this, it's kind of lame how old everything is, but then again two things: 1) this is OF ALL TIME and 2) I've been a jaded, cynical rock critic for a long time, meaning that any impressive song from the last few years is pretty much lacking in sentimentality and memories, something I found indispensable and tantamount in the execution of this near impossible task.

1) Aerosmith — *Draw the Line*
2) Deep Purple — *Highway Star*
3) Led Zeppelin — *In My Time of Dying*
4) Black Sabbath — *The Writ*
5) Queen — *Liar*
6) Dio — *We Rock*
7) Judas Priest — *Tyrant*
8) Led Zeppelin — *The Rover*
9) Black Sabbath — *Megalomania*
10) Aerosmith — *Sick as a Dog*
11) Queen — *Keep Yourself Alive*
12) Ozzy Osbourne — *Over the Mountain*
13) AC/DC — *Walk All over You*
14) Black Sabbath — *Heaven and Hell*
15) Thin Lizzy — *The Pressure Will Blow*
16) Thin Lizzy — *Baby Please Don't Go*
17) Judas Priest — *Burnin' Up*
18) Scorpions — *Virgin Killer*
19) Van Halen — *And the Cradle Will Rock . . .*
20) Blue Öyster Cult — *Tattoo Vampire*
21) Megadeth — *Symphony of Destruction*
22) UFO — *Letting Go*
23) Max Webster — *Paradise Skies*
24) Love/Hate — *Yucca Man*
25) Rush — *Subdivisions*